Great Outdoor Guide

to

Northern California

Also available:

Frommer's Great Outdoor Guide to New England

Frommer's Great Outdoor Guide to Southern California & Baja

Frommer's Great Outdoor Guide to Washington & Oregon

rommer's ®

Great Outdoor Guide
to
Northern California

by Andrew Rice

MACMILLAN • USA

MACMILLAN TRAVEL USA
A Pearson Education Macmillan Company
1633 Broadway
New York, NY 10019

Find us online at www.frommers.com

ISBN 0-02-863308-3
ISSN 1522-8134

Design by Amy Peppler Adams, designLab
Digital Cartography by Ortelius Design

Special Sales
Bulk purchases (10+ copies) of Frommer's
travel guides are available to corporations and
selected Macmillan organizations, mail-order
catalogs, institutions, and charities at special
discounts, and can be customized to suit
individual needs. For more information
write to Special Sales, Macmillan General
Reference, 1633 Broadway, New York, NY
10019.

Manufactured in the United States of America

Andrew Rice tries to spend as
little time indoors as possible. When
not on the road for *Outside, Islands,* and
a number of other magazines, he lives
in San Francisco.

Contents

List of Maps xi

What the Symbols Mean xiii

Map Legend xiii

Introduction xiv

1 The Basics 1

Getting Underway   2

Ballooning 2
Bird Watching 2
Boardsailing 3
Canoeing 3
Cross-Country Skiing 4
Downhill Skiing &
  Snowboarding 6
Fishing 7

Hikes, Bushwhacks &
  Backpack Trips 7
Horseback Riding 8
Kayaking 9
Mountain Biking 10
Road Biking 11
Rock Climbing 12
Sailing 12

Scuba Diving 12
Sea Kayaking 13
Surfing 13
Swimming 13
Walks & Rambles 13
Whale Watching 13
Whitewater Rafting 14

Outfitters   14

Schools   17

Maps   17

Books   17

Spas   18

A Note on Camping   18

Features:

- *Backcountry Equipment Checklist   4*
- *Backpacking for Beginners   9*

2 The San Francisco Bay Area 19

The Lay of the Land   21

Orientation   23

Parks & Other Hot Spots   26

The Peninsula ◆ What to Do & Where to Do It   36

Bird Watching 37
Boardsailing 37
Fishing 38
Hikes, Bushwhacks &
  Backpack Trips 39

Mountain Biking 40
Road Biking 41
Rock Climbing 41
Sailing 42

Scuba Diving 42
Surfing 42
Walks & Rambles 43
Whale Watching 43

Marin County ◆ What to Do & Where to Do It   45

Bird Watching 45
Boardsailing 45
Fishing 48
Hikes, Bushwhacks &
  Backpack Trips 48

Mountain Biking 51
Road Biking 52
Sailing 52
Sea Kayaking 52

Surfing 53
Walks & Rambles 53
Whale Watching 53

The East Bay ◆ What to Do & Where to Do It   54

Bird Watching 54
Boardsailing 54
Fishing 54

Hikes, Bushwhacks &
  Backpack Trips 54
Mountain Biking 55

Road Biking 56
Sailing 57
Walks & Rambles 57

Campgrounds & Other Accommodations   57

Features:

- *The Presidio   38*
- *Shark Watch   44*
- *Point Reyes National Seashore   46*
- *Muir Woods National Monument   50*

3 The Monterey Bay Area 61

The Lay of the Land   63

Orientation   64

Parks & Other Hot Spots   68

What to Do & Where to Do It   74

Bird Watching 74
Boardsailing 75
Fishing 75
Hikes, Bushwhacks &
   Backpack Trips 76

Kayaking 79
Mountain Biking 79
Road Biking 80
Rock Climbing 80
Sailing 80

Scuba Diving 81
Sea Kayaking 81
Surfing 82
Walks & Rambles 83
Whale Watching 84

Campgrounds & Other Accommodations   85

**4 Big Sur, the Ventana Wilderness &
    Pinnacles National Monument** 89

The Lay of the Land   90

Orientation   91

Parks & Other Hot Spots   94

What to Do & Where to Do It   97

Bird Watching 97
Boardsailing 98
Fishing 98
Hikes, Bushwhacks &
   Backpack Trips 98

Horseback Riding 103
Mountain Biking 103
Road Biking 104
Rock Climbing 105
Scuba Diving 106

Sea Kayaking 106
Swimming 108
Surfing 108
Walks & Rambles 108
Whale Watching 110

Campgrounds & Other Accommodations   111

Features:

◆ *Pinnacles National Monument   102*

5 The Wine Country & Delta 117

Orientation   118

Parks & Other Hot Spots   118

What to Do & Where to Do It   121

Ballooning 121
Bird Watching 121
Boardsailing 121

Fishing 121
Hiking 124

Mountain Biking 124
Road Biking 125

Campgrounds & Other Accommodations   126

Features:

◆ *Touring the Wineries*   *122*
◆ *Soil Yourself: Take a Calistoga Mud Bath*   *128*

6 The Sierra Nevada 129

The Lay of the Land   130

Orientation   133

Parks & Other Hot Spots   143

Northern Sierra: Lake Tahoe to Yosemite ◆ What to Do & Where to Do It   151

Bird Watching 152
Boardsailing 152
Canoeing 154
Cross-Country Skiing
   & Snowshoeing 154
Downhill Skiing &
   Snowboarding 155

Fishing 158
Hikes, Bushwhacks &
   Backpack Trips 158
Kayaking 160
Mountain Biking 162

Road Biking 163
Rock Climbing 163
Walks & Rambles 164
Whitewater Rafting 164

Southern Sierra: Yosemite to Sequoia/Kings Canyon ◆ What to Do & Where to Do It   164

Bird Watching 165
Boardsailing 165
Canoeing 165
Cross-Country Skiing
   & Snowshoeing 166
Downhill Skiing &
   Snowboarding 166

Fishing 167
Hikes, Bushwhacks &
   Backpack Trips 167
Horseback Riding 177
Ice-Skating 177
Kayaking 177

Mountain Biking 180
Road Biking 180
Rock Climbing 180
Walks & Rambles 181
Whitewater Rafting 182

Eastern Sierra ◆ What to Do & Where to Do It   183

Ballooning 183
Bird Watching 183
Boardsailing 184
Bobsledding 184
Canoeing 184
Cross-Country
   Skiing 184

Dogsledding 189
Downhill Skiing &
   Snowboarding 189
Fishing 190
Hikes, Bushwhacks &
   Backpack Trips 191
Horseback Riding 195

Hot Springs 195
Mountain Biking 196
Road Biking 198
Rock Climbing &
   Mountaineering 198
Snowshoeing 198
Walks & Rambles 199

Campgrounds & Other Accommodations   200

Features:

- *The Cow & the Cowbird   153*
- *Are Those Mountains the Sierra or the Sierras?   157*
- *Mountain Words   161*
- *Yosemite National Park   168*
- *Sequoia & Kings Canyon National Parks   178*
- *Belated Gold Rush: Settling the Eastern Sierra   185*
- *California's Great Salt Lake   187*
- *The Owens Valley Water Wars   193*
- *Swim at Your Own Risk   199*

7 The Gold Country 209

The Lay of the Land   210

Orientation   210

Parks & Other Hot Spots   212

What to Do & Where to Do It   212

Bird Watching 212	Hiking 214	Road Biking 217
Fishing 214	Kayaking 215	Walks & Rambles 217
Gold Prospecting 214	Mountain Biking 216	Whitewater Rafting 218

Campgrounds & Other Accommodations   219

Features:

- *How to Pan for Gold   215*

8 The Northern Mountains 223

The Lay of the Land   224

Orientation   225

Parks & Other Hot Spots   228

What to Do & Where to Do It   231

Bird Watching 231	Fishing 233	Road Biking 241
Canoeing 231	Hikes, Bushwhacks &	Rock Climbing &
Cross-Country Skiing	Backpack Trips 234	Mountaineering 241
& Snowshoeing 231	Horseback Riding 237	Spelunking 241
Downhill Skiing &	Kayaking 237	Walks & Rambles 242
Snowboarding 232	Mountain Biking 240	Whitewater Rafting 243

Campgrounds & Other Accommodations   244

Features:

- ◆ *Lava Beds National Monument   235*
- ◆ *Otter Bar Lodge   238*
- ◆ *Climbing Mount Shasta   242*
- ◆ *Lassen Volcanic National Park   246*

❾ The North Coast 251

The Lay of the Land   253

Orientation   253

Parks & Other Hot Spots   255

What to Do & Where to Do It   258

Bird Watching 258
Canoeing 258
Fishing 259
Hikes, Bushwhacks &
   Backpack Trips 259

Kayaking 264
Mountain Biking 265
Scuba Diving 266

Sea Kayaking 266
Walks & Rambles 267
Whale Watching 267

Campgrounds & Other Accommodations   268

Features:

- ◆ *Redwood National Park   262*
- ◆ *Thar She Blows!   268*

Index 271

List of Maps

The Bay Area—The Peninsula & East Bay   **24**

Marin & Angel Island   **27**

Golden Gate National Recreation Area   **30**

Monterey Bay Area   **66**

The Central Coast   **92**

The Wine Country   **119**

Lake Tahoe to Yosemite   **134**

The Yosemite Area   **138**

The Sequoia and Kings Canyon National Parks Area   **148**

The Gold Country   **213**

The Mount Shasta Area   **226**

The Lassen Area   **232**

The Northern Coast   **254**

Redwood National Park   **264**

Acknowledgments

WRITING A GUIDEBOOK IS DIFFERENT FROM MOST OTHER KINDS OF WRITING: SINCE you're traveling alone through far-flung territory you come to depend on the kindness of strangers for help, for companionship, and for support. To all the strangers—many of whom are now valued friends—who shared their trails, rivers, mountains, waves, and homes with me while tolerating my incessant questions and requests, I am deeply grateful.

I owe special thanks to my editors at Macmillan, Ian Wilker and Jim Moore, and my editor at *Outside*, Leslie Weeden, for grace under pressure; to Jim Buckley, without whom I'd have never gotten this job in the first place; and most of all to Lisa Palac for her love and moral support through all of it.

TO MY PARENTS

For teaching me the value of wild places early in life and allowing me to roam.

Invitation to the Reader

In researching this book, I crisscrossed the state in search of the very best places to get outside. I'm sure you have your own favorite spots, or at least will find new ones as you explore. Please share your secrets with me, so I can pass them on in upcoming editions. If you were disappointed with a recommendation, I'd love to know that, too. Please write to:

Andrew Rice
Frommer's Great Outdoor Guide
to Northern California
Macmillan Travel
1633 Broadway
New York, NY 10019

An Additional Note

Please be advised that travel information is subject to change at any time. Every effort has been made to ensure the accuracy of the information provided in this book, but we suggest that you write or call ahead for confirmation when making your travel plans. The authors, editors, and publisher cannot be held responsible for the experiences of readers while traveling. Outdoor adventure sports are, by their very nature, potentially hazardous activities. In doing any of the activities described herein, readers assume all risk of injury or loss that may accompany such activities. The Publisher disavows all responsibility for injury, death, loss, or property damage which may arise from a reader's participation in any of the activities described herein, and the Publisher makes no warranties regarding the competence, safety, and reliability of outfitters, tour companies, or training centers described in this book.

What the Symbols Mean

🚶	Backpacking	🐎	Horseback Riding	🤿	Scuba Diving
🏄	Boardsailing	📖	Inns & Lodges	🏂	Snowboarding
🏕	Camping	🚣	Kayaking	🎾	Snowshoeing
🛶	Canoeing	🚴	Mountain Biking	🪖	Spelunking
🦩	Coastal and Wetlands Birding	🚤	Powerboating	🏄	Surfing
🎿	Cross-Country Skiing	🦅	Raptoring and Woodland Birding	🛟	Tubing
⛷	Downhill Skiing	🚲	Road Biking	🏊	Swimming
🎣	Fishing	🧗	Rock Climbing	🛶	Whitewater Rafting
⛳	Golfing	🚣	Rowing	🦌	Wildlife Viewing
👟	Hiking	⛵	Sailing	🐋	Whale Watching

Map Legend

══⟨35⟩══	Interstate highway	▨▨▨	Metropolitan area
══⟨53⟩══	Primary road	○ ○	City
⟨27⟩⟨A16⟩	Secondary road	☂	Beach
= =⟨A25⟩= =	Unimproved road	↶	Dam
══╪══	Interchange	▲	Peak
••••••••	Specialized trail	■	Point of interest
··········	Trail	▭ ♣	National/State/County park
⊢—⊢—⊢	Railroad	▭	National/State forest
– · – · –	State boundary	▭	Indian/military reservation
– – – – –	County boundary	✕ ✈	Airstrip/Airport
———	Park/wilderness area boundary	·············	Ferry route

Introduction

WHEN MY EDITOR CALLED AND ASKED ME TO WRITE THIS BOOK, I leapt at the chance. And why not? My assignment: Go travel around Northern California. Hike, mountain bike, backpack, snowboard, surf, ski, climb, kayak, and anything else I thought was relevant. Live the outdoor lifestyle. More than anything the mandate was to explore, to go out there and traipse around, then come back and write about what the hell is out there.

Well, that's what I did. And believe me, there's a lot of "out there" out there. I grew up in Northern California and have spent the better part of my life poking around some of the state's most remote regions, yet there were literally hundreds of places I hadn't visited yet. In the process of researching this book I put more than 20,000 miles on my car. I went through a couple pairs of hiking boots and a pair of sport sandals. My mountain bike has been flogged to death, ruined. I was snowed in for four days after a storm dropped 14 feet of snow overnight and an avalanche buried the snowplow. Learning to snowboard I earned a concussion in a high-speed wipeout. I lived on energy bars, black coffee, and granola. I even got poison oak. But I also had magical experiences like climbing Mount Shasta, swapping hilarious stories with a good friend the whole way up. I snorkeled with spawning salmon while on a whitewater kayak trip. I surfed Santa Cruz on a huge south swell pushing 10 feet in the middle of summer.

A few weeks later I was sitting quietly by a high alpine lake watching a black bear eat berries while a golden eagle circled overhead.

And I met great people. More than once people walked over to my campsite and asked what I was doing as I hunched over my laptop computer typing out the day's adventure. At first I was reluctant to say I was writing a guidebook. "Won't they think I'm some sort of psychic vampire, running around learning all the great spots and publishing them?" I asked myself, "Won't the surly backwoods locals want to lynch me for talking about *their* lakes, *their* rivers, *their* trails?" Those fears proved to be totally unfounded. The only place I encountered any "localism" at all was in an online computer forum when a guy from Oakland of all places opined that parasite travel writers like me were responsible for the demise of the American wilderness and that I better just stay the heck away from *his* spots. But more often than not, when the people I met found out I was writing a book, I was invited into their homes, taken on hikes, or ushered into the back of a bike shop to talk about favorite trails, places I'd been, and places I should go. If it hadn't been for those people and their generosity this book never would have been completed.

So here it is, your starting place to adventure. With this book in your pack or your glove box, you can go anywhere in Northern California and find a good trail, a rich bird watching spot, a mountain guide to take you climbing, a stream full of native trout, or a roaring whitewater river. Let it point you in the right direction, then go. Have a good time. I did.

—Andrew Rice

1

The Basics

NO WAY COULD ANYONE WRITE THE DEFINITIVE GUIDE TO EVERY outdoor activity between Big Sur, Mount Whitney, and the Oregon border even if they had 10 years, much less just one. But I've given it a good whack. The *Great Outdoor Guide to Northern California* isn't the end of my journey; it should be a starting point for your own personal adventure, like a trail sign pointing you down an inviting path. It's arranged in eight regions following the natural boundaries between different areas of Northern California. Some particularly hefty chapters are broken down even further into smaller regions. The core of each chapter is the "What to Do & Where to Do It" section (or sections, if there are several regions), an A to Z list of sports or activities from bird watching to whitewater rafting, with a whole lot of hiking, fishing, kayaking, and other things in between. If you're in, say, Mount Shasta and want to go mountain biking, look under "Mountain Biking" in the Northern Mountains chapter. There you'll find an assortment of good rides around Mount Shasta, plus tips on where to find local wisdom and more rides. But maybe your thing is whale watching and you're in Half Moon Bay, not Mount Shasta? Or you want to snowboard and you're headed to Mammoth Lakes?

Well, I've covered that too, plus rock climbing in Yosemite, diving in Monterey, boardsailing in the San Francisco Bay, and a whole lot more.

Under each sports heading, you'll find specific trails, routes, waterways, and activities chosen because they are the best in Northern California. These featured activities are described in detail. Distance, time, level of difficulty, terrain, location, and availability of maps have all been included when appropriate. Of course, time and level of difficulty are relative terms, but if you're in decent condition you should do just fine following these recommendations. Level of difficulty also varies from sport to sport. For example, all Walks & Rambles are easy, but a hike designated as easy is more strenuous, since hikes denote a climb uphill or more rugged terrain. A difficult cross-country ski trail or whitewater kayak run is something that no one should attempt unless they are sure of their technical ability, whereas a difficult road biking trip mainly involves lots of hard huffing and puffing.

Introductory essays precede the sports and activities in each regional chapter. Since I don't think these kinds of sports and activities take place in a vacuum, I've tried to say something about the natural character of each region—its biology and geology, and how people have interacted with the land over the years; most of the time I've put my thoughts about these subjects into a section called "The Lay of the Land."

Because it's important that you know where you are in relation to where the action is, each chapter also contains a section that maps out the most important towns, roads, and other features of an area—if you're trying to figure out how to cross the Sierra, or what town would make a good base camp, look at "Orientation."

Because it's important that you know *where* the action is, each chapter contains a long annotated list of "Parks & Other Hot Spots": the state forests, wilderness areas, beaches, rivers, lakes, and mountains that you'll be in, or on, as you paddle, hike, ski, etc. And to ensure that you sleep well after all this action, each chapter concludes with a list of recommended campgrounds and a list of special inns and lodges for those who prefer to sleep in a bed but want to wake up with someplace wild right outside the door.

Getting Underway

By far the largest chunk of this book is broken down by sport, telling you just what you can do and where you can do it. Where is the best mountain bike ride in Marin County (they were invented here after all)? How do you go about getting a California fishing license? Who's the best whale-watching tour operator? Below is a list of most of the sports covered in this book.

BALLOONING

I haven't the slightest idea how to go up in your *own* hot-air balloon, but there are plenty of companies waiting to take you up in *theirs*. If you plan on flying with one of the numerous outfitters in Northern California, all you'll need is a camera, sunglasses, and perhaps a sweater. **Mammoth Balloon Adventures** (tel. 760/934-7188) in Mammoth Lakes and **Adventures Aloft** (tel. 707/944-4408) in Napa Valley are two of the better options.

BIRD WATCHING

Very few places on earth have the biological diversity of California. Because it has so many different types of habitat, California is either home or a temporary stopover for literally thousands of species of birds. In each chapter you'll find a list of some of the distinctive species in that area, plus recommendations of places to go birding. If there are any special activities like ranger-led bird tours or a seasonal migration through a particular area, I've tried to include that too, plus particularly good local guidebooks.

There are so many special places to view birds in Northern California that it's almost impossible to list them all. Due to the nature of the sport, on any given day, one spot could be far better than the next. However, you can hardly go wrong with these five locales:

◆ **Point Reyes** If the weather allows, you can see more different species here than any other place in North America. It's often foggy, and Point Reyes is huge, so plan on spending a few days to really explore all the different environments of the park. A great place for sighting pelagic seabirds blown off course.

◆ **Mono Lake** Strange as it may seem, most of the gulls in California are hatched here on the east side of the Sierra Nevada, not on the Pacific Coast. The birds nest on two small islands, visible with powerful spotting scopes or accessible by canoe, though you must stay at least 200 yards away to avoid stirring up the nesting birds.

◆ **Pinnacles National Monument** Raptor heaven. The towering volcanic spires of this little-known coastal range park are a stunning backdrop and, more importantly, offer nesting sites for many birds of prey. The surrounding mountains are completely undeveloped, a wonderful hunting ground. You can see golden eagles, peregrine falcons, Cooper's hawks, black-shouldered kites, and numerous other species here.

◆ **Tule Lake National Wildlife Refuge** Tule Lake is synonymous with huge numbers of waterfowl. Canada geese, snow geese, canvasbacks, and sandhill cranes wing over this huge wetland complex. To top things off, this is also a major bald eagle nesting habitat. A self-guided canoe tour and a self-guided auto tour make seeing this 40,000-acre refuge easier than you'd think.

◆ **Elkhorn Slough** This huge tidal estuary feeding into Monterey Bay is one of the most spectacular birding spots around. You can either hike the surrounding hills, or better yet, take to the slough in a canoe or kayak. The record for the most species spotted in one place in one day was set here. Besides the marsh birds and waterfowl you'd expect, you'll also see numerous hawks and songbirds.

BOARDSAILING

Boardsailing is a sport with a steep learning curve, and complex and expensive equipment, and by its very nature you're dependent on two fickle variables—wind and water. With that in mind this book assumes that you're either a beginner looking to get some introductory lessons, or you're an experienced sailor passing through the area and just need to be pointed to a local spot. Though obviously you can boardsail on just about any body of water, I only list spots where it is actually done on a fairly regular basis. Crissy Field on the San Francisco Bay is probably the best spot in the state, but Waddell Beach, just west of Santa Cruz, and the Berkeley Marina are also worth checking out.

CANOEING

There was a time when canoes were the premier craft for exploring wild waterways,

Backcountry Equipment Checklist

Below is a list of things you'll need for a backcountry trip of 2 or more days. This is more or less a backpackers' list, for a 4- to 7-day summer or fall trip on a Northern California long-distance trail. But the list will also do for canoeing, back-country skiing, whatever—there will be a few extra items of equipment you'll want for different kinds of trips, but this is a good checklist from which to start packing.

KITCHEN

- ☐ lightweight water filter pump (Pür, First Need, Sweetwater Guardian)
- ☐ 2–3 Nalgene quart-size water bottles
- ☐ 5-gallon camp water bag
- ☐ stainless steel cook set
- ☐ wooden spoon
- ☐ backpacking stove (like MSR Whisperlite or Coleman PEAK 1)
- ☐ 1.5–2 quarts stove fuel
- ☐ kitchen matches
- ☐ biodegradable soap
- ☐ scouring pad
- ☐ washcloth/potholder/towel

PANTRY

- ☐ coffee singles or tea bags
- ☐ breakfast foods, like instant oatmeal
- ☐ lunch items, such as peanut butter and jelly, crackers, cheese, hard sausage
- ☐ trail snacks, like gorp, beef jerky, dried fruit
- ☐ dinners—macaroni and cheese, freeze-dried dinners, couscous and Knorr gravy, other one-pot meals, in Ziploc bags
- ☐ spices/seasonings
- ☐ big chocolate bar
- ☐ separate sacks for lunch/snacks and breakfast/dinner foods

BEDROOM

- ☐ waterproof groundcloth
- ☐ tent (roomy 3-season, Moss, North Face, or Sierra Designs)
- ☐ sleeping bag rated to 20°F
- ☐ sleeping pad (Therm-A-Rests are great)

CLOTHES CLOSET

- ☐ boots (Vasque Sundowners, Salomon 8's)
- ☐ 2 pairs heavy socks
- ☐ polypropylene socks
- ☐ polypropylene long johns
- ☐ shorts or swimsuit
- ☐ baseball cap, or other sun hat
- ☐ knit wool cap

but in recent years the sea kayak seems to have taken over, even in fresh water. I've listed places where canoes are still king, such as Lake Alpine in the Sierra, and outfitters who will rent you a canoe or take you on a paddling tour. For more canoeing information contact the American Canoe Association, P.O. Box 1190, Newington, VA 22122 (tel. 703/451-0141). They have a website at http://world.std.com/~reichert/aca.html

CROSS-COUNTRY SKIING

Cross-country skiers seem to be evenly split between those who love nothing more than gliding down a freshly set mechanical track at a Nordic ski area and those who much prefer to bust their own trail along snow-covered logging roads, meadows, and trails. Accordingly, in the cross-country skiing section you'll find some of both: listings and descriptions

- [ ] bandanna
- [ ] water/wind-resistant, breathable shell (Gore-Tex or equivalent)
- [ ] rain pants
- [ ] cotton/synthetic t-shirt
- [ ] fleece jacket
- [ ] fleece pants
- [ ] sport sandals
- [ ] clothes stuff sack

ALL-PURPOSE ESSENTIALS
- [ ] maps/compass
- [ ] bug repellent
- [ ] lighter
- [ ] whistle (for bear country, or rescue)
- [ ] sunglasses
- [ ] watch
- [ ] toothbrush, razor, other toilet gear
- [ ] Mini-Mag flashlight, or headlamp
- [ ] extra batteries
- [ ] battery-powered or candle lantern
- [ ] Swiss army knife
- [ ] 75–100-foot rope (parachute cord), for hanging food, etc.
- [ ] toilet paper
- [ ] toilet trowel
- [ ] extra quart Ziplock bags
- [ ] extra gallon Ziplock bags
- [ ] extra stuff sack
- [ ] notebook/pen
- [ ] a good book

FIRST-AID KIT
- [ ] 2-inch by 3-inch moleskin
- [ ] pair small shears
- [ ] thermometer
- [ ] safety pins
- [ ] acetaminophen/ibuprofen/aspirin
- [ ] diarrhea pills
- [ ] antacid tablets
- [ ] sunscreen
- [ ] sting-relief pads
- [ ] iodine solution
- [ ] iodine ointment
- [ ] triple antibiotic ointment
- [ ] antiseptic towelettes
- [ ] single-edge razor blade or scalpel
- [ ] 1-inch by 3-inch fabric bandages
- [ ] fabric knuckle bandages
- [ ] sterile wound-closure strips (butterflies)
- [ ] 4-inch by 4-inch sterile gauze pads
- [ ] adhesive tape
- [ ] elastic (ace) bandage
- [ ] 5-inch by 9-inch combine dressings
- [ ] irrigation syringe
- [ ] wire mesh splint

LUXURIES
- [ ] GPS (global positioning system) device
- [ ] camera gear
- [ ] binoculars
- [ ] fishing gear

of commercial resorts in that area, plus a selection of backcountry trail listings with distance, difficulty, recommended map, and trailhead directions, plus a running description of the terrain, wildlife, and other characteristics of each trail. The phone numbers and addresses of any local agencies that offer trail information and recommendations are included.

Cross-country skiing can be totally relaxing—an easy shuffle around a mountain meadow—or it can be extremely demanding. Some of the more difficult trails involve steep climbs and speedy descents. If you haven't cross-country skied in a while, you're in for a big surprise. There are now a variety of skis to tackle the variety of terrain. First, there's the old touring ski, good for diagonal striding on groomed trails. Skating skis or racing skis are shorter and more narrow than the traditional track skis and are used with a speed-skating technique for quickness. Backcountry skis are wider than touring skis to give extra maneuverability on ungroomed trails. Telemark skis are similar to backcountry skis with the addition of metal edges. Telemarking is a gracefully lunging turning technique that gives freewheelers something close to the kind of control on steep slopes that alpine skiers have. Finally, there are *randonee* skis with lock-down heel bindings enabling you to climb a slope like a cross-country skier and descend using downhill parallel technique, bridging the gap between cross-country and downhill skiing.

The most obvious and popular destination for cross-country skiers is the Sierra Nevada, particularly the Lake Tahoe Region and Yosemite, and those places are rightfully deserving of the attention they get. Often overlooked is the great cross-country skiing in the northern mountains: the Trinity Alps and the Cascades. Mount Lassen and Mount Shasta are especially beautiful destinations and receive tons of snow. You can often ski Mount Shasta well into June and even July.

DOWNHILL SKIING & SNOWBOARDING

There's both too much and not enough to say about downhill skiing in California. Obviously it's an important sport or there wouldn't be so many resorts. You could write an entire book describing every single California ski resort in endless detail and people would probably line up to buy it, but this isn't it. We've tried to give you a feel for the personalities of some of the various resorts in each area, and to make recommendations about which are good for experts, where to take a beginner, who allows snowboards, or which mountain has a particular type of ski school, but we don't presume to be a

comprehensive encyclopedia of endless detail. If you want that, *California City-Sports* magazine publishes an annual ski preview issue every November with the latest prices, rules, snowmaking equipment, number of lifts, trails, new programs, vertical drop, and phone numbers, plus special tips on each mountain. Reach them at 214 South Cedros, Solana Beach, CA 92075 (tel. 619/793-2711) or find the magazine in any California ski shop.

Here's a list of my favorite skiing/snowboarding hills:

◆ **Squaw Valley** It's a little big and glitzy for my taste, but Squaw has unarguably the most radical terrain in the Tahoe area. Tons of steeps and moguls. Also miles and miles of easy cruising runs.

◆ **Sugar Bowl Ski Resort** Like many European resorts, you take a chairlift to get to the *base* of the mountain. Cars are kept on the other side of a hill. It's a small detail, but one symptomatic of what is right about Sugar Bowl—this is a skiers' hill, not a fashion show or a nightclub. Lots of steep, not so much intermediate, terrain.

◆ **Northstar-at-Tahoe** This north shore resort is one of the best managed in California. Tons of high-speed lifts whisk you up the mountain. Coming down is generally a well-groomed intermediate run. Good family mountain.

◆ **Kirkwood Ski Resort** Kirkwood is just far enough outside of the Tahoe area to avoid the crowds. Much of the mountain is above the tree line. A clear day is striking; a stormy one is awful.

◆ **Bear Valley Ski Area** I grew up skiing Bear Valley and went from stem christies to gonzo cornice drops here. The view into the Mokelumne River Canyon is one of the best anywhere. The back side is intermediate heaven. Below the lodge are two little-known and incredibly steep bowls served by the Kodiak and Grizzly lifts. A very diverse mountain.

FISHING

If it has fins, you can probably find it swimming somewhere in California. Fishing is big-time fun in this state, where people catch everything from trophy-sized largemouth bass and salmon to the small and extremely rare golden trout—the state fish. In each area you will find a description of the chief fishery there, as well as some recommendations about guides or shops, but remember that there are literally thousands of tackle shops, boat rentals, and fishing guides, and fishing schools are just waiting for you to give them a call or drop by. To help make sense of the huge numbers, get your hands on a copy of the *Cal/North Boating–Fishing–Diving Directory*, a wonderful phone book–style directory of all kinds of different services relating to, you guessed it, boating, fishing, and diving. The price is right—free. Contact Cal/North Marine Publishing Company, P.O. Box 410483, San Francisco, CA 94141 (tel. 415/243-0426).

If you're over 16 you need a license to fish anywhere in California waters and you must display it at all times. The only exception is fishing from recreational piers in the Pacific, but only from piers. Cast from the beach or a boat and you need a license. California has an extremely complicated license program where you buy a base license for a certain price and then have to buy different stamps for different types of fishing and different areas. To make things even easier, they change these stamps and areas just about every year, so you need a degree in rocket science just to figure out what kind of license to buy. For nonresidents they keep it a little more simple: you can buy a fishing license for a single day, 10 days, or a year.

For up-to-date license information contact the California Department of Fish and Game License Section, 3211 S St., Sacramento, CA 95816 (tel. 916/227-2244).

HIKES, BUSHWHACKS & BACKPACK TRIPS

This is consistently the biggest part of each chapter: the list of hikes and possible overnight backpacking trips for each area. Each recommended hike listing will give you the approximate mileage, difficulty, recommended map, and trailhead access, plus a description of each hike including terrain, wildlife you might see, points of interest, and things to look out for. For overnights I've also included a lot of possible side activities, and where you should go to get current trail conditions and wilderness permits. Bear in mind that these listings are not an exact description of every fork in the trail or every rock where you should turn right, cross a stream, and crawl over three logs before climbing 300 feet and turning southwest. If you don't know how to follow a trail or use a map, this book isn't going to save you. It's intended to give you the information you need to decide which hikes you want to do, not to take the place of backcountry skills and a good map. Once you leave the trailhead you're on your own.

The great thing about hiking in California is that you can do it year-round and you can do it everywhere. You can hike to isolated wilderness beaches on the north coast, find a backcountry hot spring in Big Sur, or trek to a granite-shrouded lake in the High Sierra. It's the best way to really see the state: slow enough to catch the details, but you're walking through a changing landscape with every ridge and valley.

FAVORITE DAY HIKES

◆ **High Peaks Trail, Pinnacles National Monument** A wonderful day hike in the coast range mountains of the Pinnacles. The remnant volcanic spires here are more reminiscent of New Mexico than California, and the trail winds through a wild formation of hoodoos and wind-carved rocks.

◆ **Steep Ravine Trail, Mount Tamalpais State Park** Set in a lush creek canyon, Steep Ravine connects the state park station at Pan Toll to the beach just south of Stinson Beach. In between is a wonderful series of cascades and second-growth redwoods.

◆ **Tuolumne Meadows to Glen Aulin High Sierra Camp, Yosemite National Park** Beginning with a hike across one of the largest alpine meadows in the state and ending at a spectacular waterfall, this hike is a good introduction to one of the most important watersheds in the Sierra Nevada. Lots of wildlife along the route.

◆ **Giant Forest, Sequoia & Kings Canyon National Parks** Numerous short loops will let you see the giant sequoia trees here, but if you want to really see the forest, take one of the longer hikes into the far corners of this spectacular grove. There you can be alone with the towering sequoias, the largest living things on earth.

FAVORITE OVERNIGHTS

As nice as day hiking is, nothing compares to the experience of spending a few days or even weeks away from the rat race. Literally thousands of good weekend backpacking trips can be done year-round in California. If you have more than a weekend, several long-distance trails cross Northern California:

◆ **John Muir Trail** This 200-plus-mile trek through the heart of the Sierra Nevada is the most famous backpacking trail in Northern California. It begins in the Yosemite Valley and ends at the summit of Mount Whitney. In between is the finest high country hiking in California. Plan on at least 3 weeks to cover the whole route.

◆ **Pacific Crest Trail** Running the length of California from near Mount Shasta, through Lassen National Park, and down the spine of the Sierra, the PCT links Canada, the United States, and Mexico. Most people hike it in small segments, but a few thru-hikers trek the whole length.

◆ **The Lost Coast** This 25-mile-long stretch of roadless wilderness coastline in Humboldt County is the finest coastal backpacking in the Lower 48. It's a longer 25 miles than you might think. Steep and densely wooded mountains soar out of the stormy Pacific. Lots of clambering over rocks, slogging through soft sand, and waiting for the tides to let you pass make 5 to 6 miles a day a reasonable goal.

HORSEBACK RIDING

More than 100 different dude ranches, pack horse guide services, and livery stables are dispersed around the northern half of the state, with options ranging from 1-hour trail rides to week-long wilderness adventures. While virtually anyone is capable of short day rides, some riding experience is useful before setting out on a multi-day packstock trip. Contrary to the movie *City Slickers*, horseback riding is not a sport where you ride for 4 days straight unless you have some idea of what it's like to sit in a saddle. Otherwise, your visions of *High Noon* might turn into great doom and you could be walking bowlegged for the next month.

In each area I've tried to include one or two outfitters when they offered something out of the norm or were highly recommended. For a complete list of the commercial outfitters and stables operating in California, write to the California Trade and Commerce Agency, 801 K St., Suite 1700, Sacramento, CA 95814. Include a self-addressed stamped envelope.

Backpacking for Beginners

No other activity requires more preplanning than backpacking. You have to eat and sleep for days or weeks without the luxury of a refrigerator, oven, and bed. Obviously, the first items you need are good hiking boots and a backpack. You'll also want a good sleeping bag and sleeping pad. As far as packs go, the debate over the merits of the old-fashioned external-frame pack and the more newfangled internal-frame pack has raged on for years. External-frame packs are generally a little cheaper; they're well suited to carrying heavy loads on fairly straight-ahead trail. But internal-frame packs have clearly outdistanced their rivals in most ways. They're more stable over rough going—rock-hopping and steep-and-twisty switchbacks—because they distribute the weight more evenly across your hips and shoulders and cinch more snugly to your back. They let you carry greater loads with more comfort, a combination that I find hard to beat. Whichever you choose, get one that really fits you—don't try to fit yourself to a pack. A good pack will have plenty of padding and support; a wide, firm hip belt; a lumbar support pad; and will feel good.

Now comes the hard part—trying to pare down your load so you don't feel purely like a beast of burden on your hike. All the essentials are listed in the "Backcountry Equipment Checklist" feature. I'm a terrible gear hound and a pack rat and always want to take everything. I indulge myself the luxury of pulling out every bit of gear I think I need and trying to fit it in my backpack; then I go put 80% of it away. I used to haul a lot of stuff around I never used. These days I'm a big proponent of going *very* light—leave the extra pants, three fishing reels, 10 pounds of chocolate, and encyclopedia set at home.

My meals on the trail are a mixture of dried foods (rice, beans, lentils, pastas, dried meats, dried fruits); Swiss-type crackers; plastic jars of peanut butter and jelly; cereal; trail mix of nuts, carob, and raisins; granola bars; cookies; and premade meals from Lipton's cup-a-soups to freeze-dried backpacker dinners. Water, of course, depends on where you're going. Most places in the Sierra Nevada or Northern Mountains have plentiful water. In the backcountry around Big Sur water can be scarce in summer. Take lots of containers and inquire at the ranger station before heading out. No matter where you are in California, treat your water to remove *Giardia*.

KAYAKING

I'd been an ocean kayaker for several years before realizing how great California is as a whitewater kayaking destination. The beauty of the kayak is its ruggedness, portability, and maneuverability, and California can put all these characteristics to the test. A good kayaker is the epitome of grace under pressure, and a bad kayaker is, well, swimming.

The advent of the sit-on-top kayak has opened the sport to casual dabbling, mostly in the ocean and lakes, and to a much smaller degree in whitewater rivers. Instead of sitting in the kayak, where beginners tend to feel claustrophobic and the consequences of tipping are much more serious, you sit on the kayak in a molded cockpit or well. That way if you tip over (and you just might) there's no panicked fear session hanging upside down while trying to Eskimo roll. You just take a nice dip and climb back on top of your boat. Of course, you give up a lot of handling and performance when you use a sit-on-top; I'd never recommend them for serious adventuring, but they're a great way to get a taste of the sport.

Whitewater kayaks are to sea kayaks what a Ferrari is to a school bus. The level of performance here is much higher, as is the steepness of the learning curve. You can become a competent kayaker in Class III (screw up and you won't die) rapids with a week's worth of classes, but you may never be able or have any desire to run Class IV (screw up and you *might* die) and Class V (screw up and it is *likely* that you will die) whitewater. The problem is that there's a lot of hard Class IV and V whitewater out there mixed in with all that forgiving Class III water, making it imperative that you know what lies below before you venture down any stretch of river. With that in mind each whitewater kayaking entry describes the general nature of an area's rivers, along with overall descriptions of the popular runs, but stops short of giving you mile-by-mile or rapid-by-rapid descriptions. This is not a river guidebook. *Read this very carefully:* We by no means intend this book to be used as the primary source of information for any whitewater run. That is why we list local experts and local guidebooks that do give extremely detailed descriptions of each run tailored to your individual level of skill.

I don't mean to imply that kayaking is terribly dangerous or scary. It's not, and done right it is one of the purest thrills I've ever felt. But if you've never kayaked in whitewater before, take it from me—go get at least a couple basic lessons. The fundamental building blocks of the sport are incredibly subtle and counterintuitive. Let someone show you how.

There are three main kayaking schools in California. The most deluxe and widely acclaimed is Otter Bar Lodge on the Salmon River (see chapter 8, "The Northern Mountains"), a wilderness resort and intensive kayaking program that operates in week-long sessions. The other two are Sierra South in Kernville (see chapter 6, "The Sierra Nevada") and California Canoe and Kayak on the American River (see chapter 7 "The Gold Country"). The latter two are both highly recommended schools with no lodging or resort features where you can take classes as short as a single day or as long as you like.

MOUNTAIN BIKING

It's no great mystery why the mountain bike was invented in California. We've got good weather and lots of back-country fire roads and trails, and distances in this state are huge. There are a lot of places you can reach in an easy 25-mile mountain bike ride over the course of an afternoon that would take days to reach on foot. Unfortunately the sport is in a major flux right now. Many trails are being closed to bikers because of conflicts with hikers and horses. Please do what you can to ease the tension: ride within your ability to stop quickly if you see a hiker or horse; dismount and let horses pass you instead of whizzing past them; don't shortcut or otherwise thrash trails; smile, say hi, and kill them with kindness.

Single tracks, double tracks, and dirt roads dominate the mountain biker's terrain. Dirt roads can range from hard-packed gravel logging roads to sandy fire roads. Double tracks vary in width from former railroad beds to old carriage paths. They are ideal trails for the beginner to intermediate biker. Single track—narrow trails created by hikers or horseback riders—whisk you in and out of the forest, within arm's length of trees and bushes on both sides. Unfortunately for us mountain bikers, the number of available single tracks has declined drastically since many of the national and state parks began banning mountain bikes from most of their trails. So-called "technical" single-track trails are the most challenging. They wind up and down hills, over rocks, roots, and soft mud that often feels like quicksand. On these trails, it is not uncommon to get off your bike and walk around or over an obstacle.

In my opinion the best mountain biking in the state is in the coast range, much of which has unfortunately been declared off-limits. Still, great places like Wilder Ranch State Park near Santa Cruz and Forest of Nisene Marks State Park near Aptos continue to allow largely unfettered mountain bike access to their fantastic networks of trails and roads. All across the state, national forest lands are crisscrossed with an elaborate network of logging roads and fire roads that double as the world's hugest mountain bike park. Within each chapter you'll find descriptions of individual rides including difficulty, distance, trailhead access information, and recommended maps, plus listings of good local mountain biking guidebooks and helpful bike shops where you might rent a bike or seek expert advice.

Here's a list of my favorite rides:

◆ **Deadman Creek to June Lake** This backcountry route between Mammoth Lakes and June Lakes epitomizes mountain biking in the eastern Sierra—changing terrain, spectacular views, and challenging conditions. You'll probably get lost, but so what—wherever you end up will be really nice.

◆ **Flume Trail, Lake Tahoe** Once the route of an old logging flume, this trail is the gem of all Tahoe area mountain biking. It's a strenuous, all-day event but the sight of the lake below while you whiz down perfect single track is enough to make the most jaded biker smile.

◆ **Wilder Ranch State Park, Santa Cruz** My favorite coastal biking within a day's drive of the Bay Area. Wilder is an explorer's dream. Lots of fire road and single track through redwood groves, creeks, and open grasslands. Endless ocean views.

◆ **Mount Shasta** So many trails surround Mount Shasta that you could ride for weeks. What sets this area apart from others, of course, is the looming presence of the mountain. Wherever you go, Shasta is there and always changing. One of the most difficult rides in the state is a single-day circumnavigation of the mountain using a combination of fire roads, paved road, and railroad grade.

◆ **The Lost Coast** In an era when mountain bikers seem to be losing their right to ride from all sides, the Lost Coast in Humboldt County is one of the last places you have to worry about access battles. What you do have to worry about is the incredible steepness and difficulty of the hundreds of miles of old logging roads through this redwood-encrusted wilderness.

ROAD BIKING

The biggest problem with road biking, in my opinion, is the existence of the automobile, and California, more than any other, is a state in love with the automobile. Nothing scares me more than biking along the margin of some busy highway just hoping that nobody is going to run me down. As a result, I've focused the road-biking coverage on how to get away from heavy traffic and onto the lesser-known country roads and byways that make a great ride. When applicable the rides are broken down into individual listings with distance, difficulty, recommended map, and suggested starting point.

The routes in this book are geared toward every type of biker imaginable. Whether you bike more than 100 miles a week or haven't been on two wheels in two years, whether you want a serious workout or want to go sightseeing at a slow pace, there are rides in each region that pertain to your level of biking.

If you're looking to go with an organized tour, the largest outfitter for California road biking is Backroads (tel. 800/245-3874), a Berkeley-based outfit running tours all over the state. Numerous other operators offering guided tours of the wine country and other regions are listed in those chapters.

ROCK CLIMBING

From sandstone outcroppings overlooking the Pacific Ocean to the huge granite walls of the Yosemite Valley, California is studded with great climbing spots. That's good, because people here are just crazy about climbing. Listing all the different routes and rocks would have been impossible, so the rock-climbing coverage is designed to give you an idea of what each climbing area is like and point you in the direction of what you hope to find.

As with whitewater kayaking, I cannot emphasize enough how important it is to know what you are doing when rock climbing. Screw up and you *will* get hurt. There's no other way around it. Wile E. Coyote can fall off a cliff and walk away because he is made of paint—you are not. There are numerous excellent schools and guides throughout Northern California that will teach you everything from the definition of *belay* to how to place protection in a finger-wide crack. They are also great sources of information on local climbing options—at the end of the rock-climbing section in each regional chapter you will find a list of local schools and guides.

SAILING

The two great sailing spots of Northern California are Monterey Bay and the San Francisco Bay. Monterey Bay is less sheltered from the open sea with higher winds and bigger waves. San Francisco Bay is a sailor's dream even though it does have heavy recreational and commercial traffic. If you're looking to learn how to sail, we've listed several schools in both areas that will teach you. If you're already an experienced skipper looking to rent a bareboat by the day or week, you'll find listings to help you locate the best one.

SCUBA DIVING

People have been known to scuba dive just about everywhere on the Northern California coast, but there's a huge difference between where you can dive and where you'd really want to dive. Monterey and its surrounding area offer some of the finest coldwater diving in the world. Within the Monterey chapter you'll find a description of some of the most popular dives and informational listings for the best dive shops and boats. The other good Northern California diving is in Sonoma and Mendocino counties, but access is severely restricted to just a few state parks that we list and describe.

Though scuba diving isn't particularly difficult or dangerous, there are some safety techniques that aren't naturally intuitive. As a result, instruction is not only strongly advised, it's mandatory. You must be certified by the National Association of Underwater Instructors (NAUI) or Professional Association of Dive Instructors (PADI) to rent scuba equipment, get tanks filled, or go on dive boats. This only goes for scuba diving, though. To snorkel or free-dive, you just need to be a confident swimmer.

SEA KAYAKING

The most popular sea kayaking area in Northern California is the waterfront of Monterey, followed closely by the bay shore of Marin County, but you can have a blast on a sea kayak just about anywhere (including lakes—don't take the name that seriously). Since an ocean kayak trip depends so much on weather, surf conditions, tides, and how energetic you're feeling that day, what you'll find here is a description of local conditions and a list of good places to put in with general trip suggestions. Since many people don't have their own boats or are looking for some guidance, you'll also find local outfitters listed in the areas that have them.

SURFING

When people think of surfing and California, they think of Malibu, Huntington Beach, San Onofre, Blacks Beach, and other famous Southern California surf spots, but they rarely think of Northern California. "It's cold up there," they say. "There are sharks." Well, they're right on both accounts: It is cold up here, full wetsuits are the prescription year-round, and in winter you'll probably want a hood, gloves, and booties. Yes, there are sharks. On the average, one surfer gets bitten by a great white shark each year in Northern California. Considering how many people go in the water, though, your odds of getting bitten by a shark are a lot less than getting killed crossing the street on the way to the beach. Santa Cruz is surf city, the center of all Northern California surf culture. Other popular spots are Pacifica, just south of San Francisco, and Ocean Beach, located in the San Francisco city

limits. North of Marin County on the real north coast there are hundreds of secret little breaks hidden at the bottom of a cliff or down a winding trail, some of which you even have to backpack to.

SWIMMING

Sometimes it's nice just to go for a swim, float around, and practice your dog paddle. With thousands of lakes, rivers, and miles of ocean, California has no shortage of places to swim. And don't overlook the Hot Springs section in the Sierra chapter.

WALKS & RAMBLES

The difference between Walks & Rambles and Hikes, Bushwhacks & Backpack Trips is the degree of physical exertion. Whereas hikes involve sweating, sore feet, etc., Walks & Rambles are generally short (between 0.5 and 2.0 miles) and relatively flat. Most involve some sort of destination: a landmark, historic building, or vista. Others are interpretive trails, marked along the route with interpretive signs explaining a particular natural feature or ecosystem. The listings contain distance and trailhead directions, but no listing of difficulty—by definition they are all easy. You could take your grandmother or your toddler on most of these, and probably should.

WHALE WATCHING

Every spring and fall more than 17,000 California gray whales swim through state waters on their annual migrations between the Gulf of Alaska, where they feed in summer, and secluded lagoons in Baja California, where they breed and give birth in the winter. The best season is the fall migration, when mothers and their calves travel up the coast in pods of five or six, sticking close to shore to avoid predators like the orcas that sometimes will attack the young calves. During the height of the migration it is not uncommon for whale-watching boats out of Monterey, Santa Cruz, Half Moon Bay, and San Francisco to spot 20 or 30 whales in one day. You don't need to go to sea to witness this huge migration, however. Along the entire coast it is possible to pick any spot with a good view of the ocean (look for someplace with a high cliff or hill to give you some height and perspective) and see just as many whales go by. The difference, of course, is that they're a lot farther away—pack your binoculars. Favorite places include Garrapata Beach in Big Sur, the Davenport Bluffs northwest of Santa Cruz, and Point Reyes in northern Marin County. In each regional chapter along the migration route we list commercial whale-watching tours as well as suggest places to spot the whales from shore.

WHITEWATER RAFTING

Last time I counted there were more than 40 different outfitters offering trips in California, on about 20 different major runs. It's a big business here, and getting bigger. The reason is that over the last five to ten years, innovations in raft design and improvements in technique have made it possible to run virtually anything in self-bailing paddle rafts, which are a hell of a lot of fun. The difference between a paddle raft and an oar raft is that in a paddle raft you, the client, are part of the paddling team coached by a guide who sits in the stern barking directions and trying to steer. Riding in an oar raft is more leisurely; the guide rows the boat from the middle and you just sit there looking pretty without having to lift a finger—a little like watching the Discovery Channel in a cold shower. Most people prefer to go

in paddle rafts for the sense of camaraderie and group achievement.

With minor exceptions most of the good whitewater runs in the state are in the Gold Country, the Southern Sierra Nevada, and the Northern Mountains. The single most popular river in the state is the American River, east of Sacramento. The most exciting? Well, these days they're running just about everything: Burnt Ranch Gorge on the Trinity, the Salmon, Cherry Creek, the Forks of Kern Run. Any of these will jack your adrenaline levels through the roof.

It'd be easy to get confused with so many rivers and outfitters to choose from. Luckily, the state's whitewater guides are a fairly organized bunch. California Outdoors, P.O. Box 401, Coloma, CA 95613 (tel. 800/552-3625) is the statewide professional organization of whitewater guides and outfitters. Don't hesitate to call with questions about a particular river or outfitter. River Travel Center, Box 226, Point Arena, CA 95468 (tel. 800/882-RAFT) is a free, centralized booking service for every outfitter on every river in California.

Outfitters

"Yeah, yeah. All these sports, I love them, but the problem is I don't have time. I don't have time to buy a bike. I don't even have time to pedal. Listen, I get two weeks off a year and then it's back to the floor of the Stock Exchange. For those two weeks, I'd like to breathe in some fresh air while I'm outside. A nice bike trip in Sonoma, hiking in the Sierra, you know what I mean. And I don't want to take care of a damn thing— no flat tires, no rentals, no accommodations, no food, nothin'. Ya got it?"

So you want to participate in some sort of outdoor activity in the day and be pampered at night? You want someone to guide you on your sporting excursion and you don't want to be bothered with equipment problems, finding a trailhead, renting a canoe, or, as the case may be, setting up a tent and cooking over a fire? You want someone to deal with all your arrangements, but you still want to take the best trips as outlined in this book? Then you'll need to find an outfitter.

The irony is that even finding a good outfitter and trip takes time. Hopefully, I'll save you hours of research by listing my favorite outfitters under each sport heading in the regional chapters. However, certain questions should always be asked. Most are commonsensical. Some are related to specific sports:

1. *What's the cost and what's included in the price?*

First and foremost, discuss the type of accommodation and whether all meals are included. Some companies skip lunch or an occasional dinner. Is liquor included? Then ask about shuttles to and from airports, cost of rentals, bikes, skis, etc.

2. *What level of fitness is required?*

By far, the most important question. Get a feeling for the tour. Is this an obstacle course better suited for Marines, a walk in the park for couch potatoes, or something in between? Do I have to bike 20, 40, or 60 miles a day? Do I have options for each day? Can I go shopping or sightseeing one day while my wife bikes to her legs' delight?

3. *How long have you been in business?*

Good outfitters stay in business; bad ones don't. If they've been around a long time you can expect that they're doing things right.

4. *What's the experience level of the guides?*

Many outfitters are desperate enough to hire guides who, until very recently, had no experience in that sport or are from an entirely different part of the country. The American River is notorious for having whitewater "guides" with only marginally more experience than most of the clients. Depending on the intensity level of the activity, this can be a real problem.

5. *How many people are in the group?*

What is the guide-to-client ratio? Do I have to compete with 30 or 5 other people for the guide's attention?

6. *Is it mostly singles or couples?*

Guided tours are a great place to befriend other singles or couples. Make sure you find out which trip best suits your needs.

7. *What equipment is required? What type of equipment can I rent?*

Some outfitters, particularly fly-fishing companies, request that you bring your own equipment. Others will rent you gear. Find out what they offer, especially bikes. Do they rent 10-speed Raleighs or 21-speed Cannondales and Treks?

8. *What happens if it rains?*

Do you have alternative plans or do you expect me to bike around the Napa Valley in a downpour.

9. *How much free time do we have?*

Is every minute of the day accounted for or should I bring that new novel I've been wanting to read?

10. *How far in advance do I need to book?*

Don't miss out on a limited amount of spaces by waiting until the last minute. Some of these tours are booked a year in advance.

11. *Can I bring young children?*

Most outfitters will usually answer affirmative to this. A buck is a buck, no matter who hikes or sits on the bike. However, you should take yourself and the other guests into account. Do you really want to bring the kids along? Do the other guests really want you to bring your kids along? Is this trip appropriate for children? Will they have a good time?

The main pro to hiring a guide is the complete and utter lack of responsibility on your part. Most outfitters will find a way to relieve all your vacation worries, from accommodations to food to equipment. You also have a chance to make new friends. The con is the additional cost. Most of these trips can be done on your own for much less money. The other con is the lack of privacy. There's no place better than a mountaintop, lonely backcountry road, or tranquil river to collect your thoughts and gain a sense of serenity. On vacation, you've earned a certain amount of peace and quiet. This fragile state can easily be shattered by the woman with the shrill voice and the constantly running video camera, or the man in the next tent who snores all night. Or maybe you just won't *like* the people fate throws your way. The best way to eliminate this problem is to simply book the whole trip with a group of your friends.

Below is a list of seven of the largest outfitters in the country—it's just the tip of the outfitter iceberg, but gives you a place to start:

◆ **American Wilderness Experience,** P.O. Box 1486, Boulder, CO 80306 (800/ 444-0099). Backpacking, dude ranches, mountain biking, river running (canoes, kayaks, and rafts). Fully supported. 5–22 days.

◆ **American Youth Hostels,** 733 15th St. N.W., Ste. 840, Washington, DC 20005 (tel. 202/783-6161). Bike tours, hiking trips, and, of course, the largest selection of hostels in the state. Hostels and programs are open to all ages despite the name.

◆ **Backroads Bicycle Touring,** 801 Cedar St., Berkeley, CA 94710 (tel. 510/527-1555 or 800/245-3874). The biggest and best-organized bicycle touring operation in the world. Backroads leads weekend and week-long tours specifically geared to a special set of interests; for example, singles weekends,

family outings, wine tastings, wilderness trips. Sag wagons accompany all trips, so if you find yourself waning, you'll have a ride back to your accommodations, usually an inn or B&B.

◆ **ECHO: The Wilderness Company,** 6529·Telegraph Ave., Oakland, CA 94609 (tel. 510/652-1600 or 800/652-ECHO). Specializing in rafting trips all over the world, ECHO also runs fishing seminars and river trips in inflatable kayaks.

◆ **Outward Bound USA,** 384 Field Point Rd., Greenwich, CT 06830 (tel. 800/243-8520). Outward Bound strives to foster personal growth by pushing people to the edge of their personal physical and emotional limits through challenging outdoor experiences. Unlike most outfitters, whose job it is to make sure that your trip is a seamless montage of perfect moments, a wilderness pleasure cruise, Outward Bound teaches you to fend for yourself, then puts you in tough situations where you'll need that training. Some people love it. Some hate it. Just don't go into it with false expectations.

◆ **Sierra Club Outings,** 730 Polk St., San Francisco, CA 94109 (tel. 415/ 977-5630). Since its creation in 1892, the Sierra Club has been dedicated to protecting and enjoying the outdoors. Each year the club offers hundreds of trips and expeditions around the world: bike tours, raft trips, ski touring, canoeing, canyoneering, backpacking, you name it. Two basic kinds of programs are offered: the Travel Program and the Service Program. Both involve travel in the wilderness, but the Travel Program is more geared toward recreational enjoyment. Service trips combine volunteer work like trail maintenance, archaeological surveys, and wildlife counts with outdoor enjoyment.

◆ **The Nature Conservancy**, 4245 N. Fairfax Dr., Arlington, VA 22203 (tel. 703/ 841-5300). Primarily dedicated to purchasing and preserving large tracts of endangered land, the Nature Conservancy also offers trips and work-study options for people wishing to explore their extensive holdings.

Schools

Instruction is an important aspect of outdoor recreation. For sports like sailing, scuba diving, sea kayaking, whitewater kayaking, and rock climbing, schooling is imperative. Lessons in cross-country or downhill skiing, mountain biking, horseback riding, fishing, and canoeing can only improve your skills and make the sport more enjoyable.

The same questions asked to outfitters above apply to schools. Group size is extremely important. You want to be in a small group where you get personal attention. Be blunt with your questioning. If you want to be able to bareboat charter a sailboat in Monterey Bay or kayak down a Class III river, inquire whether you'll be able to achieve those goals by the end of the course. Also ask how much time is spent in the classroom compared to time spent actually participating in the activity. Lectures are one thing, but nothing compares to the lessons of hands-on experience. I've found that the best schools and instructors impart their knowledge through guided activities rather than abstract theories. Throughout the regional chapters, I have pointed out schools that pertain to each activity.

Maps

As anyone who has ever gone backcountry hiking knows, a good map can be your best friend. For that reason, I have listed under each featured trip how to locate maps. Many hikes simply have maps at the trailhead or park visitors center. In other cases, I have mentioned the appropriate United States Geological Survey (USGS) maps—topographical maps designed by the U.S. government. Many of these maps can be found at local bookstores or sporting goods stores. If you can't locate the map for a particular section, go to the source, **U.S. Geological Survey,** Federal Center, Building 810, P.O. Box 25286, Denver, CO 80225 (tel. 800/USA-MAPS).

Books

For many activities covered in this book, particularly whitewater kayaking or hiking the John Muir Trail, a specialized guidebook is absolutely indispensable. In many of the sports listings, I refer to specific books. Below is a list of more generalized books about Northern California:

◆ *California Coastal Resource Guide* California Coastal Commission (University of California Press, 1987). An unbelievably detailed inventory of the coastal resources in the state. Arranged north to south, the resource guide will tell you everything from what that weird salamander is to where to go surfing. The Coastal Commission has also published a *Coastal Access Guide.* The only problem with both these books is their unwieldy size. They don't really fit into a travel pack.

◆ *California State Parks: A Complete Recreation Guide* Rhonda and George Ostertag (The Mountaineers, 1995). An excellent guide to California state parks including hikes, camping information, history, wildlife, and practical travel information.

◆ *Great Hot Springs of the West* Bill and Ruth Kaysing (Capra Press, 1993). It's unfortunate that this book is bound in a large-page format because it is such a handy travel resource. Hot springs throughout the west are included with good maps and accurate descriptions.

Not very comprehensive but it will get you to the major springs.

◆ *Roadside Geology of Northern California* David Alt and Donald Hyndman (Mountain Press, 1994). What's neat about this book is that it doesn't speak in generalizations: it points to specific features along Northern California roadways and explains what they mean and where each particular region of the state fits into the big geological picture.

◆ *The High Sierra: Peaks, Passes and Trails* R. J. Secor (The Mountaineers, 1992). Ostensibly a book of climbing routes and backcountry trails, this volume is one of the best researched and most authoritative books about the history, geology, and practicalities of traveling in the High Sierra.

Spas

There's a hard way and an easy way to do everything. If you like the easy way, Northern California's spa scene is the thing for you. Usually centered around natural hot springs or in out-there resort areas, most California spas offer massage, hot pools, mud baths, and comfortable lodging and great food. Though largely centered in the Napa and Sonoma valleys, there are several spas, or at least hotels with spa services, in Big Sur and in the Sierra Nevada.

What's great about combining, say, a bike trip to the Napa Valley with a stay at some of the spas in Calistoga is that you'll experience the satisfaction that can only come from working your muscles until they're sore, then turning your body over to expert hands to feel better again.

One of the best resources for finding spas is *California Spas and Urban Retreats* by Laurel Cook (Foghorn Press, 1993). Though Cook doesn't really get into outdoor sports at all, her information about the spas themselves can be really useful.

A Note on Camping

It's an unfortunate fact of life that in a state with 20 million residents and millions more visitors, it's sometimes a little tough to find the perfect campsite. There are two main approaches to the problem. One is to get your reservations far in advance. The state parks (tel. 800/444-PARK), national parks (tel. 800/365-CAMP), and large national forest campgrounds (tel. 800/280-CAMP) all have centralized reservation numbers. Unfortunately they are all managed by a reservation service called MISTIX, based out of Florida or somewhere, that appears to be run entirely by computers. Not hardworking, trustworthy computers, mind you, but computers that only work during normal business hours and follow a bizarre system of logic. For the pleasure of dealing with seemingly endless multiple-choice computerized voice loops to reserve your campsite, you get to pay MISTIX the cost of your site, plus a $6 to $8 reservation fee. Know the exact name of the park you are visiting, the exact campground, and hopefully, the exact campsite you're seeking, and have your credit card ready, or dealing with MISTIX is pretty much a lost cause.

The second method, which is the one I usually subscribe to, is flexibility. Instead of camping at the famous national park on a busy weekend, I find some tiny national forest campground nearby that doesn't take reservations, or I camp in the most far-flung corners of Yosemite or Kings Canyon. Show up around noon, when people are leaving. Think back roads and out-of-the-way places, many of which are actually more beautiful and more relaxing than the overrun "famous" spots. I've won some and lost some this way, but at least I didn't spend 45 minutes on the phone with a computer only to end up camped next door to the annual Hell's Angels road rally.

2

The San Francisco Bay Area

PERHAPS NO OTHER MAJOR METROPOLITAN REGION IN THE UNITED States is as blessed with plentiful and nearby outdoor recreation as the Bay Area. From its defining feature—the bay itself—to Golden Gate Park, the mountains of Marin County, wild Pacific beaches, and the inland parks and hills of the East Bay, the Bay Area attracts people from all over seeking outdoor adventure, something you just don't find in a lot of cities.

A study conducted by People for Open Space, a San Francisco–based environmental group, counted more than 700,000 acres of open space within San Francisco, Marin, San Mateo, Santa Clara, Alameda, and Contra Costa counties. Those acres include several national parks, monuments, and seashores, a dozen state parks, watershed preserves, and many excellent county and city parks. The survey didn't include the bay itself as open space, which adds another 400 square miles of potential sailing, fishing, boardsailing, kayaking, and swimming.

A number of factors played an important role in preserving so much open land. When the area first began growing rapidly around the turn of the century, city planners realized that if they wanted to develop the bay waterfront, which lacks any sort of good groundwater, they would have to preserve the high watersheds of the surrounding hills to provide water. As a result, thousands of acres were preserved for the sake of catching rainwater runoff. Today these lands offer some of the best mountain biking and hiking in the region.

Other large tracts of land were set aside by private landowners and early environmentalists who foresaw the need to preserve large areas of pristine land long before most realized it would someday be such a scarce commodity. Muir Woods is one such example where a wealthy philanthropist outbid a lumber company to purchase this dramatic grove, narrowly saving it from becoming redwood siding in some San Francisco Victorian.

Weather and dramatic geology also conspired to keep parts of the Bay Area protected. Not many people live on the Pacific side of the peninsula simply because it is remote, windy, and foggy much of the year. Marin County, now a swanky bedroom community to San Francisco, was separated from the city by the current-swept channel of the bay mouth until the Golden Gate Bridge was completed in 1937. Most people in the Bay Area are clustered in a relatively narrow strip of land around the tip of the peninsula and along the inside edge of the bay. Some sprawl spills over the eastern hills, and the South Bay suburbs around San Jose seem to go on forever, but for most Bay Area residents a large undeveloped tract of land is only a short distance away.

The two big urban park districts in the Bay Area, the Golden Gate National Recreation Area and the East Bay Regional Parks District, have done an admirable job of connecting the region's urban areas with the necklace of wild parklands that surrounds them. As a result, it is possible to bike from the city's crowded Marina District across the bridge to the wild and scenic Marin Headlands in about 15 minutes. Pedaling another 15 to 20 minutes will take you to the old-growth redwoods of Muir Woods. Try that in New York City, Los Angeles, or Chicago.

The climate is conducive to utilizing all that space. Though San Francisco Bay went undiscovered by Europeans until 1769 because the omnipresent marine fog shrouding the Golden Gate kept early Spanish explorers from seeing the great harbor entrance, you shouldn't let the famous San Francisco fog keep you away too. Fog is only one of the Bay Area's many faces. While on any given day it can be foggy and cold somewhere in the Bay Area, this is a region of dramatic microclimates. It might be freezing at Golden Gate Park but sunny and beautiful on Angel Island. An open mind and a flexible schedule are the key. If it's too hot to go mountain biking on Mount Diablo, head to Point Reyes for a hike. If the surf is too big at Ocean Beach to go out, go kayaking in Richardson Bay instead.

Though San Francisco owes its status as a city to the Gold Rush of 1849—one of the worst disasters man has ever inflicted on California's natural surroundings—since then it has historically been a city with a green conscience and a hankering for environmental action. The Sierra Club, formed here by John Muir and a number of his San Francisco friends to protect their favorite hiking and climbing areas, went on to become one of the world's most influential environmental groups. Greenpeace, Forest Action Network, and the Earth Island Institute are all based in the Bay Area. Like any big metropolitan area, the Bay Area has its environmental horror stories (such as the City of San Francisco drowning Yosemite's Hetch Hetchy Valley under a reservoir, or the continual air pollution of the East Bay), but it has also been a leader on the progressive edge of urban planning and environmental preservation.

San Francisco in particular is a place that emphasizes quality of life over convenience. When the 1989 Loma Prieta earthquake knocked down the Embarcadero freeway through town, city voters elected not to rebuild it on the grounds that getting through town quickly wasn't nearly as important as the quality of life in the neighborhoods that would be affected by the freeway. Other expressions of anti–status quo thinking are more overt: one Friday each month hundreds of Bay Area cyclists converge on Market Street in an informal ride called Critical Mass. The goal is to stop all automobile traffic downtown in symbolic opposition to the tyranny of the automobile. This takeover of city streets is not only tolerated by City Hall, but it is provided with a police escort to make sure nobody gets hurt.

The Lay of the Land

The Bay Area is so diverse that it is difficult to talk about as a single entity. The very bay that defines the area also serves to separate and distinguish between the surrounding communities and geographic features. The coastal mountains of Marin County and the peninsula are a lush mix of oak woodland, rolling grassland, and dramatic redwood and Douglas fir forest. In the canyon bottoms, an understory of poison oak and blackberry vines grow alongside ferns, dogwoods, and bay laurel under a covering of first-growth, or more likely second-growth, redwoods or Douglas fir. Along the bay shore, wetlands were once predominant, but most of the bay's marshy habitat (300 square miles, worth) has been filled in to build airports, housing tracts, and shopping malls, and only a few undeveloped miles of shoreline remain, mostly in the East Bay and Marin.

Because they lie in the rain shadow of the coastal mountains and are farther from the temperature-moderating effect of the Pacific, the hills of the East Bay are relatively hot and dry. The highest point in the Bay Area is the East Bay's 3,849-foot Mount Diablo, visible for hundreds of miles on a clear day and a great lookout. When conditions are right you can see as far as Mount Lassen in the Cascades or make out the distinctive shape of Half Dome in the Yosemite Valley. Diablo, like the rest of the East Bay mountains, is covered by rolling grass, oak savannah, and brushy chaparral, and a few more heavily vegetated areas occur where stream canyons concentrate the runoff. One species, the eucalyptus tree, tends to dominate as it's particularly well adapted to the East Bay's climate. Imported from Australia in the 19th century, the exotic blue gum eucalyptus took off, eventually crowding out native species. Recently, the eucalyptus has fallen into disfavor after several wildfires fueled by the volatile wood devastated homes and parkland in the East Bay. An ongoing debate between those who want to remove the trees because they don't belong in the area and those who think they're a historically and ecologically important part of the California landscape flares up every time one of the park districts cuts down a eucalyptus grove. Eucalyptus or not, many excellent hiking and biking areas are hidden in the folds of the East Bay's rolling hills.

The Pacific coast of Marin, San Francisco, and San Mateo counties is a completely different world from the more urbanized parts of the Bay Area. Other than a short stretch of developed coast inside the San Francisco City limits and into Pacifica, you'd never know that millions of people live within a 20-mile radius. Point Reyes National Seashore anchors one end of this beautiful coast with 65,000 acres of protected land, 32,000 of it designated wilderness. From here south to the Golden Gate, the Marin coast is a wild mix of long sandy beaches popular with surfers and sunbathers, and sheer, rocky ocean cliffs that ward off even the most daredevil adventurers.

Across the Golden Gate, San Francisco has some incredible coastline within city limits. Baker Beach in the Presidio is a favorite summertime hangout. Ocean Beach, a 4-mile sandy beach between the Cliff House and Fort Funston, is a world-renowned surfing spot made even more famous by a two-part *New Yorker* piece a few years ago profiling San Francisco surfer Mark "Doc" Renneker. South of San Francisco the coast quickly becomes wild again, passing through the precipitous Devil's Slide just south of Pacifica. The main town between San Francisco and Santa Cruz is Half Moon Bay, a small port backed by steeply rising forested hills. Once a hardscrabble fishing town, Half Moon Bay has become something of a tourist destination. Whale-watching tours and salmon fishing out of Pillar Point Harbor are big business here now, and bed and breakfasts are springing up all over town. Maverick's, the once-secret big wave riding spot, is located just outside the north harbor jetty—it became the center of a worldwide media feeding frenzy when professional surfer Mark Foo died there after wiping out on a 20-foot wave on Christmas Eve, 1994.

Other beaches near Half Moon Bay are popular for camping and swimming though the water is chilly. From Half Moon Bay along the shore, a number of state beaches, such as San Gregorio, Pompanio, and Bean Hollow, line the west side of the Highway 1 strip and draw flocks of visitors on busy summer weekends. Other times of year they can be nearly deserted. On the inland side of Highway 1, many of these state parks reach into the coastal hills and forests for great hiking, biking, and camping that is often overlooked by visitors intent on spending the day at the beach.

Then there's the bay itself. The mile-wide Golden Gate is the largest break in the California coast range, yet the looming headlands on either side are so dramatic they nearly obscure the bay entrance. Four times a day the tides pour in or out through this narrow channel, surging past the pillars of the Golden Gate Bridge at what can be a terrifying clip if you've misjudged your kayaking ability or broken some vital piece of equipment on your sailboard just as the tide begins going out. Which is not to discourage anyone; hundreds of board-sailers put in at Crissy Field to sail the bay every time the wind blows, and people swim across the Golden Gate every year. Just be extremely cautious: know the limits of your ability and time your voyage to coincide with slack or incoming tides so you don't end up halfway to the Farallon Islands. Look out for busy ship traffic too if you venture into the open bay.

Other parts of the bay are more forgiving and better suited to casual exploration. Aquatic Park in the Marina District is a favorite with swimmers, many of whom swim here every day without wetsuits even though the water is a chilly 52° to 58°F. A small sand beach makes getting in easier than staying in. Richardson Bay is the catchall name for the protected waters of the Marin Coast between Sausalito, Tiburon, and Angel Island. Ideally suited to sea kayaking and sailing, this is a great area for all ability levels to get on the bay. Angel Island, the largest and most pristine of the bay islands, is accessible by ferry or private boat. A military garrison between the Civil War and World War II, Angel Island is now a state park. You can set up a tent at the island's environmental campsites, and hike or bike the old

San Francisco's Average Temperatures and Precipitation											
	Jan	Feb	Mar	Apr	May	June	July	Aug	Sept	Oct	Nov	Dec
High (°F)	56	60	61	63	64	66	66	66	70	69	64	57
Low (°F)	46	48	49	50	51	53	54	54	56	55	51	47
Precipitation (in.)	4.1	3.5	2.9	1.5	0.5	0.2	trace	trace	0.2	1.1	2.6	3.9

military roads to the top of Mount Livermore, the highest point on the island. Though pollution and cutbacks in the amount of fresh water pouring into the bay have left some species reeling, fishing is still a popular pastime when large game fish like striped bass, salmon, and steelhead come through the bay on the way to their spawning or feeding grounds in the rivers of Northern California's central valley and delta. A number of long piers provide fishing access in Berkeley, San Francisco, and the South Bay.

Orientation

THE PENINSULA

San Francisco

Surrounded on three sides by water, the city lies at the northern end of a 50-mile-long peninsula dividing the bay from the Pacific. The city has a reputation for fog and fierce weather drawn in off the ocean by the Golden Gate's break in the coast range. While it is true that the city gets more than its fair share of bad weather, it also gets more than its fair share of wonderful ocean breezes, amazing scenery, and plentiful outdoor activities. In the last decade the city has become the center of a high-tech youth culture, full of computer and information workers who labor behind computers all day and play hard all weekend. The list of activities that

go on all the time within the city limits ranges from base jumping (skydiving from a stationary object) of financial district skyscrapers, to surfing at Ocean Beach, to trout fishing in Lake Merced.

Within the city are numerous large parks, including the Presidio, Land's End, Golden Gate Park, Ocean Beach, Lake Merced, the Marina Green, Aquatic Park, Baker Beach, and Fort Funston, where you can fish, hang glide, boardsail, surf, sail, hike, or have a picnic. The largest park authority in the area is the Golden Gate Recreation Area (tel. 415/556-0560), headquartered in Fort Mason on Marina Boulevard, which manages the bay islands and the entire coast from the Golden Gate to Fort Funston. A fantastic book put out by the Golden Gate National Parks Association is the *GGNRA Recreation Area Park Guide*. A hip-pocket-sized reference, the 100-page book is a valuable source of the historical, the practical, and the trivial; in short, just about anything you could want to know about outdoor recreation in the city. The thousand acres of Golden Gate Park (hiking, picnicking, playing fields, fly-casting ponds, museums, . . .) are managed separately by the City of San Francisco. Park Headquarters (tel. 415/556-0560) are located in McLaren Lodge at Fell and Stanyon where you can get maps and activity schedules.

Pacifica

Once south of the city and county limits of San Francisco, the coastal zone of

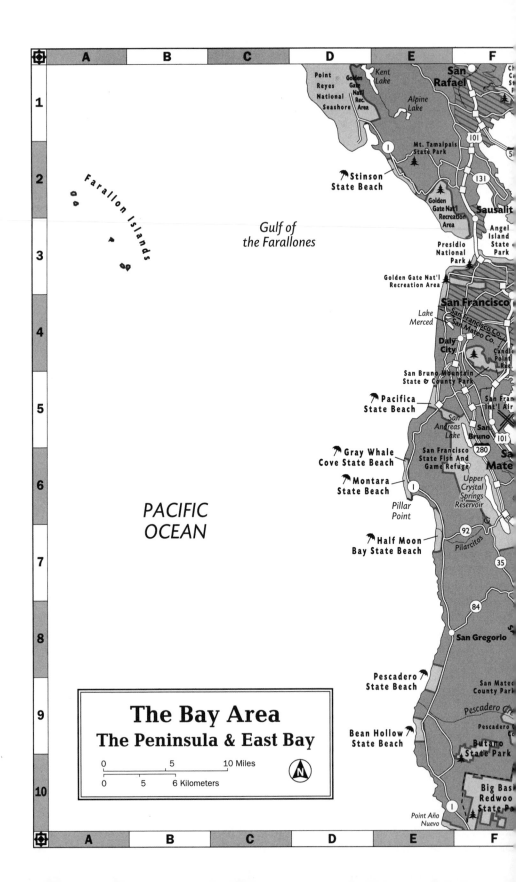

The Bay Area
The Peninsula & East Bay

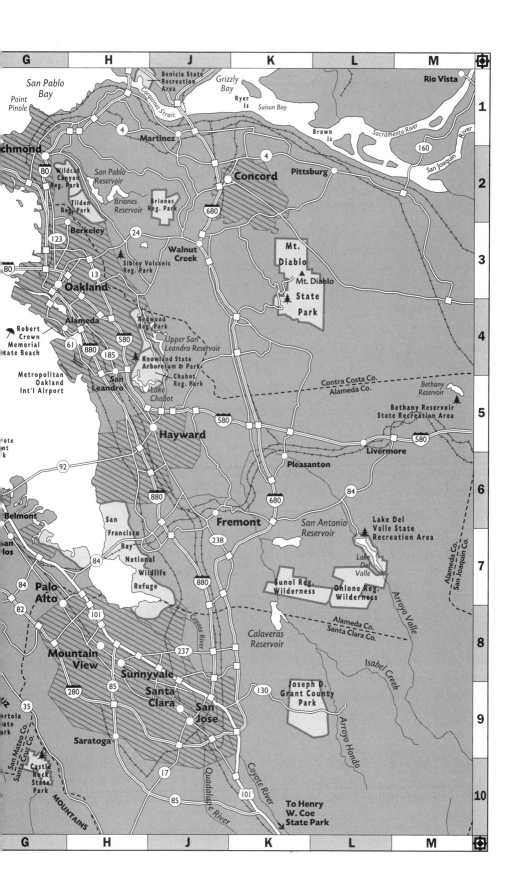

San Mateo County passes through Pacifica, a ticky-tacky little town of trailer parks and 1950s tract homes, and then quickly becomes less populated. Sharp Park Beach and Pier is a popular fishing and surfing spot right in Pacifica. The pier stretches a quarter mile out and is open 24 hours a day for fishing. Rockaway and San Pedro beaches are also popular, and the Sweeney Ridge segment of the GGNRA rises above Rockaway where you can find miles of hiking trails into the coastal mountains. The main Sweeney Ridge Trailhead starts near the nursery at 2,000 Cabrillo Hwy. (Highway 1).

Devil's Slide

Exactly 1 mile south of San Pedro Point, Highway 1 passes through the Devil's Slide, an aptly named stretch of road on the shoulder of one incredibly unstable area of coastal cliff. The road here, hundreds of feet above the ocean, is in a state of perpetual repair as it slides downhill after nearly every heavy rain. There is talk of replacing it with a tunnel through Sweeney Ridge.

MARIN COUNTY

Bolinas

North of Bolinas Lagoon on Olema-Bolinas Road. Back about 30 years in time.

Bolinas is the town that time forgot, circa 1968. Less than 1,000 people live in this wonderful throwback where dogs and children run wild and loose in the four streets that make up this tiny town surrounded by Bolinas Lagoon, Point Reyes, and the Pacific Ocean. They've got everything they need here: a bar, a good cafe, an organic grocery, sandy beaches, and virtually no traffic. To keep

it this way they tear down the street signs from Highway 1 as soon as Caltrans puts them up. Now if only they could change the name of the Bolinas Lagoon they could really hide out. Several good trailheads into the southern reaches of Point Reyes leave from Mesa Road.

Panoramic Highway

From Mill Valley to Stinson Beach, this windy two-lane road goes over the crest of Mount Tam instead of sticking to the coast like Highway 1. Many great hikes and vistas are reached from here including the summit of Mount Tam.

Parks & Other Hot Spots

THE PENINSULA

The Presidio

Southern base of the Golden Gate Bridge. For information call the Presidio Army Museum (tel. 415/561-4323) or the GGNRA Headquarters (tel. 415/556-0560). Hiking and biking trails, beaches, golf course, historic buildings, restrooms, outdoor showers, picnic areas.

For more than two centuries the Presidio was a huge military base guarding the Golden Gate. Though it has long been open to the public, it is now in the process of being converted into a National Park. Baker Beach, Fort Point, and Crissy Field are popular for sunning, surfing, and windsurfing. Wooded paths and dramatic views of the Bay and the Golden Gate make hiking and walking in the Presidio very rewarding—one of the best urban nature experiences in the

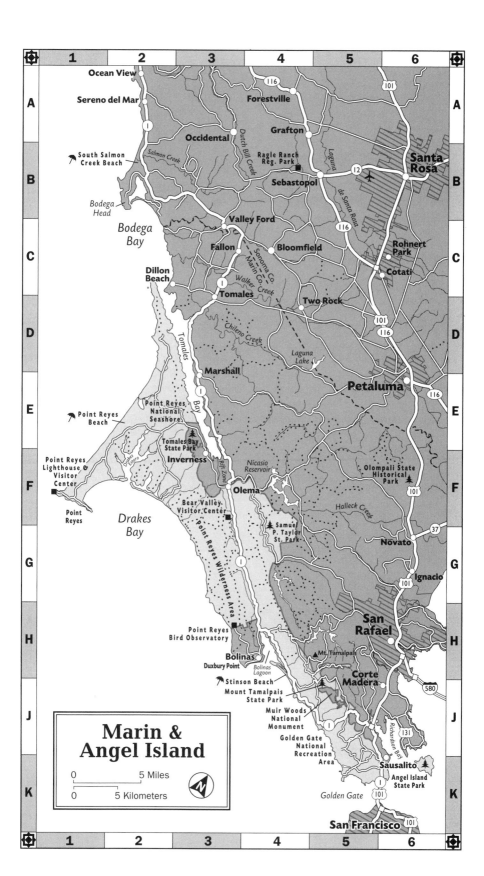

Marin & Angel Island

United States. See the feature on the Presidio a little later in this chapter.

San Bruno Mountain State and County Park

Access from Guadalupe Canyon Parkway from Bayshore Boulevard or I-280. Tel. 415/355-8289. Hiking and biking trails, restrooms, picnic area.

What's remarkable about this park is that it is here at all. At one time the mountain was targeted to be torn down, dumped in the bay, and used as fill for an airport (mind you, we're talking about a mountain, not just a hill). Other plans would have covered the mountain with condos. Two endangered butterflies, the Mission Blue and San Bruno elfin, are responsible for the preservation of these 2,700 acres of the last large coastal scrub habitat on the peninsula.

Coyote Point Recreation Area and Museum

Access from U.S. 101 southbound exit at Poplar Avenue and follow signs to park, which is on Coyote Point Drive. Tel. 650/573-2592. Natural history museum, beach, showers, restrooms, restaurant, bike path, marina, rifle range.

This is one of the few actual waterfront beach accesses on the bay, but the main reason for coming here is the incredible Museum for Environmental Education (tel. 650/342-7755). The museum is designed to allow visitors to explore fully the six biotic communities in San Mateo County: broadleaf forest, coniferous forest, chaparral, grassland, badlands, and

seacoast. Computer games, working beehives and ant colonies, food-chain dioramas, and a continually changing list of exhibits are displayed in a high-tech, environmentally friendly building.

Montara Area Beaches and Parks

Both sides of Highway 1 between Devil's Slide and Half Moon Bay. Tel. 650/573-2592. Hiking, beaches, parking, restrooms, outdoor showers.

South of the Devil's Slide the coast turns inland, but a number of state beaches provide ocean access. Most of them have parking and restrooms. Some, but not all, charge day use or parking fees. None have camping. Gray Whale Cove State Beach (tel. 650/728-5336) is the first, a beautiful sandy cove beach reached by a stairway. Montara State Beach comes soon after, a particularly popular mile-long stretch of sand that is matched on the other side of Highway 1 by 2,000-acre McNee Ranch State Park, the site of some great mountain biking and hiking. The Montara Lighthouse (tel. 650/728-7177) just south of Montara is a popular youth hostel. South of here about a mile is the James V. Fitzgerald Marine Reserve (tel. 415/728-3584), a wonderful zone of rocky intertidal reefs and tide pools where, since its declaration as a reserve in 1969, scientists have found 25 new species. Interpretive programs and tide pool walks are led by park docents on a regular basis; call for current schedules.

Pillar Point Harbor

West of Highway 1 and Capistrano Road. Tel. 650/728-3377 for harbor activity information.

You can't miss Pillar Point; it's the huge headland with a huge radio telescope and satellite tracking station just west of Highway 1. The harbor here in the lee of the point is an important fishing and boat-building port; plus it's the only safe harbor between San Francisco and Monterey Bay. Charter fishing boats and whale-watching cruises leave from the port town of Princeton daily. A nice wetland and beach are found in the northernmost corner of the harbor—perfect for children.

Half Moon Bay State Beaches

West of Highway 1 in Half Moon Bay. Tel. 650/726-8820. Picnic tables, restrooms, motorhome and hike/bike campsites, beach, outdoor showers.

Half Moon Bay stretches from Pillar Point to Miramontes Point about 5 miles south. In between, this 3-mile-long stretch of several adjacent beach parks allows public access to the longest uninterrupted sand beach on the San Mateo Coast. El Granada Beach is a popular beginning surfers' hangout as well as a motorhome campsite. Farther south you come to Roosevelt, Dunes, Venice, and Francis beaches, all of them broad sandy beaches linked by the blufftop Coastside Trail.

Southern San Mateo Coast Beaches and Parks

Both sides of Highway 1 between Half Moon Bay and Año Nuevo. Tel. 650/879-0227. Wild beaches and parks with nonflush restrooms, picnic areas, lighthouse, hostel, campground, wildlife viewing.

From Half Moon Bay to the San Mateo County line, Highway 1 passes through one of the best concentrations of state parks anywhere. The state beaches, Bean Hollow, Pomonio, Pescadero, and San Gregorio, provide fantastic ocean access in this otherwise rugged coast. On the mountain side of the road, Pescadero Marsh, San Gregorio estuary, Bean Hollow State Park, and Butano State Park offer great hiking, bird watching, and camping. The wetlands and redwoods of this area are a good example of what much of the peninsula looked like prior to development.

San Mateo Memorial County Park and Pescadero Creek County Park

8 miles inland of Pescadero on Pescadero Road. Tel. 415/879-0173. Hiking, creek swimming, camping, nature museum.

Altogether more than 6,000 acres of virgin redwoods and the upper watershed of Pescadero Creek. Trails connect the two parks and Portola State Park.

Portola State Park

From State Route 35 (Skyline Boulevard) go west on Alpine Road 3.5 miles to State Park Road. Tel. 415/948-9098. Camping, restrooms, showers, visitors center, hiking, mountain biking, wildlife viewing.

In the upper headwaters of Pescadero Creek, Portola State Park is a hidden jewel of San Mateo County. The second-growth redwood forest, creek, and campground get much less use than

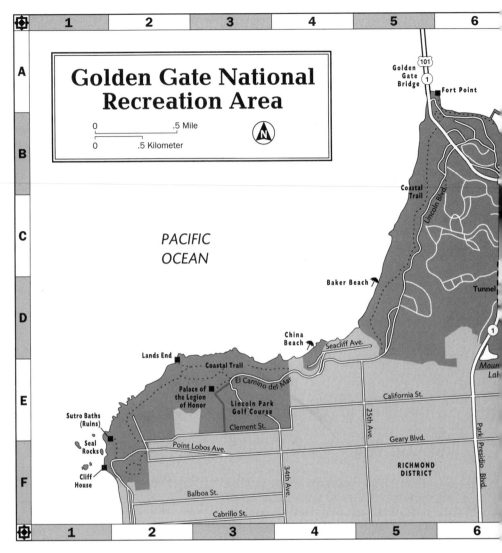

Golden Gate National Recreation Area

0   .5 Mile

0   .5 Kilometer

PACIFIC OCEAN

Golden Gate Bridge

Fort Point

Coastal Trail

Lincoln Blvd.

Baker Beach

Tunnel

China Beach

Seacliff Ave.

Lands End

Coastal Trail

El Camino del Mar

Palace of the Legion of Honor

Lincoln Park Golf Course

California St.

Sutro Baths (Ruins)

25th Ave.

Clement St.

Seal Rocks

Point Lobos Ave.

Geary Blvd.

Cliff House

34th Ave.

RICHMOND DISTRICT

Park Presidio Blvd.

Balboa St.

Cabrillo St.

Moun Lak

---

other Santa Cruz mountain redwood parks.

Castle Rock State Park

From State Route 9, take State Route 35 south 2.5 miles. Tel. 408/867-2952. Backcountry camping, picnic tables, hiking and horse trails, rock climbing, nonflush toilets, water.

Known mostly as the closest rock climbing to the South Bay (on Castle and Goat Rocks, 100-foot-high sandstone outcroppings), Castle Rock is also the starting point of the 37-mile Skyline to the Sea Trail that traverses the Santa Cruz mountains and is a popular spot for picnics and short walks.

Point Reyes National Seashore

Access from Highway 1 or Sir Francis Drake Boulevard. Tel. 415/663-1092. Flush toilets, running water, restaurant, museums, 100 miles of hiking trails, bird and whale

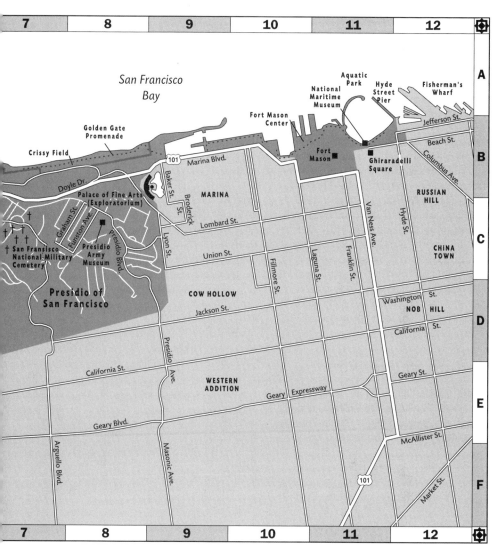

San Francisco
Bay

A

Aquatic
Park

National
Maritime
Museum

Hyde
Street
Pier

Fisherman's
Wharf

Fort Mason
Center

Jefferson St.

Golden Gate
Promenade

Beach St.

Crissy Field

101 Marina Blvd.

Fort
Mason

Ghiraradelli
Square

Columbus Ave.

B

Doyle Dr.

Baker St.

MARINA

RUSSIAN
HILL

Palace of Fine Arts
(Exploratorium)

Broderick St.

Lombard St.

Hyde St.

Van Ness Ave.

C

Graham St.

Funston Ave.

Lyon St.

Union St.

Fillmore St.

Laguna St.

Franklin St.

CHINA
TOWN

San Fransisco
National Military
Cemetery

Presidio
Army
Museum

Presidio Blvd.

Presidio of
San Francisco

COW HOLLOW

Jackson St.

Washington St.

NOB HILL

D

California St.

Presidio Ave.

California St.

WESTERN
ADDITION

Geary Expressway

Geary St.

E

Geary Blvd.

McAllister St.

Arguello Blvd.

Masonic Ave.

101

Market St.

F

watching, 44-bed hostel, Native American history exhibits, horse farm. Open year-round. No fee.

Point Reyes, set aside as a national seashore in 1962 by President John F. Kennedy, is paradise found for birders, whale-watchers, beachgoers, and hikers. The best backcountry camping in the Bay Area is here in the wooded southern part of the seashore (36,000 acres of which are designated wilderness). Other areas are set aside as agricultural preserves, continuing an old tradition of coastal dairy farming on the ocean bluffs, and some areas are used for commercial oyster farming. For information see the feature on Point Reyes later in this chapter.

Tomales Bay State Park

Access from several points on Bear Valley Road or Highway 1. Tel. 415/669-1140. Beaches, hiking, bike-in and walk-in camping, bird watching, restrooms, parking, picnic tables. No fee.

Tomales Bay *is* the San Andreas Fault. This shallow rift bay caused as the fault runs out to sea is more than 13 miles long yet only a mile wide and often less than 10 feet deep. At low tide large mudflats are exposed. Relatively undeveloped, the bay is an important wildlife breeding and feeding area as well as a popular fishing, clamming, and kayaking spot. Birders have identified more than 100 different water birds in the bay. The state park encompasses several different properties on the waterfront and ridges around the bay.

Samuel P. Taylor State Park

5 miles east of Olema on Sir Francis Drake Boulevard. Tel. 415/488-9897. Camping, hiking trails, showers, flush toilets, running water, creek, picnic grounds.

The closest good car camping to Point Reyes, Samuel Taylor is also a great destination on its own with redwood groves and hiking into the headwaters of Lagunitas Creek.

Point Reyes Bird Observatory

Mesa Road. Tel. 415/868-1221. Ornithological research station open to the public. Call for hours. Small donation requested.

Visitors can observe and participate in some of the fieldwork going on at this cutting-edge ornithological research station. The visitors center explains the birds' habitat and behavior.

Audubon Canyon Ranch

Access from Highway 1 between Stinson and Olema. Tel. 415/868-9244. Open to public on weekends and holidays. Fee required.

This 1,500-acre ranch owned by the Audubon Society is best known for its egret and great blue heron nesting trees, visible from the Henderson Overlook at the end of a half-mile trail.

Stinson Beach

Access from Highway 1 north of intersection with Panoramic Highway. Tel. 415/868-0942 (Ranger Station). Picnic grounds, restrooms, showers. Open 9am to 10pm.

This long sandy beach is the most popular weekend getaway for Marin residents and many visitors from the city. In addition to the state beach, there is the small town of Stinson with a few B&Bs, a surf shop, grocery store, and private homes.

Mount Tamalpais State Park

Access from Panoramic Highway between Mill Valley and Stinson Beach. Tel. 415/388-2070. Camping, hiking, picnic grounds, scenic drive, group camp. Fees charged.

The buffer between developed east Marin and wild and scenic west Marin is this 6,200-acre state park. Encompassing most of Mount Tamalpais (known simply as Mount Tam), the park is most famous for the network of trails that lace its high ridges and wooded flanks, connecting the summit to the sea. Camping is severely limited and fills up fast.

Muir Woods National Monument

Muir Woods Road, 3 miles north of Highway 1. Tel. 415/388-2595. Interpretive trail, visitors center, restrooms, wheelchair accessible. No fee.

Completely enclosed by Mount Tamalpais State Park, Muir Woods was the first part of Marin set aside to protect the old-growth redwoods, in 1908. Short trails loop through the park; other longer ones extend into the state parklands.

Golden Gate National Recreation Area: Marin Headlands

From San Francisco, take the Alexander Avenue exit off of U.S. 101 just over the Golden Gate Bridge. Southbound traffic should take the second Sausalito exit after the Waldo tunnel. Tel. 415/331-1540.

The GGNRA, a branch of the National Parks Service, manages a number of facilities on the Marin Headlands, the striking northern half of the Golden Gate. Hiking trails, backcountry campsites, beaches, a marine mammal rescue center, youth hostel, and old military installments are all tucked away in these steep and wild headlands.

Richardson Bay and Angel Island

Take the ferry from Tiburon or San Francisco. Tel. 415/435-1915. Hiking, biking, camping.

Inland from the harsh conditions of the Golden Gate, Richardson Bay stretches back into a long harbor and tidal basin that is the best sea kayaking in the entire bay. Raccoon Strait separates 740-acre Angel Island from Richardson Bay and the Marin mainland. The island has served various roles from the West Coast version of Ellis Island to prison produce gardens for Alcatraz, but today it is maintained by the GGNRA and left virtually wild to be enjoyed by hikers and bikers. Several environmental campsites dot the island. Slips and mooring buoys are available for private boaters and a ferry runs to the island several times daily from San Francisco or nearby Tiburon.

THE EAST BAY

East Bay Regional Park District Headquarters

2950 Peralta Oaks Ct., Oakland. Tel. 510/562-7275. 60,000 acres of parks, trails, preserves, shorelines, bike paths, wildlife corridors, camping areas, and lakes. Fees vary from none to $3 per vehicle.

The East Bay Regional Parks District controls most of the large open space in the East Bay and is a wonderful resource for hikers, bikers, and equestrians. The major trails, important parks, and wild places managed by the EBRPD are listed individually below, but for general information, reservations, or advice call or visit the headquarters.

Skyline and Ohlone Trails

For access and other info, contact the EBRPD. Tel. 510/562-7275.

Managed by the EBRPD, these two trails connect the six biggest wilderness parks together. The Skyline Trail is open to bicycles, hikers, and horses and follows the crest of the Berkeley/Oakland hills for 31 miles. The Ohlone Trail is a wilder path. Much of the 29-mile trail runs through remote areas and over 3,817-foot Rose Peak. It is not open to bicyclists and is used mostly by backpackers en route to the several backcountry camps.

Point Pinole Regional Shoreline

From I-80, exit Hilltop Drive west to San Pablo Avenue, go right on Atlas Road, then left on Giant Highway, which will take you to the park. Fishing pier, bird watching, hiking, water, restrooms, picnic areas.

The square mile of Point Pinole was left relatively intact while the rest of Pinole and Richmond became an industrial hell for the simple reason that it was the site of an explosives factory from the 1880s until 1960. The plant occupied only a portion of the point and the rest was left open as a safety buffer. Now it is the site of the best fishing pier in the whole bay, a 1,225-foot-long mother that puts you right over the migration routes of salmon, striped bass, and sturgeon. It also puts bird-watchers right under the flightway of waterfowl migrating into the Delta from the bay.

Wildcat Canyon Regional Park

In Berkeley take Arlington Boulevard to Park Avenue. Several other more remote entries exist too. Water, picnic areas, restrooms, hiking, views, creek.

Wildcat Canyon is one of the least developed East Bay Regional Parks. At 2,000 acres it is plenty big enough to wander off into wooded canyons and across the grassy hillside pretending you're not, in fact, on the edge of a huge metropolis. The Skyline Trail begins here.

Tilden Regional Park

Surrounds Berkeley. Use a Berkeley street map to find any number of entrance points. Camping, picnicking, archery range, botanic garden, beach and lake with swimming, restrooms, environmental education center.

Tilden Park is the most developed and well-used park in the whole EBRPD with everything from merry-go-rounds to a golf course. Fortunately it also holds miles of nice hiking and numerous quiet picnic grounds. The Environmental Education Center is the headquarters for the EBRPD's naturalist program and home to numerous educational displays, maps, and brochures. A small farm with pigs, rabbits, goats, horses, and chickens gives kids a look at the rural life.

Robert Sibley Volcanic Regional Preserve

1.5 miles north of Skyline Boulevard. Shepherd Canyon junction. Water, restroom, picnic tables, hiking.

The hill in the center of this park used to be a volcano. Years of quarrying by a sand and gravel company revealed many old volcanic features that are now explained with a great self-guided walking tour, maps, and brochures provided in the park.

Huckleberry Botanic Regional Preserve

Adjacent to Oakland at 7090 Skyline Blvd. No water, one toilet, nature trail.

This small preserve was set aside to protect rare plants that grow on the hillside above urban Oakland. In addition to the namesake huckleberry, here would-be botanists can check out a rare blend of chaparral community plants including three distinct species of manzanita and the endangered western leatherwood.

Redwood Regional Park

Redwood has several entrances; the most commonly used one is on Redwood Road (Take the 35th Avenue exit off I-580 southbound. East 35th becomes Redwood Road.) Picnic ground, restrooms, swimming pool, hiking trails, bicycle trails.

It's hard to believe now, but once the East Bay was covered with redwoods, the two tallest of which were located here, reputedly so tall that sailors entering the bay used them as a landmark to steer by. The demand for redwood lumber after the Gold Rush quickly caused the forests to be razed, but more than 100 years later the second-growth forest here is pretty nice, too. This is also the spot where the rainbow trout was first identified as a separate species in Redwood Creek. Tons of good hikes roam the hills and canyons. Big trout swim in Redwood Creek but fishing is prohibited.

Anthony Chabot Regional Park

Several entrances off Redwood Road and Skyline Road. Campground, picnic area, livery stable, lake, marina, restrooms, showers.

Lake Chabot, a popular fishing and boating lake (no private boats, rent them at the marina), is the main draw of this large park. At 315 acres it's large enough for a nice afternoon of canoeing. Hikers can follow the trail around the lake and others within this 5,000-acre park.

Black Diamond Mines Regional Preserve

End of Somersville Road in Antioch. Tel. 925/757-2620. Water, restrooms, picnic tables, underground mining museum, nature walks, 30-plus miles of hiking trails.

Once a working coal mine, the Black Diamond Preserve is an interesting example of land turning back to nature. Once there was a town, mill, and huge mine here. Now there are 30 miles of trails, incredible bird watching, and a fascinating tour of the old mine tunnels (by reservation only; phone the park before coming).

Briones Regional Park

Bear Creek entrance is accessible from Orinda exit off State Route 24. Tel. 925/370-3020. Water, restrooms, picnic tables.

This 5,000-acre park is mostly open ranchland, where cattle still graze to keep the grass and subsequent fire hazard down. Many hikes in the 2- to 8-mile range are here and the view from Briones Peak is spectacular.

Mount Diablo State Park

From I-680 in Danville take Diablo Road 3 miles to the park's south entrance. Tel. 925/837-2525. Campsites, horse camp, picnic ground, restrooms, hiking trails, equestrian trails, mountain bike trails, observation tower on summit of Mount Diablo.

Miwok Indian myth held 3,849-foot Mount Diablo to be the home of Eagle and Coyote, two of their most sacred spirits. The Spaniards put a negative spin on this spirituality and named the mountain after the devil. Today this 29,000-acre park has not just a little for everyone but a lot. Fifty miles of backcountry hiking trails, miles of unpaved fire roads for mountain biking, three year-round campgrounds, winter-only backcountry camps (closed in summer due to fire hazard), and some of the most stunning spring wildflowers you'll ever see. The summit can be reached by car, and after a rain you can see as far as Mount Lassen in the north.

Henry W. Coe State Park

From U.S. 101 in Morgan Hill, exit at East Dunne Avenue. Go east 13 miles. Road is extremely narrow and winding. Tel. 408/779-2728. Car, horse, and backpacking camps; visitors center/ranch museum; restrooms and water at the visitors center.

This park, once a private ranch homesteaded by the Coe family, is the second largest in the state. Its 79,500 acres are little visited, and the harsh elements of the Diablo range make it unlikely that it will be overrun anytime soon. The park has become popular with mountain bikers in recent years, and given the considerable distances involved, a bicycle is the ideal way to cover ground, but the terrain is not for beginners. Steep rough trails, long distances, and scarce potable water make this a spot for the experienced backcountry rider.

The Peninsula ◆ What to Do & Where to Do It

There's a lot to be said for keeping the city in the city and the country in the country without a lot of in-between, and San Francisco says it well. Though the city is extremely densely populated, within a 15-minute drive or even a short walk you can be in—if not exactly wilderness—places that can safely be called nature—places like the Presidio, Fort Funston, Lake Merced, Land's End, and Ocean Beach. As you progress down the peninsula, the same holds true: cities like Palo Alto, Atherton, and Sunnyvale line the inside of the bayshore, but once over the mountain crest the land is still wild evergreen forests, flower farms, and wild, wild beaches. The ridgeline that divides the peninsula is a steep and powerful barrier to suburban spillover; development is largely contained on the east side of U.S. 280.

As a result of this division, much of the sporting scene on the peninsula relates directly to the sea: hikes along coastal marshes, beachfront bike paths, surfing the beautiful waves of Ocean Beach, or boardsailing at Crissy Field. Even when you're high in the hills of the southern peninsula, the occasional glimpse of blue, or sometimes a smothering cloud of gray ocean fog, will remind you that you're playing on the edge of the continent.

BIRD WATCHING

The variety of ecosystems on the peninsula is reflected in the variety of birding— the bay provides important **shorebird** habitats, the high ridges and forests offer feeding and nesting areas for **raptors,** and the wild Pacific coast is home to many **pelagic** and **near-shore species.**

Sweeney Ridge Preserve is a great **raptor** watching spot. During a 95-hour survey by the Golden Gate Raptor Observatory in 1988, volunteers saw 143 turkey vultures, 4 osprey, 2 bald eagles, 31 northern harriers, 58 sharp-shinned hawks, 49 Cooper's hawks, 2 red-shouldered hawks, 1 golden eagle, 24 American kestrel, 1 prairie falcon, and 47 other unidentified raptors. All this within line-of-sight of downtown San Francisco.

The **wetland marshes** around the southern San Mateo County beaches are known for their incredible variety of **migratory species.** At **Pescadero Marsh,** just inland of Pescadero State Beach, 230 separate species have been counted and 66 species are known to nest in the marsh and surrounding woodlands. Commonly seen are rare varieties of sandpipers, great blue herons, Virginia rail, willet, marsh wrens, and downy woodpeckers. The state park maintains a checklist.

BOARDSAILING

For anyone with a car and the appropriate wave-riding and high-wind skills, the entire Pacific coast of the peninsula is a potential playground. The two most popular spots on the peninsula, however, are inside the bay.

Crissy Field, the former airport of the U.S. Army Presidio and now a national park, is arguably the best high-wind spot in the state, and unarguably the most beautiful urban windsurfing site in the country. As you tack back and forth in the steady 20- to 30-knot winds that blow through the Golden Gate almost every afternoon, the Golden Gate Bridge towers over you, the mountains of Marin frame your view to the north, and the skyline of downtown offers a stunning backdrop while you jump whitecaps and tanker wakes. This is only a spot for confident sailors; blow it and you can find yourself on a collision course with a Titanic-sized ship, only this time it'll be you going down for good. The current through the Golden Gate whips up to 4 knots on an outgoing tide, so don't get caught becalmed in the center of the bay as the tide turns around.

Coyote Point is at the southern boundary of the city in the shadow of Candlestick Park. The same bad winds and weather that make the Giants pout and threaten to leave San Francisco every year blow happy boardsailors to their heart's content. The park has good parking, rigging space, and bay access. Because it is located in a shallow part of the bay, ship traffic is not a worry here and the currents are no big deal.

Several good shops sell and rent equipment in the city. **Bay Area Bike and Car Rentals** (tel. 415/441-4779), 599 Post St., is good for people flying into town. They'll rent you a car and board package and everything you need. **The San Francisco School of Windsurfing** (tel. 415/753-3235) is located on Lake Merced, where they offer 2-day beginning lessons on weekends for $95

The Presidio

In 1989 the Department of Defense announced what many had long thought impossible: The army, which had held the Presidio as a military base since before the Civil War, was pulling out and leaving the most prized piece of real estate in San Francisco to the National Parks Service as an example of post–Cold War retrofiting. At press time, the last soldiers were leaving and a new Presidio era was beginning.

Frankly it's too early to tell what will become of the conversion, but some signs are promising: The Clinton administration has mandated that the Presidio should become a global center for the study of environmental policy, technology, and sustainability. Many details remain to be hammered out and there is much fighting over who will get to do what and where, but an optimism that positive change is happening hangs over the place. "The Presidio," said Vice-President Al Gore, "will be a special place where environmental policies for the future will be shaped and translated into action."

Unlike many military complexes with their machine-gun-toting guards and high fences, much of the Presidio has always been open to the public, and city residents have long escaped San Francisco's teeming streets into the base's forests and beaches. Now those uses will be encouraged even more. The base golf course is going public (Yes, they had their own golf course), former military buildings are being leased out, and the base theater is opening as a private repertory theater. Many bicyclists like to use the Presidio roads as a warm-up before venturing across the Golden Gate Bridge and into the Marin hills.

Walkers and joggers will enjoy the forests of the Presidio. Once a bleak field of windblasted rock, sand, and grass, the area is now a thriving woodland habitat. In a strangely humanitarian gesture that can only be chalked up as some sort of foreshadowing to San Francisco's future, 60,000 trees were planted in the 1880s to make the place more livable for the troops. Today, on the 2-mile **Ecology Loop Trail,** walkers can see more than

including board, wetsuit, and 8 hours of instruction. They also offer intermediate and advance lessons at Candlestick (Coyote Point) during the spring, summer, and fall. In the South Bay, **Spinnaker Sailing** (tel. 650/956-7474) at Shoreline Park in Mountain View has a full shop of equipment plus an extensive instruction program located on the water.

FISHING

Pier and shore fishing for halibut, surf perch, and the occasional striped bass is a popular pastime all over the bay, but the big **saltwater fishing** news around here is chasing **salmon.** When they run, numerous charter boats will take you outside the Golden Gate to fish the rich waters between Point Reyes and Half Moon Bay, or to wherever the fish are running in the bay. The fleet makeup changes regularly, but some of the long-time charter operators are **Hot Pursuit Sport Fishing** (tel. 415/567-7610), Fisherman's Wharf, San Francisco; **Wacky Jacky** (tel. 415/586-9800), Fisherman's Wharf, San Francisco; **Captain John's Deep Sea Fishing** (tel. 800/391-8787), Half Moon Bay; **New Easy**

30 different species of those trees including redwood, spruce, cypress, and acacias. Other good walks are the 2.5-mile **Coast Trail,** which follows the blufftop from Baker Beach to the southern base of the Golden Gate Bridge, and **Lover's Lane,** a short and romantic walk from ritzy Pacific Heights straight downhill to the former officers' housing.

Anyone interested in the military history of the Presidio must stop at the **Presidio Army Museum,** loaded with military arcana from 200 years of base history. Another interesting chunk of military history is **Fort Point,** a National Historic Site that lies directly under the Golden Gate Bridge. During the Civil War the brick Fort Point was manned by 140 men and 90 pieces of artillery to prevent a Confederate takeover of California. Rangers in Civil War regalia lead regular tours and sometimes fire the old cannons. Call 415/556-1693 for schedules and information.

Two of the most popular beaches in San Francisco lie in the Presidio. **Baker Beach,** a small and beautiful strand just outside the Golden Gate, is packed on sunny days with sunbathers and fishermen. Because of the cold water and the roaring currents that pour out of the bay twice a day, swimming is not advised here for any but the most confident. On very low tides it is possible to walk all the way from here to the Golden Gate. On the other side of Fort Point is **Crissy Field,** a former airfield that in recent years has become known as one of the see-and-be-seen proving grounds of California's windsurfing culture. Between March and October, hundreds come to try their hand. The Crissy Beach provides easy water access and plenty of room to rig up. This is also a popular place for joggers en route from the Marina District to Fort Point and back. At the west end of Crissy Field is a pier that can be used for fishing and crabbing.

For schedules, maps, and general information about ongoing developments at the Presidio, the best source is the **Golden Gate National Recreation Area Headquarters** at Fort Mason, Building 201, San Francisco, CA 94123 (tel. 415/556-0560).

Rider (tel. 415/285-2000), Berkeley Marina; and **Emeryville Sport Fishing** (tel. 510/654-6040), Emeryville.

Freshwater fishing is surprisingly popular and good in the many small lakes in several of the **East Bay Regional Parks,** several of the **Mount Tamalpais water district lakes,** and at **Lake Merced** in San Francisco. Lake Merced regularly delivers up trophy-sized (5- to 10-pound) trout and bass. Access to the lake is difficult on most of the shoreline because of steep banks and reedy shoreline. At Harding Park, at the south end of the Great Highway, **Lake Merced** **Boating and Fishing Co.** (tel. 415/753-1101) rents boats and canoes, and there is bank fishing as well.

HIKES, BUSHWHACKS & BACKPACK TRIPS

DAY HIKES

Sweeney Ridge

4.8 miles round-trip. Moderate. 2 to 3 hours. Access: Take Fairway Drive from Highway 1 in Pacifica to the dead end near a nursery. Map: GGNRA hiking map.

Sailors had missed the Golden Gate for over 200 years before the bay was discovered by Captain Gaspar de Portola on November 4, 1769, and he discovered it by hiking. Portola was looking for Monterey Bay when he climbed Sweeney Ridge that day, but quickly realized the potential of this huge natural harbor. The rest, as they say, is history. The Sweeney Ridge Trail climbs about 600 or 700 feet to a scrub and grassland ridgeline from which you can see the entire Bay Area: Mount Diablo, Mount Tam, the Golden Gate and Bay bridges, and the Farallon Islands 25 miles out to sea. Stand here and imagine Portola's surprise when he crested the ridge.

Jackson Flats Trail, Butano State Park

3.5 miles round-trip. Easy. 2 hours. Access: Near Butano State Park Headquarters on Cloverdale Road. Map: Butano State Park map.

Butano State Park protects a series of lush forests mixed with vernal pool wetlands, small seasonal ponds caused by geologic slumping that are important breeding habitat for many amphibians. The Jackson Flats Trail passes through a small redwood forest and then follows the side of a ridge for about a mile. At about 1.5 miles from the trailhead you can see a few small ponds and a large marsh on a flat plain of forest. A few hundred yards more brings you to an awesome stand of virgin redwoods. The trail continues further, but this is where we turn around and head back the same way we came.

OVERNIGHTS

Butano Trail Camp, Butano State Park

13 miles round-trip. Moderate. Access: Butano State Park Headquarters, Olmo Fire Trail. Map: Butano State Park map.

It's hard to find a place you can hike almost 7 miles through first- and second-growth redwoods and over running creeks, and then camp in a primitive trail camp this close to a big city, but this hike is it. The flora, fauna, and geography here are otherworldly, from the earthquake fault to the periodic ocean views. The camp itself has a single pit toilet, no water, and no fires allowed.

MOUNTAIN BIKING

It's unfortunate that the place that invented mountain bikes should become the epicenter of the backlash against them, but that's exactly what has happened. Ten years ago just about every trail in the Bay Area was open to bicycles; now they are prohibited from most trails and strictly regulated on fire roads. On Mount Tamalpais in Marin, rangers actually use radar guns to enforce the 15 mph speed limit. Ever tried descending a huge mountain at 15 mph? It sucks. Ever been ticketed or had your bike taken away for riding on single track? Me neither, but I bet it sucks too. The truly committed have taken to poaching trails at night under full moons or using halogen lamps. Others just drive to Santa Cruz or into Sonoma and Mendocino. It's out there, but not nearly as convenient as it once was. If you arrived without your bike, a couple of places in the area will rent you one. **American Bike Rental** (tel. 415/931-0234), 2715 Hyde, rents tandems as well as mountain bikes.

Old Haul Road, Portola State Park

13 miles. Moderate. Access: Portola State Park Headquarters.

From the parking area at the state park headquarters pedal down the road, over a bridge, and through the service road gate. In about three-fourths of a mile you'll pass employee housing and come to another gate—this one is the boundary with Pescadero Creek County Park. Turn right here onto Old Haul Road. It's about 6 miles from here to Memorial County Park through rolling evergreen woodlands, and the total elevation gain is only 400 feet, though you do it twice since it comes in the middle. At the Memorial Park Trailhead turn around and pedal up and over that hill again. From there it's a coast back to your car.

Butano State Park Ranger-Led Rides

11 miles round-trip. Easy to moderate. Fire roads and wide trails. Access: Ride begins at the Butano State Park Visitors Center. Map: Butano State Park map.

This is a beautiful ride, and sadly, the ranger-led ride is the only way to go. Park staff have made arrangements with private landowners inside and surrounding the park to open access to a 5.5-mile-long logging road that leads through dense, tall stands of redwoods and Douglas fir. At several points the trail passes onto open ridges with views of the surrounding coast range and the ocean below. Along the way you'll stop several times to rest and to hear your ranger guide talk about natural history. The rides are only offered on summer weekends and fill up quickly. Make reservations in advance at the Butano State Park ranger station (tel. 650/879-2040).

ROAD BIKING

Despite its hills, San Francisco is actually a really bike-friendly city, and the open country in southern San Mateo County is even better. The best resource for anyone interested in doing a lot of road rides here is *Touring the San Francisco Bay Area by Bicycle* by Peter Powers

(Terragraphics, 1990). Small enough to stick in a jersey pocket yet incredibly detailed, this book shows hundreds of potential routes in the city and all over the Bay Area. *Bay Area Bike Rides* by Ray Hosler (Chronicle Books, 1994) is also very good for outlying areas, but not nearly as detailed in the city.

San Francisco Ocean Front and Golden Gate Bridge

20–30 miles depending on turnaround point. Moderate. Access: Park in lot at Sloat and Great Highway on Ocean Beach. Follow bike path north. Map: San Francisco city map or GGNRA trail and road map.

One of my favorite rides here follows the oceanfront path between Fort Funston and Golden Gate Park along Ocean Beach, weaves through the woods of Land's End, drops down through the Presidio, and then crosses the Golden Gate Bridge to Sausalito. It's easy to get confused getting on the bridge because the bike path from Lincoln Boulevard heads toward the west (ocean) side of the bridge but a seemingly hidden tunnel then ducks under the toll plaza to the east (bay) side. Be patient and you'll find it. On weekends the bay side is closed to cyclists, but I like to do this ride early in the morning on a weekday so I can ride with the view of the city. Usually the fog is lifting when I hit the bridge. You can see the ships entering and leaving the bay below and the sun rising behind the city skyline. Pedestrians aren't really a problem this early, but as you round the bridge pillars, watch for bicycles coming the other way. Once on the Marin side I ride into Sausalito, fuel up on scones and coffee, then ride home.

ROCK CLIMBING

Rock climbing is one thing there just isn't a lot of around here. Most serious climbers either trek over to Yosemite or down to the Pinnacles. **Castle Rock State Park** (tel. 408/867-2952) is the closest decent-sized rock to the peninsula and it is nothing to write home about. To stay in shape for those Yosemite treks, a lot of San Francisco climbers go to **Mission Cliffs** (tel. 415/550-0515), 2295 Harrison, in the Mission District. This newly constructed climbing gym in a converted garment factory has numerous difficult routes and seems to be in a growth phase. They also offer introductory and beginning lessons, good for getting the basics down or refreshing after a few years away from climbing.

SAILING

The bay is one of the finest sailing grounds on the West Coast—the Golden Gate allows Pacific winds through but stops much of the open ocean's rollicking swell. A number of charter fleets and sailing schools make it pretty easy to get on the water whether you're an experienced skipper or a rank beginner. **A Day on the Bay** (tel. 415/922-0227) will arrange charters or lessons on a number of large sailboats out of the San Francisco Marina. **Sailing Educational Adventures** (tel. 415/775-8779) is a nonprofit community sailing program with lessons at all levels and a member fleet based at Fort Mason. **Atlantis Yacht Charters and Management Co.** (tel. 415/499-7707; e-mail atlantis@yachtcharter.com) maintains a fleet of privately owned yachts at several locations around the bay that are leased out bareboat or skippered for anywhere from an afternoon to a week. **Spinnaker Sailing** (tel. 415/543-7333) is based at Pier 40 along the south beach harbor near the Bay Bridge. They rent boats from 22 to 80 feet and offer complete lessons from basic sailing to open-ocean cruising. In the Berkeley Marina the **Olympic Circle Sailing School**

(tel. 800/223-2984) rents bareboats and skippered charters and offers a full spectrum of American Sailing Association certified courses.

SCUBA DIVING

Given that the area between Point Reyes, Point Año Nuevo, and the Farallon Islands is commonly known as the "Blood Triangle" because of all the great white sharks that live here (see "Shark Watch" feature) plus the fact that the water is generally murky and rough, not many people go diving here. The exception is the large number of people who go **abalone diving** on the ocean side of **Tomales Point** in Point Reyes. You can't really call it diving, though, since most of them just poke around in large tidepools looking for abs. I don't blame them at all. Biologists have seen more white sharks at Tomales Point than any other mainland spot.

SURFING

San Francisco was an underground surfing scene, a deeply held secret until the late 1980s. The water here is really cold year-round, which scared off all but the most diehard surfers. Then, a vast explosion in the sport's popularity, coupled with improvements in wetsuit materials, made this coldwater kingdom more accessible. It's still not a cakewalk: the main break on the peninsula is **Ocean Beach,** a hollow, unforgiving beach break known for breaking boards and basically kicking ass. **Fort Point, China Beach,** and **Baker Beach** are all semi-point breaks inside the Golden Gate with smaller but still unforgiving conditions. Only when you get down to **Pacifica** and **Rockaway Beach** will you find anything approaching beginner- or intermediate-level surf breaks. Of course the big hype in the surfing world now is **Maverick's,** the Half Moon Bay reef break where professional big-wave rider Mark Foo died in 1994. On a good day, 20- to 25-foot sets roar through Maverick's with a sound approaching that of a jet on takeoff. The lineup is pretty far out in the ocean, but nearby cliffs offer a good viewpoint. Just follow the trail around Pillar Point from the parking area below the radar station. If Maverick's is breaking, you can't miss it.

The main surf shop in San Francisco is **Wise Surfboards** (tel. 415/750-9473), 800 Great Highway, which also runs the San Francisco surf hotline (tel. 415/273-1618). The staff is taciturn almost to the point of unfriendliness, but the place stays in business despite itself simply because it stocks the best selection of boards on the North Coast.

WALKS & RAMBLES

Cliff House to Land's End

Access: Park at the Cliff House at the junction of Geary Boulevard and the Great Highway.

Perched on a rocky outcrop at the northern headland of Ocean Beach, the Cliff House is a historic restaurant and museum overlooking the sea. Park here and follow the sidewalk a short distance until you come to the ruins of the Sutro Baths on the shore below. Pass through the Merrie Way parking area and pick up the Coastal Trail. Actually a series of interweaving trails, the Coastal Trail curves through the cypress forest and along the clifftop until the Golden Gate Bridge comes into sight. Across the channel you can see the Marin Headlands and Point Bonita Lighthouse. Several ships have run aground on the rocks below Land's End and are sometimes visible during low tides. At several points benches and coin-operated telescopes are placed along the trail.

Pescadero Marsh Trails

Distance varies. Access: Pescadero State Beach.

Two trails with numerous observation decks allow nature lovers and birders to get a good look at the wealth of wetlands here. Bring binoculars and park at either of the main Pescadero Beach parking lots. The marsh is across Highway 1 and stretches up this striking coastal valley for what seems like miles. You, however, only need to go a few hundred yards before you'll start seeing the hundreds of species of birds that use the marsh as their breeding ground and shelter.

Fort Point

2 miles. Access: Park at Marina Green.

Beginning in the swanky Marina District of San Francisco, this walk follows the best of the bayfront from near the Saint Francis Yacht Club through Crissy Field and the Presidio to end up at Fort Point. This Civil War–era emplacement was designed to keep Confederate ships from taking over California. It must have worked. Construction of the Golden Gate Bridge, which passes directly over the fort, was headquartered here. Originally the fort was slated for demolition to make way for the bridge but was spared when project engineer Joseph Strauss decided it should stay. The walk to the fort is level but often windy. The view back to the city from here is one of the best.

WHALE WATCHING

Whale watching isn't quite the big deal on the peninsula that it is in Monterey

Shark Watch

In a skiff bobbing off the Farallon Islands, some 30 miles west of San Francisco, Scot Anderson watches a 16-foot great white shark approach a battered surfboard floating nearby. The surfboard is a decoy, modified to hold an underwater video camera. The shark is familiar, one Anderson calls Stumpy because of its chopped-off tail fin. Stumpy seizes the decoy like a dog fetching a stick. Then, no longer interested, the shark is suddenly gone.

Great white sharks come to the Farallons specifically to feed, mostly on elephant seals, which find these rocky, windswept, deserted islands an ideally located refuge. On land the seals are safe, but in the surrounding waters it's another story.

As a result, the seals and their predators form a natural marine laboratory for students of the great whites: In a single 3-month span last year, the scientists from the Farallon Islands Shark Project witnessed almost 80 attacks by great whites.

One of the things the Farallon researchers have learned is that the sharks arrive at the same place every year on a predictable schedule. One shark, called Half-fin because it is missing the top of its dorsal fin, has come to the same rocky point between October 7 and October 10 for 3 of the last 4 years. After feeding, it disappears. Other sharks in the Farallons follow similar patterns of arrival and departure.

The surfboard decoy is one of the project's most useful research tools. Seen from below—the shark's view—the decoy resembles the silhouette of a young elephant seal. White sharks regularly approach Anderson's unbaited contraption, bumping, biting, or just eyeing it. Their curiosity satisfied, they vanish back into the depths.

September to November is the project's observations season. "What really goes on most of the time," Anderson says, "is that we go up to the lighthouse and look around the island all day long. You look at the nearshore waters for gulls or blood or whatever catches your eye."

A shark attack triggers a rapid sequence of actions. First the observer takes a location fix from the lighthouse, then turns on a telephoto-equipped video camera calibrated to register the size of the shark. Word of the sighting is relayed to others on the island. If ocean conditions allow, researchers race out in a small boat to get a better view of the feeding shark. The scientists try to gather as many details as possible: type of prey, weather, tide, time of day, and—using visible scars and marks—the identification of the shark.

In coming years the scientists hope to attach sonic tracking devices to individual sharks. This will help them learn more about what sharks do the rest of the time because, as marine animal behaviorist Peter Klimley explains, "Right now we only know where they are when they feed or hit the decoy."

Bay to the south or Point Reyes to the north. The whales tend to be farther offshore here and the weather and coastline aren't as hospitable to clifftop viewing. Several San Francisco and Half Moon Bay area charter companies run trips to see the whales as they pass offshore. My favorite are the trips run by the **Oceanic Society** (tel. 415/474-3385), a nonprofit research organization based in Fort Mason. These multifaceted trips on an 85-foot boat leave the San Francisco Yacht Club and last 8 or 9 hours, sometimes traveling as far as Point Reyes or the Farallon Islands. Trained naturalists explain many different aspects of the marine environment on each trip, so even if you don't see whales, you'll come back satisfied. Departure time is 9am on Saturday and Sunday.

Marin County ◆ What to Do & Where to Do It

Marin County's most famous inventions are the mountain bike and the hot tub: It's hard not to like a place with that kind of initiative. From the top of Mount Tamalpais (known simply as Mount Tam) to the seaward tip of Point Reyes, Marin is the most fabulous natural playground near any major U.S. city. Grassy ridges and forested ravines dominate the high country while steep sea cliffs alternate with occasional long sand beaches on the coast. The people who live here do so because they value their surroundings and hold fierce opinions as to how those surroundings should be used. Mostly this is a good thing; just look around—it's hard to argue with success. But other times it leads to factionalism and infighting such as the ongoing war between hikers and mountain bikers that has closed so much of Marin to offroad bicycling and resulted in actual fisticuffs and arrests. Because it is so close to San Francisco, the backcountry of Marin can sometimes be overrun on summer weekends or big holidays. The off-season—fall, winter, and spring—is often the best time to visit. Between winter storms are long stretches of warm weather when there is nothing better than a long hike on Mount Tam or a trip to Stinson Beach.

BIRD WATCHING

No two ways about it, Marin County is the single best place in California for birders to buff out their life list while seeing numerous species in a still-wild setting. Practically anyplace in the North Bay you stand a good chance of seeing something interesting, but **Point Reyes** is the Chartres Cathedral of birding. The park's 100 square miles contain plentiful and varied habitats, which as the result of a geological quirk have been thrust miles out into the Pacific Ocean. Because of this, the point is both a magnet for migrating birds coming down the Pacific Coast, looking for land, and also the landing place of a lot of vagrants that were separated from their flock and blown wildly off course. Many East Coast and Siberian species are spotted here on a regular basis. An amazing total of 430 recorded species, ranging from the Cooper's hawk to the Cape May warbler, are listed on the park's bird list, available at the **Bear Valley Visitors Center** (tel. 415/663-1092).

Located just south of the park on Mesa Road near Bolinas, the **Point Reyes Bird Observatory** (tel. 415/868-0655) is a good place to get up close and personal with many land birds. The staff here offer tours and special programs. They also run year-round netting and banding operations and welcome public participation. The observatory is a privately supported, nonprofit ornithological research organization and welcomes any donations.

Audubon Canyon Ranch (tel. 415/868-9244), located in a forested canyon across Highway 1 from the Bolinas Lagoon, is an important nesting area for egrets and the great blue heron. The birds congregate by the hundreds in high tree branches on the south side of the canyon while a vista point on the other side offers a perfect place to set up a spotting scope.

BOARDSAILING

The Marin side of the bay is less windy and less accessible than most other corners of the bay. Richardson Bay is almost

Point Reyes National Seashore

The national seashore system was created to protect rural and undeveloped stretches of the coast from the pressures brought on by soaring real estate values and increasing population, preserving both the natural features and unique culture of the coast. Nowhere is the success of the system more evident than at Point Reyes. Seventy road-miles north of San Francisco, Point Reyes is a 100-square-mile peninsula of dark forests, wind-sculpted dunes, endless beaches, and plunging sea cliffs. It offers a window to California's coastal history: lighthouses, turn-of-the-century dairies and ranches, Sir Francis Drake's 1579 landing, plus a complete replica of a coastal Miwok Indian village.

Layers of human history coexist peacefully here with one of the world's most dramatic natural settings. Residents of the surrounding towns, **Inverness, Point Reyes Station, and Olema**, have steadfastly resisted runaway development. You'll find no strip malls and fast food here, but rather a laid-back culture of cafes, country inns, and gentle living. The park, a 65,000-acre hammer-shaped peninsula jutting 10 miles into the Pacific and backed by Tomales Bay, is loaded with wildlife ranging from tule elk, birds, and bobcats, to gray whales, sea lions, and white sharks. During Audubon's annual Christmas bird count, Point Reyes regularly scores the largest concentrations of bird species in the continental United States—as many as 350.

This is also shaky ground. The infamous **San Andreas Fault** separates Point Reyes, the northernmost landmass on the Pacific Plate, from the rest of California, which rests on the North American Plate. Should the legendary "Big One" hit, it is Point Reyes, not Los Angeles, that will probably shear off into the sea. Until then, however, Point Reyes will continue its steady movement toward Alaska at about 2 inches per year. In 1906, though, Point Reyes jumped north almost 20 feet in an instant, leveling San Francisco and jolting the rest of the state.

The **Bear Valley Visitors Center** (tel. 415/663-1092) just outside Olema is the best place to begin a visit to Point Reyes. In addition to the **Earthquake Trail** (see "Walks & Rambles" later in this chapter), here you'll find all the maps and information you could possibly hope for plus great natural history and cultural displays. Two particularly fascinating features of the center are **Kule Loklo**, a recreated Miwok Indian village that often hosts displays of dancing, basket making, Native American cooking, and indigenous art; and the Park Service's **Morgan Horse Ranch**, the only working horse-breeding farm in the national park system. The best time to visit Kule Loklo is during July when it hosts an annual **Native American Celebration** and the whole village comes to life. Classes in Native American crafts and skills are offered intermittently throughout the year. Call the Visitors Center (tel. 415/479-3281) for more information.

Beachgoers have their work cut out here. The **Great Beach** is one of California's longest sand strands. It is also one of the windiest and home to large and dangerous waves—a mixed blessing since you can't swim here, but the beachcombing is some of the best in the world. Tidepoolers should go to

McClures Beach at the end of Pierce Point Road on a low tide or hike out to **Chimney Rock**. Swimmers will want to stick to **Limantour Beach** or **Drakes Beach** in the protected lee of Point Reyes. **Drakes Beach** is home to the **Kenneth C. Patrick Visitors Center** with exhibits about the area's whale fossil beds and **Drakes Beach Cafe,** the only food concession in the park (famous for great oysters). Sir Francis Drake reputedly careened the *Pelican* (later rechristened the *Golden Hind*) on the sandy shore of Drake's Bay in June 1579 for repairs and replenishing of supplies before sailing home to England.

At the **Point Reyes Lighthouse** it is sometimes possible to see 100 whales in an afternoon. Even if the whales don't materialize, the lighthouse itself, teetering high above the sea at the tip of a knife-backed promontory, is worth a visit. The Lighthouse Visitors Center (tel. 415/669-1534) offers great displays about whale migration and maritime history.

There's a little of everything for hikers here: 32,000 acres of the park containing 70 miles of trails are set aside as wilderness where no motor vehicles or bicycles are allowed. One great sight that's worth the hike required to see it is **Alamere Falls**. The falls, which lie near Wildcat Camp on the Coast Trail, plummet 40 feet down to the beach and into the Pacific Ocean from an ocean bluff. The falls can also be reached via the Palo Marin Trail or Five Brooks Trail in the south of the park. Bicycles are permitted in the park but not on the wilderness area trails, making for complicated navigating. Check with the visitors center for specific information.

Rangers lead special programs year-round from wildlife hikes and history lessons to habitat restoration. All are free and open to the public. Call the Bear Valley Visitors Center for up-to-date schedules. Other groups such as the Marin chapter of the **Sierra Club** (tel. 510/526-8969), **Golden Gate Audubon Society** (tel. 510/843-2222), and **Oceanic Society Expeditions** (tel. 415/474-3385) run special excursions and outings to the park.

JUST THE FACTS

Seasons. Weather at Point Reyes is very fickle. The point itself is the foggiest place on the West Coast. Inland, however, it can be warm and balmy while the coast is socked in. Generally the seasons here are reversed, summer cold and foggy, winter clear and, if not exactly warm, often at least tolerable. There is no hard-and-fast rule about the weather though. Winter storms can rage for weeks and sometimes the summer fog stays away. The best bet is to take advantage of variations in local weather by being flexible with your itinerary. It's better to hike the hills in the sun than sit on the beach in the fog.

Avoiding the Crowds. Though the park is heavily visited, crowds are only a problem at a few places and only during certain times. If you must visit the lighthouse on a weekend or holiday during whale season, be prepared to wait for the shuttle at Drakes Beach and deal with a lot of people. Trails leaving from Bear Valley tend to be more crowded on weekends than others. Try the Five Brooks or Palomarin trailheads to avoid backcountry hordes.

always tranquil, which can make for a good beginning spot, but getting to the water through the maze of waterfront developments, parking lots, and fences can be a real chore. Most experienced Marin boardsailers simply hoof it over the Golden Gate Bridge to Crissy Field, where lots of parking, large lawns for rigging, and gobs of wind make for the best boardsailing in the bay.

FISHING

There are a wide variety of saltwater and freshwater fishing options available all over the Bay Area. For more specific information, see "Fishing" under "The Peninsula ◆ What to Do & Where to Do It" earlier in this chapter.

HIKES, BUSHWHACKS & BACKPACK TRIPS

DAY HIKES

Mount Tam to Stinson Beach Loop

7 miles. Moderate. 4 to 5 hours. Access: Pantoll Ranger Station on Panoramic Highway, Mount Tamalpais State Park. Map: Mount Tam trail map available at trailhead.

This 7-mile hike dishes out a little of everything Marin has to offer: It begins just below the summit of Mount Tam but quickly plunges downhill in the thickly wooded Steep Ravine Trail (one portion of this trail is a ladder, if you were wondering how it got the name). The trail follows Web Creek and crosses five or six wooden bridges under the cover of redwoods and California laurel. When you come to the junction with the Dipsea Trail, bear right. Steep Ravine continues to the ocean and a nice campground, but for the sake of making a loop you want to go right. The Dipsea

will take you through hillsides of open chaparral with stunning views of Stinson Beach, San Francisco, and even the Farallon Islands on a clear day. You'll hit paved roads at the junction of the Panoramic Highway and Highway 1 just above Stinson. Once in town you can stop for an ocean swim or lunch at a cafe, or else start the long climb home.

The Matt Davis Trail begins just above Highway 1 at the other end of Stinson Beach. From this trailhead it is almost 4 miles home. After the first mile or so of hiking through the heavy forest above Stinson, you'll break out onto an open ridge with more amazing vistas of the beach below and the city to your south. After several steep switchback sections the trail descends and crosses the Panoramic Highway back at Pantoll.

Muir Woods Lose-the-Crowd Loop

4-plus miles. Moderate. 2–3 hours. Access: Trail begins near Muir Woods Visitors Center. Map: Muir Woods map. Mount Tamalpais State Park hiking map.

More than a million people every year come to Muir Woods, but 98% of them walk the 1-mile Redwood Creek Loop. To get away from the crowd while still enjoying the redwoods, take the trail that bears uphill from the Gifford Pinchot Tree. Depending on which map you use it may be called either the Ocean View Trail or the Panoramic Highway Trail. Either way, this trail will take you through Muir Woods and past a nice waterfall. Before reaching the Panoramic Highway (and the ocean view) you'll come to a junction with the Lost Trail. Go left and follow it downhill to Fern Creek. The Fern Creek Trail follows its namesake until you reach the Bootjack Trail, which will shortly deposit you back at the visitors center.

Hassle Free Loop, Muir Woods

5 miles. Moderate. Access: Trailhead is off the Panoramic Highway in Mount Tamalpais State Park. Map: Muir Woods map. Mount Tamalpais State Park hiking map.

On busy weekends and summer vacation when Muir Woods's 200-space visitors center parking area can be a real headache, consider avoiding the traffic jam with the Hassle Free Loop. It begins on the Panoramic Highway in Mount Tamalpais State Park and descends into the redwood grove and fern canyon via the Panoramic Trail, Ocean View Trail, and Fern Canyon Trail, a total of about 5 miles. It is also a short but steep hike from this parking area to the top of Mount Tamalpais, one of the best views in the bay area.

Bass Lake

5.8 miles round-trip. Moderate. Allow 4 to 5 hours to give yourself swimming time. Access: Palomarin Trailhead at end of Mesa Road north of Bolinas. Map: Point Reyes map or USGS Double Point topo.

This relatively flat hike takes you through rolling oak forest and grasslands where deer are common, past striking ocean overlooks, and into a cool and wooded freshwater swimming lake. From the trailhead the route is obvious. The trail skirts several steep cliffs and then heads over a steep ridge and inland. At about 2 miles you are faced with an unsigned fork. Go left. Soon you will pass a few small ponds and meadows. If it is a hot day you'll probably sense Bass Lake before you see it; it always seems to exude a cool, wet smell. The trail passes Bass Lake and a short spur trail will take you left to a grassy area and several steep trails to the water. Though

there isn't any real beach, there is a rope swing, and the water is perfect for swimming. When you've had enough, return the way you came.

Bear Valley Trail, Point Reyes

8 miles round-trip. Easy. Compressed rock Park Service road. Allow 4 hours. Access: Bear Valley Visitors Center. Map: Park map or USGS Inverness topo.

The Bear Valley Trail leads through wooded hillsides and past Divid Meadow until it reaches the sea at **Arch Rock** where Coast Creek splashes into the sea through a "sea tunnel." While the compressed rock trail takes away a bit from the nature experience, it does make the trail wheelchair accessible.

Estero Trail, Point Reyes

Various trails ranging from 4 to 8 miles round-trip. Easy to moderate. Access: Estero Trailhead in Point Reyes. Map: Park map or USGS Drake's Bay topo.

This relaxing group of trails is a favorite with birders. They meander along the edge of Limantour's Estero and Drake's Estero. Estero is the Spanish word for estuary, and the brackish waters of these two draw flocks of waterfowl and shorebirds as well as many raptors and smaller species.

Tomales Point Trail, Point Reyes

11 miles round-trip. Easy to moderate. Access: Trailhead is at the Pierce Ranch parking area in Point Reyes. Map: Park map or USGS Tomales topo.

The Tomales Point Trail is one of the best hikes in the state to see wildlife. In addition to the views of rugged shoreline,

Muir Woods National Monument

Leave San Francisco, cross the Golden Gate Bridge, and within 20 minutes you can be in Muir Woods experiencing the old-growth coastal redwoods of Northern California much as they were prior to the influx of European settlers in the 19th century. While the rest of Marin County's redwood forests were being devoured to feed the building spree that was San Francisco around the turn of the century, Muir Woods's trees in a remote ravine on the flanks of Mount Tamalpais escaped destruction in favor of easier pickings. By 1905, however, lumber companies had designs on the 200-foot-tall, 800-year-old giants. They were thwarted when farsighted congressman, philanthropist, and conservationist William Kent purchased the grove for $45,000. But only 2 years later the trees faced a different threat: the local water agency sought to condemn the land and build a dam on Redwood Creek, which would have inundated the forest. Kent appealed to President Theodore Roosevelt and in 1908 secured the National Monument status that the woods enjoy today. It was on Kent's request that the park was named after John Muir.

Muir Woods is a small park, only 553 acres tucked in a V-shaped canyon, but the national monument is completely encircled by enormous Mount Tamalpais State Park, lending it a wildness beyond its size. Most visitors know the park for the easy paved loop trail that leaves from the visitors center and circles along the banks of Redwood Creek into the heart of the monument's **Bohemian and Cathedral groves**. Hikers seeking more solitude should consider the longer trails such as **Fern Creek Loop**, 4 miles of spectacular canyon and redwood views, or the more strenuous **Dipsea Loop,** an 8-mile mix of shady creekside, high ridges, and ocean views.

The monument is 17 miles north of San Francisco with well-marked signs leading from U.S. 101. From 101 you can enter the park from either Highway 1 or the Panoramic Highway. The National Monument Visitors Center and the state park both sell good hiking maps for a small fee. Muir Woods is open every day from 8am to sunset. Admission is free. For more information contact **Muir Woods National Monument,** Mill Valley, CA 94941 (tel. 415/388-2595). There is no picnicking, camping, or accommodations in Muir Woods. The nearest campground is a first-come, first-served 13-site walk-in camp at Pantoll Station or the heavily wooded Alice Eastwood Group Camp, reservations required (tel. 800/444-7275), in **Mount Tamalpais State Park.**

---

the watering hole 3 miles into this hike is home to the park's herd of tule elk. Elk trails lead off the main trail, offering many side-trip possibilities. Keep an eye out for poison oak's waxy three-leaf clusters. Also be sure to check for ticks as the Lyme disease–carrying black-legged tick is common here.

OVERNIGHTS

Wildcat Camp and Beach, Point Reyes National Seashore

11.4 miles. Moderate to difficult. Allow 2 or 3 days. Access: Palomarin Trailhead at end of Mesa Road north of Bolinas. Map:

Point Reyes trail map or USGS Double Point topo.

This continuation of the Bass Lake day hike passes three more freshwater lakes, the largest of which, Pelican Lake, is enhanced by having its own ocean view, but is almost impossible to reach because of thick brush. The coastal trail here winds through the eucalyptus and past thick berry vines. In the spring and summer the whole trail is lined with sticky monkey flowers and lupine. Almost 6 miles of hiking from the trailhead you'll reach Wildcat Camp, a large meadow with running water. Several picnic tables mark the campsites, and sandy Wildcat Beach is a short walk away. Reservations to camp here are required and are available from the park headquarters at Bear Valley (tel. 415/663-1092).

MOUNTAIN BIKING

The mountain bike was officially invented here in 1977, and well into the 1980s Mount Tam was the hub of the off-road biking world. When mountain biking really took off, the pressure became too much for Marin to bear, and the forces of hiking and horseback riding united to ban bikes from all Mount Tamalpais single-track trails. Luckily numerous fire roads web the mountain, and those remain open, though a 15 mph speed limit is enforced. For maps of bikeable areas in **Mount Tamalpais State Park,** contact the visitors center (tel. 415/388-2070). The Marin Municipal Water District also owns much of Mount Tam, though they also enforce the single-track ban and speed limit. For maps of trails outside the state park area contact the **Bicycle Trails Council of Marin** (tel. 415/456-7512), P.O. Box 13842, San Rafael,

CA 94913. If you arrived without your bike, a couple of places in the area will rent you one. Try **Start to Finish** (tel. 800/600-BIKE), which has several locations around the Bay Area, or **Mike's Bike Center** (tel. 415/454-3747) at 1601 Fourth St. in San Rafael.

Old Railroad Grade to Mount Tam Summit

13 miles round-trip. Strenuous. Steep with tons of switchbacks. Access: West Blithdale Avenue, Mill Valley. Map: Mount Tam State Park.

This ride is the most popular route to the summit (other than the paved road). Following the bed of an old narrow-gauge railway that served a mountaintop hotel, it switchbacks over 100 times on the way to the summit. Pick up the Old Railway Grade about a mile out of Mill Valley on West Blithdale Avenue at the Blithdale Summit Gate. From here you just put it in a low gear, crank, and try to enjoy the scenery. After about 5 miles you reach the Panoramic Highway and the West Point Inn. Cross the highway and pick up the grade again on the other side. From here it gets *steep* and switchbacky. Don't worry—it's only about 1.5 miles more, most of it straight up. You'll get there eventually and after a long rest it is all downhill. If riding down at 15 mph sounds just too boring for you, there is always the paved road, but watch out for traffic there.

Bolinas Ridge Trail

28 miles. Moderate. Access: Highway 1 near Audubon Canyon Ranch and Bolinas Lagoon. Map: None needed.

Mountain biking is pretty much verboten in Point Reyes since most of the good trails are in the wilderness sections, but this trail just on the other side of Highway 1 gives you the same sort of terrain and no headaches. From the intersection of Bolinas Road and Highway 1, follow the Fairfax-Bolinas Road to the 1,300-foot summit overlooking the lagoon, Stinson Beach, the San Andreas Fault, and Point Reyes. Here you turn left on the Bolinas Ridge Trail, a wide path. For almost 10 miles you ride through redwoods, keeping pretty much to the ridgeline. The road begins to descend and breaks out into grazing land. Watch for cattle and shut all gates behind you. About 4 miles after leaving the redwoods you'll reach Sir Francis Drake Drive, giving you two return options. One is to simply go back the way you came. The other is to turn left on Sir Francis Drake into Olema and then take Highway 1 south to your car. The road is pleasant but traffic sometimes whizzes through the windy curves here.

Over the Hill and Around Muir Woods

30 miles. Strenuous. Steep climbs, fast descents. Access: Park at Vista Point on north side of Golden Gate Bridge. Map: Marin County road map or GGNRA trail and road map.

From Vista Point, a bike path descends down Sausalito Lateral and then weaves through Sausalito along the waterfront, where it is simply a bike lane, not a separate path. Soon a separate path branches off. Follow it until it forks left under U.S. 101. From here just follow the signs to Panoramic Highway, Stinson Beach, or Mount Tamalpais. After passing through Mill Valley, the Panoramic Highway catapults up the side of Mount Tam,

alternating hideous climbs with outrageous views of the surrounding countryside and of the Pacific. Once you pass Pan Toll Station it's a solid downhill blast to the intersection of Panoramic Highway and Highway 1. This stretch of road is winding, steep, and narrow. If you're up for the speed, I'd try to ride a little faster than the prevailing car traffic down the hill to avoid getting run off the road. Once you reach Highway 1 above Stinson Beach, you'll follow it south along one of the most stunning coastal roads in the world. Muir Beach is the last oceanfront on this ride and a good resting point. Then Muir Woods Road will take you back to the Panoramic Highway just outside Mill Valley. Turn right and return through Sausalito the way you came.

SAILING

The bay is one of the finest sailing grounds on the West Coast—the Golden Gate allows Pacific winds through but stops much of the open ocean's rollicking swell. For a list of charter fleets and sailing schools in the Bay Area, see "Sailing" under "The Peninsula ♦ What to Do & Where to Do It."

SEA KAYAKING

Marin is a sea kayaker's dream come true. In addition to the bay itself, Tomales Bay, Drakes Bay, Bolinas Lagoon, and Richardson Bay are all classic sea kayaking adventures. **Sea Trek Ocean Kayaking Center** (tel. 415/488-1000) in Sausalito teaches sea kayaking and has a rental fleet of sit-on-top and closed cockpit boats right on the edge of Richardson Bay. They also offer guided night kayaking tours in Richardson Bay nearly every full moon. **Pacific Currents** (tel. 800/465-2925) also leads trips, particularly at north county spots like Tomales Bay and Drakes Bay.

SURFING

Unlike San Francisco's fierce conditions, Marin is somewhat tame by comparison. **Stinson Beach** and **Bolinas** are the main spots. They are generally small and mushy since both lie in the shelter of Duxbury Reef. A few certifiable nut cases of my acquaintance, who think Maverick's has gotten too crowded, surf an even gnarlier giant reef break north of here near a seal rookery (See "Shark Watch" feature above), but they'd break my legs if I told you where. **Livewater Surf Shop** (tel. 415/868-0333) on Highway 1 in the heart of Stinson Beach rents wetsuits, surfboards, and boogie boards. For wave info, call the **Marin Surf Report** (tel. 415/868-1922).

WALKS & RAMBLES

Redwood Creek Trail, Muir Woods National Monument

1 mile. Access: Muir Woods headquarters.

Muir Woods is the striking remnant of the virgin redwoods that once covered Mount Tamalpais. The Redwood Creek Trail is a great way to get acquainted with these 400- to 800-year-old giants. The tallest tree in the park is 253 feet tall. Many others top 200 feet. Perhaps the most charming feature of this short trail is its proximity to Redwood Creek. The gurgling of the creek and the wind in the trees is a wonderful white noise filter to cover up the sounds of others on this popular (over a million visitors a year) trail.

Slide Ranch Tidepools

Short but steep. Access: Driveway on ocean side of Highway 1, 2 miles north of Muir Beach.

Slide Ranch is possibly the best tide-pooling spot in Marin. Several large pools here contain nudibranchs, starfish, urchins, anemones, crabs, and tiny fish. Don't be intimidated by the steep driveway—you'll make it. Also on site is a small organic farm and environmental education center. Closed from November to February. Call 415/381-6155 for information.

Earthquake Trail, Point Reyes National Seashore

0.6 miles. Access: Bear Valley Visitors Center, Point Reyes.

The earth is alive here, and the Earthquake Trail will illustrate it. The trail takes you through a brief but fact-filled informational tour of the San Andreas Fault as it slices through Point Reyes. You'll see sink ponds left when the earth collapses, slumping hillsides, broken fences, and a barn knocked off its foundation—all caused by the gradual but relentless movement of the fault.

WHALE WATCHING

Point Reyes juts nearly 10 miles out to sea from the surrounding coastline, creating an incredible bottleneck for coast-hugging whales on their migration. As a result you can see more whales in a day here than any other place in the state. Of course that presumes that the fog cooperates. On a good day hundreds of visitors gather at the **Point Reyes Lighthouse** for the chance to spot 50 to 60 whales in an afternoon. Bring binoculars as the point is several hundred feet tall and you'll be looking a long way down. During peak season, from December to March, the Park Service runs a shuttle from Drake's Beach to the light house. Two other spots in Point Reyes,

Chimney Rock and Tomales Point, offer just as many whales without the crowds. Other favorite lookouts are the **Muir Beach Overlook** and the **Pacific blufftops** between Muir Beach and Stinson Beach on Highway 1.

During whale season **Oceanic Society Expeditions** (tel. 415/474-3385) takes naturalist-led whale-watching boats from the San Francisco Marina to Point Reyes every weekend that the weather permits. The all-day trip costs $48 for adults and $46 for kids and senior citizens. No children under 10 are allowed.

The East Bay ◆ What to Do & Where to Do It

The East Bay differs dramatically from the peninsula and Marin County. The terrain here is more rolling and the climate much drier. The cities also tend to be more sprawling, fingers and strands of development fragmenting the wildlands. Still, the parklands of the East Bay Regional Parks District and the State Parks System hold many square miles of wonderful hiking and biking opportunities here. The bay shore is another outlet; boardsailing, fishing, and sailing are extremely popular.

BIRD WATCHING

The **East Bay Wilderness System** operated by the East Bay Regional Parks District is an important nesting and feeding zone for numerous species, especially the larger raptors. Though this part of the bay is often developed right to the water's edge, a few preserves like **Point Pinole Regional Shoreline** have sheltered the last remaining salt marshes. Migratory species heading into the Delta are often seen passing through here too. The EBRPD maintains a bird list and offers bird watching interpretive programs at several regional parks. Call the main office (tel. 510/635-0135) for more information.

BOARDSAILING

With predictable high winds that funnel in through the Golden Gate, but little surf to speak of, the East Bay Area is a popular hangout for boardsailers looking for a speed fix or beginners working on their oceangoing skills. Access to the bay, however, can be tough in many spots. The **Berkeley Marina** is one spot where it is easy to get on the water. **Berkeley Windsurfing and Snowboards** (tel. 510/843-9283), 1601 University Ave., is the largest East Bay boardsailing shop and offers a full line of new, used, and rental gear; plus they teach lessons of all levels. Inland a bit more, **Windsurf Del Valle** (tel. 925/455-4008) on Lake Del Valle near Livermore is a well-regarded school for beginning and intermediate sailors.

FISHING

There are a wide variety of saltwater and freshwater fishing options available all over the Bay Area. For more specific information, see "Fishing" under "The Peninsula ◆ What to Do & Where to Do It" earlier in this chapter.

HIKES, BUSHWHACKS & BACKPACK TRIPS

DAY HIKES

Around Mount Diablo

7-mile loop. Strenuous. 6 hours. Access: Juniper Camp Trailhead, 2.5 miles up the summit road from south entrance. Map: Mount Diablo State Park map.

For good reason most visitors flock to the summit of Mount Diablo for the incredible view, but to get a good look at the different ecosystems and geological zones on the mountain, this hike is better. Mount Diablo can get scorching in the summer and has little to no water, so get an early start on the day and bring more water than you think you'll need. The trail begins in a forest of giant live oaks, passes through chaparral, into a digger pine forest, over grassland, through more chaparral, more oaks, and of course, tons of poison oak. As you crest each ridge you'll get a sample of what the view is like from the summit before plunging back into the next canyon. Eventually you'll have done a complete circle and will be back at Juniper Camp.

Little Yosemite

3.5 miles round-trip. Easy. 2 hours. Access: Canyon View Trailhead at Sunol Regional Park Headquarters. Map: Sunol trail map available in park.

This short trail crosses several creeks and wanders through an oak and wildflower wonderland on a hillside overlooking Alameda Creek. After a junction with an old ranch road you'll descend to Little Yosemite, a boulder-strewn, rock-walled canyon that seems more Sierra Nevada than Alameda County.

OVERNIGHTS

Oristimba Wilderness, Henry W. Coe State Park

22-plus miles round-trip. Strenuous. Allow 3 or 4 days. Access: Henry Coe State Park Headquarters, Pacheco Route Trailhead. Map: Henry Coe State Park map.

This state park is the largest wild tract of public land in the East Bay, and this hike will take you to the most remote

corner. Because the park was formerly a ranch, many of the trails are old ranch roads. That's actually a good thing, because the area is steep, and poison oak lines the trail in many areas so the extra width is a nice buffer. You'll go through an interesting dry woodland of Digger pines, laurel, buckeye, and several different kinds of oak. The destinations, though, are the three biggest lakes in the park: Coit, Kelly, and Mississippi reservoirs. With plentiful water, good swimming, and sometimes spectacular bass fishing, these lakes are a good place to spend a couple days in the spring or fall.

MOUNTAIN BIKING

Lucky for mountain bikers the backcountry of the East Bay is laced with an elaborate network of fire roads and water district maintenance grades that link the major East Bay parks. Due to heavy use, however, there is virtually no single track open to bikes. Still, it is great to be able to do a nice fire road ride within an easy pedal of Berkeley and Oakland. For info on renting a bike try **Start to Finish** (tel. 800/600-BIKE), which has several locations throughout the Bay Area, or **Missing Link Bicycles** (tel. 510/843-7471) at 1988 Shattuck Ave. in Berkeley.

Tilden and Wildcat Canyon Regional Parks

16 miles. Moderate. Access: Wildcat Canyon Drive in Tilden Park. Map: Tilden and Wildcat Canyon maps.

From the Lone Oak Picnic Area take the Meadow Canyon Trail to the Curran Trail. Soon you'll reach Wildcat Gorge Trail, which veers right. Both these trails run in a beautiful and narrow canyon lined with springs and lush riparian growth. They are often closed in the rainy season in which case you should simply detour on the Meadow Canyon Trail. Either way you end up on the Wildcat Creek Trail edging along the boundary of Tilden Nature Area, an ecological study area, and Jewel Lake. Bikes aren't allowed in the nature area. After almost 5 miles of pedaling along Wildcat Creek, the Belgum Trail veers right and uphill almost to the top of "No Way Hill." At this point you're on the San Bruno Ridge Trail, which soon hooks up with Nimitz Way and a smooth coast down to your starting point.

Henry W. Coe State Park

Distance is as long or short as you want. Strenuous. Access: Park Headquarters 20 miles southeast of San Jose. Map: Henry W. Coe State Park map.

Some of the roughest, toughest mountain biking in California is here in the ranch country of this huge coast range park. More than 200 miles of old ranch roads and single track climb and plunge over, down, and around the neck-straining topography of the park. Almost all of it is open to bikes with the exception of the Orestimba Wilderness in the east end of the park. This is not the place for a first-time ride or a new-bike shakedown cruise. The terrain is extremely unforgiving, the climate can be positively brutal, and if you blow it and break something it's going to be a long walk home or a long wait for rescue. That said, this is heaven for solid riders. There is little hiker traffic, and the distances between points of interest are perfect for the pace of mountain biking. In spring the weather is best, the creeks are flowing (lots of swimming holes in Coyote Creek), and the wildflowers are amazing.

Mount Diablo State Park

Distance is as much or as little as you can take. Moderate to strenuous. Access: South Park entrance near Danville. Map: Mount Diablo State Park map.

Until 1990 bikes were banned on Diablo, a terrible waste of some of the best fire roads in the Bay Area. Thanks to the constant lobbying of the Bicycle Trails Council of the East Bay and other mountain biking advocates, the park officials relented and threw most fire roads and a few short sections of single track open. Park elevations range from the 3,849-foot summit to down around 500 feet, and fire roads range all over the mountain. If you're looking to pound some vertical it is possible to bike up the summit road on asphalt and then drop down the Summit Trail or North Peak Trail. Not looking for that much of a thrill? Well, then the Wall Point Road near Sentinal Rock and Barbecue Terrace Road makes a nice 7-mile loop. Bring lots of water bottles as it gets really hot here, and a supply of tubes, patch kit, etc.

ROAD BIKING

Mount Diablo Summit Ride

29 miles (14.5 up, 14.5 down). Access: Downtown Danville. Map: Diablo State Park map.

Begin in downtown Danville, a pleasant little town with plenty of cafes and water fountains to fuel up for the grind ahead. Take Diablo Road to the south entrance of the state park, marked by two stone pillars and a sign. From here, South Gate Road begins climbing at a steady but not oppressive 6% grade. Eventually you turn right on Summit Road and the climb continues. From Summit Road turnoff, it is 5 miles and 1,500 feet to the summit parking lot and observation building, all but the last 300 yards a gentle climb. (The last 300 yards is a killer, but it's only 300 yards.) Hopefully it is a clear day and you can soak up the view while resting. I'm not sure if I believe them, but according to people who tally these kinds of things, Mount Diablo is second in the world to Mount Kilimanjaro for the number of square miles of land you can see from its summit, something like 400,000 square miles. When you're good and ready, check those brakes and whoosh home.

SAILING

The bay is one of the finest sailing grounds on the West Coast—the Golden Gate allows Pacific winds through but stops much of the open ocean's rollicking swell. For a list of charter fleets and sailing schools in the Bay Area, see "Sailing" under "The Peninsula ◆ What to Do & Where to Do It."

WALKS & RAMBLES

Mount Diablo Fire Interpretive Trail

0.7 miles. Access: Summit Observation Tower, Mount Diablo State Park.

Best done in spring, this short hike circles just below the summit of Mount Diablo through an area swept by wildfire in 1977. A brochure that you can purchase at the summit visitors center will explain the fire recovery process, now nearly completed. From February through May, wildflowers bloom on the slope that the fire once charred.

Monument Trail, Henry W. Coe State Park

1.6 miles. Access: Headquarters, Henry W. Coe State Park.

After exploring the 19th-century ranch headquarters at the visitors center, this

brief but interesting trail leads up to a good view knoll that overlooks much of this huge park. Like Mount Diablo, spring is the best time to visit here. The wildflowers and clear days make for spectacular views of the Sierra Nevada to the east and the Santa Cruz Mountains to the west.

Campgrounds & Other Accommodations

CAMPING

THE PENINSULA

As you might imagine, camping on the San Francisco Peninsula is less than plentiful and in high demand. There is no official camping in San Francisco, so if you must stay in the city, see "Inns & Lodges" later in this section for the little I have to say about sleeping indoors. It's still possible to find a nice place to camp on the peninsula outside of San Francisco, however, if you're willing to make reservations through the dreaded PARKNET service or to travel in the off-season, which really isn't as bad as it might be since the weather is better here in winter than summer anyway. San Mateo County, which controls most of the wild area in this chapter, has draconian laws against sleeping in your car. As tempting as it might be to pull your van to the side of the road along Highway 1 and crash in the back, don't do it unless you're prepared to deal with rude cops with bright spotlights. You're much better off paying for a site in Butano or Half Moon Bay State Park, if you can get one, or guerrilla camping in a residential neighborhood or remote mountain road. Better yet, plan your visit to leave time to get to either Marin or Santa Cruz before nightfall.

Half Moon Bay State Beach

7 miles south of Pillar Point Harbor on Highway 1, turn west on Kelly Avenue to park. Tel. 650/726-8820. 51 tent or motorhome sites. Flush toilets, water, fire pits, pets okay. First come, first served. No reservations. $16 per night.

The beach is a short walk from this level and unfortunately wide-open campground. On weekends it's a little too crowded here for my taste. Still, the beaches of San Mateo County stretch in both directions, Pillar Point Harbor is a few miles north, and the mountains rise in the background.

Butano State Park

Just west of Pescadero Beach and south of the tiny town of Pescadero on Cloverdale Road. Tel. 415/879-2040. 40 sites. Flush toilets, running water, fire pits, pets okay. Reservations: PARKNET (800/444-PARK). $16 per night.

The best real camping on the peninsula. You can hike for miles from here or take the short drive down to Pescadero State Beach for a day by the sea. Also really interesting is the Pescadero Marsh nature preserve, miles of undisturbed freshwater creek and estuary at the mouth of Pescadero Creek.

MARIN COUNTY

Angel Island

Reached by ferry from San Francisco Fisherman's Wharf or Tiburon Landing. Tel. 415/435-1915. 9 environmental walk-in campsites. Tables, water, pit toilets, no fires. Arrange ferry transport through Blue & Gold Fleet (415/705-5555). $7–$9 per night plus ferry (ferry runs weekends only).

The most unique camping option in the whole Bay Area is the Angel Island walk-in sites. It requires planning far in advance to get reservations, but where else can you be practically alone on a several-square-mile wild island with the Golden Gate Bridge, Bay Bridge, and San Francisco skyline all practically within reach? The closest sites are a mile from the ferry landing, so bring your gear in a backpack and go light.

Olema Ranch Campground

Junction of Highway 1 and Sir Francis Drake Boulevard in Olema. Tel. 415/663-8001. 200 sites. Running water, flush toilets, showers, laundry, pets okay. Reservations accepted. $18–$25 per night.

Since Point Reyes doesn't have any car camping within park boundaries, this private campground picks up most of the business. Nearby is Olema, a quaint little town, and Tomales Bay to the north.

Samuel P. Taylor State Park

Sir Francis Drake Boulevard, 6 miles east of Highway 1. Tel. 415/488-9897. 60 sites. Restrooms, running water, fire pits, food lockers. Pets okay in campground but not on trails. Reserve through PARKNET (800/444-PARK). $12–$16 per night.

Samuel P. Taylor is the closest public campground to Point Reyes but is also a great destination in its own right. The sites are right in a forested creek canyon. It can get cold here in winter as the sites get little sun through the trees.

Pan Toll Campground, Mount Tamalpais State Park

Panoramic Highway, Mount Tamalpais State Park. Tel. 415/388-2070. 16 walk-in sites. Flush toilets, running water, fireplaces, tables, wood for sale. No reservations. $12–$16 per night.

The little-known secret of camping on Mount Tam is that the best campground doesn't take reservations or fill up early. If you are willing to hoof it up a small hill, you can camp at the beginning of the Steep Ravine Trail and within a short hike of the mountain summit. I've camped here on busy weekends and had no problem getting a site as long as I arrived before dark.

Point Reyes Campgrounds

Point Reyes National Seashore. Tel. 415/663-1092. 50 walk-in sites total. Water, pit toilets, fire pits, food lockers. No pets. Reservations accepted. Free.

Camping within the park is limited to four hike-in camps. Two, **Wildcat Camp** (6.5-mile hike) and **Coast Camp** (1.8-mile hike), sit just above the beach. They are often foggy and damp, so bring a good tent and sleeping bag. **Sky Camp** (1.7-mile hike) and **Glen Camp** (4.6-mile hike), set in the woods away from the sea, are more protected from the coastal elements. Individual sites hold up to 8 people. Camping is free, but permits are required and stays are limited to 4 days. Sites can be reserved

up to 2 months in advance, Monday through Friday, 9am to noon only.

THE EAST BAY

Mount Diablo State Park

South Gate Road outside Danville. Tel. 925/673-2890. 60 sites in three separate campgrounds. Running water, flush or pit toilets, showers. Reservations through PARKNET (800/444-PARK). $12–$15 per night.

Hot and dry in summer, this is a great winter or spring getaway. The view from Diablo's summit is clearer, and you won't roast.

Anthony Chabot Regional Park

Redwood Road in Castro Valley. Tel. 510/562-2267. 10 walk-in and 35 regular sites. Running water, showers, flush toilets. Pets okay. For reservations call East Bay Regional Park District (tel. 510/635-0135).

With 5,000 acres and a large fishing lake, Chabot is a popular local camping getaway. Fishing is great in the winter and spring, as is the hiking.

Henry W. Coe State Park

Exit Dunne Avenue from U.S. 101 in Morgan Hill. Go east 13 miles to end of road. Tel. 408/779-2728. 7 walk-in and 13 regular sites. Pit toilets, water available at the visitors center. $8–$12 per night.

Few people bother to drive all the way out to this huge state park, leaving more of it for the rest of us. The mountain biking is amazing here, as is the spring and winter hiking. Also of interest are the early California ranch buildings and equipment.

THE PENINSULA

If you want to stay in San Francisco, the best place to look for hotel or other accommodation information is the **San Francisco Convention and Visitors Bureau** (tel. 415/391-2000), P.O. Box 429097, San Francisco, CA 94142, or stop by their **Visitors Information Center** at 900 Market Street downtown.

Montara Lighthouse Hostel

Located just off Highway 1 on 16th Street in Montara. P.O. Box 737, Montara 94037. Tel. 650/728-7177. Reservations by mail only. Rates $9 and up.

The Montara Lighthouse Hostel is a beautiful conversion of the old Coast Guard buildings into simple lodgings. Everything is deliberately simple but functional. It's always hard to beat a lighthouse for a view, and this is no exception.

MARIN COUNTY

Steep Ravine Cabins

Rocky Point, south of Stinson Beach on Highway 1. Reserve 8 weeks in advance through PARKNET (800/444-PARK). $30 per night.

Once the getaway of wealthy and powerful San Franciscans, these 10 simple redwood cabins on Rocky Point south of Stinson are now available to the general public. Overlooking the raw surf as it strikes the rugged Marin shoreline, these simple two-room cabins are a deal you just can't beat—$30 per cabin per night, and they sleep four or five. With wood stoves, outhouses, and no electricity, you'll be transported back to a different century.

Point Reyes Hostel

Limantour Road, Point Reyes National Seashore, P.O. Box 247, Point Reyes Station 94956. Reservations by mail only. $9 per night.

With a well-equipped shared kitchen, this old ranch compound is a great way to be self-sufficient while staying in the park. If you do feel like eating out, Point Reyes Station and Olema are nearby with a number of great restaurants. Within walking distance of the hostel is Limantour Beach and Drakes Estero, plus miles of great hiking. The hostel fills up early, so reservations are recommended. Maximum stay is 3 nights.

THE EAST BAY

Claremont Resort and Tennis Club

Ashby and Domingo Aves., Oakland, CA 94623-0363. Tel. 510/843-3000 or 800/551-7266. Fax 510/848-6208. 239 rms, 30 suites. $235–$395 double; from $300 suite. Packages available, including a one-night package from $281. AE, DC, MC, V.

This 22-acre resort overlooking San Francisco and the Bay straddles the municipal line between Oakland and Berkeley. The main draw is the spa, which offers five different types of massage and a variety of body care treatments—loofah scrub, mud and herbal wraps, aromabath, and Turkish scrub. Many fitness facilities are available, including an exercise room for aerobics and yoga classes, a weight room, two lap pools, and 10 tennis courts. The beauty salon offers a complete range of skin and beauty treatments. The cuisine—fairly standard—consists of nutritionally balanced menus of seafood, salad, and pasta.

3

The Monterey Bay Area

T o write about Santa Cruz and Monterey in the same chapter at first seems ironic. Santa Cruz is bohemian and loose at the seams, a throwback to a more experimental time in American culture. Monterey and Carmel, on the other hand, seem to inhabit a loftier—some would say snootier—frame of mind.

It's Monterey Bay that brings these cities and the surrounding landscape together. Besides its fringe of beaches, tide pools, sand dunes, surf breaks, and scuba-diving spots, the bay is something much more. This is one of the most alive patches of ocean you'll ever find.

Comparable in size to the Grand Canyon, the Monterey Submarine Canyon begins just offshore of Moss Landing in the middle of the bay's crescent, and extends more than 90 miles out to sea. Within a half-mile of its head the canyon is already 300 feet deep. It quickly deepens even more, and well offshore reaches a depth of more than 10,000 feet. Scientists speculate that the canyon began more than 30 million years ago as an onshore canyon (rather than a submarine trench) just west of present-day Santa Barbara.

All that cold, deep water creates a nutrient-filled soup for hundreds of species each year during the spring and summer upwelling season, when currents and wind push the warmer surface water out to sea and bring highly oxygenated water up from the canyon. That in turn creates a feeding and breeding frenzy on the lowest end of the food chain. Phytoplankton bloom in a huge bounty that doesn't stop until it reaches the highest level on the food chain: the whales, sharks, birds, and people who are the final recipients of the bay's riches.

On the northern edge of the bay, the redwood-covered Santa Cruz Mountains border a rugged coast of cove beaches and steep, fast-eroding sea cliffs. Though the mountains have been logged for over 100 years, numerous groves of beautiful *Sequoia sempervirens*, the coast redwood, were saved with the creation of Big Basin State Park in 1902 and the later creation of Henry Cowell, Wilder Ranch, and Forest of Nisene Marks state parks.

Año Nuevo Island and State Preserve just north of Santa Cruz are, together with the Farallon Islands off San Francisco, the most important breeding habitat of the northern elephant seal and an important feeding ground for the great white shark, which preys on the juvenile and adolescent seals.

Santa Cruz, a city of nearly 40,000, is known throughout California as the capital of Northern California surfing. Famous breaks like Steamer's Lane and Pleasure Point, plus numerous lesser-known spots, keep one of the world's most intensely competitive surfing scenes alive. The city gets great waves on almost any swell direction year-round and there are more surf shops per capita here than anywhere on earth. Mountain biking is another booming sport in Santa Cruz, with the fire roads and skid trails through the mountains behind town seemingly designed for long steep rides through the forest.

In Santa Cruz, manners and mores are such that people will take off their clothes or otherwise get out of hand simply to make a point. In Monterey and Carmel, by contrast, everything is neat and orderly. I'm convinced no one has done anything overtly impolite in decades. At least not since the wild and woolly days John Steinbeck documented in *Cannery Row* and *Tortilla Flats*—the sardine boom of the 1940s was perhaps the most famous (some would say notorious) period of Monterey Bay history. All those little fish made Monterey a rich town, but by 1951 the boom was over—the sardine population had been decimated by overfishing in the bay. They're only now beginning to recover, but squid, anchovy, salmon, and ling cod are all commercially fished in the bay.

Monterey Bay came by its name during the 1602 voyage of Sebastian Vizcaino, who christened it after his Mexican viceroy, the count of Monte Rey. Though it was one of the first major harbors discovered by early explorers and was an important stopover for many voyages, it wasn't settled until much later. Gaspar de Portola and Padre Junipero Serra made things permanent for the Spanish in 1770 when they built a *presidio* in present-day Monterey and a mission, the Mission Basilica San Carlos Borromeo del Rio Carmelo, in present-day Carmel.

The settlement of Monterey sounded the death knell for the culture of the Costanoan Indians who had inhabited this area for at least 10,000 years. To save their poor pagan souls (and provide a cheap and easy source of labor to construct the new city), the Spaniards rounded up the Indians in *rancherias*, small settlements where the missionaries converted them to Christianity. Syphilis, smallpox, and general despair ripped through the Costanoans and decimated their population.

The city was built and became the capital of Spanish California. From then until the Gold Rush it was the busiest port on the coast and the political and cultural center of Alta California. However, the stormy half-circle embayment was never quite sheltered enough to use as a major commercial port in later years. And it was here, of course, that the Constitutional Convention met to set up the state's first government in 1849 prior to California becoming an official U.S. state in 1850.

With the onset of the Gold Rush, statehood, and increasing traffic to California, Monterey Bay was eclipsed by San Francisco Bay, leaving it and its surroundings to the fishermen, loggers, smugglers, and scientists.

The Lay of the Land

Officially Monterey Bay extends from Point Piños in Pacific Grove to Lighthouse Point in Santa Cruz. Unofficially, it exerts a much larger influence on the surrounding land and ocean. This chapter covers the coastal area from Point Lobos just south of Carmel to Año Nuevo Island just north of the Santa Cruz/San Mateo County Line, and inland to include the Santa Cruz Mountains, which wrap down as far as Watsonville, and the Carmel Valley and surrounding hills.

Highway 1 is the main road of interest, running more or less within striking distance of the coast the entire way from Point Lobos to Año Nuevo. Between Santa Cruz and Año Nuevo the road runs right alongside the ocean with virtually no development save for the occasional Brussels sprout field or farmhouse. Several times the road climbs up to follow the top of precarious sea cliffs. Then it will plunge down to creek crossings and beautiful beaches like Scott Creek Beach or Waddell Beach.

The redwood- and pine-covered Santa Cruz Mountains stretch all the way from Santa Cruz to the sprawling cities of the south bay. In the northern county a series of marine terraces demonstrates the continuing uplift caused when the Pacific Plate and North American Plate collide. (The Forest of Nisene Marks, a state park just outside Aptos, was the epicenter of 1990's disastrous Loma Prieta earthquake that did so much damage in the Monterey and San Francisco Bay areas.) Because of this uplift, the geology of the mountains is an interesting mix of metamorphic rock blended in alternating layers with sedimentary rock formed when this land was the ocean floor. Within the mountains the two chief thoroughfares are State Route 9, a beautiful and winding two-lane road that leads to Big Basin and Castle Rock state parks, and State Route 17, connecting Santa Cruz to San Jose with a four-lane freeway.

As Highway 1 heads south around the crescent bay, affluent tourist towns like Aptos and Capitola give way to busy agricultural centers like Watsonville and Castroville, home to much of the world's artichoke-growing industry. At the same time the mountains give way to the fertile Salinas River Plain. This is some of the richest land in the state. Also here is Moss Landing, an important commercial port, and Elkhorn Slough, a huge and relatively undisturbed freshwater estuary. Between Moss Landing and Monterey is a long stretch of coastal dunes caused by the omnipresent wind.

Near Monterey, the flanks of the Carmel mountains reach down from the heights of Mount Toro in a long stretch. Monterey itself sits in the crook of a large and wooded peninsula with hills at its back and a rocky shoreline. The Pacific side of the peninsula is more windswept. Sandy beaches are here at Asilomar and Carmel, but also there is mile after mile of rocky, wave-swept coves and sheer drops into the sea. Sadly, in my opinion, this beautiful stretch has been overly commodified by the famous 17-Mile

Drive. The segment of Highway 1 just south of Carmel is equally beautiful and free of the toll booth, the busloads of tourists, and the ostentatious wealth. Carmel itself is a cute little town. Quaint almost to a fault, it is one of those former artists' colonies where the artists no longer can afford to live, but the beach here is wonderful for surfing, walking, kite flying, just about anything.

Outside Carmel you'll come to Monastery Beach, a famous diving spot (and also a rock-climbing area), then you'll reach the entrance gate of Point Lobos State Reserve, an unbelievable piece of coastal wildland. Inland from Monastery Beach, the Carmel Valley is beautiful ranchland quick becoming mini-ranchettes, and the secret accessway to much of the Ventana Wilderness.

Orientation

Pigeon Point Lighthouse

The second tallest lighthouse on the West Coast at 115 feet, the Pigeon Point Lighthouse is still an important navigational marker for boat traffic between San Francisco Bay and Monterey Bay. Located 6 miles north of Año Nuevo on Highway 1, the lighthouse is currently under renovation but should be re-opened for tours by the time this book is in print. There is also an **AYH Youth Hostel** (tel. 415/879-0633) at the lighthouse's base.

Santa Cruz Surfing Museum

You can buy a T-shirt saying "real surfers don't have real jobs," or check out the very first wetsuits (invented by Santa Cruz's Jack O'Neill) in this old lighthouse building. With its collection of historic and modern boards and a great exhibit of photographs and videos, the tiny museum (tel. 831/429-3429) is perfectly located on West Cliff Lane at Lighthouse Point—about 50 feet from Steamer's Lane, Northern California's most famous surf spot. Hours vary and donations are appreciated.

Santa Cruz County Conference and Visitors Council

The best source of practical information like hotel reservations, restaurants, and businesses is the Visitors Council office downtown at 701 Front Street (tel. 831/425-1234). They're not great for outdoor recreation queries but can probably point you to a local person who can answer your question.

Capitola Town and Wharf

Distinct from Santa Cruz, Capitola is probably a little too quaint for its own good. Its Victorian cottages and 1920s bungalows are beautiful, but Capitola seems to be succumbing to the kind of civic narcissism that allows a town to base its economy and self-image on T-shirts and coffee cups with the city name emblazoned on them because it's just so damn cute. The municipal pier is good for fishing and there is a nice sandy beach. If you visit after a storm, look for the fossilized shells that erode out of the cliff at the Capitola bluffs.

Moss Landing

For a look at what Monterey was really like during the Cannery Row era, go to Moss Landing. Named after Charles Moss, a New England sea captain who sailed these waters in the 19th century and turned Moss Landing into a whaling port, the little town is home to one of the largest commercial fishing fleets in California. Fishing boats are built here in large numbers and every day the fleet

Monterey's Average Temperatures and Precipitation											
	Jan	Feb	Mar	Apr	May	June	July	Aug	Sept	Oct	Nov	Dec
High (°F)	60	62	62	63	64	67	68	69	72	70	66	61
Low (°F)	43	44	45	45	48	50	52	53	53	51	47	43
Precipitation (in.)	3.8	2.7	3.1	1.6	0.4	0.2	0.1	0.1	0.3	0.8	2.5	2.9

sets out to fish the rich waters of the Monterey Submarine Canyon, which begins about 200 feet beyond the harbor mouth. This is a town that instinctively faces the sea. It smells like fish, looks like fish, and is full of fish, most of which are immediately whisked to markets around the state. The California State University Marine Biology Laboratories offer undergrad and graduate level fieldwork at the laboratory complex on Sandholdt Road. On a clear day the huge 500-foot twin smokestacks of the Moss Landing Power Plant make it easy to spot the harbor from anywhere in the bay.

Fisherman's Wharf

A major fishing pier during the sardine boom, Monterey's Fisherman's Wharf is now where they set the hook on huge schools of tourists. Seafood restaurants, art galleries, barking sea lions, deep-sea fishing trips, and a constantly changing array of nautical-theme kitsch are the bait. It is located at the foot of Oliver Street and Del Monte.

Cannery Row

One of the most famous streets in the world as a result of John Steinbeck's novel *Cannery Row*, this street in Monterey was actually named after the book rather than the other way around. Once the home to more than 20 separate canneries, the area is now a tourist trap anchored on one end by the Coast Guard Breakwater and by the Monterey Bay Aquarium on the other. Several small beaches and stairways provide water access to some of the best shore-launched scuba diving anywhere, but parking is tough.

Monterey Bay Aquarium

886 Cannery Row, Monterey. Tel. 831/648-4888 for information, 831/648-4937 for advance tickets. Open 10am to 6pm every day.

The best way to understand the workings of Monterey Bay and its surroundings is to spend an afternoon in this amazingly designed aquarium. From a three-story-tall kelp forest exhibit to the first successful jellyfish display, the staff of the Monterey Bay Aquarium keeps on the cutting edge of aquarium design. Particularly notable is the way the museum displays ecosystems rather than individual species. Indoors and outoors interact beautifully in the sparsely constructed building: the kelp forest, tide-pool tank, and shorebird aviary lead to outside decks where you can watch whales go by and sea otters play. The museum is extremely popular on weekends and holidays, so make reservations if you can.

Pacific Grove Museum of Natural History

Often overshadowed by the Monterey Aquarium is this great natural history museum (tel. 831/648-3116). With a large collection of area birds, fish, and mammals, you can learn a lot about terrestrial flora and fauna and the Monterey Bay area. They also have

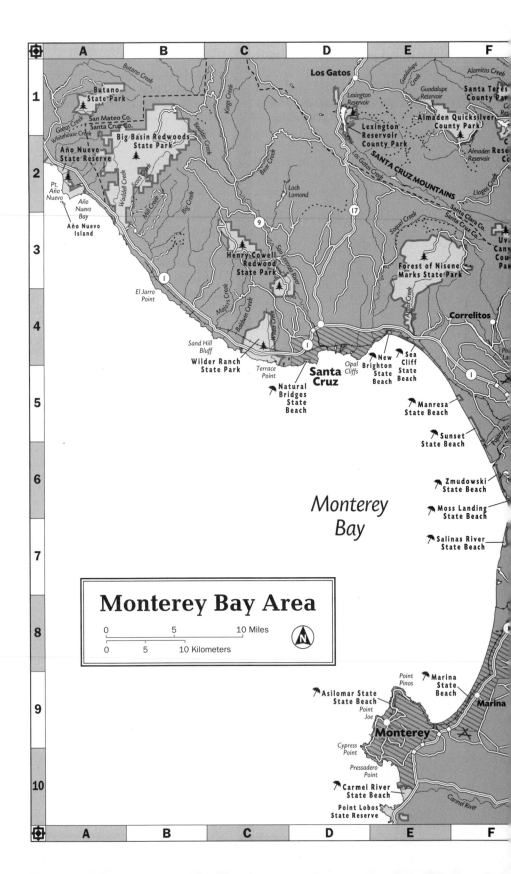

Monterey Bay Area

0   5   10 Miles
0 5 10 Kilometers

Monterey Bay

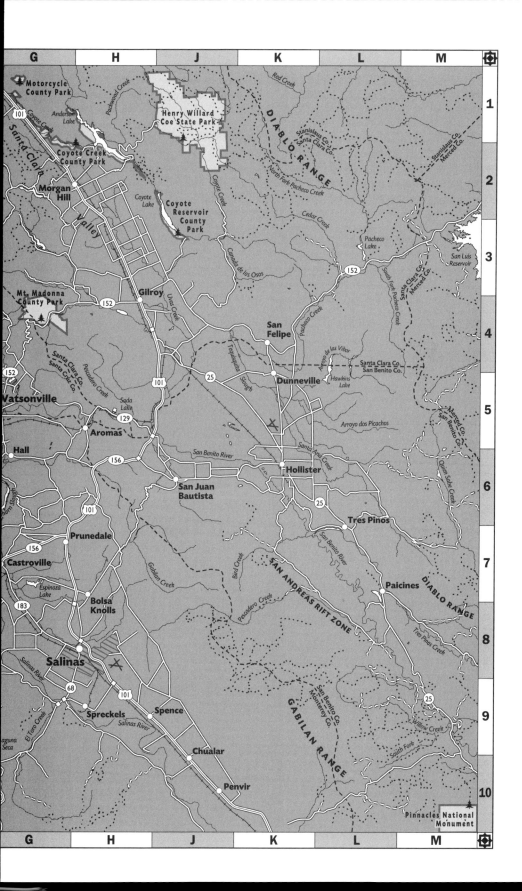

a selection of Native American arti-facts. The museum is located at 165 Forest Avenue in Pacific Grove and is open Tuesday to Sunday from 10am to 5pm.

Point Piños Lighthouse

Marking the southern boundary of Monterey Bay, the Point Piños Light-house, Asilomar Avenue and Lighthouse Avenue in Pacific Grove (tel. 831/ 648-3116), is the longest operating on the West Coast—since 1855. The point is a great tide-pool area and also home to some small dunes. Whales are often sighted from the point. The lighthouse and museum are open for tours Saturday and Sunday from 1pm to 4pm.

17-Mile Drive

Travel writers love to gush about the beautiful, scenic, glamorous, quaint, dramatic, extravagant, natural, other-worldly 17-Mile Drive through the Del Monte Forest between Pacific Grove and Carmel. Well, in my humble opin-ion, it is way overrated. Basically, a bunch of filthy rich people have success-fully monopolized a beautiful—but by no means the most beautiful—stretch of coastline and are charging you money at five separate toll booths to drive through their neighborhood and look at their ostentatious wealth under the guise of checking out a bunch of natural wonders. I'm not denying that there are nice beaches, vistas, etc., here, but I think that these people should be hung by their gilded thumbs for trying to cut you and me off from beaches and ocean-front that by law we own. To do that they've promoted a road as a tourist attraction. Come on, its just a road. We already own the beaches and ocean. Just let us drive to them.

Carmel-by-the-Sea

I'm waiting for the hyphenators in City Hall to change the name to Ye-Olde-Scenic-Carmel-by-the-Sea-Great-Paradise-of-all-Arty-and-Quaint-Plus-Lots-of-T-Shirt-Shops-Scenic-Area-and-Historical-Zone-Aren't-We-Cute? But then again that would be too hard to fit on a T-shirt. Nonetheless, Carmel is actually a nice place to go to the beach. The city beach at the foot of Ocean Avenue is backed by great dunes and is a really fun place to fly a kite, run down the dunes, roll in the sand, and splash in the waves. During the winter, surf can get really good here.

And if you look past entrepreneurs' attempts to capitalize on the town's inherent quaintness, some of the charm that made it an artists' colony in the first place still remains. Walk some of the narrow residential streets of small beach cottages. Street numbers aren't allowed in Carmel, so many of the houses have distinctive names to match their look. Call 831/624-2522 for information.

Parks & Other Hot Spots

Año Nuevo State Preserve

21 miles north of Santa Cruz on High-way 1. Tel. 650/879-0227. Open 8am to sunset. Fee and reservations required for guided elephant seal colony tours (tel. 800/ 444-PARK), also available first come, first served. Other park areas and beaches open at no fee. Bathrooms, visitors center, picnic tables, water.

This former dairy farm is most popular now as the site of California's largest breeding colony of elephant seals. From late fall to early spring, throngs of tourists come to see one of the most amazing close-up views of these gigantic seals as they breed and give birth. The park is also great for hiking, bird watching, picnicking, and (if you aren't afraid of the great white sharks who cruise the area looking for tender seal pups) surfing. The old ranch buildings and visitors center give a look back to a more slow-paced time on the California coast.

Waddell Beach and Creek

2 miles south of Año Nuevo on Highway 1. No fee. Parking on road only.

Actually part of Big Basin State Park, this beautiful beach is popular with surfers and boardsailers who come to ride the waves and bird-watchers or nature lovers who come to explore the beautiful wetland habitat of Waddell Creek.

Big Basin State Park

9 miles west of Boulder Creek on State Route 236. Tel. 831/338-8860. Open daily year-round. Entrance and camping fees. Camping, grocery store, picnic grounds, natural science museum.

Created in 1902, Big Basin was the first California state park. With more than 14,000 acres, beaches, waterfalls, virgin redwoods, and 40 miles of hiking trails, it is also one of the nicest. Rising from the ocean to high redwood forests, the park encompasses the entire Waddell Creek drainage and is home to all sorts of wildlife.

Wilder Ranch State Park

2 miles north of Santa Cruz on Highway 1. Tel. 831/423-9703. Open daily year-round. Parking fee inside park. Plenty of free parking on Highway 1.

One of the newest state parks, Wilder Ranch is paradise for mountain bikers. Where other state parks ban bikes from all but a few roads, Wilder encourages them to ride on almost all the trails, including miles of single track through redwood forests and open meadows. The beach here is closed to protect snowy plover nesting habitat, but the bike and walking trail along the coastal bluff is magnificent. The old ranch headquarters are operated as a historical site several days a week.

Henry Cowell Redwoods State Park

Main park 3 miles north of Santa Cruz on State Route 9. Fall Creek unit 2 miles further. Tel. 831/335-4598. Fee for day use and camping.

Covering more than 6,000 acres of forest land, the two units of this park have numerous short trails through the redwoods and along the headwaters of the San Lorenzo River. There are 15 miles of hiking trails and swimming and fishing holes on the river.

Natural Bridges State Beach

2531 W. Cliff Dr., Santa Cruz. Tel. 831/423-4609. Open daily, year-round. Fee.

Named for a pair of natural rock bridges that once adorned the eastern end of this pocket beach, only one bridge remains at Natural Bridges State Beach, and with the current rate of erosion, its days are numbered. The cove beach and eucalyptus grove in the center of the park aren't going anywhere though. Visitors are split between those who come to use the biggest sandy beach on the west side of Santa Cruz and those who come here to see the monarchs that nest in the butterfly grove every winter. It is also home to good tide pools and the Secret Lagoon, a small freshwater wetland where you can find ducks and geese.

Steamer's Lane

West Cliff Lane at Lighthouse Point.

Steamer's Lane is one of the best surf spots in Northern California—a long point break set off by dramatic water-carved cliffs. Because it is sheltered from most prevailing winds yet exposed to virtually all swells, the Lane is great in everything from 2-feet to 15-feet. When the surf gets big, the waves crashing on the cliffs make entry and exit a bit dicey—plus it gets crowded. But if you can manage those factors the waves more than make up for it.

Santa Cruz Yacht Harbor

Sailing is a huge sport in Santa Cruz, and the Yacht Harbor on East Cliff Drive (tel. 831/475-6161) is where you'll find it. Several charter sailboats and deep-sea fishing companies operate out of the harbor. *Chardonnay*, a Santa Cruz 70 racing yacht, is available for $500 an hour for tours of the bay in unimaginable style. UC Santa Cruz teaches summer sailing classes here that are

open to the public (see "Sailing" in "What to Do & Where to Do It"). The harbor itself is nothing special; winter storms shoal up the harbor mouth for weeks at a time, and the entrance can be really hairy on a big swell. Call for harbor information.

Inland Arana Gulch, the wetland from which the harbor was dredged in the 1950s, continues back and is a great spot for birding.

Schwan Lake

Once a brackish estuary, Schwan Lake at East Cliff and 9th Street is now a freshwater lagoon adjacent to a beautiful beach. A number of important wetland habitats occur here and a corresponding number of birds come here to take advantage of the biological bounty. Canoes and kayaks are allowed on the lake.

Pleasure Point

When the macho chest beating at Steamer's Lane is too much to bear, Pleasure Point on East Cliff Drive between 32nd and 41st avenues usually lives up to its name. Santa Cruz is famous for mean locals and hassles in the water, but I've never felt anything but good vibrations at Pleasure Point. The waves are good too. During big winter swells the entrance and exit can be spooky because there is no beach; you leap off rocks and clamber back up when you want to leave.

New Brighton State Beach

1500 Park Ave., off Highway 1. Tel. 831/464-6330. Camping and beach activities. Fee. Reservations accepted for camping.

From New Brighton to Monterey the bay is practically one long sandy beach. The State Beach here is really two separate parks. The beach is a popular swimming and play beach with restrooms. On top of the bluff is the campground. Wooded with Monterey pines, the campground is quiet, shady, well laid out—arguably the best in the immediate Santa Cruz area.

Forest of Nisene Marks State Park

Aptos Creek Drive off Soquel Drive in the town of Aptos. Tel. 831/763-7063. Hike-in camping, hiking, biking.

This primitive 10,000-acre state park is a favorite with mountain bikers and hikers looking for a bit of solitude. The formerly logged forest is now mature second-growth redwood. Though stripped bare by 1923, 70 years later the forest is starting to diversify back to a more complex redwood forest with layers of dogwood, bay laurel, Douglas fir, and tanbark oak. The Loma Prieta earthquake that demolished much of downtown Santa Cruz as well as huge portions of the Bay Area was focused here and you can hike to the epicenter—fissures and fallen trees marked the spot for a few years, but these signs seem to have faded after heavy rains and erosion.

Seacliff and Rio Del Mar Beaches

State Park Drive, Rio Del Mar. 5 miles south of Santa Cruz. Tel. 831/685-6442. Trailer camping, fishing pier, picnic grounds, interpretive center, sandy beach.

These two beaches stretch 2 miles from the 500-foot pier made out of a former World War I supply ship to the mouth of Aptos Creek. Wide and sandy, they are a popular summertime hangout for people from the inland valleys and nearby neighborhoods of Aptos and Rio Del Mar.

Manresa Beach State Park

Sand Dollar Drive off San Andreas Road exit from Highway 1, Watsonville. Tel. 831/724-3750. Fee for day use and camping. Camping, surf fishing, surfing, 64 tent camping sites.

Extremely popular with both locals and visitors from out of town, Manresa is a stunning park set on a bluff overlooking the bay. The bluff is covered by a mature grove of Monterey pines where you find picnic grounds and campsites.

Sunset Beach State Park

201 Sunset Beach Rd., Watsonville. Tel. 831/763-7063. Fee for day use and camping.

Sunset Beach will always have a special place in my heart as the first place I ever camped on the beach as a kid. On the northern edge of the huge dune fields that line the back of Monterey Bay, Sunset Beach has the best preserved coastal dune habitat in Santa Cruz County. Important dune and beach plants like the mock heather, sea rocket, and the endangered Monterey paintbrush occur here in healthy quantities. It is rare to find such a well-preserved dune habitat with all its strata intact from the water line to upland bluff. The beach is often windy as it lies right in the crux of Monterey Bay, and fog is not uncommon. Birds, dolphins, whales, and sea otters are frequently seen offshore.

Pajaro Valley Wetlands

Between Watsonville and the sea.

This 21-square-mile expanse of five sloughs is one of the most important wetland habitats in the Monterey Bay area after Elkhorn Slough near Moss Landing. The five sloughs here—Gallighan, Hanson, Harkins, Struve, and Watsonville—however, are freshwater rather than brackish and support a different type of ecosystem.

Moss Landing State Beach

End of Jetty Road on north side of Moss Landing Harbor. Parking fee within the park, plenty of free parking a short walk away.

This relatively small beach park offers an inordinate number of things to do in the park or the waters surrounding it. Located on a sandy isthmus between Moss Landing Harbor, Elkhorn Slough, and the bay, the park is popular with surfers, surf casters who fish off the rock jetty, bird-watchers for whom this is one of the most popular spots to view huge numbers of shorebirds in the exposed low-tide mudflats, boardsailers, and kayakers and canoers who use the east side of the park as a convenient launch point to begin exploring Elkhorn Slough.

Elkhorn Slough

East of Highway 1 at Moss Landing, reaching inland 7 miles to Watsonville.

The largest relatively undisturbed wetland in California, Elkhorn is a complex tidal embayment covering 2,500 acres of tideland, and several more thousand acres of grasslands and rolling oak woodland habitat.

Archaeological evidence suggests this was an important center for the Ohlone Indians who subsisted on the incredible population of tule elk and waterfowl that congregated here. The elk are gone but the waterfowl still come in huge numbers. More than 250 bird species congregate here during the winter and spring migrations, often crowding the back bays. Exposed tidal mudflats are an incredible source of food for both indigenous and migratory shorebirds on their way elsewhere. The **Monterey Bay Area Rare Bird Alert** (tel. 831/375-2577) posts a recorded message of interesting bird sightings in the slough and bay area each week. Many saltwater fishes use the slough as a breeding ground, including leopard sharks, halibut, starry flounder, bat rays, and smaller species like the northern anchovy.

Thirteen hundred acres of the slough are owned by the state as part of the **Elkhorn Slough National Estuarine Research Reserve and State Ecological Reserve** (tel. 831/728-2822). There is a visitors center, hiking trails, guided walking tours, kayak tours, fishing access, and displays about the slough and Monterey Bay Marine Sanctuary. Located at 1700 Elkhorn Slough Rd., the visitors center is in the middle of nowhere. Follow signs from Moss Landing and don't give up; it's a long way out here, but it is the best place to see and understand the slough in a single visit. **Kirby Park** (tel. 831/633-2461) on Kirby Road is the best place to get your own kayak or canoe to the water.

Salinas River Wildlife Area

1 mile west of Del Monte Avenue exit from Highway 1. Tel. 831/649-2870. No fee.

The Salinas River flows 170 miles, mostly underground, to surface and enter the ocean here. A large and important nesting and feeding area for shorebirds that occupy a number of small islands in the river, the river mouth is also an important resting and congregating area for brown pelicans, gulls, and terns. Several endangered species of plants and animals are found here, including the Smith's blue butterfly and the snowy plover, which nests on the beach. South of here are miles of private sand dunes accessible only by hiking down the beach.

Marina State Beach

Dead end of Reservation Road, Marina. Tel. 831/384-7695.

Hang gliders have turned a Marina curse—constant onshore winds—into a blessing here. When the onshore breezes encounter the huge dunes, they create a powerful updraft. A hang-glider launch area and concession with equipment rentals and lessons is located here (tel. 831/384-2622). Even if you aren't here to fly, it is fun to watch and explore the dunes.

Jacks Peak Regional Park

End of Olmstead County Road off Highway 168, Monterey. Tel. 831/647-7799. $2–$3 per vehicle.

Monterey Jack cheese is named after David Jacks, an early dairy farmer after whom this park is also named. Equestrian and hiking trails lead through Monterey pines to views of the bay and Pacific.

Coast Guard Breakwater

Southern end of Cannery Row, Monterey. Parking, diving, restrooms, boat ramp. Fee for parking.

The Coast Guard Breakwater marks the southern end of Cannery Row. Sea lions haul out on the jetty, and little San Carlos beach is a popular entry spot for scuba divers. Parking is up the hill with only a few spots for unloading gear at the beach.

Lover's Point

A dramatic headland with granite boulders and wandering trails, Lover's Point, Ocean Boulevard at 17th Street, is a fantastic dive spot on calm days and a stunning place to watch the waves crash on other days. From the grassy hilltop, park trails lead down to Pacific Grove Beach, Lover's Point Beach, and Otter Cove. All three are used by divers to access the **Pacific Grove Marine Gardens Fish Refuge,** an underwater reserve reaching from the mean high-tide line down to 60 feet, all the way from the aquarium to Asilomar Beach. No collecting is allowed other than taking fin fish with a valid license. Shoreline Park runs the same distance between Ocean View Boulevard and the bay. One of the few **hyperbaric chambers** (tel. 831/372-6660 in case of emergency), a recompression device used to treat diving accidents, on the West Coast is just to the east of Lover's Point.

Asilomar State Beach

Sunset Drive and Asilomar Avenue in Pacific Grove. Tel. 831/372-4076.

Sandy beaches are few and far between south of Point Piños, but Asilomar Beach is one of the most exceptional beaches anywhere. The fine-grained sand interspersed with granite rocks and tide pools has a brilliance unrivaled by any other nearby beach. Sandbars and offshore rock reefs form the best surfing waves on the Monterey coast. Diving can be good on calm days. In the 1970s a diver was killed by a great white shark here and his body was never recovered. The attack, chronicled in a *Rolling Stone* magazine story, began an era of shark attack hysteria that has only faded in recent years.

Monastery Beach

South of Carmel on Highway 1. Tel. 831/624-4909. No fee.

Part of Carmel River State Beach, Monastery Beach is one of the most fantastic dive spots in the world. The Carmel Submarine Canyon starts literally a few yards from shore, and dives on the canyon wall can be really spectacular. Surf conditions can be really scary here when trying to go diving. Swells come up out of the deep water with virtually no warning and whomp in a crashing shorebreak. To avoid this, enter on the northern end of Monastery Cove, not in the middle. This is an ecological reserve, so all marine invertebrates and plants are protected. Fin fish may be taken with a license. Rock climbers often climb on the 15- to 20-foot-tall granite boulders on the beach below Ribera Road, some of which are bolted.

Point Lobos State Reserve

4 miles south of Carmel off Highway 1. Tel. 831/624-4909. Open 9am to 5pm. Fee.

Point Lobos is everything the 17-Mile Drive is supposed to be but isn't. Wild and pristine, the landscape here is so beautiful that everywhere you turn you'll feel like crying. Entrance into the park is limited to only 450 people to preserve the solitude of the place, and a line often forms as people wait for one group of visitors to leave so rangers will let another enter.

The 1,300-acre site includes several rocky headlands, several coves, a creek, rocky beaches, offshore rocks, and Monterey pine forests. Though short, the hiking trails here are like walking through a magic forest. Divers can enter the water in Whaler's Cove by reservation or by lining up for entry early in the morning. It's worth the hassle. Underwater, the granite rocks and spires are covered with extravagant numbers of sea anemones, nudibranchs, and gorgonians. Schools of bluefish, ling cod, and red snapper are seen in the kelp forests along with seals and sea otters. Proof of certification is required before entering the water.

What to Do & Where to Do It

BIRD WATCHING

The world record for most bird species seen in a single day from one spot was set on the **Five Fingers Loop Trail** at **Elkhorn Slough** with 116 separate species sighted in one day in 1982. The combination of the rich marine and wetland environments with the nearby mountains and forests makes this a particularly rich area for spotting diverse species.

Raptors such as the golden eagle, osprey, and peregrine falcon regularly hunt the grasslands surrounding all of Monterey Bay's wetland areas. Thousands of **waterfowl** use these same grasslands as an important layover on the Pacific Flyway, and all along the bay shore you'll find sandpipers, curlew, snowy plovers, brown pelicans, gulls, shearwaters, grebes, stilts, and avocets, to name just a few.

The **Interpretive Center** at Elkhorn Slough, 1700 Elkhorn Rd. (tel. 831/ 728-2822), keeps a master list of species sighted there, and also leads canoeing and kayaking trips into the heart of the slough. To find out the latest sightings in the area, call the **Monterey Bay Area Rare Bird Alert** (tel 831/ 375-2577), a recorded message of recent spottings and their location. **Moss Landing Beach** and the **Salinas Rivermouth** are particularly good for **shorebirds**.

BOARDSAILING

With fairly reliable wind and good waves, the beaches northwest of Santa Cruz are the best bet for wave jumping and surfing. **Waddell Beach** just south of Año Nuevo often has huge surf and sideshore winds. Parking is along the road and free. From here you can see Año Nuevo Island, home to the state's thickest concentration of great white sharks. Think about that the next time you get dismasted on a 15-foot day at Waddell.

For more leisurely sailing **Cowell's Beach** at the base of the Santa Cruz wharf is a good training ground. This calm cove is sheltered from really big waves and really big gusts, perfect for learning the basics on a floater board. **Club Ed** at Cowell's Beach (tel. 831/ 459-9283) rents sailboards and other beach paraphernalia.

FISHING

Inland fishing is pretty limited. The creeks and rivers of the northern half of the bay are either closed to fishing because of endangered runs of steelhead trout, or simply don't have any fish. The **San Lorenzo River,** which runs through Santa Cruz, is an exception with decent but not extraordinary fly fishing all along its reach.

Ocean and surf fishing is another story. Monterey Bay is one of the richest fisheries in the world and with a little conviction you can catch just about anything here. The fall catch of **ling cod** is a great deep-sea fishing adventure with party boats pulling up fat 30-pounders every day. **Salmon** also run in the bay on an unpredictable schedule. Surf casters will find plenty of rocky points from which to cast their lines, but beware, fishermen die almost every year in Santa Cruz and Monterey when they are swept from the rocks by rogue waves: Stay well above danger's reach.

Greyhound Rock County Park between Waddell Beach and Scott Creek is a popular surf fishing area with free parking and a trail down the bluffs. The **Santa Cruz, Capitola,** and **Monterey piers** are all popular with crabbers and bait fishermen after halibut and other game species. And an added benefit of fishing from these piers is that no license is required.

Sport fishing boats operate out of Santa Cruz, Moss Landing, and Monterey harbors to chase salmon, ling cod, and other sport species. In Santa Cruz, **Stagnaro's Fishing Trips** (tel. 831/ 423-2180) operates off the wharf and **Shamrock Charters** (tel. 831/476-2648) runs trips out of the yacht harbor. **Monterey Sport Fishing** (tel 831/ 372-2203), and **Randy's Fishing Trips** (tel. 831/372-7440) are all located on or near Fisherman's Wharf and lead half-day and full-day trips into the bay. Randy's takes trips as far south as Point Sur on calm days.

HIKES, BUSHWHACKS & BACKPACK TRIPS

DAY HIKES

Point Año Nuevo Elephant Seal Colony

2.5 miles. Easy. Mostly flat. Allow approximately 4 hours. Access: Año Nuevo Main entrance off Highway 1. Map: Park map. Hike is docent led from December to April. By permit other times.

The elephant seal breeding colony at Año Nuevo is truly amazing. Beginning in November, the 16-foot, 6,000-pound elephant seal bulls begin staking out their turf on the beach and dunes of Año Nuevo Point. By January the females, comparatively small at only 1,500 to 2,000 pounds, arrive to give birth and to mate. Yes, that's right—they give birth and then are almost immediately impregnated again. An elephant seal cow spends most of her adult life pregnant.

The mating ritual is the most dramatic wildlife display I've ever witnessed. The huge alpha male bulls stake out a harem of anywhere from 2 to 20 cows and proceed to mate with as many as possible. All that sex makes them tired and vulnerable to attack from younger bulls waiting to sneak in and steal their harem. The vocal and physical conflicts between these 3-ton monsters literally shake the ground. Meanwhile the cows and pups are just trying to stay out of the way. By the peak of the elephant seal season as many as 1,000 seals line the dunes of the point.

Docents lead hikers within what seems like a few feet of the seals and share a wealth of biological information. The hike itself is easy, a flat couple miles round-trip along a beautiful coastal bluff and over a few dunes. Reservations (tel. 800/444-7275) are required for the hikes from December to April. A number of slots are kept open every day for people who show up early in the morning, but they go quickly. Call the state park (tel. 650/879-0227) for more information.

During the rest of the year some elephant seals are in residence but not in the same numbers. Still, this beautiful dune landscape is one of the wildest oceanfront hikes in the area. You can enter the wildlife protection area with a permit from the state park visitors center.

Skyline to the Sea/Sunset Trail Loop, Big Basin State Park

10.5 miles round-trip. Strenuous. Allow 6 to 8 hours. Access: Big Basin Park Headquarters. Map: Big Basin trail map.

By combining a portion of the famous Skyline to the Sea Trail with a return via Big Basin's Sunset Trail via the Berry Creek Falls cutoff, you can see the best of Big Basin's backcountry in a single hike. The trail runs through lushly vegetated redwood forests and through a canyon adorned with several beautiful falls. The forest is very primordial after a winter rain, and 65-foot Berry Creek Falls is a roaring torrent. This is old-growth rather than second-growth redwood forest; some of the trees here reach 240 feet tall and are as large as 17 feet in diameter. There is an understory of dogwood and azalea and, like everywhere in the Santa Cruz Mountains, poison oak is common.

From the Park Headquarters take the Redwood Trail (itself a great short hike) to the Skyline to the Sea Trail. Skyline to the Sea follows Kelley and Waddell creeks until you come to the Berry Falls Trail. Continue up Berry Creek to Sunset Trail and return to the headquarters.

Ridge Trail, Henry Cowell State Park

3 miles round-trip. Moderate. Allow 2 hours. Access: Main entrance to park, off State Route 9 just south of Felton. Map: Henry Cowell State Park map.

Though the redwood forests along the creek bottoms in Henry Cowell State Park are the most popular attraction, the Ridge Trail is an interesting hike that passes through the redwoods and then climbs to a high ridge and former fire tower with observation deck. Along the way you pass through several different plant communities: the redwood forest, chaparral, and finally oak and pine forest. From the observation deck you can see for miles down into Santa Cruz and surrounding mountain canyons. There are so many crisscrossing trails in this park that it is difficult to stay on the right one. Just keep bearing uphill and you'll eventually get to the ridgetop.

Loma Prieta Grade–Bridge Creek Loop, Forest of Nisene Marks State Park

7.5 miles. Moderate to difficult. Access: Porter Family Picnic Area. Main entrance of Forest of Nisene Marks State Park. Map: Park map.

This hike takes you up a dramatic creek canyon through second-growth redwoods, then up a steep ridge and back down to the trailhead through the hillside that is the namesake of the October 17, 1989, Loma Prieta earthquake, which was centered near here. Begin by hiking up the Bridge Creek Trail from the picnic area. The trail follows Aptos Creek a short distance until heading up the lush canyon of Bridge Creek. After about a mile you are forced to choose between a clockwise or counterclockwise loop. Counterclockwise gives you a better perspective as you go up the creek canyon. After about 3 miles you

come to an old homestead site, now mostly gone after floods carried away the ruins. Here the Loma Prieta Trail veers left. It is possible to hike up the creek another half mile to delicate Maple Falls by rock hopping and bushwhacking along a faint trail. After switchbacking up a steep ridge the Loma Prieta Grade will carry you back down to the trailhead.

Wilder Ranch Old Landing Cove Trail

3.6 miles. Easy. Flat and wide. Access: Wilder Ranch parking lot. Map: Park brochure trail map.

This flat and wide trail allows some of the best lateral access along the blufftops north of Santa Cruz. You'll walk out along a farm road through flower and Brussels sprout fields until you come to Wilder Beach. This beautiful beach is off-limits to protect nesting habitat for the endangered snowy plover. The trail veers north along the coastal cliffs and in about a mile a trail leads down to the old landing cove. A fern grotto below a clifftop spring is a unique site here only 25 feet above the Pacific. The very next cove north contains Seal Rock, a flat offshore rock popular with harbor seals and the occasional sea lion. Several trails descend to Sand Plant Beach. Most hikers turn around here and return to the park headquarters. However, the trail continues upcoast for another 3 miles to the 4-mile beach at Wilder Ranch's northern boundary. From there you can walk back along Highway 1 to your car.

Point Lobos Perimeter Trail

6.5 miles. Moderate. Access: Whaler's Cove, Point Lobos. Map: Point Lobos Park map.

Actually several shorter loop trails strung together to allow a hiker to traverse the entire waterfront of Point Lobos in a day, the perimeter trail is an ambitious hike. Not that it is so difficult; there is just so much to see. You'll want to go slow and stop for lots of lookouts. The perimeter trail is accessible from seven different spots along the park road, so don't feel obligated to do the whole thing. My favorite portion of the trail is the segment near Sea Lion Cove and Point Lobos. A spur trail leads out to the dramatic headland of Point Lobos where churning surf meets the harsh granite coast. Sea lions and seals play in the water and haul out on the rocks in Sea Lion Cove. Whale-watchers flock to this point in winter to see gray whales that sometimes come within 100 feet of the point. South of here along China Cove the water is more tranquil in the lee of the point and the beach is sandier. Pelicans, gulls, and cormorants are visible in large numbers in the air and on offshore Bird Island.

Skyline Nature Trail, Jacks Peak Regional Park

2 miles. Moderate. Access: Olmstead County Road off Highway 168 south of Monterey. Map: None needed.

Though only a 515-acre park, Jacks Peak is the highest point on the Monterey Peninsula at 1,068 feet. The Skyline Nature Trail leads you up through oak forests and poison oak to a forest of Monterey pines and the summit where you can see all of Monterey Bay and the Carmel Valley on a clear day.

OVERNIGHTS

Skyline to the Sea
(Big Basin Headquarters to Waddell Beach)

11.5 miles. Difficult. 2 or 3 days. Access: Big Basin Headquarters. Park second car or arrange pickup at Waddell Beach on Highway 1, 18 miles north of Santa Cruz. Map: Big Basin trail map.

Big Basin is a remarkable park because it encompasses nearly the entire watershed of Waddell Creek from mountain crest to the sea. This trail takes you from the lush old-growth redwood forests near the park headquarters to stunning and wild Waddell Beach, following the creek most of the way. Several overnight camps make this a great 2- or 3-day hike; Camp Herbert is closest to midway at 7.5 miles. The other camps are within 2 miles of Highway 1 but are great for camping one last night before an early-morning shuttle. In summer you must make reservations to use any of the three backcountry camps along this route by calling the park (tel. 831/338-8860) at least 2 weeks prior to the date you wish to use them. Fires are prohibited and there is a charge for camping. Though you can hike this trail either way, do it from headquarters down to the sea and save yourself a lot of climbing.

Sand Point Overlook,
Forest of Nisene Marks State Park

12 miles round-trip. Difficult. 2 days. Access: Aptos Creek Trailhead in Forest of Nisene Marks State Park. Map: Nisene Marks trail map.

This 6-mile-each-way hike up the west ridge of the Aptos Creek drainage has many things to recommend it. Besides the hike up through mature second-growth redwoods and Douglas firs, you end up at Sand Point Overlook, one of the most dramatic vistas in the Santa Cruz Mountains. The view from here stretches all the way across Monterey Bay and down into the Bridge Creek and Aptos Creek drainages. The trail camp is a short distance north on the West Ridge Trail.

From Sand Point it is also possible to return down the Aptos Creek fire road and China Creek. Though this extends the hike to nearly 20 miles, it does allow you a different return route through some interesting terrain. Mountain bikers use this road a lot, so keep your ears open for descending cyclists.

KAYAKING

The only **whitewater** kayak run in the Monterey Bay area is the **San Lorenzo River** between Henry Cowell State Park and town. An extremely reactionary river, it flows very dramatically with even a small rain. The best time to run it is a few days after a good rain when the river calms down again. The rapids on this run are all Class II and III, but the potential for logjams and strainers makes the run potentially dangerous for inexperienced boaters. Be careful.

MOUNTAIN BIKING

Santa Cruz is to Northern California mountain biking what Marin County once was. One positive aftereffect of the unfortunate logging history of the area is a vast network of old and new logging roads deep into the Santa Cruz Mountains. With the crackdown and closure of most good Mount Tamalpais trails, many of California's top-level mountain bikers have moved here for the plentiful backcountry roads and trails that remain largely unrestricted. Two state parks, **Wilder Ranch** and **Nisene Marks Forest,** are extremely friendly to mountain bikers. Wilder, in fact, seems to cater to bikers more than hikers. Many rides outside the two parks are semisecret and trespass on private lands. Because of the active competitive and casual biking scenes around the area, several good bike shops do a booming business, including **The Bicycle Trip,** 1127 Soquel Ave. (tel. 831/ 427-2580).

Wilder Ranch

30 miles of trails. Easy to difficult. Access: 1 mile north of Santa Cruz on Highway 1. Map: Wilder Ranch has a special bike trail map.

Wilder Ranch is one of my favorite places in the world to mountain bike. The first time I rode here I was stunned. I'd passed the park on Highway 1 for years and dismissed it as another state beach. What I didn't realize was that the park stretches for 3,900 acres up into the forest highlands of the Santa Cruz Mountains. The 30 or so miles of trails and fire roads loop and intersect their way up the hills, passing meadows, redwood forests, old barns, a eucalyptus grove, creeks—all with a striking view of the bay. That first day I covered at least half the trails and saw everything from a bobcat to banana slugs. This place is amazing. From gently meandering fire roads to hairy switchbacked single track, Wilder has it all. My favorite trail is any trail that takes you to the very top of the ranch where the Charcoal Trail and Sequoia Trail loop around a eucalyptus grove, marking the park boundary with Gray Whale Ranch. (Also a popular but illegal riding area. Won't talk about that here.)

From the top of the park any number of loops and forks will eventually lead you back down to your car or the road to town. I'm particularly fond of the Peasley Gulch Trail, a steep single track through a creek bottom. Don't, however, get hung up on following any one "ride" because eventually you'll get where you're going anyway. Enjoy.

Forest of Nisene Marks State Park

Distances and difficulty vary. Access: Aptos Creek Trailhead. Map: Park map.

Almost as popular as Wilder Ranch is the Forest of Nisene Marks State Park (or

Nisene Marks for short). Though the regulations say bikes are only allowed on the Aptos Creek fire road, I've seen bikes all over the park when I was hiking and nobody seems to be complaining, perhaps because horses are not allowed here. The best ride in the park, however, is on the Aptos Creek fire road anyway. From the trailhead the fire road ascends China Ridge, a steep workout. The epicenter of the 7.1-on-the-Richter-scale Loma Prieta quake of 1989 was right here. Fissures and fallen trees marked the spot for a few years but seem to have faded after heavy rains and erosion.

As you climb China Ridge you'll alternate between shade and stretches of sun. Bring plenty of water because there's none available in the park. After what seems like endless miles uphill through redwood and tan oak forest, you'll pass a small meadow and soon come to the Sand Point Overlook. Drink in the huge view and then bomb the road home. An option is to overnight at the trail camp about a mile farther along the fire road and ride down the next day.

Soquel Demonstration Forest

Distances and difficulty vary. Access: To reach the forest you must take Old San Jose Road up from Soquel, turn right on Stetson and then right again on Comstock Mill Road in another 1.5 miles. You can also reach the area from State Route 17 by turning east on Summit Road, south 2.4 miles on Old San Jose Road, then left on Stetson. Map: Forest map.

Attached to Nisene Marks is a 3,000-acre forest owned by the State Department of Forestry as an experimental timber forest. Though not technically a park, all the forest trails are open to hikers and bikers. A number of trails loop through the forest and some connect down to Nisene Marks. The Sulfur Springs and Tractor Trail connect to the Ridge Trail. It in turn can connect you to the Sand Point overlook and eventually all the way down to Aptos. For information about the forest, call 831/475-8643.

ROAD BIKING

With all these roads and all these beautiful mountains and coastline, Santa Cruz and Monterey are prime road biking territory. The obvious ride is **Highway 1** from Año Nuevo to Santa Cruz. In Monterey the **17-Mile Drive** is another favorite as is the loop along **Ocean Front Boulevard** around Point Piños and down through Asilomar.

ROCK CLIMBING

Most rock climbers from here travel to the Pinnacles to do any serious climbing, but there are a few small outcroppings in the Monterey Bay area to practice on. **Castle Rock State Park,** State Route 35 between State Route 17 and State Route 9 (tel. 831/867-2952), offers large sandstone outcroppings with numerous top-roped routes. **Monastery Beach** in Monterey is another great practice area with a formation of granite outcropping rising right out of the sand at the northern end of the beach. The beach is best reached by driving to the end of Ribera Road and walking down a short access trail. **Bugaboo Mountain Sports** (tel. 831/429-6300) in Santa Cruz is by far the most knowledgeable source of local climbing information and has a great selection of gear.

SAILING

Monterey Bay is often incredibly windy, perfect for learning to sail in open ocean conditions. **UC Santa Cruz** teaches basic and intermediate sailing each summer on their fleet of Lasers, Flying Juniors, and Moore 24s through the physical education department (tel. 831/459 2531). **Pacific Yachting** (tel. 831/423-7245) offers daily charters, sailing les sons, and a multi-day skippering class. **Chardonnay Sailing Charters** (tel. 408 423-1213) is a great chance to see how the other half-percent lives. Their million-dollar racing yacht, *Chardonnay*, a Santa Cruz 70, is one of the fastest and sexiest boats on the water today. Since most of us probably will never be able to afford one, Chardonnay Charters rents theirs out fully crewed for a basic rate of $500 per hour (2-hour minimum from Santa Cruz, 3-hour minimum from Monterey). With tons of deck space, a bar, stereo, cellular phone, and all the other amenities a boat can have, the *Chardonnay* is a great way to throw a party while touring the bay in style.

SCUBA DIVING

Monterey and Carmel are without a doubt the best and most well-known diving sites in Northern California. The incredible concentration of marine life here in combination with relatively good visibility (averaging 20 to 60 feet) makes putting up with chilly bay waters seem like a treat, not a burden.

Almost without fail you will be diving in areas with thick kelp. The **kelp forest** is one of the most beautiful underwater environments, but it takes some getting used to. It is important to have a good sense of where your body and equipment are at all times to avoid getting tangled. Also, be more conservative with your air supply. Instead of waiting until you are nearly out of air and then looking for the boat or your path to shore, it is vital that you make sure you have enough air to swim under any kelp beds between you and your destination. One time crawling across the surface of a huge kelp bed wearing full scuba gear will teach you why this is important.

One of the best things about Monterey is how easy it is to dive from the shore. You can find great diving just a few hundred feet off **Cannery Row, Monastery Beach,** or **Point Lobos.** Several diving boat charter companies run out of Monterey to sites within the bay and harder-to-reach spots like the **Ocean Pinnacles** in Carmel Bay or **Chase Reef** off Point Piños.

Aquarius Dive Shop (tel. 831/375-1933) has two locations in Monterey: 32 Cannery Row and 2240 Del Monte Ave. Besides running charters in the bay they offer rentals, equipment sales, certification classes, photography tours, and a wealth of local information. **Twin Otters, Inc.** (tel. 408/656-9194) is another well-run scuba charter operation running trips as far south as Granite Canyon off Big Sur and numerous sites in the bay and off Carmel.

All of the above shops will give recommendations of what they think is the best dive site for current conditions and season. If you want an invaluable description of all the shore-accessible dive sites on the Monterey Peninsula, as well as great photos and natural history essays, the *Diving and Snorkeling Guide to Northern California and the Monterey Peninsula* by Steve Rosenberg (Pisces Books, 1992) will set you up with enough potential dive sites to last years.

SEA KAYAKING

Kayaks have blossomed as the watercraft of choice for explorers in the last few years, and Monterey Bay is no exception. Especially in the more sheltered southern part of the Monterey Bay coast—near Carmel and Monterey—kayaks are perfectly suited for exploring the rocky coastline. **Monterey Bay Kayaks,** 693 Del Monte, Monterey (tel. 831/373-KELP), is one of the biggest dealers of ocean kayaks in the world. They have a complete line of rental boats and lead tours and classes on a regular basis.

In Santa Cruz, **Venture Quest,** 125 Beach St. (tel. 831/427-2267), is both a shop and a rental and teaching facility. The **Kayak Connection** (tel. 831/ 479-1121) in the yacht harbor rents and sells equipment plus offers guided bird watching and moonlight bay tours. Some of the above companies run trips to explore the wetlands of **Elkhorn Slough,** and the State Park system (tel. 831/728-2822) periodically offers kayak tours of the slough.

Getting your kayak to the water without too much of a hike can be a challenge in parts of the bay. **Davenport Landing Beach** about 8 miles north of town is one popular launching point. In Santa Cruz, **Twin Lakes, Seabright,** and **Capitola beaches** are commonly used. To access the Elkhorn Slough **wetlands** you can either launch at **Moss Landing State Beach** and paddle up the slough through a large tidal basin or put in at **Kirby Park,** at the end of Kirby Road off Elkhorn Road (tel. 831/633-2461), in the heart of the slough. Monterey kayakers deal with huge parking hassles along the bayfront to unload their boats. The **Coast Guard Breakwater** at the south end of Cannery Row is the closest you can get your car to the water and has loading zones. Parking is up the hill in the city lot. **Lover's Point** is another possibility, though you'll have to carry your boats a little farther.

SURFING

Santa Cruz is situated in such a way as to allow in both north and south swells while sheltering the main surf breaks from prevailing winds and chop. This miracle of geography makes it the most consistently good surf town on the entire California coast. Summertime south swells break fast and playful on the numerous rock reefs and points. Big wintertime norths roar into the bay like freighters. A big day at **Steamer's Lane** can be a lesson in humility for even the best surfer. Best of all are those cold clear winter days after a big storm when you can see Monterey across the bay to the south and the redwood-covered slopes of the Santa Cruz Mountains rising behind town to your north while you drop in on head-high waves at the Lane or **Pleasure Point.** The beaches west of town like **4-Mile, Scott Creek,** and **Waddell Beach** are even wilder; the closer you get to Año Nuevo the more exposed and sharky it becomes.

Año Nuevo State Reserve itself has a fantastic surf break—within a few hundred yards of the elephant seal rookery. A wildlife biologist once told me that elephant seal pups from the rookery suffer a 50% mortality rate between the time they enter the water and the time they pass Año Nuevo Island about a half mile offshore. The reason? Predation by great white sharks and orcas. I've seen how I look sitting on a surfboard and it's much too close to a seal pup for my comfort.

South of town the surf poops out pretty quickly. The long sandy beaches stretching all the way to Moss Landing have periodic good surf, but just as often they're windblown and sloppy. The exception is **Moss Landing** itself. Because the submarine canyon comes right up to shore here, deep-water swells reach the sandbars around the harbor mouth relatively unimpeded and jack up. When the surf is really big in Santa Cruz, Moss Landing is unrideable. When the surf is small in Santa Cruz, it can be glassy, head high, and so hollow you'll think you're in Hawaii at the Moss Landing harbor mouth. It is wide open to the wind though, so if you're going to get it, you'll have to get on it early.

Monterey is well known for diving, not surfing, and there's a reason. The surf here pretty much sucks, with two notable exceptions: **Asilomar Beach** and **Carmel Beach.** While neither offers anything like the point break perfection of Steamer's Lane to the north or some of the secret Big Sur spots to the south, they are fun and playful beach-break and rock-reef waves.

During the summer, **Club Ed** (tel. 831/459-9283) at Cowell's Beach in Santa Cruz is a very successful concession that rents boogie boards, surfboards, and wetsuits; plus they teach beginning surfing on Cowell's gently breaking waves. This is one of the few breaks in the area really gentle enough to make that first ride a pleasure instead of a white-knuckle drop. **Freeline Design** (tel. 831/476-2950) at the corner of 41st and Portola near Pleasure Point rents wetsuits and surfboards ranging from hybrid mini-longboards to 9-foot BZ softboards for first-timers. They also carry a good selection of boards and wetsuits for sale.

WALKS & RAMBLES

Redwood Nature Trail, Big Basin State Park

0.6-mile loop. Access: Across from Park Headquarters a 10-foot-tall sign marks the trailhead.

This tiny loop trail is a microcosm of what you'd see in much of the rest of the Big Basin backcountry: redwoods, tan oaks, lush creek corridor full of berry vines and poison oak, maybe even a few banana slugs. Like any other microcosm you are missing the richer, more diverse experience of the whole, but the big attractions are here. The tallest tree in the park, 329-foot tall Mother of the Forest, is here, as is the Chimney Tree, a naturally hollowed- out redwood formed

> "If I had more influence, or if I had my way, I'd zone Santa Cruz as a special conservation area where people from more crowded and polluted regions could come to see what human beings can do with their environment, nurtured with love and compassion. I envision Santa Cruz even more beautiful, in a better future than it is now. . . . I would rather live with the white shark more prevalent because we protect its primary food—sea lions and sea otters—than have to surf or swim in the disease-ridden sewer outlets I learned to surf in Santa Cruz in the 50's. In my mind Santa Cruz has done more than maintain its environment. It is a progressive and controversial county—an area where the potential for a paradise continues."—Fred Van Dyke, early California surfer, from his book *30 years of Riding the World's Biggest Waves* (Ocean Sports International Publishing Group, 1989)

when a fire burned out much of the trunk but left the living outer layers of the tree standing.

Butterfly Grove, Natural Bridges State Beach

0.5 miles. Handicapped-accessible boardwalk. Access: Park at the state beach parking lot on West Cliff and follow the signs.

Every fall and winter thousands of monarchs come to Natural Bridges for shelter. This spot is special in that it offers two important monarch habitats: the eucalyptus trees they favor for congregating and the milkweed that monarch caterpillars feed on before turning into butterflies. Milkweed is highly toxic to most animals, so scientists speculate that by eating the plant monarchs gain a lifelong protection from predators.

Elkhorn Slough Interpretive Trail

1 mile. Access: Park Headquarters at 1700 Elkhorn Rd.

Several miles of trail leave from the visitors center, but before hiking any others it is useful to walk the short interpretive trail with informational signs that will help a first-timer identify some of the upland plants that surround the slough as well as plants and animals that live in the slough. The visitors center also has some great exhibits explaining the complex workings of this large wetland.

Cypress Grove Loop, Point Lobos State Reserve

0.8 miles. Access: Information station inside Point Lobos.

The short Cypress Grove Loop shows off a little of everything Point Lobos has to offer in one walk. The grove of Monterey cypress on South Point, for which this walk is named, is one of only two spots in the world where this tree grows naturally. These grizzled old-growth cypresses on their dramatic headland seem the perfect icon for the Monterey area. Beyond the grove the trail passes an overlook where sea lions are often spotted playing near the Devil's Cauldron. The trail then passes a swirling tidal surge channel and exits into the open at South Point, a favorite whale-watching site.

WHALE WATCHING

As the gray whale population has increased in the last 15 years, it has begun to seem as if there is no longer a whale-watching season. Indeed, as the population recovered, it reached a point where now some whales are beginning to migrate south by the time others are migrating north. Now 17,000 whales make the trip every year, providing a constant treadmill effect. You may be able to find a whale at any time of the year, but the best season is still from December through April when pods of whales (generally two to six individuals traveling together) hug the California shoreline en route between their winter calving grounds in Mexico and their summer feeding grounds off Alaska.

Several spots on the Monterey Bay coast are well suited to whale watching. **Lighthouse Point** in Santa Cruz and all of **West Cliff Drive** up to Natural Bridges is a good area to walk while keeping an eye out for the telltale spout of passing whales. Monterey has many good lookouts on its rocky coast. The **Point Piños lighthouse grounds** is one great spot as the whales make the turn into Monterey Bay. **Point Lobos** just south of Carmel is another spot where the whales come extremely close to shore and give whale watchers a good look. The cliffs at Point Lobos are the perfect size to give you a little height to look out at the whales without placing you so far away you can barely see.

Of course the best way to really see a lot of whales and to see them up close is to join a whale-watching tour on any of the boats that run out of Santa Cruz and Monterey. Over the years the whales have become accustomed to being watched and often will swim right up to an idling boat. The following companies run whale-watching tours during the winter season out of Monterey: **Chris' Fishing Trips** (tel. 831/375-5951), **Monterey Sport Fishing** (tel. 831/372-2203), **Randy's Fishing Trips** (tel. 831/372-7440), and **Sam's Fishing Fleet** (tel. 831/372-0577). In Santa Cruz try **Chardonnay Sailing Charter** (tel. 831/423-1213), **Santa Cruz Sport Fishing** (tel. 831/426-4690), or **Shamrock Charters** (tel. 831/476-2648).

Campgrounds & Other Accommodations

CAMPING

SANTA CRUZ

Big Basin State Park

9 miles west of Boulder Creek on State Route 236. Tel. 831/338-8860. 100 car campsites, 45 walk-in sites. Also has rustic, reasonably priced cabins for rent. Store, showers, flush toilets, running water. Fees vary by site from $6 to $18. Call 800/444-PARK (the cursed service) to make a reservation.

Big Basin is California's oldest and most popular state park, so be prepared for (a) a pain in the butt getting a site, and (b) a crowd once you're here.

But it is still one of the most beautiful places within an hour's drive of the teeming millions who call the Santa Clara Valley home. Since you didn't come here looking for solitude, enjoy the whole Ranger Rick ambiance of Big Basin—the campfire programs, the interpretive signs, the kids screaming as their marshmallows catch fire. If you *did* come here looking for solitude you better put on your hiking shoes and start walking.

Henry Cowell Redwoods State Park

On the outskirts of Felton just north of Santa Cruz. Tel. 831/335-4598. 112 sites. Piped water, flush toilets, showers, store in Felton. $14–$18 per night excluding reservation fee ($7.50). Reservations are through 800/444-PARK.

Henry Cowell is often considered the ugly stepsister of Big Basin, which is really unfortunate. Though not nearly as wild as Big Basin, Henry Cowell is a great park, especially for a family with kids. The trails around the park are manageable by all ages and clearly marked, and summer swimming holes are plentiful on the San Lorenzo River. If you need a mechanical distraction, a narrow-gauge railroad leftover from the logging days runs from here to the Santa Cruz Boardwalk and back (it's very slow; take it for the ride, not to actually get there quickly).

New Brighton State Beach

Right in the middle of Aptos and Capitola. Take New Brighton exit from Highway 1. Tel. 408/429-2850 or 408/464-6329. 105 car camping sites, 2 bike-in sites.

Running water, flush toilets, disposal station, propane, grocery store, laundry, and showers. $3–$23 per night. Reservations through 800/444-PARK.

This is one of the prettiest state beach campgrounds. The sites are spread around a wooded glade that seems as if it were in the wilderness, even though it is surrounded by homes. From the campground trails descend to the sandy beach below.

WATSONVILLE

Manresa Beach State Park

On Sand Dollar Drive, 8 miles south on the San Andreas Road exit from Highway 1. Tel. 408/429-2850 or 408/761-1795. 64 tent sites, some with ocean views. Running water, flush toilets, showers. $14–$18 per night. Reservations through 800-444-PARK.

Manresa and Sunset Beach just to the south are the two most beautiful camping beaches in the Monterey area. Surrounded by farmland and the occasional beach house, these two gems are perfect for a quiet weekend by the sea. Manresa is extremely popular with day users from the surrounding towns who come here to surf and fish. Sunset is a big hit with kids who like to run or roll down its huge dunes. Both these parks are within easy driving distance of Elkhorn Slough, which lacks any good camping in its immediate vicinity.

Sunset Beach State Park

San Andreas Road exit from Highway 1. Follow signs to state park. Tel. 408/429-2850 or 408/763-7063. 90 tent and motorhome spaces. Flush toilets, showers. $14–$18 per night. Reservations through 800/444-PARK.

Wonderful dunes and well-laid-out campsites make this beach campground a welcome break. Some sites have ocean views. The others are just a short walk away from the beach. It can be very windy here, so sometimes the more sheltered sites are a better choice than the ones with great views.

MONTEREY

Saddle Mountain Recreation Park

5 miles from Carmel at the end of Schulte Road. Tel. 831/624-1617. 25 tent sites and 25 motorhome sites. Running water, flush toilets, showers, pool, playground, and store. $20–$35 per night.

Monterey and Carmel are really hurting for good camping options near town. Saddle Mountain is a nice park on the banks of the Carmel River, which is less of a draw than you might think since the river is dry most of the year. Even though it is nothing special, the park is only about a 15-minute drive from anywhere in Monterey—Point Lobos, Carmel, Fisherman's Wharf, etc.—and is a pleasant, cheap alternative to staying in a high-priced motel.

INNS & LODGES

Pigeon Point Lighthouse AYH Youth Hostel

210 Pigeon Point Rd. Tel. 650/879-0633. 52 beds. $15 nonmembers, $12 members, children half-price when accompanied by an adult. MC, V. Reservations mandatory. Hostel office open year-round from 7:30 to 9:30am and 4:30 to 9:30pm.

This area has literally hundreds of nice hotels, bed-and-breakfasts, and small inns; but most of them are set right in town, a far cry from the wilderness experience you're probably seeking. This hostel offers the wildest accommodations in the area. Consisting of several old Coast Guard buildings clustered at the base of 115-foot-tall Pigeon Point Lighthouse, the hostel is very basic but the location is unreal: Año Nuevo is just a few miles south and the ocean is right outside the window. And how many other hostels have a hot tub?

Pleasure Point Inn

2-3665 East Cliff Dr., Santa Cruz (right across from Pleasure Point). Tel. 831/475-4657. 2 rooms, 2 suites. $125–$145. MC, V.

Surfers and fishermen looking for a deluxe weekend might splurge and stay at this small B&B in a neighborhood of residential homes. It offers several rooms with ocean views, fireplaces, and surfboard storage on site. The owners also charter a large motor cruiser out of the Santa Cruz harbor.

Mangels House

570 Aptos Creek Rd. Tel. 831/688-7982. 6 rooms. $120–$160. MC, V.

This B&B sits right on the edge of the 10,000-acre Forest of Nisene Marks State Park. Though this pleasant country inn doesn't really promote itself as a wilderness retreat, it is located on its own 4 acres smack in the middle of some of the best mountain biking and hiking in the Santa Cruz Mountains and only a mile or so from New Brighton Beach.

Asilomar

800 Asilomar Blvd., Pacific Grove. Tel. 831/372-8016. 308 rooms. $74–$92 double. MC, V.

Monterey and Pacific Grove have more B&Bs than you can shake a stuffed teddy bear and a dish of potpourri at, including several along Ocean Front Boulevard, but this old YMCA located right in the middle of a beautiful state park and beach is probably the best place for an action-figure type to stay. Asilomar is now a conference center owned by the state, but it still rents out some rooms to the general public. Several of the old cottages have kitchens and fireplaces. Make reservations well in advance.

4

Big Sur, the Ventana Wilderness & Pinnacles National Monument

BIG SUR'S RESIDENTS PUT UP WITH WHAT SOME WOULD CONSIDER great inconveniences—road-closing mudslides, fires, terrible television reception, wild storms, and a meager economy—in order to live a life of simplicity lost to most of the rest of California. Henry Miller, while living high above the ocean on Partington Ridge, put his finger on it in his 1957 novel *Big Sur and the Oranges of Hieronymus Bosch:* "Whoever settles here hopes he will be the last invader. The very look of the land makes one long to keep it intact— the spiritual reserve of a few bright spirits."

It's still the spiritual reserve he wrote of, but anyone hoping to be the last invader is going to be severely let down. During peak tourist season (March to October), Big Sur swarms with out-of-towners, most of them blowing through on their way from Monterey to points south and figuring they'll pull over at a few vista points and say they've seen Big Sur. Stupid mistake. Big Sur is as much a state of mind as it is a place, and the way to find that is to get out in the deep quiet of the woods or scramble down an eroding bluff to the ocean edge—anywhere away from the rush of Highway 1—and experience the wildness of this beautiful place.

When the Spanish settled Monterey Bay they didn't know what to make of the coastline to the south. This grizzly filled, vertiginous landscape of plummeting sea cliffs and towering mountains didn't have much to recommend it by their standards, so they left it alone, calling it *El País Grande del Sur*—the big country of the south. By the time the first homesteaders moved into the area in the early 19th century to ranch cattle, Big Sur's original inhabitants, the Esselen Indians, once estimated to number about 1,000, were already extinct from European diseases. Mining and gold panning brought more settlers during the 1850s. In 1899 the Point Sur Lighthouse was built, lit by a kerosene lamp at the top of 395 wooden steps. Tourism to Big Sur began about the same time, centering on Pfeiffer's Resort, which opened in 1908 at the present site of the Big Sur Lodge in Pfeiffer Big Sur State Park. Florence Pfeiffer ran the place until 1934, when it became part of the state park; Big Sur's reputation as something of a Bohemian enclave rests with the guests she lured—Stanford professors, writers, artists, and nature lovers.

There are still a lot of people here living the back-to-the-land, bohemian life. Though the permanent population for all of Big Sur is less than 4,000 people, the region is home to the Esalen Institute (home of the Human Potential Movement), the Tassajara Zen Buddhist Retreat Center, a Benedictine monastery, numerous inns and lodges, and more than its share of artists, recluses, and geniuses who prefer to be left to their own devices.

Farther inland, the Salinas Valley is one of the richest agricultural areas in the world, and towns like Soledad, Greenfield, and King City reflect that heritage; hardscrabble field-workers and agribusiness money share a common bond with the land here. To the east lie the Gabilan Mountains and Pinnacles National Monument. In the Salinas Valley lettuce is king and broccoli queen, but this is hard-core cattle country. Most of the land is tied up in private ranches; the exception is Pinnacles National Monument, which was set aside during the early part of this century because of its unique geology and important wildlife habitat.

The Lay of the Land

Where is Big Sur? Ask 10 people and you'll get 10 different answers. Several state parks, a river, and a smattering of landmarks bear the name, not to mention stores, motels, and a post office, but it seems like no one can agree on where Big Sur begins and where it ends. The subject provides fodder for an arcane and never-ending debate among residents to whom it is a point of pride. We'll let them work it out. For the sake of simplicity, Big Sur is everything south of Point Lobos near Carmel, north of Willow Creek and Cape San Martin, and west of the Salinas Valley. Pinnacles National Monument falls outside this boundary, but we've put it with Big Sur because of their relative proximity.

Northern California's coastal mountains peter out when they hit Monterey Bay, but rise again on the southern end, this time in the form of the Santa Lucias, a rocky range of dry chapparal peaks that rise out of the sea at an angle so steep you feel like you're not just standing on the edge of a continent but actually over it. To illustrate how steep the Santa Lucias really are, consider the case of Cone Peak, the summit of which rises to 5,155 feet within 3.2 miles of the ocean. That's a 30.5% gradient, steeper than even the steepest parts of the Sierra Nevada. The highest peak in the Santa Lucias is 5,750-foot Junipero Serra Peak. Numerous other peaks exceed 4,000 feet.

Though they look foreboding at first, covered as they are by brushy, thick chapparal, the Santa Lucias are also interspersed with redwood-lined valleys, pine forests, meadows, and numerous creeks. Most land here is owned by the federal government as part of the northern section of Los Padres National Forest. Of nearly 200,000 acres that make up Big Sur, only about one-quarter is privately owned. Big Sur, of course, is famous for its coastline, a rocky plunging stretch of often inaccessible beaches and sheer rocks. Two main rivers, the Big Sur and Little Sur, drain the range's west slope. Runoff from the east enters the Salinas River and eventually Monterey Bay. All creeks and waterways here can dry up in the summer, and once away from the major creeks, water is scarce. Across the agriculturally rich Salinas Valley to the east, the Gabilan Mountains are home to the otherworldly Pinnacles National Monument, a remnant volcanic plug of towering rock spires and cool tunnel caves. The two parallel ranges run in a north–south orientation for over 100 miles between Monterey and San Luis Obispo.

The climate is moderate year-round. Precipitation falls mostly in the winter months and is extremely localized, falling mostly on the immediate coastal strip. Inland a few miles, less than a third as much rain falls. Rarely snow falls on the higher peaks. Summer brings coastal fog and hot inland temperatures. The beach can be drizzly and cold while 5 miles away on the ridgeline it is 90°. Inland, it gets much hotter. The Pinnacles and the back reaches of the Ventana Wilderness often reach 100° during the dry summer months.

Though the grizzly bears that kept early settlers guessing are gone now, plenty of wildlife remains. Deer, red-tailed hawks, bobcats, cougar, wild turkeys, squirrels, raccoons, and other animals are common. So are poison oak,

ticks, and rattlesnakes. The area is also home to several wildlife recovery success stories. It was along the Big Sur coast in the 1920s that California Fish and Game biologists found the isolated colony of California sea otters—long thought to be extinct—from which the population recovered to now occupy the entire northern coast. In the remote backcountry of the Ventana Wilderness, wildlife biologists have reintroduced bald eagles and hope to soon have four breeding pairs. The Big Sur and Little Sur rivers, the largest wild rivers in central California, are home to winter runs of endangered steelhead trout. Gray whales, once hunted to near extinction, are now numerous in the waters off Big Sur as they migrate from their feeding grounds in Alaska to their calving grounds in Baja California.

More than 400 miles of hiking trails cut through the Big Sur area of Los Padres National Forest and another 30 or so miles traverse the Pinnacles. Main trails into and through the Ventana Wilderness are Pine Ridge Trail, Carmel River Trail, and the Arroyo Seco Trail.

Orientation

Highway 1, the famous coast highway, provides the main access to the Big Sur coastline and accompanying state parks. Most visitors to the Big Sur Valley come down the 29-mile stretch from Carmel and Monterey. Others drive the entire 90-mile stretch from Carmel to San Simeon. There are no roads east to west over the Santa Lucias with the exception of Nacimiento Road through Hunter Liggett National Guard Base. Underutilized are the eastern accesses into the Big Sur backcountry from Arroyo Seco Road and Carmel Valley Road. Here, those in search of true solitude can access the most remote parts of the Ventana Wilderness by coming in

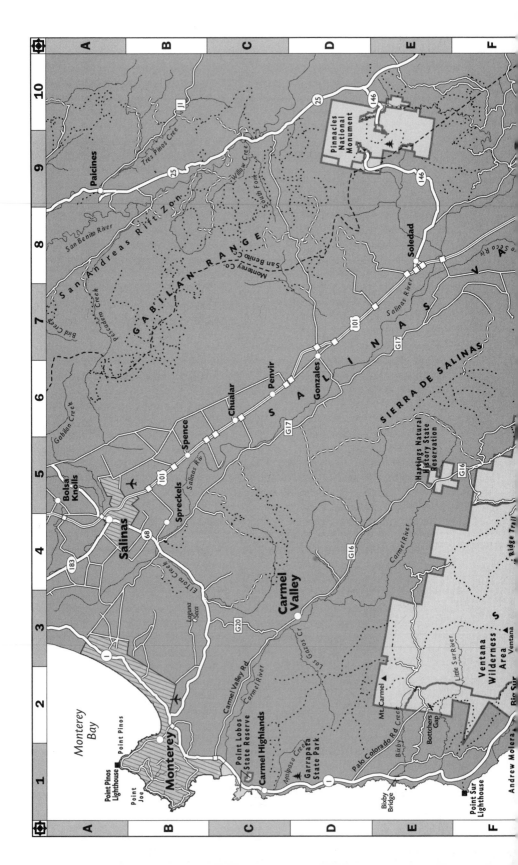

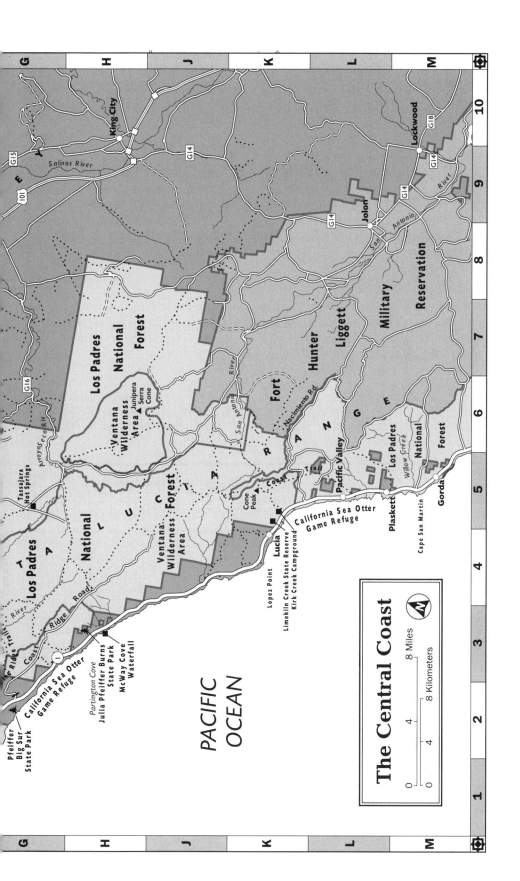

The Central Coast

PACIFIC OCEAN

Pfeiffer Big Sur State Park

California Sea Otter Game Refuge

Partington Cove
Julia Pfeiffer Burns State Park
McWay Cove Waterfall

Los Padres

National

Forest

The Ridge Trail

Coast Ridge Road

Ventana Wilderness Area

Tassajara Hot Springs

Arroyo Seco Rv

Ventana Wilderness Area

Los Padres National Forest

Junipera Serra Cone

Cone Peak

Coast Trail

Lopez Point
Limekiln Creek State Reserve
Kirk Creek Campground

Lucia

California Sea Otter Game Refuge

Plaskett

Cape San Martin

Gorda

Los Padres National Forest

Willow Creek

Pacific Valley

Nacimiento Rd

Fort Hunter Liggett

Military Reservation

San Antonio River

San Antonio River

Jolon

Salinas River

King City

Lockwood

San Antonio River

R A N G E

PACIFIC OCEAN

The Central Coast

0   4   8 Miles
0   4   8 Kilometers

the back way, away from the tourist crush. Pinnacles National Monument does have a west entrance just a few miles from Soledad, but is best reached via State Route 25, a beautiful winding two-lane road that threads through miles of ranch country between Hollister and King City and leads to the eastern entrance of the Pinnacles, where the most interesting features and visitor services are located.

Palo Colorado Road

This narrow two-lane road 6 miles south of Carmel on Highway 1 leads 8 miles into the hills to Bottcher's Gap, a major trailhead for the Ventana Wilderness as well as a national forest car camp.

Bixby Bridge

Fallacious local legend claims Bixby Bridge, 12 miles south of Carmel on Highway 1, as the longest concrete arch in the world. It's not, but the beautiful span is one of the few man-made features that actually enhances the already outrageous scenery. Before the bridge was open, travelers had to traverse miles up-canyon before continuing down the coast. Park on the north side and walk about 100 yards up the Old Coast Road for an unbeatable view of the bridge and river mouth below. It is risky but possible to scramble down the rocky slope to the pocket beach below.

Urban Big Sur

A misnomer if there ever was one—there's no such thing as an urban center in Big Sur; however, the 5-mile stretch of Highway 1 through the Big Sur Valley is the closest thing you'll find to a town. Residents do all their shopping in Carmel, 24 miles to the north. You should too, but anything you've forgotten can probably be found, outrageously

overpriced, at one of the small gas stations, markets, motels, or restaurants along this stretch. The **River Inn** (tel. 408/ 625-5255) has a **BP** gas station, restaurant, grocery store, and outdoor espresso cart. Locals perform music and theater here during winter months. Adjacent is **Big Sur Garage and Towing** (tel. 408/ 667-2181). **Big Sur Health Center** (tel. 408/667-2580) offers emergency treatment. Just before leaving the Big Sur Valley to the south, you'll find the **Big Sur Post Office** (tel. 408/667-2305), a **Chevron** gas station, and a store.

Arroyo Seco Road

This beautiful country road loops from U.S. 101 in the Salinas Valley near Soledad, deep into the back side of the Los Padres National Forest, and exits near King City, providing trailhead access to the most remote portions of the Ventana Wilderness.

Parks & Other Hot Spots

The spots along Highway 1 are listed in north to south order, with Pinnacles National Monument at the end of the section.

Garrapata State Park

5 miles south of Carmel on Highway 1. Tel. 408/667-2315. Pit toilets, no water. Open daily year-round, dawn to dusk. No fee.

Heading south from Carmel, the first coastal access you'll come to after 4 miles of high cliffs is Garrapata, an undeveloped 2,800-acre park with a beautiful-sounding Spanish name that means, no kidding, wood tick. Though the park extends on both sides of Highway 1 for 4 miles, most visitors come for the beaches. As one of the few places in the northern part of Big Sur where you can actually get to the water, Garrapata draws fishermen, surfers, skinny-dippers, picnickers, and beachcombers. More than 30 numbered gates lead from roadside pullouts to vistas, and beaches, on one side of Highway 1, and hiking trails, redwood forests, and chapparal-covered mountains on the other. The mountain side of the park is little used and a boon for hikers seeking solitude. A map and brochure of the park are available for sale at the entrance kiosk at Andrew Molera State Park 15 miles south.

Point Sur Lighthouse State Park

17 miles south of Carmel on Highway 1. Tel. 408/625-4419. Visitors center, pit toilets, no water. Open to guided tours only, year-round Wed 10am, Sat 10am and 2pm. $5 per person. Meet 15 minutes before tour at locked gate on Highway 1. Reservations accepted.

Jutting 200 feet in the air like a fantasy castle at the end of a long sandpit, Point Sur, a huge solid rock monolith, provided the perfect place to situate a lighthouse along this treacherous coast. Though only open 3 days a week, and even then by docent-led tours only, it's worth setting aside a weekend morning to tour the 40-foot-tall lighthouse built of stone blocks, picnic on the grounds, and scan the ocean for passing whales. Built in 1889, the lighthouse provides great insight into what life was like on this part of the coast before Highway 1 was opened in 1937.

Andrew Molera State Park

22 miles south of Carmel on Highway 1. Tel. 408/667-2315, or 408/625-8664

for horseback-riding concession. Walk-in campground (reservations not accepted), picnic area. Open daily year-round. Fee.

Just south of Point Sur, Highway 1 leaves the ocean's edge and for almost 10 miles is cut off from the sea by Pfeiffer Ridge. Most of the land here is extremely private and off-limits, but fortunately the beautiful Andrew Molera is a 4,800-acre exception. The park is almost entirely undeveloped and a hiker's paradise. At the Big Sur River mouth on the park's northern end, surfers find some of the best waves in the area and access to Big Sur's longest beach. A private concession (tel. 408/625-8664) leads horseback trail rides for a real-life ranch experience.

Pfeiffer Big Sur State Park and Big Sur Station

26 miles south of Carmel on Highway 1. Tel. 408/667-2315 (state park); 408/667-2423 (Big Sur Station). Public campground, showers, flush toilets. Fees for day use and camping.

Pfeiffer's old-growth redwoods, a waterfall, cool swimming holes, and numerous trails make it Big Sur's largest public campground, the epicenter of tourist-season Big Sur. You'll find a grocery store, restaurant, and laundromat here, as well as Big Sur Lodge, a bleak example of what goes wrong when park concessionaires with no real investment in the physical property of a hotel defer maintenance and cut corners.

One half mile south of the state park on Highway 1 is Big Sur Station, a multi-agency administrative center for both national forest and state park needs; it has the best information about the backcountry, as well as wilderness and fire permits. Several major trails into the Ventana Wilderness leave from here and parking is provided.

Pfeiffer Beach

Sycamore Canyon Road, 25 miles south of Carmel on Highway 1. Tel. 408/667-2423. Pit toilets, parking. Open dawn to dusk year-round. Fee.

Though you can't look 10 feet in Big Sur without seeing the Pacific Ocean, getting to the water is notoriously difficult. Pfeiffer Beach is the closest you can get your car to the beach—about one-quarter mile, flat—so it's popular with everyone from picnickers and nude sunbathers to kayakers and surfers. At low tide climb the two huge seaward rocks for a majestic view of the waves. Locals regularly steal the Sycamore Canyon Road sign that leads to Pfeiffer Beach in order to confuse visitors, so just keep your eyes peeled for the only paved road on the west side of Highway 1 after you pass Big Sur Station.

Ventana Wilderness/Los Padres National Forest

Access from Highway 1 or Arroyo Seco Road. Tel. 408/385-5434 or 408/667-2423. Open daily year-round. Fees may apply.

Within this wilderness lie 161,000 acres of varied geography ranging from redwood forests to desolate, dry ridgelines. With 400 miles of trails, lots of backcountry camps, three major rivers, hot springs, and numerous high peaks, the Ventana Wilderness offers the best winter backpacking in Northern California; wilderness permits required to enter (available at Big Sur Station—see above). Most hikers enter through the popular Pine Ridge Trail at Big Sur Station, but numerous trailheads lead into the wilderness from all sides. The Ventana Wilderness Recreation Map ($4.25) can point you to them. In mid-to late summer be sure to ask about trail closures to due to fire danger. Los Padres National Forest also manages several beaches, campgrounds, and day-use areas in the southern reaches of Big Sur. *Hiking the Big Sur Country: The Ventana Wilderness*, by Jeffrey P. Schaffer (Wilderness Press, 1991), is an excellent, if a bit dry, guidebook to the more obscure trails of the Ventana Wilderness.

Julia Pfeiffer Burns State Park

37 miles south of Carmel on Highway 1. Tel. 408/667-2315. Two walk-in campsites. Picnic area, restroom. Open daily year-round, dawn to dusk.

If you haven't figured it out already, the Pfeiffers, an early homesteading family, were the originators of tourism in Big Sur and their name is everywhere. Julia Pfeiffer Burns State Park is a small but remarkable park encompassing a lush redwood forest, two clifftop environmental campsites, a sheltered cove, and what park literature claims is the only waterfall in California to fall directly into the Pacific Ocean. The environmental campsites here are some of the best in the state and consequently hard to get. Kayakers willing to schlepp their boats down a short but steep trail and through a 200-foot-long solid rock tunnel can launch at the remains of the old Partington Cove loading dock to explore miles of otherwise inaccessible coastline. Divers (experienced only!) are required to register with the rangers in advance to explore this designated marine sanctuary.

Limekiln Creek State Park

52 miles south of Carmel on Highway 1. Tel. 408/667-2315.

A brand-new addition to the state park system 26 miles south of the Big Sur Valley, Limekiln holds a waterfall, historic lime kilns, redwoods, and a small sheltered beach. The name refers to a lime-making operation set up here by settlers in the 1870s. At the time of operation it was known as Rockland Landing. Because programs, facilities, and access are all being worked out at the time of publication, visitors should contact the State Parks at Big Sur Station (see above) for up-to-date information.

Pacific Valley Area

58 miles south of Carmel on Highway 1. Tel. 408/385-5434 for national forest information; tel. 408/927-8655 for store or gas station. Gas, phones, store, ranger station, campgrounds, trails, beaches.

Between 28 miles and 38 miles south of the Big Sur Valley is a stretch of coastline containing several Los Padres National Forest beaches, campgrounds, picnic areas, and a small community (Pacific Valley). The most remote part of the Big Sur coast, this stretch doesn't bear the same tourist burden as the northern parks. Great diving, kayaking, and hiking. Also noteworthy because the Nacimiento–Fergusson Road between Kings City and Kirk Creek is the only east–west road through the Santa Lucias.

Pinnacles National Monument

For best results enter the park from State Route 25 on the east side. A secondary entrance exists just outside Soledad from U.S. 101 but leads to a dry and dreary part of the park. Tel. 408/389-4485. Public and private campground, visitors center, picnic area, toilets, trails, climbing, caving. Open dawn to dusk year-round. Fees.

Located in the rolling hills of the Gabilan Range ranch country east of the Salinas Valley, the Pinnacles are a geological anomaly, half the remains of a volcanic plug that left jutting rock spires and caves in the middle of this otherwise nondescript landscape. The other half of the volcano sits more than 300 miles south near Tehachapi—testimony to the San Andreas Fault's influence over this landscape. Popular with climbers, Pinnacles is also a great springtime destination to catch the wildflower bloom and is home to California's largest breeding population of hawks, eagles, and falcons. See the Pinnacles National Monument feature later in this chapter.

What to Do & Where to Do It

BIRD WATCHING

The list of birds you can see on the central coast is pretty much endless, given the variety of ecosystems and climatic zones that meet in this part of the state. Particularly noteworthy is the large variety of **raptors** common here. **Pinnacles National Monument** is the largest nesting area of raptors in California; you'll often see kestrels, black-shouldered kits, red-tailed hawks, Cooper's hawks, and the occasional peregrine falcon or golden eagle soaring over the volcanic towers that make such fine nesting sites. Much zoological and ornithological study has been done on the Pinnacles, and the visitors center at **Bear Gulch** (tel. 408/389-4485) has extremely detailed species lists available.

Big Sur is also a **raptor** hot spot. Bald eagles and peregrine falcons have been reintroduced into the **Ventana Wilderness** (tel. 408/385-5434). Other **woodland birds** commonly seen are the chestnut-tailed chickadee, California towhee, hermit thrush, lesser goldfinch, and Lewis woodpecker. The coastal river mouths like **Andrew Molera State Park** (tel. 408/667-2315) or the **Little Sur River** are a great place to look for **sea and shorebirds** like willets, snowy plovers, sanderlings, pelicans, grebes, and numerous migratory species. A list of birds in the area is available for 25 cents at the Andrew Molera State Park entrance.

BOARDSAILING

One thing you can say about the Big Sur coast is that the wind always blows and it blows hard. Unfortunately, most of the 60-plus miles of coastline are inaccessible except by foot, and the trails to the beach are often precipitous. That pretty much eliminates Big Sur as a boardsailing destination except for the most hard-core. It's not that far, however, to Cambria, San Simeon, and Cayucos, beaches south of here popular with advanced, high-wind sailors.

FISHING

Inland, the fishing here is pretty limited. The **Big Sur and Little Sur rivers** both offer some beautiful fly-fishing water in the winter and spring, but are subject to closure due to runs of endangered steelhead trout that use these rivers to spawn. Higher up the Big Sur River near **Sykes Hot Spring** I've caught and released small trout on flies and lures. Always

check with the Forest Service at Big Sur Station to find out the most recent regulations here before casting, as the fishery seems to be in a state of flux.

The **Pacific** is a different story. Cold nearshore water, rich and rocky habitat, and relatively light use make Big Sur a surf fisherman's dream come true. It's not uncommon to catch large ling cod, cabezon, and red snapper straight off **Willow Creek, Pfeiffer Beach,** or **Garrapata Beach.** Like all coastal-dependent sports in Big Sur, the hardest thing is getting to the water. That, and the often adverse wind and surf conditions. Only at Willow Creek in the southern end of Big Sur can you launch a small inflatable or skiff.

Randy's Fishing Trips, Fisherman's Wharf, Monterey (tel. 831/372-7440), offers full-day deep-sea fishing trips down to the waters off Point Sur.

HIKES, BUSHWHACKS & BACKPACK TRIPS

DAY HIKES

Mount Carmel Trail, Ventana Wilderness

10 miles round-trip. Strenuous. Access: Bottcher's Gap Trailhead, Ventana Wilderness. Map: Ventana Wilderness trail map (Forest Service topo maps are available, but you won't need them—the brush here is much too thick to bushwhack).

This trail leads through some of the least-used backcountry of the Ventana Wilderness to the summit of Mount Carmel. Thickly covered with scrub oak, this 4,417-foot peak would be viewless were it not for a rock outcropping that fortuitously graces the summit. From the top of the rock the 360° views take in the Carmel Valley, Salinas Valley, Monterey Bay, and much of the Ventana backcountry. If the view from here isn't enough, a mysterious telephone pole with rungs is located on the summit

(Just a pole, no lines. Go figure.) and juts about 3 feet higher.

Bluff–Panorama Ridge Loop, Andrew Molera State Park

9 miles. Moderate. Access: Andrew Molera State Park; trailhead at beach at the mouth of the Big Sur River (see "Beach and Headlands Trail," below, under "Walks & Rambles"). Map: Andrew Molera State Park map.

The Bluff Trail circles most of the high points of the 4,800-acre park. It skirts the top of the ocean bluff for almost 2 miles. To the north is Point Sur and the lighthouse. South is Cooper Point. This coastal grassland blossoms with numerous wildflowers during the spring and early summer including lupine, sage, poppies, and Indian paintbrush. Before the trail circles left, crossing the ridge and returning to the parking area, a spur trail leads down to the beach, offering the chance to hike 2 miles back to the river in lieu of the loop trail. Hikers who opt to stay on the loop will cross the ridge via a switchbacked path and return through a deeply shaded oak grove. Look for circling vultures and hawks cruising the updrafts. As the loop heads back, another cutoff, Hidden Trail, leads down to the Big Sur River. Many lush meadows carpet the river valley here. Deer are common and summer footbridges allow you to cross over to Highway 1. Otherwise remain on the ridge trail until you return to the river mouth and beach, then hike the short ranch road back to the parking lot.

Coast Ridge Road, Los Padres National Forest

10 miles to Terrace Creek Trail, round-trip, returning to Ventana Inn; 12 miles to Big Sur Station via Terrace Creek Trail and Pine Ridge Trail. Moderate. Steep but smooth. Access: Los Padres National Forest. Park in the clearly signed Vista Point lot at the Ventana Inn or in the pullout on Highway 1; please don't park in the restaurant lot or the Ventana Inn lot itself. Trailhead just below the inn. Map: Los Padres National Forest map.

The Coast Ridge Road climbs steeply to the crest of the Santa Lucias and then heads south, switchbacking over the ridge with alternating views of the ocean and wilderness. While the road is almost 25 miles long, it's the first 4 or 5 miles you're interested in. Just below the restaurant you'll see a locked gate swathed in threatening-looking NO TRESPASSING signs. Take note, then head on—the Coast Ridge Road has been at the center of a public-access battle for several years now. The Forest Service owns and maintains the graded dirt road; thus, taxpayers own it and have the right to walk, bike, or horseback ride on it. Several private property owners who use the road feel differently about public access, however, and do everything they can to keep you out. The best policy is to be extremely careful not to trespass on private land, but if anyone hassles you for being on the road, politely tell them that Coast Ridge Road is a public easement; you pay for it, and you plan on using it. Almost immediately after passing the gate, you'll enter a cool redwood grove. Several spur roads lead above and below the road. These are driveways. Stay off! In half a mile you'll come to one of the most interesting-looking waterfalls around. Marble from upstream dissolved and subsequently resolidified as it trickled down the face of a 40-foot cascade, forming a sort of stalactite hanging from the hillside.

Almost immediately after the falls you'll exit the trees and begin traversing grassy hillsides. In spring, this area is carpeted with poppies, lupine, Indian paintbrush, and blooming yuccas. The view north is the best perpective on the Big Sur Valley I've ever found, with Point Sur and Molera Point capping the course of the winding river valley. The road heads south, leading to dramatic ridgelines and canyons where you can peer down onto Partington Ridge, an ultra-private cluster of homes where author Henry Miller lived upon his return to the United States after years in Paris. In 4.2 miles you'll come to a grove of red-barked madrones. Here you'll find the trailhead for the Terrace Creek Trail, which drops down to the Pine Ridge Trail, allowing the opportunity to loop back to Big Sur Station. But the walk back down Coast Ridge Road is shorter and just as nice.

Tan Bark Trail, Julia Pfeiffer Burns State Park

6.6 miles round-trip. Moderate. Access: Julia Pfeiffer Burns State Park; trailhead uphill from the parking pullout for Partington Cove, about a mile north of the McWay Falls parking lot. Map: Ventana Wilderness or Los Padres National Forest map.

The Tan Bark Trail is the remnant of a skid-trail system used to haul tan oaks and redwoods down to Partington Cove to be loaded onto schooners bound for San Francisco to the north. It's a fairly short trail but climbs more than 2,000 feet in 3.3 miles. The drainage of Partington Creek is home to a lush forest of tan oaks and several redwood groves. You'll switchback through many different plant communities on the way up—including plenty of poison oak, so watch out. On a clear day the top, near an interesting-looking tin house, offers great views and is a good place to stop for a picnic before heading down.

Vicente Flat Trail, Ventana Wilderness

6.8 miles round-trip. Moderate. Access: Trailhead at Kirk Creek Campground,

Ventana Wilderness. Map: Los Padres National Forest map.

Beginning at Kirk Creek Camp on Highway 1 in the southern reaches of Big Sur, this gives some of the most consistently stunning ocean views of any trail in the region as it climbs into the Ventana Wilderness. It's a simple hike. Just find the Vicente Flat Trail (also sometimes called Kirk Creek Trail though it doesn't follow Kirk Creek) across the road from the car campground and head on up. For 3.4 miles you'll switchback through fields of wildflowers and mixed oak and bay trees. Occasionally you'll traverse gullies lined with redwoods. Overall you'll gain 2,000 feet in elevation from the starting point only 164 feet above sea level. By the time you reach Espinosa Camp, the views up and down the coast will make you dizzy. Below lie Hare Creek and Limekiln Creek canyons, home to some of Big Sur's best redwood groves. When you've had enough, return the way you came.

High Peaks Trail, Pinnacles National Monument

6 miles. Moderate. Bring a flashlight for Bear Gulch Cave. Access: Pinnacles National Monument; trailhead at visitors center. Map: Pinnacles National Monument trail map.

This wonderful day hike allows you to see almost all of Pinnacles National Monument in a single day: caves, rock spires, circling raptors, and stunning views of the Salinas Valley and San Andreas Fault. Take Condor Gulch Trail from the visitors center. As you climb quickly out of the parking area the Pinnacles' wind-sculpted spires seem to grow taller. In less than 2 miles you are among them and Condor Gulch intersects with the High Peaks Trail. The view from the top spans miles: the Salinas Valley to your west, the Pinnacles below, and miles of coast range to the east. After traversing the high peaks (including stretches of footholds carved in steep rock faces) for about a mile, the trail drops back toward the visitors center via a valley filled with eerie-looking hoodoos. In another 1.5 miles you'll reach the reservoir marking the top of Bear Gulch Cave. You'll need your flashlight and might get wet, but this 0.6-mile-long talus cave is a thrill. From the end of the cave you're just a short walk through the most popular climbing area of the park away from the visitors center. If the cave is closed due to rain or earthquakes, then return via Moses Spring Trail.

OVERNIGHTS

Pine Ridge Trail, Ventana Wilderness

18.4 miles round-trip. Strenuous. Access: Big Sur Station Trailhead, Ventana Wilderness. Map: Ventana Wilderness map.

This is the most popular trail in the Ventana Wilderness by far. The reason? Sykes Hot Spring, 9.2 miles up the Big Sur River. If hot water and backcountry crowds aren't your thing, then this isn't your trail. However, if the thought of soaking in a 104° pool on the banks of a gurgling river after a hard day's hike appeals to you, aim for midweek or a wintertime weekend and check Sykes out. From the Big Sur Station Trailhead the path climbs directly up the mountainside, skirting the Big Sur River Gorge. Steep and hot, this is the worst part of the entire trip. Once beyond sight of the Big Sur Valley, you'll climb up and down ridges, sometimes near the river, often high above. Midway to Sykes is the Barlow Flat Camp, a perfect place to stop and swim on your way in or a nice layover if you're planning a longer trip. You'll come to the river a second time

9.2 miles after leaving the road. Here the trail crosses and heads away from the river. You're there. The hot spring is about 0.25 miles downstream on the south bank. The number and size of pools vary seasonally. Campsites are strung up and down the river. Good trout fishing in both directions. Wilderness permits required.

Bottcher's Gap to Ventana Double Cone, Ventana Wilderness

30 miles round-trip. Strenuous. Access: Bottcher's Gap (Palo Colorado Road). Map: Ventana Wilderness map.

This 30-mile round-trip takes you through the loneliest part of the Ventana Wilderness and to the summit of 4,853-foot Ventana Double Cone, the highest peak in the wilderness reachable by trail. Along the way you'll take in some of the most expansive country in the coast range. Unfortunately this is one of the driest areas of the wilderness too. You'll depend on tiny creeks and the occasional spring for water, and the second half of the hike is even drier. For this reason it's often better to hike one day into Puerto Suelo Camp (11.5 miles) where there is a spring and shade, then day hike to the summit and back (15 miles round-trip), allowing you to blast up and back with just water and food. On top of the higher southern summit you'll find the remains of an old fire lookout and occasionally a windbreak of scrap wood. From here you can see virtually all of the Ventana Wilderness. To the east-southeast you'll spot a mountain that is considerably higher than any other. That's Junipero Serra Peak, at 5,862 feet the highest in the central coast range. Because of its dry nature it is best to do this hike in the early spring when you'll catch blooming wildflowers and running creeks. Later

Pinnacles National Monument

Once a little-known outpost of the national monument system, Pinnacles National Monument has become one of the most popular weekend climbing destinations in central California over the last 10 years. The mild winter climate and plentiful routes make this a perfect off-season training ground for climbers. It's also a popular haven for campers, hikers, and nature lovers. One of the most unique chaparral ecosystems in the world supports a large community of plant and animal life here, including California's largest breeding population of raptors.

The Pinnacles themselves, hundreds of towering crags, spires, and hoodoos, are seemingly out of place in the voluptuously rolling hills of the coast range. And they *are*, in fact, out of place, part of the eroded remains of a volcano formed 23 million years ago 195 miles south in the middle of the Mojave Desert. It was carried here by the movement of the San Andreas Fault, which runs just east of the park. The other half of the volcano remains in the Mojave. Because of this distinctive geology, Pinnacles was set aside as a national monument on January 16, 1908, though it wasn't developed for visitor use until the 1930s and 40s.

You could spend days here without getting bored, but it's possible to cover the most interesting features in a weekend. With a single hike you can go from the lush oak woodland around the Bear Gulch Visitors Center to the dry and desolate crags of the high peaks, then back down through a half-mile-long cave complete with underground waterfalls (see the **High Peaks Trail** listing under "Day Hikes"). If you're coming into the park from the west entrance, there are a couple of other day hike options. The **Juniper Canyon Trail** is a short (1.2 mile) but very steep blast to the top of the high peaks. You'll definitely earn the view. Otherwise, try the short **Balconies Trail** to the monument's other talus cave, **Balconies Cave** (bring a flashlight). Beware of poison oak, particularly in Bear Gulch. Rattlesnakes are common throughout the park but rarely seen. Bikes and dogs are prohibited on all trails, and there is no backcountry camping allowed anywhere in the park. Daytime temperatures often exceed 100° in summer, so the best times of year to visit are spring, when the wildflowers are blooming, followed by fall. Crowds are common during spring weekends.

Two entrances lead to the park. The **West Entrance** from Soledad and U.S. 101 is dry, dusty, and much less attractive than the **East Entrance.** Unless you're coming from nearby, take the longer drive on Highway 25 to enter through the east. Because the peaks of the Pinnacles face east, and the watershed drains east, most of the interesting hikes and geologic features are on this side. No road crosses the park.

The first place you should go upon entering the park from the east is the **Bear Gulch Visitors Center** (tel. 408/ 389-4485). This small center is rich with exhibits about the park's history, wildlife, geology, and also has a great selection of nature handbooks and climbing guides for the Pinnacles. Climbers should register here before heading out: many routes are closed during hawk and falcon nesting season, and rangers like to know how many climbers are in the park.

Adjacent to the visitors center, the Bear Gulch picnic ground is a great place to fuel up before setting out on a hike or, if you're not planning on leaving your car, the best place to gaze up at dramatic spires of the high peaks.

in the season it is hot beyond belief and the flies will eat you alive.

OUTFITTERS

There are no backpacking outfitters in Big Sur, though the **Sierra Club** (tel. 415/977-5630) runs a week-long trek through the Ventana Wilderness every spring at the peak of wildflower season; cost is approximately $360. The **Esalen Institute** (tel. 408/667-3005) also runs one or two wilderness backpacking courses each summer.

HORSEBACK RIDING

A private concession operating from the old barn and corral inside Andrew Molera State Park, **Molera Trail Rides** (tel. 408/625-8664) leads 2-hour trail rides through the park. Reservations required for all rides. **Ventana Wilderness Expeditions** (tel. 408/659-2153) offers 3- to 7-day pack-stock trips into the Ventana Wilderness.

MOUNTAIN BIKING

Big Sur would be a world-famous mountain biking destination but for one thing, the Ventana Wilderness. Many Ventana trails would be great rides but, alas, they're off limits to bikes so we're out of luck.

Single track it lacks, but fortunately Big Sur has some great fire roads that make for unforgettable rides. Since the Los Padres National Forest has many inholdings (privately held land within the forest's boundaries), you'll have to be on the alert for vehicles on all the backcountry roads.

Coast Ridge Road

10–40 miles round-trip. Moderate. Graded dirt road. Access: Ventana Inn. Please do not park in restaurant or inn parking lot. Map: Los Padres National Forest map.

I just can't say enough about this ride. It's steep enough to be a workout, stable enough to be doable, and has the best views of any ride in Big Sur. Stretching back for almost 20 miles along the edge of the Ventana Wilderness, it is also the longest ride beginning in the Big Sur Valley. Unfortunately, the Coast Ridge Road, which begins just below the famous Ventana Restaurant and scales to the crest of the Santa Lucias in a powerhouse 4.2 miles, is reportedly now closed to mountain bikes. The only reason I could get from the Forest Service, which maintains this dirt road as a fire accessway and a trail easement into the Ventana Wilderness, is that private landowners along the route complained about bike traffic. Frankly, the Forest Service maintains this road with your tax dollars, and it is historically a public easement. You should be allowed to ride here. The whole thing smells like yesterday's fish to me. Call the Forest Service (tel.408/385-5434) and tell them what you think. Write them a letter. I'm not advocating trespassing, but I rode it anyway and no one said a word.

Old Coast Highway

14 miles one way. Strenuous. Graded dirt road. Access: Begin at the roadside pullout just above Andrew Molera State Park; Old Coast Highway to Bixby Bridge; Highway 1 loops back to where ride begins. Map: Los Padres National Forest map.

Before Bixby Bridge was completed at the end of 1932, travelers heading south into Big Sur from Carmel detoured 14 miles up Bixby Creek, through the Little Sur River Valley, over a few ridges, and then were deposited at the head of the Big Sur Valley at the entrance to current-day Andrew Molera State Park. Today travelers whiz south along the coast road, cutting 9 miles and many hours off a once harrowing journey. In a rare incidence of what's good for cars is good for mountain bikers, the virtual abandonment of the Old Coast Highway other than as an accessway to a few remote homes and ranches left cyclists with a splendid dirt road all to themselves.

The Old Coast Highway steeply ascends over the ridge into the Little Sur Valley. You'll wind through ranch country and drop along a few ridges before curving past a beautiful turn-of-the-century ranch compound and entering the lush river valley. Watch for wild turkeys in the open rangeland. Often they'll run in front of you for a mile or more, gobbling and clucking in a panic. In the river bottom, stop and absorb the scents and sounds of the Little Sur River running through an old-growth redwood forest. It's up and over another steep ridge from here, then down a long fast hill. You'll pass a cluster of houses including a geodesic dome. If you were a drop of water you'd be only a short distance from the bridge and ocean, but the road takes a radical detour up the seemingly vertical north side of Bixby Canyon. Just when you think the climb is going to do you in, boom, there you are, coasting down to Bixby Bridge and the Pacific Ocean. From here you can ride the 5 miles down Highway 1 to your car with the wind at your back or get a ride with a friend. This is my favorite way to do this ride. The loop can be done in reverse, but the climbs are steeper that way, and the wind is in your face as you head north on Highway 1.

Andrew Molera State Park

Several short but sweet rides. Easy. Old ranch roads. Access: Molera Parking Area. Map: Molera trail map.

As a former ranch, 4,800-acre Molera is crisscrossed with numerous old dirt roads and trails. Some, but not all, are open to mountain bikes, and those

designations keep changing. You're not going to find any long rides here, but if a short trail in beautiful surroundings is what you seek, ask at the front entrance which trails are currently open to bikes.

Nacimiento Road/Cone Peak

28 miles round-trip. Strenuous. Graded fire road and potholed pavement. Access: 1 mile south of the Kirk Creek Campground you'll come to Nacimiento–Fergusson Road. Map: Los Padres National Forest map.

This is the only east–west link across the Santa Lucias. *Nacimiento* is the Spanish word for childbirth, and you'll feel like you've given birth after climbing this mother. Beginning at 48 feet above sea level, the road climbs a towering series of switchbacks to the crest of the mountains. After the first 7 miles, which are on paved (though not well-maintained) county roads, you'll be at 3,106 feet and see Cone Peak Road forking off to the left. Don't worry—it's only about another 2,049 feet of altitude and 10 to 15 miles of steep dirt road to the summit of 5,155-foot Cone Peak. Only 3 miles as the crow flies from the Pacific, Cone Peak's western escarpment is one of the steepest on the West Coast, more than a 30% incline. That's steep. It's all downhill from here. Hope you have good brakes.

ROAD BIKING

If you want to ride a road bike in Big Sur, you'll be doing a lot of riding along **Highway 1** since it's the only paved road that goes more than a few miles. Bicycle companies, like car companies, like to shoot photos of their products crossing Bixby Bridge or wheeling down the backside of Hurricane Point on Highway 1. Ooh, how romantic! you think, fingering through the new Trek or

Bianchi catalogue. I want to do that! This entire stretch of coast is a legendary bike tour, what with its incredible views, plentiful inns and campsites, and plenty of places to fill a water bottle, but those glossy images and romantic notions leave something unsaid, namely the ponderous motorhomes, amphetemine-crazed sports car drivers, and rubbernecking tourists too swept up in the views to watch out for anything as insignificant as a cyclist. With no shoulders and places where getting run off the road can mean a 400-foot fall into the drink, I've always found biking Highway 1 to be more hair-raising than worthwhile. A lot of people ride in worse places for worse reasons every day in urban California, but I'm just a country boy from Santa Barbara and the traffic here really freaks me out more than the view enchants me.

People touring through Big Sur, like all of the West Coast, generally ride from north to south to have the prevailing winds at their back and the ocean that much closer. If you really want to bike this stretch, my advice is to do it midweek, and do the Carmel to Big Sur stretch early in the day (I mean sunrise) when you can get a jump on southbound tourist traffic. Once south of the Big Sur Valley the traffic situation is better though the road gets narrower and the cliffs taller.

Locally no one is leading bicycle trips or renting equipment. Several of the larger statewide outfitters listed in the beginning of the book lead road-biking trips through the area.

ROCK CLIMBING

The rotten and crumbly rock of the coast range limits the options for climbers, but this region is not without its attractions. Most climbers head to **Pinnacles National Monument**, the central coast's most famous climbing destination and home to the area's only long routes.

Many routes are closed during the spring nesting season of several endangered raptors, including the peregrine falcon and golden eagle. The volcanic rock is soft and crumbly—always double-check holds before trusting your life to them. Most routes are bolted. If you're climbing a new route, be aware that protection can and will pull out of situations here where it wouldn't on better rock. The Park Service requests that all climbers check in at the Bear Gulch Visitors Center (tel. 408/ 389-4485) on their way in. That's not a big problem since Bear Gulch is where you'll find most of the well-marked and bolted routes. The visitors center has a free climbing supplement as well as an excellent selection of descriptive climbing guidebooks to the park.

A couple groups and individuals lead guided climbing trips and classes to the Pinnacles: **Epic Adventures,** 993 9th St., Albany, CA 94710 (tel. 510/528-9884); and **Pacific Edge Climbing Gym,** 104 Bronson, Santa Cruz, CA 95062 (tel. 831/454-9254).

The **Big Sur Coast** also has a few short but exceptional climbing spots. The most well known of these are the granite outcroppings at **Garrapata Beach, Granite Creek,** and **Sea Otter Rocks** with many 5.8 to 5.10 routes. None are more than 30 feet high, and most are bolted top-rope situations. In winter the high waves take away the sand beach below many of these routes, making for bad landings into rocky surf if you fall. Frankly, the climbing is much better elsewhere, but the fact that you're hanging out over the edge of the Pacific makes up for a lot of what the rock lacks. Several similar granite outcroppings exist down the coast at **Partington Cove** and points beyond. There are no really formal routes and the area is waiting to be explored.

SCUBA DIVING

With the world-famous diving of Monterey Bay to its north, Big Sur gets almost no visiting divers. On those rare occasions when the wind and waves cooperate, Big Sur is home to some of the wildest underwater habitat on the Central Coast. Large fish, thick kelp, and numerous marine mammals are the norm. Only dive here if you're really in shape and confident with your surf entries; the currents and surf here are extremely powerful.

DIVE SITES

Willow Creek and Mill Creek

38 miles south of the Big Sur Valley, just past Pacific Valley.

Though often rocked by large surf, Willow Creek and Mill Creek a few miles north are the only places you can beach launch an inflatable boat or dive board on the entire coast. Immediately north of the launch site are several rock reefs and nice cobblestone areas with thick kelp. Several more coves extend up the coast, with offshore sea-stack Plaskett Rock standing to the north. Jade is not uncommon in this area of Big Sur. In 1971 a team of three divers pulled up a 9,000-pound nephrite jade boulder near here that was valued at almost $200,000 after working for months to raise it from 30 feet. This state beach has restrooms and picnic areas.

Partington Cove

36 miles south of Carmel on Highway 1, 1 mile north of the main entrance to Julia Pfeiffer Burns State Park.

By permission only (tel. 408/667-2315) divers are allowed to explore the rich environs of this sheltered cove. It's a fairly steep quarter-mile walk from Highway 1, and you'll have to enter and exit the water by clambering down a steep rock face. Still one of the nicest dives in the area.

OFFSHORE BOAT DIVES

When conditions permit, boats from Monterey race down the coast to dive some rarely utilized spots, including several offshore rocks, and Granite Canyon in the northern edge of Big Sur.

OUTFITTERS

Sisters Laura Cuzner and Leslie Moran operate **Aquatic Adventures of Big Sur,** P.O. Box 398, Big Sur, CA 93920 (tel. 408/667-2914). They teach scuba certification classes at the River Inn in Big Sur and lead beach dives in the area. All equipment is provided. Prices vary depending on how many tanks and where you go.

DIVE BOATS

Aquarius Dive Shop, 2040 Del Monte Ave., Monterey, CA 93940 (tel. 408/375-1933 or 800/833-9992), and **Twin Otters, Inc.,** P.O. Box 8744, Monterey, CA 93943 (tel. 408/394-4235), both sometimes run trips down to Big Sur. Aquarius is also the nearest full-service dive shop to Big Sur for rentals and equipment sales.

SEA KAYAKING

With its miles of beautiful, inaccessible coastline, Big Sur is perfectly suited to exploration by sea kayak. First, however, you have to get your boat to the water—no small feat itself—and then you have to deal with Big Sur's unpredictable wind, icy water, and waves. If you can handle that, you're in for the paddle of a lifetime.

One sunny February day, Leslie Moran (see Aquatic Adventures of Big Sur below) and I set out from Pfeiffer Beach to paddle a couple miles down-coast to Wreck Beach, an isolated beach reachable only by boat. Once we punched through the surf, it was smooth paddling offshore by huge sea cliffs and over eerie, surging, sucking rock boils. Pulling into the lee of a small point, we watched as migrating whales headed past. Several curious sea lions circled our boats. Back at Pfeiffer, the wind had come up and so had the swell. I got lucky and caught the first wave of the set and made it almost to the beach, got flipped in the shorebreak, and stood up in time to see Leslie scrambling over a big clean-up set. The waves kept getting bigger until eventually she just took off on one, making it halfway to the beach before the wave closed out and whitewater rolled her; then she swam in with her boat. We both laughed hard at our icy dunkings, but if getting wet isn't your idea of kayaking fun, then Big Sur on anything other than a totally calm day probably isn't the best place for you.

It's always prudent to head north from your put-in point. That way when the prevailing winds come up in the afternoon, they'll be at your back for the return trip.

It's possible to do overnight kayak camp trips down the coast here, though very few people do. If you decide to, be aware that though the beach below the high tide line is public, most of the land along here is private. Be as subtle and discrete as possible when choosing a campsite.

LAUNCHING POINTS

Andrew Molera State Park

Molera, with it's point-sheltered river mouth and long beach, would be a great launching point but for one thing—it's a mile from the parking lot to beach here. Still, a few people do it.

Pfeiffer Beach

This beautiful sandy beach, located at the end of Sycamore Canyon Road, is the easiest spot to carry your boats to the water in northern Big Sur—only about a quarter-mile and flat. The coast in either direction is a mixture of high cliffs and secluded cove beaches. Pfeiffer is also a popular surfing spot, which tells you something about the launch. The second cove down is better; if there is a swell, you can paddle out in the lee of the rocks and scramble through the breaker zone during a lull.

Partington Cove

A mile north of the main entrance to Julia Pfeiffer Burns State Park a small dirt road leads down a canyon, through a 200-foot tunnel blasted through stone, and out into rocky Partington Cove. You can still see huge eyebolts in the rock and the remains of a high lead here where schooners once tied up to take on loads of tanbark and redwood logs. The same sheltered conditions that let them come in so close let you launch the kayaks you just carried a quarter-mile down that steep road. Bring a rope to help lower your kayaks into the water. Then it's just a matter of scrambling down the rocks and getting in. Down-coast is a large beach and beautiful McWay Falls. North is Fuller's Cove, a popular surfing spot and beautiful bay with a tumbling creek pouring down a side canyon.

Willow Creek

When it's windy and bumpy up in northern Big Sur, Willow Creek is often still calm and flat. That's all relative of course, but the other plus is that you can drive your car within striking distance of the ocean here, saving you the hike with a boat on your head. Paddle upcoast from here and explore the other coves to the north. If it's really calm, paddle out to Plaskett Rock with a mask and snorkel.

OUTFITTERS

The Moran sisters of **Aquatic Adventures of Big Sur,** P.O. Box 398, Big Sur, CA 93920 (tel. 408/667-2914), take as few as 2 and as many as 12 out on open-cockpit kayaks—wetsuit, boat, and paddle provided. They'll also take you diving off a kayak if that strikes your fancy. Most trips go to Willow Creek or Point Lobos, but they're flexible and specialize in small, custom adventures. **Monterey Bay Kayaks,** 693 Del Monte Ave., Monterey (tel. 408/ 373-KELP), concentrates mostly on the Monterey Bay but offers occasional tours of the Big Sur area.

SWIMMING

With its cold ocean temperatures, the beaches of Big Sur aren't exactly cut out for leisurely swims. The most you'll want to do is jump in to cool off on a rare hot day. Inland, however, the **Big Sur River Gorge** offers a number of great summer swimming holes. To reach them, park at Pfeiffer Big Sur State Park and walk the short Gorge Trail. From the deep pool at the bottom it's only a matter of your determination how high up the creek you go. There are numerous nice swimming holes and jumping rocks. The nicer hotels in Big Sur all have pools, but the only one open to the public is at the **River Inn** (tel. 408/667-2700) and requires a small day-use fee.

SURFING

Big Sur's surf is fickle, but not in the usual sense of the word; here it's often too big rather than too little. Most of the really good spots are secret spots—hard to find, hard to reach, and heavily localized. **Fuller's Cove**, an insane left point-reef setup, is the hot Big Sur surf spot, and consequently the site of many ugly confrontations between extremely proprietary locals and people with less-than-perfect wave etiquette. Stay away unless you are an adept lineup diplomat. Spots that are more open to outsiders are **Willow Creek, Kirk Creek, Pfeiffer Beach**, and **Molera Point**, though localism runs strong just about everywhere here. Big Sur breaks better on a summertime south swell than during wintertime norths, when the stormy conditions often make it unsurfable.

WALKS & RAMBLES

Soberanes Point Trail, Garrapata State Park

1.7-mile loop. Access: Garrapata State Park, Gate 13 on the west side of Highway 1, about 4 miles south of Point Lobos. Map: Los Padres National Forest map.

Once through the gate veer left at the junction onto this loop trail. In another 0.1 miles you can veer right or left depending on whether you prefer to do the loop clockwise or counterclockwise. The inland leg of the trail offers great views down the coast toward Point Sur and beautiful wildflowers in spring. A short side trail leads 0.3 miles to Whale Saddle, with short paths to the dual summits of North and South Whale Peaks. A viewing bench marks the spot. During winter months, particularly in early January, this spot and the two summits are some of the best places to spot passing gray whales who cut close to Soberanes Point as they migrate south to calve. The seaward leg of the loop offers more intimate views of the crashing waves, tide-pool rocks, and seastacks and arches. Hikers often spot sea otters, seals, and sea lions in the rich feeding waters just offshore. In spring, nesting seabirds colonize offshore rocks, and you can catch the whales on their way back north.

Beach and Headlands Trail, Andrew Molera State Park

2.8 miles round-trip. Access: Trailhead at parking lot near main entrance of Andrew Molera State Park. Map: Molera State Park map.

The Big Sur river mouth is one of the best birding spots on the central coast and the headlands of Molera Point are a perfect place to sit and watch a sunset and the plentiful wildlife of both the ocean and river estuary. This flat, 2.8-mile round-trip follows the Big Sur River through a beautiful riparian habitat in its last miles before the Pacific and also provides great beach access. Follow the trail on the north side of the river. In about 0.3 miles you'll pass through the walk-in camp with more than 100 sites, toilets, and running water. Continue on along the wide path past a cabin on your right. This is Cooper's cabin. Built in 1861, it's the oldest building in Big Sur. Just past here the trail curves left, following the river through a grove of willows, blackberry, and poison oak. In about a mile a fork to the left leads over a narrow summer-only footbridge to the beach. The right fork climbs a coastal bluff and leads out to Molera Point. Many species of shorebirds and seabirds take shelter from Pacific winds in the lee of the point and migratory steelhead trout can sometimes be spotted making their way upstream. On your way back, cross the footbridge to the long beach. During low tides it is possible to walk for miles downcoast over beautiful water-polished cobbles and past several small headlands, but you must be extremely aware of the incoming tide or it'll be a wet, cold, and potentially dangerous walk back. From the beach, return to the parking lot along an old ranch road through the beautiful riparian meadow trail south of the river.

Nature Trail, Pfeiffer Big Sur State Park

0.6 miles. Access: Just off the park road inside the entrance of Pfeiffer Big Sur State Park. Map: State Park map from front kiosk.

This trail introduces hikers to many of the plant species and habitats of the Big Sur region. Pick up the interpretive brochure at the park kiosk on your way in.

Gorge Trail, Pfeiffer Big Sur State Park

2 miles round-trip. Access: Trailhead is 0.1 miles from the Pfeiffer campground site 202, in Pfeiffer Big Sur State Park. Map: Los Padres National Forest map or State Park map.

The Gorge Trail leads you to a deep pool at the foot of the Big Sur River Gorge. Upstream from here are many more pools and falls, popular as a swimming and sunbathing destination with locals and visitors alike in summer months, but you'll have to rock-hop and scramble to get there.

Pfeiffer Falls—Valley View Trail, Pfeiffer Big Sur State Park

1.8-mile loop. Access: Trailhead near Pfeiffer Big Sur State Park Nature Center; follow the signs. Map: State Park map.

This loop trail leads you through a beautiful redwood grove to delicate 60-foot-tall Pfeiffer Falls. In the creek bottom below the falls is a lush verdant mixture: sword fern, five-finger ferns, chain ferns, lichen, and tan oak all contribute to a rich green hue. Several footbridges cross the creek before you'll come to the tiny but beautiful ribbon of water contrasted against a dark cliff. Beyond the falls the Valley View Trail leads onto the nearby ridge for a panoramic view of Pfeiffer Big Sur State Park.

McWay Falls, Julia Pfeiffer Burns State Park

0.5 miles. Access: Trailhead at parking lot inside Julia Pfeiffer Burns State Park. Map: Los Padres National Forest map.

Regardless of its diminutive length, the half-mile trail to the overlook of McWay Falls is worth stopping for. From the parking lot inside the park descend the stairs and follow a wide path through a tunnel under Highway 1. At the trail's end, watch McWay Creek splatter itself onto the beach below in one of the most ridiculously beautiful falls you'll ever see—depending on the tide it sometimes actually falls straight into the turquoise-hued Pacific. A short detour on the way back leads to the Pelton Wheel, an early water-powered generator that provided the first electricity for the Pfieffer homestead.

Bear Gulch Trail, Pinnacles National Monument

1.5 miles. Bring a flashlight for Bear Gulch Cave. Access: Trailhead at visitors center of Pinnacles National Monument. Map: National Monument trail map.

This short trail leaves right from the visitors center on the east side of the park and goes through the most shaded and lush part of this otherwise harsh landscape. Numerous climbing routes exist on the overhanging walls of the canyon. Eventually you'll come to Bear Gulch Cave. If you've thought ahead to bring a flashlight, you can explore this 0.4-mile-long talus cave. Some chambers are pitch dark. Others are spacious grottos with diffuse light seeping in through high-up entrances. A creek and several falls run through the cave. One of the most unique short hikes in California.

WHALE WATCHING

Nowhere on the California coast have I seen as many whales as at Big Sur. Particularly in the southern stretches of Highway 1, near Kirk Creek, it seems like every time you look at the ocean a whale spouts. The winter months when the **gray whales** are headed north to their summer feeding grounds off Alaska are the best times to spot a spout, but whales are present here year-round. Almost any roadside pullout makes a good whale-watching perch, but several spots are perennial favorites.

Molera Point, Andrew Molera State Park

At the mouth of the Big Sur River, this elevated headland gives a good perspective on passing whales that cut near shore on their way around Point Sur. It's a mile hike from the Molera parking lot to the point.

Point Sur Lighthouse

This 19th-century lighthouse is only open 3 days a week by guided tour, but the top of Point Sur is one of the most amazing spots to watch whales as they round the corner formed by the point, even if only for a few minutes. Call 408/625-4419 to reserve tour space.

Pfeiffer Beach

It lacks the expansive views of many other spots in Big Sur, but one of my favorite spots to watch the whales go by is from the top of either of the two huge rocks sticking up out of Pfeiffer Beach. You'll have to climb hand over hand to get up, but the intimate view more than compensates you for the struggle. Not for the faint-hearted.

Soberanes Point

This large expanse of oceanfront land in Garrapata State Park is a favorite whale-watching perch, either from the cliffs or from the top of aptly named Whale Peak. (See "Soberanes Point Trail" under "Walks & Rambles" earlier in this section.)

Campgrounds & Other Accommodations

CAMPING

More than just about any other region in California, Big Sur is hospitable and well equipped for just about every kind of camping. In contrast to many parts of the state, where pulling off the road in your VW bus on the cliff above your favorite surf break, popping the top, and crawling into a sleeping bag for the night is probable cause for arrest and police harassment, or an invitation to every sociopath for 100 miles, here it is an ages-old and well-respected tradition; no one will hassle you at all. Heck, they might even bring you breakfast.

Obviously most campers in Big Sur still choose a more official approach to lodging, and there are plenty of choices ranging from the deluxe to bare bones. Two of my favorite coastal campsites in the state are here: one, the **clifftop environmental campsite** at the top of McWay Falls in Julia Pfeiffer Burns State Park, is extremely hard to get; the other, **Andrew Molera's walk-in campground**, is uncrowded even on a popular weekend. The following are my selections for the best public and private campsites in the Central Coast, Salinas Valley, and Pinnacles National Monument.

Bottcher's Gap

8 miles up Palo Colorado Road, which leaves Highway 1 ten miles south of Carmel just past the Rocky Point Restaurant. Palo Colorado dead ends into the campground. 20 sites; 9 tent-only, 11 tent or small RV. Pit toilets, running water, picnic tables, fire pits, food lockers. Open year-round. Fee charged. Dogs okay on leash. Call Big Sur Station (tel. 408/667-2423) for information.

Bottcher's Gap Camp is nothing special, but I'm listing it because this is the trailhead to some of the more remote hikes into the Ventana Wilderness such as Mount Carmel or the overnight to Ventana Double Cone. It's also one of the least crowded camps on a busy weekend. Other than hiking, it's pleasant, but there's nothing much here.

Andrew Molera Walk-In Campground

21 miles south of Carmel in Andrew Molera State Park. Tel. 408/667-2315. More than 100 sites. Running water, chemical toilets, picnic tables, fire pits, and food storage boxes. Pets okay on leash. Bring your own wood or buy it at entrance station. Open year-round. First come, first served. $3 per night.

Amazing the difference a quarter-mile walk makes. Though the campsites themselves are nothing to write home about and the chemical potties will make you think twice before sucking down that second cup of coffee, Andrew Molera is one of the most spectacular settings anywhere with its wild beach and thousands of acres of undeveloped land. This campground is often desolate when Big Sur's car camping sites are totally booked, but it's a good idea to call and find out if the campground is full before coming on a busy weekend. It's extremely laid back—I'm absolutely phobic about calling PARKNET to reserve campsites in advance, so I depend on Molera for those impromptu journeys up the coast.

Fernwood Park, Big Sur Campground, and Riverside Campground

On the Big Sur River between Andrew Molera and Pfeiffer Big Sur State Parks. Facilities: You name it, these three privately owned campgrounds at the heart of the Big Sur River have it: The usuals, like showers, fireplaces, and restrooms, are almost overshadowed by stores, laundromats, several playgrounds, dump stations, etc. Dogs are fine at all three if leashed. Reservations and fees: A resounding yes to both. Sites in these campgrounds range from $24–$42 per night. Ouch! All accept reservations by phone. Fernwood, 408/667-2422 ($24–$27); Big Sur, 408/667-2322 ($24–$42); and Riverside, 408/667-2414 ($25–$28).

I wouldn't have included these except for the fact that they are the last car camping sites in the Big Sur Valley to fill up (no doubt because they cost a small fortune) and are a good option as a last resort. I have to admit to a certain bias against most private campgrounds; they're often cramped, overpriced, and shoddy. Well, none of these three are shoddy; in fact, they're well kept and managed, but the sites are too close together and way too expensive for what you get. They're surrounded by private (no trespassing!) land, so hiking from camp is out, and they're just too

overdeveloped for my idea of a nature experience. Also, because of their location in the shadow of Pfeiffer Ridge, they don't get a lot of daylight.

Pfeiffer Big Sur State Park

29 miles south of Carmel on Highway 1 in the Big Sur Valley. 217 campsites for tents and RVs up to 32 feet. Primitive bike-in camp. Piped water, flush toilets, showers, fireplaces, tables. Nearby in the park is a laundromat, grocery, restaurant, gas and propane. Pets permitted on leash. Car sites $14–$23 per night. Bike sites $3. Pets $1. Call PARKNET at 800/444-PARK to reserve sites.

This is the mother of all car camping sites in Big Sur and one of the most heavily used in the state. If it weren't such a beautiful spot, I'd tell you to just keep on driving, but the hikes, river, and redwoods here are so beautiful it's worth the hassles. Pfeiffer Beach is a short drive, the Ventana Wilderness begins at the park boundary, and Big Sur Station—the joint agency headquarters for federal and state information services—is a half-mile stroll. PARKNET will nail you for a $6.75 reservation fee on top of the cost of the site, but reservations are a necessity on any summertime weekend here.

Ventana Campground

About 2 miles south of Pfeiffer Big Sur State Park below the famous Ventana Inn. P.O. Box 206, Big Sur, CA 93920. Tel. 408/667-2688. 70 tent sites. Restrooms and showers. Small store across the highway. Four-star Ventana Restaurant up the hill. Pets okay on leash. $20 per site. Open year-round.

Okay, so it's expensive. Otherwise this is one of the most beautiful car camping sites in the Big Sur Valley with none of the usual negatives of a private campground. Spacious sites interspersed throughout a towering redwood grove.

Julia Pfeiffer Burns State Park Environmental Walk-In Campsites

About 10 miles south of the Big Sur Valley on Highway 1. Tel. 408/667-2315. Two walk-in sites (0.25 miles, level). Pit toilets, picnic tables, million-dollar view. Since it's a walk-in campground, the fees here aren't the problem, only about $14; it's getting the sites that is a challenge.

I'd sleep on a bed of nails to wake up with the view these two sites have from their perch under cypress trees at the top of McWay Falls, a 60-foot-tall ribbon of water that catapults out of McWay Canyon and lands on the beach below. Crashing waves, birds, whales, and otters will be your only neighbors here at night. During the day it can be a little bit of a drag dealing with all the people who haplessly wander down "your" private trail to this choice spot. Oh well. Call the park for information on how to reserve these two special sites.

Kirk Creek, Los Padres National Forest

4 miles south of Lucia on Highway 1. 33 sites for tents or RVs. Bike-in sites. Flush toilets, running water, picnic tables, fireplaces. $16 per site; $5 for bike sites. Call Los Padres National Forest (tel. 805/683-6711) for reservations. Open year-round.

Located on a high bluff overlooking a cobblestone beach of gemlike agates and other exotic-looking rocks, Kirk

Creek has such outrageous views you won't even notice the sites are a little too close together and the people next door are watching *The Simpsons* on their satellite TV instead of the sunset. Besides the beach, great hiking (Kirk Creek Trail) and biking (Nacimiento Road) begin just across Highway 1. Surfing and fishing are sometimes great from the beach below. Lucia, 4 miles north, is a quaint little town with most services.

Arroyo Seco, Los Padres National Forest

On the edge of the Ventana Wilderness 19 miles west of Greenfield and U.S. 101. 33 tent or motorhome sites. 1 group site. Running water, pit toilets, fireplaces, picnic tables, bathrooms, showers. Pets okay. $15 per night. No reservations. Open year-round.

This campground in the pretty ranch-lands of the Arroyo Seco area is a major trailhead into the back side of the Ventana Wilderness as well as a beautiful spot in its own right.

Pinnacles Campground, Inc.

Just outside the east entrance of Pinnacles National Monument 2.5 miles off State Route 25 between Hollister and King City. 125 sites for tents and motorhomes. Flush toilets, showers, running water, picnic tables, fire pits, firewood for sale, store, swimming pool, RV disposal station. Pets okay. Group camps can be reserved by calling 408/389-4462. $4 reservation fee. Sites are $7 per person per night with a $28 maximum. Group sites $60 minimum.

I've included this campground and not the actual National Monument Campground on the west side of Pinnacles

because the east side is where all the action is and the west side is dry and desolate. Rangers from the monument hold interpretive programs here weekend nights. It's a long hike but a short drive or bike ride from here to the main park attractions around Bear Gulch. Perhaps because it's popular with climbers and hikers more than motorhomers, this is the nicest private campground I've seen: lots of room between sites, ranchlike setting, natural vegetation, minimal road system, and a nice, on-site manager. The pool can be a blessing because it gets scorching at the Pinnacles.

INNS & LODGES

Nobody (I hope!) goes to Big Sur to hang around inside a hotel, so the people here have developed their own style to bring the lodging outdoors and the outdoors inside: natural landscapes, plentiful glass to frame captivating views, fireplaces, and wood construction.

Deetjen's Big Sur Inn

5 miles south of the Big Sur Valley on Highway 1. Tel. 408/667-2377. 20 rooms. $75–$180 per night.

With 20 highly individual rooms and several buildings including a barn, this eclectic, funky historical inn is one of the coolest places you'll ever stay at: no locks on the doors, handmade furniture, and a wildly overgrown garden as well as great food and company. The restaurant and bar are open to nonguests as well. Castro Creek runs through the grounds. Julia Pfeiffer Burns State Park is a few miles south. Very bohemian, very Big Sur. Don't make the mistake of confusing Deetjen's Big Sur Inn with the poorly operated Big Sur Lodge in Pfeiffer Big Sur State Park.

The Ventana Inn

28 miles south of Carmel on Highway 1. Tel. 408/624-4812. 62 rooms, 3 villas. $260 and up per night. All major credit cards.

The Ventana Inn is very Big Sur in a different way. This laid-back love nest of the rich and famous is ultradiscreet and luxurious in a way only a four-star hotel on the edge of a wilderness can be. With two 25-meter pools, Japanese whirlpool baths and sauna, staff masseuse, and a clothing-optional sun deck, this is a fabulous place to lie in the sun and iron out those kinks in your pysche. The landscaping is all native plants. Hammocks hang in the trees. Deer graze outside your room and the first thing that wakes you in the morning will probably be a wild turkey gobbling outside your window. Though most people don't leave the grounds, some really great hiking surrounds the inn, and the staff will advise you or arrange for a guide.

The Ventana Restaurant (expensive) has the best dinner in Big Sur and a great view from its outside decks. Breakfast (complimentary) is a delicious mix of California fruits, homemade granola, croissants, fresh bread, juices, and hot coffee or tea. Tip: Don't come here by yourself unless you feel like being the odd person out; this is very much a lovey-dovey couples sort of place, and even if you weren't lonely when you came, you'll feel like a hermit by the time you leave. I speak from experience.

Esalen Institute

10 miles north of Lucia. Tel. 408/667-3005. Rooms begin at $80 per night.

Once a hippie hotbed where Joan Baez, Hunter Thompson, Carlos Castenada, and many others of that generation hung out to get back to nature, Esalen is still a counterculture haven, though now it leans more toward the crystal-clutching New Age than the good old days of gobbling acid and roaring down the coast on motorcycles. Still, Esalen is the site of many interesting seminars and workshops ranging from shamanic healing and psychosynthesis to massage (Esalen has its own style of massage named after it) and wilderness trips. You can also come here just to chill out. Simple accommodations in a variety of buildings on the oceanfront Esalen campus include lunch and access to the famous Esalen hot springs. The hot springs here are some of the nicest in the world—terraced into a sea cliff, clothing optional. Don't come if you are uncomfortable with nudity. Call for information about programs or reservations.

Tassajara Zen Monastery

East edge of the Ventana Wilderness between Carmel and Greenfield. $65 for dorm accommodations; $115–$200 for a single.

Tassajara is a meditative and quiet place to get back to nature, think, hike, swim, and eat healthy vegetarian food. A working monastery and Zen center, it's not for everyone. There is no electricity or phone. Bathhouses are communal. You are responsible for housekeeping and must provide your own linens. It's all about simplicity, and if that's what you seek, there's no better place to find it than here. Not everything is ascetic though—the large outdoor pool is heated by thermal spring water, other rock pools of varying temperature (clothing optional) are perfect to soak sore hiking muscles, and the surroundings are perfect. All prices include buffet-style meals of gourmet "Zen-style" cooking made with the best organic vegetables and ingredients. Call the San Francisco Zen Center at 415/431-3771 to make reservations.

5

The Wine Country & Delta

T HE WINE COUNTRY OF NAPA, SONOMA, LAKE, AND MENDOCINO counties has achieved a worldwide fame in the last 20 years for giving even the finest wine-making regions of France a run for their money. The climate and soil here are perfect for growing high-quality wine grapes, and an entire culture has been built up around it. Each weekend swarms of visitors descend to trek from tasting room to tasting room, sometimes causing traffic jams on the main roads. Though it can all seem a little too precious—too much money, too many European sports cars, and too many affected accents—the rolling hills and country roads of the wine country are ideal for world-class bicycle touring. Several bike shops offer rentals, and almost all the big bike touring companies, like Backroads, offer multiday trips through the area. The main roads can be a little hairy with all that traffic, but once on the rural side routes, bicycling here is a ride in heaven.

Another quirk of nature has turned the entire area into Spa Central. Numerous hot springs underlying area towns like Calistoga, Geyserville, and Middletown have been tapped to create a mecca for the sore-muscled or the stressed out—the perfect denouement to a hard weekend in the saddle or on the trail. Besides biking, the wine country is also blessed with great

Napa's Average Temperatures and Precipitation											
	Jan	Feb	Mar	Apr	May	June	July	Aug	Sept	Oct	Nov	Dec
High (°F)	56	61	64	69	73	79	81	81	82	76	67	58
Low (°F)	38	40	41	43	47	50	52	52	50	47	42	39
Precipitation (in.)	4.9	4.2	3.3	1.7	0.8	0.2	0.0	0.0	0.4	1.2	2.4	4.4

hiking in the several state parks here, and is home to Clear Lake, one of California's largest natural lakes.

If the wine country is southern France in California, the Sacramento River Delta, at the confluence of the San Joaquin and Sacramento rivers, is Holland. Once a huge series of tule marshes richly populated with wildlife that covered hundreds of square miles, the Delta is now a diked-off maze of sloughs, below-water-level "islands," deepwater channels, and huge farms of sunflowers, rice, and soybeans. The towns in this part of the state are usually nothing more than a gas pump and a post office. Most visitors come by boat anyway, not by land, the houseboat being the best way to travel. In this Huck Finn swamp, you can hide away in a quieter time and place, whether you've officially come to fish, houseboat, bicycle the levees, camp, or bird-watch.

Since the Delta is the largest break in the coast range, winds off the San Francisco Bay and Pacific Ocean funnel through the narrow straits and hit the western edge of the Delta full force. Rio Vista has become a popular speed boardsailing spot as a result. With flat water and howling winds, plus little other boat traffic, this could be the next Columbia Gorge.

Orientation

Sonoma Valley

The **Sonoma Valley Visitors Bureau,** 453 First St. East, Sonoma, CA 95476

(tel. 707/996-1090), is a great source of lodging and service information for the entire Sonoma Valley and surrounding region.

Napa Valley

The **Napa Chamber of Commerce,** 1556 First St., Napa, CA 94559 (tel. 707/226-7455), offers the best general service information for the Napa Valley.

Heraldsburg

The **Heraldsburg Area Chamber of Commerce,** 217 Heraldsburg Ave., Heraldsburg, CA 95448 (tel. 707/433-6935), provides good maps and other resources about the Russian River Valley and Heraldsburg proper.

Rio Vista

The **Rio Vista Chamber of Commerce,** 75 Main St., Rio Vista, CA 94571 (tel. 707/374-2700), is a great source of information about the backwaters of the Delta. It's near here at Sandy Beach County Park that some of the best boardsailing takes place on the Sacramento River.

Parks & Other Hot Spots

Annandel State Park

Channel Drive, via Mission Boulevard and Montgomery Drive, east of Santa Rosa and south of State Route 12. Tel. 707/539-3911. Picnic tables, museum, water,

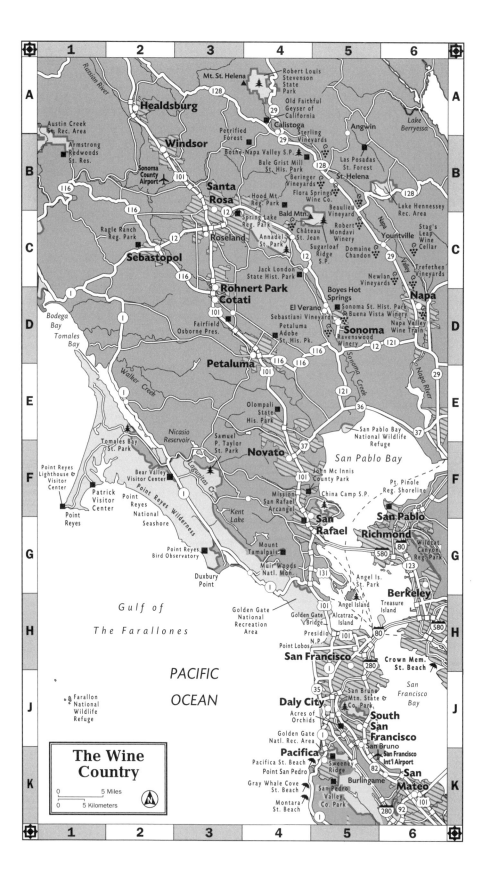

The Wine Country

pit toilets, ghost town. No dogs. Open 9am to sunset. No fee.

Just east of Santa Rosa, this 5,000-acre park is woven with an elaborate web of trails that intersect and cross so often it's easy to get lost. Luckily the park map is good. Lake Ilsanjo, a man-made 26-acre pond, is good for catching black bass and bluegill in the spring. Of particular note is the Ledson Marsh, a neat little pocket wetland that is often home to migrating waterfowl, herons, and grebes.

Sugarloaf Ridge State Park

Adobe Canyon Road, 7 miles east of Santa Rosa, north of State Route 12. Tel. 707/833-5712. 49 campsites. Picnic tables; hiking, horse, and mountain bike trails; pit toilets; flush restrooms; water. Day-use and camping fee. $12–$16.

Midway between Santa Rosa and Sonoma, Sugarloaf Ridge State Park contains almost the entire upper drainage of Sonoma Creek—lined in places by redwoods—and mile upon mile of hiking and biking trails. The high point of the park is 2,729-foot Bald Mountain, which offers an incredible view of the surrounding wine country.

Jack London State Park

Glen Ellen, about 20 minutes north of Sonoma. Tel. 707/938-5216. Picnic tables; museum; hiking, horse, and mountain bike trails; pit toilets; water. 10am to 7pm summer; 10am to 5pm winter. Fee.

Jack London may be most famous for writing about the Arctic, but he lived much of

his life here, just outside the tiny town of Glen Ellen. Besides its interesting literary history and wonderful museum of London's life, filled with memorabilia from his wide-flung travels, the park is also a great outdoors spot, with plenty of hiking and nature. Horse lovers will get a kick out of the 2-hour trail rides ($45) offered by **Sonoma Cattle Company** (tel. 707/996-8566) on the trails here.

Clear Lake State Park

Soda Bay Road, 3.5 miles northeast of Kelseyville. Tel. 707/279-4293. 147 campsites. Picnic tables, hiking trails, swimming area, restrooms, showers, water, boat launch. Camping and day-use fee.

Clear Lake is almost 20 miles long and has about 100 miles of shoreline. Spring fed and fairly shallow, the lake gets into the mid-70s during the summer—perfect for swimming and boating. It's also an important bird and fish habitat. Anglers pull largemouth bass, catfish, perch, and bluegill from the lake year-round. The 600-acre park is small, but it contains some great lake frontage. In summer the water turns a brownish-green from algae blooms, but is perfectly safe; it's a result of those same 76° waters that make the lake such an inviting swim.

Delta Meadows River Park

Most accessible by boat. Limited vehicle access is via a dirt road just north of the Cross Delta Canal, 100 yards south of Locke. Tel. 916/777-6671. Trails, pit toilets, no drinking water, primitive boat launch. Daylight hours. No fee.

Want to see what the Delta looked like before it was leveed and diked into submission? Well, this is all that's left: a small expanse of wild marshland. River otters and beavers are the most common large mammals, and the birding possibilities here are endless. You can explore the park on foot, but better yet is to poke around the wild Railroad Slough in a kayak or canoe. Bring your own—there's nothing much here in the way of services.

Brannan Island and Franks Tract State Recreation Areas

Brannan Island is on State Route 160, 3 miles south of Rio Vista. Franks Tract is only accessible by boat. Tel. 916/777-6671. 102 regular campsites, 32 boat-in sites. Boat launch and slips, picnic tables, swimming area, restrooms, showers. Camping, boat launch, and day-use fees.

These two recreation areas are perfect proof that what nature giveth, nature taketh away. Bordered by the Sacramento River, Brannan Island is one of the most popular fishing and boating centers of the Delta. It offers a swimming area, camping, and access to miles of Delta waterways. Franks Tract was not too long ago a leveed-off area of farmland and homes. Now, since the levees holding back the water collapsed, it's a lake. It is one of the most wide-open expanses of water in the whole Delta, a perfect spot for waterskiers and boaters. Franks Tract can only be reached by boat, a boat that you'll most likely want to launch at Brannan Island.

What to Do & Where to Do It

BALLOONING

Floating over the grape vines is a popular Napa pastime. Several hot-air ballooning companies are based in Napa. **Adventures Aloft,** at Vintage 1870 (tel. 707/944-4408 or 707/255-8688), is Napa's oldest hot-air balloon company, with full-time professional pilots. Groups are small, and flights last about an hour. Like all ballooneries, Adventures Aloft flies in the early morning, when the wind is gentle and the air is cool. The cost, $185 per person, includes a preflight continental breakfast, a postflight champagne brunch, and a framed First-Flight certificate.

BIRD WATCHING

Both Clear Lake and the Delta are extremely important remnants of what once was a much larger expanse of marshy **waterfowl** habitat. At either place you're likely to see lots of big waterbirds: great blue heron, Canada geese, tundra swans, snow geese, greater white-fronted geese, and the full spectrum of ducks. One of the best places to explore if you have a boat is **Delta Meadows River Park** (tel. 916/777-6671). Poke around the slough quietly and you might find some great surprises.

BOARDSAILING

Rio Vista is quickly becoming an important flat-water sailing destination for the high-wind crowd. Because the Delta offers an opening to Pacific winds otherwise stymied by the coast range, the wind rages here. It pours through the opening like water through a funnel, and Rio Vista just happens to be at the center of the funnel. **Sandy Beach County Park** (tel. 707/374-2097) offers easy water access. Call the **Rio Vista Chamber of Commerce** (tel. 707/374-2700) for recommendations and current conditions.

FISHING

The Delta is a fisherman's dream. Every migratory species headed to spawning

Touring the Wineries

California's adjacent Napa and Sonoma valleys are two of the most famous wine-growing regions in the world. The workaday valleys that are a way of life for thousands of vintners are also a worthy trip for any wine lover. Hundreds of wineries are nestled among the vines of this beautiful countryside; most are open to visitors.

Tours are generally offered daily from 10am to 5pm. The tours usually chart the process of winemaking, from the grafting and harvesting of the vines to the pressing of the grapes and the blending and aging of the wines in oak casks. They vary in length, detail, and formality, depending on the winery. Most tours are free.

Conveniently, most of the large wineries are located along a single road, State Route 29, which starts at the mouth of the Napa River, near the north end of San Francisco Bay, and continues north to Calistoga and the top of the growing region. Every Napa Valley town and winery listed here can be reached from Route 29. The Sonoma Valley towns and wineries are over the ridge, due west of Napa Valley, roughly along State Route 12.

NAPA VALLEY

The wineries listed below are organized geographically from south to north along State Route 29, beginning in the village of Napa. You can't miss them; each winery bears a large sign to ensure that you won't. In addition to those listed here, be sure to stop at some of those you pass along the way. In the mom-and-pop wineries throughout the region you can make discoveries, pick up bottles that are sold nowhere else but from the proprietor's front room, and talk with the colorful people who made the wine they're selling you with their own hands. The big, commercially oriented wineries offering tours are not to be missed,

for sure, but don't pass up the other, more personal side of the Wine Country experience either.

Domaine Chandon. Founded in 1973, Domaine Chandon, California Drive at State Route 29, Yountville (tel. 707/944-2280), produces about 500,000 cases annually of *mèthode champenoise* sparkling wines—Chandon Brut Cuvèe, Carneros Blanc de Noirs, Chandon Rèserve, and Etoile.

You can take a guided tour of this California-style champagne house. Wines are sold by the bottle or glass and are accompanied by complimentary hors d'oeuvres. There's also a gift shop and a small gallery housing artifacts from the vineyard's French parent company, Moët et Chandon, depicting the history of champagnes. The Domaine Chandon restaurant is one of the best in the valley.

Flora Springs Wine Co. While this handsome stone winery just off State Route 29 at 1978 W. Zinfandel Lane, St. Helena (tel. 707/963-5711), dates back to Napa Valley's early days, the Flora Springs label didn't appear until 1978. The label is well known for its barrel-fermented Chardonnay, a Cabernet Sauvignon, and Trilogy, a Bordeaux-style blend.

Flora Springs offers an excellent two-hour "familiarization seminar," which can be tailored to all levels of wine enthusiast. Limited to groups of ten, the course is held Monday through Thursday and Saturday at 10am and is available by advanced reservation only. The program begins in the vineyards, where you'll taste the grapes. While the grapes are being crushed, you taste the must (the just-pressed juice) and see how it ultimately becomes a beautiful, clear wine. Then you're taught how to evaluate wines: You'll blind-taste different ones and learn how wines change with age and how to distinguish between them. You'll also learn to pair wines with different foods.

Beringer Vineyards. This remarkable Rhine House, with its hand-dug tunnels carved out of the mountainside, is the site of the original Beringer winery. Beringer Vineyards, 2000 Main St., St. Helena (tel. 707/963-7115), was founded in 1876 by brothers Jacob and Frederick; the family owned it until 1971, when it was purchased by the Swiss firm of Nestlè, Inc. It's the oldest continuously operating winery in the Napa Valley. ("What about Prohibition?" you might ask; Beringer made "sacramental" wines during the dry years.)

The modern working winery on the opposite side of the road is not open to the public. Tasting of current vintages is conducted during sales hours in the Rhine House; reserve wines are available in the Founders' Room (upstairs in the Rhine House). A modest fee is charged per taste. Tours are conducted by very knowledgeable guides.

SONOMA VALLEY

Sonoma is often thought of as the other valley, second to Napa, but it really isn't. In fact, even though there are far fewer wineries here, its wines have won more awards than Napa's. What makes a trip to Sonoma so pleasant is the intimate quality of so many of its vineyards; most of the wineries here are still family owned. California's first winery, Buena Vista, was founded in the Sonoma Valley in 1857; it's still in operation (see below). Today, Sonoma is home to about 35 wineries and 13,000 acres of vineyards. Chardonnay is the variety for which Sonoma is most noted; it represents almost one-quarter of the valley's acreage in vines.

The wineries here tend to be a little more spread out than they are in Napa, but they're still easy to find. The visitors bureaus listed above will provide you with maps to the valley's wineries.

Buena Vista Winery. The patriarch of California wineries is located slightly northeast of the town of Sonoma at 18000 Old Winery Rd. (tel. 707/938-1266). It was founded in 1857 by Count Agoston Haraszthy, the Hungarian émigré considered the father of the California wine industry. Haraszthy returned from Europe in 1861 with 100,000 of the continent's finest vine cuttings, which he made available to anybody who wanted them. Although Buena Vista's winemaking now takes place in an ultramodern facility outside Sonoma, the winery still maintains a tasting room inside the restored 1862 Press House.

Château St. Jean. This winery, founded in 1973, is at the foot of Sugarloaf Ridge, at 8555 Sonoma Hwy. (tel. 707/833-4134), just north of Kenwood and east of State Route 12. A private drive takes you to what was once a 250-acre country retreat, built in 1920. Château St. Jean is notable for its exceptionally beautiful buildings, well-landscaped grounds, and elegant tasting room. A well-manicured lawn is now a picnic area, complete with a fountain and benches.

There's a self-guided tour with detailed and photographic descriptions of the winemaking process. When you're done with it, be sure to walk up to the top of the tower for a view of the valley. Back in the tasting room, Château St. Jean offers several Chardonnays, a Cabernet Sauvignon, a Fumè Blanc, a Merlot, a Riesling, and a Gerwürtztraminer. Since 1984, the winery has been part of the Suntory family of premium wineries.

The toll-free, interactive Château St. Jean "wine line" (tel. 800/332-WINE) offers free recorded reports on the Sonoma Wine Country, including updated information on vineyard conditions, interviews with winemakers and growers, what's happening at the winery, and descriptions of currently available wines.

grounds upriver must pass through here, and the rich waters support numerous year-round residents too. Striped bass run in the spring and summer. Salmon run in the summer and fall. Catfish, largemouth bass, and sturgeon are caught year-round. To fish the Delta you really should have a boat. If you don't have one, there's no shortage of guides willing to take you out for a price. Look in the yellow pages under "fishing guides" or ask the local chamber of commerce to recommend someone.

HIKING

Warren Richardson Trail, Annadel State Park

7.5 miles. Moderate. Access: Trail begins at east end of parking lot at end of Channel Road east of Santa Rosa. Map: Annadel trail map.

It's actually hard to follow an exact route anywhere in this park because trails criss-cross so much and aren't always clearly marked. The basic idea is to follow the Warren Richardson Trail to Lake Ilsanjo, walk around the lake, and take Steve's Trail to Ledson Marsh. From there, follow the Quarry Trail back to your car. Along the way you're likely to see deer, plenty of interesting birds, and a wonderful landscape of rolling grasslands and oak woodland. Keep your eyes peeled for chips of obsidian. Native Americans used this site as a quarry for the valuable black-glass stone from which they fashioned many tools and weapons.

Bald Mountain Loop, Sugarloaf Ridge State Park

7 miles. Moderate to strenuous. Access: Main park day-use area on Adobe Canyon Road. Map: Sugarloaf Ridge State Park map.

Though the chief reason for doing this hike is the splendid view from the top of Bald Mountain, the process of getting there is worthwhile in itself. Parts of the hike follow fire roads, but other times you'll find yourself walking on beautifully shaded single track through huge and healthy chaparral interspersed with even healthier oak, laurel, and madrone forests. Watch for deer—there's no shortage of them here.

MOUNTAIN BIKING

Bald Mountain Loop, Sugarloaf Ridge State Park

7 miles. Moderate. Steep. Access: Main day-use area on Adobe Canyon Road. Map: Sugarloaf Ridge State Park map.

This one almost didn't cut the mustard simply because it contains a long stretch of paved service road, but since that road is so steep, I thought I'd throw it in. The strong will be reaching for their granny gear, and the weak . . . well, the weak shouldn't try it. Once you wheeze your way up the 1,500-foot climb to the summit of Bald Mountain on the paved road, you'll want to take in the view for a few minutes. Then pull out that handy map you bought back at the visitors center to decide which trail is the Gray Pine Trail (it's the one to the right, but don't trust me). Go that way and enjoy the downhill—about 30 minutes to an hour's worth of perfect curvy trail depending on how fast you ride. The Park Service would like you to ride 15 mph tops, but that's pretty hard to do on a downhill like this. Just be careful not to run over any hikers or scare any horses. A horse had to be killed here after it broke its leg when a group of mountain bikers scared it off the trail. Other than that, though, there haven't been any major trail-use conflicts here, and it would be nice to keep it that way.

ROAD BIKING

The back roads of the Sonoma and Napa valleys are just too good to pass up on a road bike. It just seems like the roads are never too hilly and never too flat. The temperature in spring and fall is perfect for cycling without overheating. Outside of the main highways, cars are actually kind of rare around here. The scenery just keeps rolling along; vineyards, beautiful houses, wild hillsides. It's great. Then to top it off, you've got a full selection of hot springs, spas, and mud baths in which to drown your sorrows after climbing a few too many of those seemingly easy hills. It doesn't get any better than this. The hill country around **Harbin Hot Springs** is a favorite with a lot of people for its secluded roads. (I hear there's a big nudist scene here—a clothing-optional resort complete with clothing-optional hiking trails, and so on; just thought you might want to know.) Others like the **Angwin** and **Saint Helena** area.

One of the most popular ways to explore the wine country is with local bicycle guides. Some of these outfitters combine wine tasting with their rides. Others are more seriously aimed at covering some distance and really exploring the wine country roads. Ask very specific questions about exactly what the goal of each tour is; some are aimed at novices who haven't been on a bike in years; others target the strong road tourer. Whichever you are, you don't want to find yourself riding with the other. The following is a list of area outfitters offering wine country tours: **Getaway Bicycle Tours,** Calistoga (tel. 800/ 499-2453), **Good Time Bicycle Co.,** Sonoma (tel. 707/938-0453), and **Napa Valley Bike Tours,** Napa (tel. 707/ 255-3377). **Backroads** (tel. 800/245-3874) in Berkeley runs multi-day supported tours of the wine country.

Easy Napa Valley Loop

12 miles. Easy. Starting point: Corner of State Route 29 and Pope Street in Saint Helena. Map: Napa Valley road map.

Park in or near the high school and head east on Pope Street. Very shortly (less than a mile) you'll cross the Napa River on a beautiful stone bridge and hit Silverado Trail. Turn south. From here you'll enjoy a smooth, gently hilly ride through the heart of the Napa Valley. Vineyards line much of the route, and on weekends you won't be alone; you'll probably see balloons flying overhead and other bicyclists. After about 7 miles you'll reach Oakville Cross Road. Here you have two major options. You can turn right, where you'll soon hook up with the main valley thoroughfare, State Route 29, and return north, passing through a 3-mile stretch with four wineries before arriving back at your car. Or, if busy road traffic makes you as insane as it makes me, turn around and return the way you came.

Best of Napa Loop

54 miles. Moderate. Starting point: Corner of State Route 29 and Pope Street in Saint Helena. Map: Napa Valley road map.

From the starting point you have to make a choice: Do I want to ride on busy State Route 29 and visit Bale Grist Mill and Bothe–Napa State Park, both interesting historic and natural landmarks between here and Calistoga, or do I want to avoid the busiest part of Route 29 and ride straight into the country in peace? If the former, go north on State Route 29. If the latter, go east on Pope Street until you reach Silverado Trail, then head north (left). Eventually the two routes hook up again in Calistoga, and you will continue the ride on Route 29. This ride will take you through some of the Napa Valley, but after Calistoga it immediately begins climbing. Here you'll find nice views of Sugarloaf Ridge and of the valley below. About 15 miles into the ride you will reach the high point of the climb, about 2,500 feet—the ride begins at about 250 feet. (If you're on a mountain bike or a sturdy touring bike, the unpaved road to the summit of 4,344-foot Mount Saint Helena offers an interesting side-trip challenge.) From here you'll descend and reach the small country town of Middletown, where you'll turn right on Butts Canyon Road. If you're going to need food or drinks on this ride, this is the place to buy them—it's a long way to anything else.

After about 10 miles on Butts Canyon the road name changes to Pope Valley, but everything else stays the same—mile after mile of beautiful rolling hill country. Watch on your left for Hubcap Ranch, the brainchild of Litto Diamonte. He collected hubcaps throughout his life, covering every inch of the house and barn and lining the fences. He died in 1983, but the ranch has been declared a State Historic Landmark and will live on as his legacy. Soon, you'll reach tiny Pope Valley; turn right on Howell Mountain Road, climb one last steep 2-mile ascent, and then it's all downhill until Saint Helena and your car.

Campgrounds & Other Accommodations

CAMPING

Brannan Island State Recreation Area

3 miles southeast of Rio Vista on Highway 160. Tel. 916/777-6671 or 916/777-7701.

102 car sites, 36 boat sites. Flush toilets, showers, boat ramp, picnic tables. $12–$15 per site. Call PARKNET (800/444-PARK) for reservations.

For waterskiing or fishing in the Delta this is the place to stay. It's nothing special as far as scenery goes, but the water access for swimming and boating is unbeatable—it's the biggest campground for year-round boating access in the heart of the Delta.

Sugarloaf Ridge State Park

Midway between Santa Rosa and Sonoma at the end of Adobe Canyon Road off State Route 12. Tel. 707/833-5712 or 707/938-1519. 49 sites. Flush toilets, running water, picnic tables. Dogs okay.

Whether you come here for the hiking and mountain biking within the park, or plan to use it as a base for exploring the surrounding region, this park is a gem. It's hands down the best camping near the wine country. Great scenery and plentiful nature.

INNS, RESORTS & SPAS

Tall Timbers Chalets

1012 Darms Lane, Napa, CA 94558. From State Route 29 North, turn left onto Darms Lane before Yountville. Tel. 707/252-7810. 8 cottages. Year-round Sun–Thurs $116.55 double, Fri–Sat and holidays $166.50 double. Extra person $20. AE, MC, V.

This group of eight whitewashed, roomy cottages surrounded by pines and eucalyptus is one of the best bargains in

Napa Valley. All the cottages are nicely decorated and well furnished; amenities include refrigerators, toaster ovens, and coffeemakers. It's really pleasant to find, on your arrival, a basket of fresh fruit in the breakfast nook, breakfast treats in the refrigerator, and a complimentary bottle of champagne. There are no phones in the cottages, but you'll have access to one in the main office. Each unit can sleep four (there's a bedroom plus a queen sofa bed in the living room); several have decks. No smoking is allowed in the cottages.

Vintage Inn

6541 Washington St. (between Humbolt St. and Webber Ave.), Yountville, CA 94599. From State Route 29 North, exit at Yountville and turn left onto Washington Street. Tel. 707/944-1112 or 800/351-1133. Fax 707/944-1617. 72 rooms, 8 minisuites. $150–$275 double; $225–$325 mini-suites. Extra person $25. Rates include continental breakfast. AE, CB, DC, MC, V.

Built on an old 23-acre winery estate in the center of town, this inn is a contemporary accommodation, although the land once belonged to pioneer George C. Yount, who received it as a Spanish land grant. Famed designer Kipp Stewart, who also designed the sybaritic Ventana Inn at Big Sur, was responsible for creating this hideaway, which boasts four villas. Rooms are well equipped, with fireplaces, ceiling fans, oversize beds, coffeemakers, refrigerators, plush bathrobes, tubs with Jacuzzi jets, and a complimentary bottle of wine. A California-continental champagne breakfast (cereals, yogurt, pastries, egg salad, and fruit) is served in the Vintage Club, as is afternoon tea, and there is a 60-foot, year-round heated swimming pool, an outdoor heated whirlpool, two tennis courts, and bikes for rent. Ballooning can also be arranged.

Meadowood Resort

900 Meadowood Lane, St. Helena, CA 94574. Tel. 707/963-3646 or 800/458-8080. Fax 707/963-3532. 99 rooms, 8 suites. April 30–Nov 21 $395–$880 double; from $550 suite. About $20 less off-season. AE, DC, MC, V.

This exquisite resort, on 250 wooded and hilly acres, resembles a New England resort on the sea. The private, quiet accommodations are scattered around the property in four-unit clusters, close to either the golf course or the tennis and pool facilities. Some 13 rooms are located in the handsome English-style croquet lodge overlooking the perfectly manicured croquet lawn. All rooms have private porches, fine furnishings, a coffeemaker, and a toaster; most have fireplaces. Guests have use of the nine-hole golf course, seven tennis courts, croquet, bicycles, hiking trails, pool and whirlpool, and health spa offering massages, facials, and body treatments.

Dr. Wilkinson's Hot Springs

1507 Lincoln Ave. (State Route 29, between Fairway and Stevenson aves.), Calistoga, CA 94515. Tel. 707/942-4102. 42 rooms. Winter $89–$139 double; summer $109–$149 double. Weekly discounts and packages available. AE, MC, V.

This spa/resort was originally established by "Doc" Wilkinson, who arrived in Napa Valley just after World War II. Today, it's a typical motel, distinguished by the mud and mineral baths on the premises. Rooms range from Victorian-style units to rather basic and functional motel-like rooms, similar to Janet Leigh's room in *Psycho*. All rooms have drip coffeemakers and refrigerators; some have kitchens. Facilities include three swimming pools (two outdoor and one indoor). Facials and all kinds of body treatments are available in the salon.

Soil Yourself: Take a Calistoga Mud Bath

One thing you should do while you're in the wine country is head for the mud. In Calistoga people have been doing it for the last 150 years. The natural mud baths are composed of local volcanic ash, imported peat, and naturally boiling mineral-hot-springs water, all mulled together to produce a thick mud that simmers at a temperature of about 104°F.

Once you overcome the hurdle of deciding how best to place your naked body into the mushy stone tub, the rest is pure relaxation—you soak with surprising buoyancy for about 10 to 12 minutes. A warm mineral-water shower, a mineral-water whirlpool bath, and a mineral-water steam room visit follow. Afterward, a relaxing blanket-wrap will cool down your delighted body slowly. All of this takes about 1½ hours and costs about $45;

with a massage, add another half-hour and $20. The outcome is a rejuvenated, revitalized, squeaky-clean you. Mud baths aren't recommended for those who are pregnant or have high blood pressure.

The spas also offer a variety of other treatments, such as hand and foot massages, herbal wraps, acupressure face-lifts, skin rubs, and herbal facials. Prices range from $35 to $125, and appointments are necessary for all services; call at least a week in advance.

Indulge yourself at any of these Calistoga spas: **Dr. Wilkinson's Hot Springs,** 1507 Lincoln Ave. (tel. 707/942-4102); **Lincoln Avenue Spa,** 1339 Lincoln Ave. (tel. 707/942-5296); **Golden Haven Hot Springs Spa,** 1713 Lake St. (tel. 707/942-6793); and **Calistoga Spa Hot Springs,** 1006 Washington St. (tel. 707/942-6269).

Beltane Ranch

1775 Sonoma Hwy., Glen Ellen, CA 95442. Tel. 707/996-6501. 6 rooms. $130–$210 double. No credit cards.

This 1892 double-porched bunkhouse is off the main road, on the slopes of the Mayacamas, surrounded by 1,600 acres. It's part of local legend, having once been owned by "Mammy" Pleasant, a former slave and abolitionist who, among other professions, was a madam and the mistress of English millionaire Thomas Bell. Mammy was suspected of his murder but was never convicted.

Since the 1930s, the Heins family used the ranch to raise turkeys, but when Rosemary Wood inherited it in 1981, she turned it into a B&B. The gardens are filled with irises and roses; a terrace surrounding the house looks out over the flowers and the fields beyond. Guests can

use the comfortable parlor with the brick fireplace and woodstove. Rooms are comfortably furnished in a homey style and with the occasional family antique. Facilities include hiking trails and a tennis court.

HOUSEBOATS

There's no better way to satisfy that Huckleberry Finn fantasy you've had all these years than to spend a week or a weekend drifting the backwaters of the Delta in a houseboat. These stable, spacious, slow-moving pontoon boats make the perfect platform for exploring the more than 70 islands and hundreds of sloughs, channels, and rivers that make up the Delta. Rates vary widely with season and size of boat. **Paradise Point Marina,** 8095 Rio Blanco Rd., Stockton, CA 95219 (tel. 209/952-1000), rents houseboats by the week as well as fishing boats and ski boats.

6

The Sierra Nevada

O EUROPEANS AND EARLY AMERICAN SETTLERS, THE NEW WORLD meant limitless expansion. They pushed west for two centuries, from the first explorations of Davy Crockett, Jim Bridger, and Lewis and Clark all the way through the Gold Rush, taking pelts, mining gold—in short, ripping through the land in search of resources to exploit. America seemed an inexhaustible resource. Kill a hundred buffalo and there were a thousand more over the next hill. Plant a thousand acres and there were a million more across the river. When the California Gold Rush of 1849 brought thousands west, America's frontier mentality crashed like a wave against the shores of the Pacific. San Francisco overtook Monterey as the most important city in California, and the huge profits of the Mother Lode drove the quick development of the state. Suddenly, there was no more "west" to head to.

To early pioneers, the Sierra Nevada was simply the last of many obstacles to overcome before reaching the shining Pacific and the gold fields of the west. But as in any final line of defense, the continent threw up every last weapon at its disposal. The Sierra was raw, untamed nature—wild and rugged and not easily bested—a lesson learned by many early settlers. The tale of the Donner party—who had to resort to cannibalism to survive a winter that came early and trapped them in the high country north of Lake Tahoe—is merely one of many.

The realization that the frontier was dead dawned slowly at first, but when it did it was here, in the peaks and valleys of the Sierra Nevada. When John Muir arrived by boat in San Francisco in the spring of 1868 he asked a passerby to point him to "any place that is wild." The answer led him across the great Central Valley and into the Sierra Nevada, where Muir found the raw nature he was looking for, and found it in danger of being eroded away by the trample of civilization. Even before reaching the range, Muir was awestruck. Looking up from Pacheco Pass in the coast range, said Muir, "it seemed to me the Sierra should be called not the Nevada, or snowy range, but the Range of Light." His experiences in the Sierra Nevada became the central focus of his writings and philosophy, which bore the seeds of the modern conservation movement.

Muir lived for years in the Yosemite Valley—which he was instrumental in having declared a national park—and traipsed the whole range, often traveling with just the clothes on his back. For Muir, the Sierra embodied light not only in the literal sense, but in the metaphysical as well. "Everything in it seems equally divine—one smooth, pure, wild glow of Heaven's love." In these mountains, Muir waxed, "you bathe in these spirit beams, turning round and round as if warming in a campfire. Presently you lose consciousness of your individual nature: You blend with the landscape and become part and parcel of nature."

Obviously, Muir fell in love with these mountains, and like any good lover he fought tirelessly to protect them. In 1892 he and 27 other men formed the Sierra Club both to promote the enjoyment of the wild and, in what was a landmark declaration for the time, "to enlist the support of the people and the government in preserving the forests and other features of the Sierra Nevada Mountains."

Every year thousands come to the Sierra Nevada with perhaps less lofty but equally enticing goals, hoping to find a place where they too can seek a little quiet repose from their hurried existence in the cities below. They find one of the world's best expanses of wilderness. Three national parks cover 1.6 million acres. Eight national forests contain another 8 million acres. In all, the publicly owned portion of the Sierra is larger than most eastern states.

That is a lot of land, but the Sierra is sometimes in danger of being loved to death. Yosemite National Park gets more than 3 million visitors a year, most to the Yosemite Valley. Sequoia and Kings Canyon National Parks is visited by another 2 million. Lake Tahoe was once a pristine wilderness. Now home to casinos, condos, and a higher concentration of ski resorts than anywhere in the nation, it staggers under more than 12 million visitors a year. Still, for every Yosemite and Lake Tahoe, there are a hundred backcountry lakes and isolated national forest campgrounds with hardly any visitors.

The Lay of the Land

Nearly 450 miles from north to south and between 60 and 80 miles wide, the Sierra is carved from a huge mass of granite. If you picture the range as a single building block beginning just below Mount Lassen and ending just below Mount Whitney, the block is tilted west, and slanted so it is almost twice as tall in the south as it is in the north. The High Sierra is the area from just north of Yosemite to the south end of the range characterized by high granite domes and peaks, alpine lakes, and little tree cover. Most of this stretch is relatively unsullied wilderness.

One hundred million years ago under an ancient sea, molten granite from the earth's mantle spewed forth and was released under a seabed of sedimentary and volcanic rock. Never to reach the surface, the molten granite cooled in the gigantic dome shapes that characterize the Sierra. From about 70 million years ago until 12 million years ago the range was uplifted by geological forces. Massive erosion of the soft sedimentary deposits exposed the huge granite batholiths. It was only in the last million years that the glacial scouring of three separate ice ages put the finishing polishes on the Sierra as we know it today.

Because of its westward tilt, the west slope of the Sierra is a gentle wedge: Grassy foothills become pine-forested mountains and finally reveal themselves as the granite-spired high peaks. Large rivers drain through numerous canyons and glacial valleys. The eastern flank demonstrates no such subtlety. Viewed from the east, a huge escarpment of strikingly sheer peaks simply shoots straight out of the sagebrush desert. No rolling foothills, no messing around, it's one of the most striking mountain walls anywhere in North America.

The Sierra is still growing. As rivers and glaciers continue to gnaw away at the western slope, the range grows from the east. A 400-mile-long fault zone along the eastern base of the Sierra is the location of some of the most active geology in California. In the last 2,000 years more than 30 major eruptions have draped a necklace of cinder cones and lava flows across the land. Geological activity is a daily fact here, not just something discussed in textbooks. And though there are obvious dangers to living in a land of earthquakes and volcanic eruptions, there are also benefits, like the hot water that gushes from the ground all over the eastern slope. There are more hot springs here than in any other part of California, some commercial but most of them free and scarcely used. Most popular is Hot Creek, near the Mammoth Lakes Airport, where boiling thermal water mixes with 40° snowmelt for perfect bathing, but there are literally hundreds more waiting to be discovered (see "Hot Springs" in "Eastern Sierra ◆ What to Do & Where to Do It" later in this chapter).

The precipitous nature of this eastern massif testifies to the continuing heartbeat of the Sierra Nevada. Some 700,000 years ago, say geologists, Long Valley just south of Mammoth Lakes was the site of an eruption so massive that one part of the flow actually crested the eastern slope and flowed down the west slope as far as the great Central Valley at speeds pushing 100 mph. The loss of that much landmass caused the caldera to collapse in the wake of the great eruption, forming 20-mile by 15-mile Long Valley.

Residents of the few towns on the east side of the range have learned to take frequent earthquakes in stride. Generally the uplift is measured in fractions of an inch per year, but a single quake in 1872 produced a 17-foot vertical shift in mountains near the Owens Valley. The resort town of Mammoth Lakes and surrounding Long Valley are built on the still-active remains of that ancient volcanic caldera, as the steam vents on top of Mammoth Mountain and hot springs in the valley illustrate. In the wake of fears raised by the Mount Saint Helens eruption the area was ranked by the U.S. Geologic Survey as the most likely place in the continental United States to experience the next volcanic eruption. When the feds went so far as to release a notice saying that the town and ski moutain at Mammoth are sitting on a powder keg of potential volcanism, the powers that be nearly blew a gasket, worried that tourism and the real estate market would suffer. Of course the U.S. Geologic Survey was speaking in geologic terms and had never meant that an eruption was imminent, simply that the odds of one happening here in the next, say, 1,000 years were much greater than an eruption happening at Mount Hood, Oregon, or Amarillo, Texas, for that matter. The warning was downgraded to appease local land speculators and chamber of commerce types, but the fact remains the same: Mammoth could blow tomorrow or it could blow in 5,000 years. The mountain sleeps, but it's not dead.

Several bands of plant species climb the mountain flank. Though distibution of plant communities varies widely following local geography, by taking rainfall, soil type, latitude, and slope orientation into consideration, some generalizations can be made.

The lower slopes from about 1,000 to 5,000 feet are covered with thick chaparral alternating with drought-resistant pine and oak species, not to mention huge patches of poison oak and blackberry vines.

Above that is what's known as the transition zone, a broad band of evergreen and deciduous forest containing the majority of timber. Douglas and white firs, incense cedar, and sugar pine are the common evergreens, while cottonwood, maple, and oak are the most common broadleaf species. Also occurring in the transition zone are the Sierra's unique groves of *Sequoiadendron giganteum*, the giant sequoia. These enormous trees are living fossils, a species that evolved 150 million years ago,

before the Sierra even existed. Some of the largest living specimens are 30 feet thick and nearly 300 feet tall. The oldest is roughly 3,200 years old. Unlike the coastal redwoods, which are good for lumber, the giant sequoias splintered when felled and the remains were good only for shingles, fenceposts, and other small items. As a result, they were less heavily logged and substantial groves remain in Yosemite, Kings Canyon, and Sequoia national parks and Calaveras Big Trees State Park.

Nearing timberline, one passes through the lower boreal belt: lodgepole, Jeffrey and silver pines, red fir, Sierra juniper, and aspen. "Above timberline" is somewhat of a misnomer; there are still trees here in what is more properly called the subalpine belt. Buried under snow most of the year and subject to cruel winters, this high-altitude region is nonetheless home to hardy and isolated populations of several pine species pushing the outer limits of their survival capacity. A head-high tree here might be as old as one that soars 100 feet in the much lower altitude of the transition zone.

Though much of the Sierra has been preserved, in many ways it is not as wild as the Sierra that Muir wandered. That bear you see on the California state flag is a grizzly, once common in these mountains but now extirpated from the whole state. Wolves too were driven out. Apparently if you're a predator big enough to eat people, you aren't welcome in California.

Black bears, though, are still common, and often get into trouble when careless tourists forget to hang or lock away their food. Other predators include mountain lions, coyotes, bobcats, ringtails, foxes, raccoons, and several species of skunks. Present, but extremely rare, is the territorial and foul-tempered wolverine. Known for its ill disposition, maliciousness, and almost legendary feats of strength and cunning, the wolverine sounds almost too good to be true.

A large population of grazers summer in the range. Mule deer are common in high-country meadows and move to the foothills before the snow settles in. Sierra bighorn sheep, nearly extinct by the 1970s, have staged a comeback since the creation of special reserves and a relocation effort. They can be seen in the jagged peaks east of Tioga Pass and at other more remote sites in the High Sierra.

The endangered spotted owl, which gained national fame for its role as the canary in a coal mine to the old-growth forest in the 1980s, is still here. Legal skirmishes over saving the bird and its habitat halted much of the clear-cutting that was taking place. Pygmy owls, gray owls, red-tailed hawks, and peregrine falcons are also to be found in the Sierra. Other birds like the three-toed woodpecker and clark's nutcracker make their home near timberline, and the whole Sierra is full of crested jays, finches, and warblers.

Ecologically the eastern Sierra is one of the great transition zones between the rugged high-country peaks and the flat sagebrush plains of the Great Basin Desert. As a result there is an incredible diversity of life here. Rivers and creeks draining this side of the range hold endangered cutthroat trout and a few of the high lakes hold golden trout, the strikingly beautiful state fish.

The plains of the desert below are filled with a whole different menagerie of wild and feral animals. Mono Lake, of course, is a whole bizarre world of bird islands, brine shrimp, and buzzing insects, but the rest of the plain is remarkable too. Perhaps because there are so few people it seems like there are more animals, or maybe it is just the lack of cover that makes them so easy to spot.

Near the former Owens Lake on U.S. 395 it is common to see herds of elk grazing near the road. Pronghorn antelope, the fastest mammal in North America, are also regularly spotted racing across the plain. You also might see one of the large groups of wild burros, descendants of mining camp escapees, who forage in the lava fields between Big Pine and Bishop.

The Bureau of Land Management has rounded up many of the burros in an effort to preserve important forage for the elk and other native animals, but the little jackass and its cousin the mule are such an ingrained part of the culture here that every Memorial Day weekend more than 40,000 people venture to Bishop for Mule Days, a 3-day bacchanal of mulish antics like mule lookalike contests, mule races, and much showing off of everyone's mules and burros, not to mention good music, food, and company. I've never done Mule Days myself, but a friend of mine swears by it.

Orientation

The first highway to cross the Sierra Nevada was the Lincoln Highway, promoted by early car manufacturers as the first transcontinental highway. It was mostly a rutted and dangerous collection of old wagon tracks and cow paths that would scarcely be called a road these days. The Lincoln Highway is gone now, buried under the roadbed of modern six-lane Interstate 80, the largest road over the Sierra, but plenty of other passes still appeal to a sense of adventure.

First to cross the range in the north, where the mountains are barely 5,000 feet high, is State Route 36. Farther

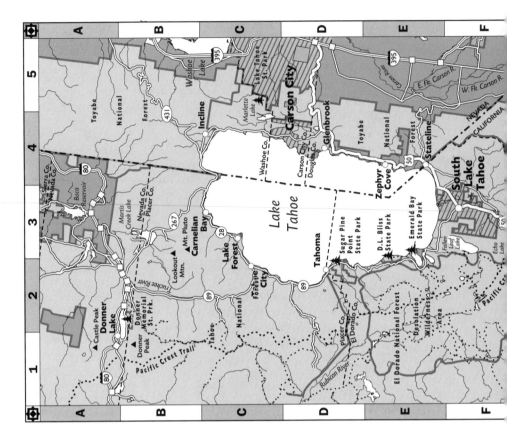

south, Beckwourt Pass on State Route 70 and Yuba Pass on State Route 49 begin to climb higher. Near Tahoe the Sierra begins to grow to a respectable size and Donner Summit on Interstate 80, Echo Summit on U.S. 50, Luther Pass on State Route 89, and Carson Pass on State Route 88 are all high and dramatic roads. Then things get really interesting: The passes from State Route 88 all the way south to State Route 178 are summertime only, and in a bad year some don't open until mid-July when the last snow is cleared from the high country. State Route 4, Ebbetts Pass, briefly leaves the timberline between Bear Valley and Markleeville, and offers astounding views of the Nevada desert. Next is Sonora Pass, State Route 108. This winding, less-than-two-lane road climbs through some of the most dramatic Sierra peaks accessible by driving. Since it's so twisted and steep, you'll find

none of the commercial traffic that plagues the northern passes. (Leave the RV at home.) Tioga Pass, State Route 120, connects the western part of Yosemite with Mono Lake and Lee Vining, traveling through high granite country and beautiful alpine meadows. In the summer of 1995, after a winter of huge snowfall, Tioga Pass did not open until nearly August. South of here, the mountains are too high and wild for year-round roads. For the 160 miles between Tioga Pass near Mono Lake and Sherman Pass (State Route 190), the Sierra is uncrossed by a single road.

The impassable wall the Sierra presents to the rest of Northern California—especially in winter—is the reason the eastern Sierra is more popular with Southern Californians than with denizens of the north. It's easy to drive up through the Mojave Desert on any given winter day. Crossing the High Sierra

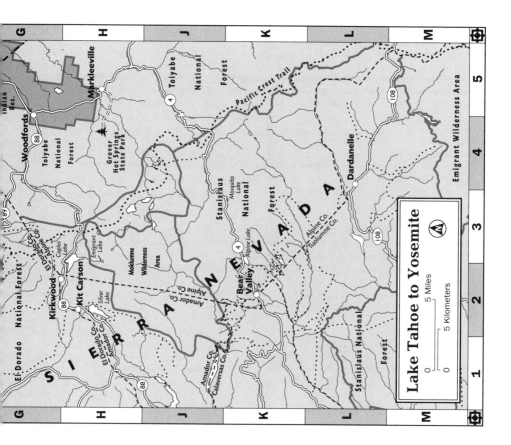

passes near Tahoe during a winter storm is a different story altogether. This lack of roads in the southern Sierra, and particularly the eastern side of the southern Sierra, creates one of the greatest wilderness opportunities in the state. Within easy striking distance of U.S. 395 are literally hundreds of hikes and backpacking trips. In the course of its run down the eastern Sierra the road passes Yosemite National Park, Mono Lake, Devils Postpile National Monument, several national wilderness areas including the John Muir and the Carson-Iceberg, two major downhill ski resorts and one major cross-country ski resort, creeks, hot springs, and lakes, and then culminates in the dramatic shadow of the Whitney Massif, the highest cluster of peaks in the Lower 48.

Running north to south, State Route 49 on the west side and U.S. 395 on the east parallel the Sierra about 80 to 100

miles apart. U.S. 395 is *the* road on the eastern side of the Sierra; it runs through varied terrain, from the desert plains of the Owens Valley to the forested summit of 7,519-foot Devil's Gate before crossing into Nevada.

Several major trails weave through the Sierra. Most famous is the Pacific Crest Trail that runs north-south through the entire range. The John Muir Trail from Yosemite to Sequoia National Park traverses almost 200 miles of High Sierra wilderness without crossing a single road. In winter, the Tioga Pass and the Sierra Haute Route through Sequoia and Kings Canyon are popular ski touring crossings.

For the sake of manageability, I've divided the Sierra Nevada into three subchapters: the northern Sierra, which includes everything north of Yosemite; the southern Sierra, which includes Yosemite National Park to Sequoia and

South Lake Tahoe's Average Temperatures and Precipitation												
	Jan	Feb	Mar	Apr	May	June	July	Aug	Sept	Oct	Nov	Dec
High (°F)	37	39	43	50	59	69	79	78	70	58	47	40
Low (°F)	17	18	22	26	32	37	43	42	38	31	25	20
Precipitation (in.)	6.1	5.4	3.9	2.2	1.2	0.6	0.3	0.2	0.5	1.6	3.1	5.4

Kings Canyon National Parks; and the eastern Sierra, which includes everything accessible from U.S. 395 on the east side. Since even then it is a long way from, say, Pinecrest Lake on State Route 108 to Bear Valley on State Route 4, activities will be clearly marked by the pass on which they occur.

NORTHERN SIERRA: LAKE TAHOE TO YOSEMITE

Lake Tahoe

One of the most positive signs that humankind isn't hell-bent on condo-izing every square inch of the great outdoors is the Lake Tahoe master plan, a 20-year development code. Even in the worst that Tahoe has to offer, South Lake Tahoe, the glitter gulch of the Sierra Nevada, city planners have launched an ambitious plan to return their town to a more natural state. It seems they've realized there's more money to be had from nature lovers than from Las Vegas cast-offs. Parks are being opened where motels used to stand, new buildings are designed in a more Alpine motif, and, amazingly, for every new hotel room being built, 1.31 old rooms are being torn town. At that rate South Lake should look like a mountain town in, say, 100 years. But at least they're headed in the right direction. For North Lake information, contact the **Tahoe North Visitors and Convention Bureau,** P.O. Box 5578, Tahoe City, CA 96145 (tel. 800/TAHOE-4-U). For South Lake information, contact the **Lake Tahoe Visitors Authority,** P.O. Box 16299, South Lake Tahoe, CA 96151 (tel. 800/AT-TAHOE).

Interstate 80

This six-lane monster road running just to the north of Lake Tahoe is the major commercial route over the Sierra, the last to close during winter storms and the first to reopen. Several ski areas line Donner Summit, and the headwaters of the American River, fall just to your south. Just past Truckee, Interstate 80 turns north and runs downhill to Reno.

Truckee

Once a wicked little Wild West outpost of bordellos and gin mills, Truckee has mellowed somewhat but is still the most, shall we say, gritty and real town in the Tahoe Basin. It was near here that the Donner party was forced to resort to cannibalism to survive the winter of 1846–47 when early snows trapped them. These days the reverse is nearly true: If it hasn't snowed by Christmas the streets of Truckee are crawling with jobless ski bums looking like they just might stick a fork into you. But the snow always comes, even in the worst years. Once it does, North Shore resorts like Squaw Valley, Alpine Meadows, Northstar, and Sugar Bowl start hiring, and you can walk the streets of Truckee without fear of winding up in somebody's stew. For the purpose of most visitors, Truckee is where you'll come to find that flashlight you forgot or to get pizza when your camp stove dies. For information contact the **Truckee-Donner Chamber of Commerce,** P.O. Box 2757, Truckee, CA 96160 (tel. 530/587-2757 or 800/548-8388).

Fanny Bridge, Tahoe City

To see the biggest trout you're ever likely to encounter, come to Fanny Bridge over the Truckee River in Tahoe City. Bend way over and look at those lunkers lurking under the bridge. (Sorry, no fishing.) Then back up a few steps, look at all the other people bending over to see those huge trout, and try to guess where the bridge gets its name.

U.S. 50

Much more modest than its brother Interstate 80 to the north, U.S. 50 provides the best direct access to the south shore of Tahoe. It's a curvy and scenic two-lane road that miraculously stays open in the winter nearly as much as Interstate 80 and seems much safer because it lacks the heavy commercial traffic of the interstate. Between Tahoe and Sacramento, U.S. 50 runs past Echo Lake with good access points into the back side of the Desolation Wilderness.

State Route 89

Running south along the west shore of Tahoe from Truckee to South Lake, State Route 89 continues south to Pickett's Junction and Sorenson's Resort, Markleeville, and finally runs into U.S. 395 along the east side of the Sierra north of Mono Lake.

State Route 88

Between the old gold mining center of Jackson and its intersection with State Route 89 at Pickett's Junction, State

Route 88 runs through high ponderosa pine forests and climbs to an elevation of 8,573 feet at Carson Pass. Beyond the summit it passes a series of small lakes and descends the Carson River Canyon to Minden, Nevada.

Sorensen's Resort, Pickett's Junction

South of Lake Tahoe and east of the Sierra Divide, at the junction of State Route 88 and State Route 89 on the east side of Carson Pass, Sorensen's Resort is the focal point of Hope Valley. With cabins, good restaurant food, sleigh rides, and its own cross-country center, there's plenty to do here without the hectic scene of the South Lake Tahoe glitter gulch. For information contact Sorensen's Resort, 14255 State Route 88, Hope Valley, CA 96120 (tel. 530/694-2203 or 800/423-9909).

Ebbetts Pass (State Route 4)

Connecting Angels Camp on the west with Markleeville on the east, Ebbetts Pass is a bridge between two of the most eccentric towns you may ever find. Angels Camp, of course, is famous for its Jumping Frog Jubilee, popularized by one-time resident Mark Twain. Markleeville, population 1,200, is one of the most insulated communities in the Sierra Nevada. It doesn't have a bank, but it does have the Death Ride: Tour of the California Alps bike rally.

In between the two extremes, State Route 4 weaves through beautiful redwoods, along the North Fork of the Stanislaus River, past the turnoff to Bear Valley Ski Resort and up to strikingly beautiful Lake Alpine. Just past here, the road narrows to less than two lanes and crosses the pass before heading down to Markleeville. For information contact the **Calaveras Ranger District,** P.O. Box 500, Hathaway Pines, CA 95233 (tel. 209/795-1381).

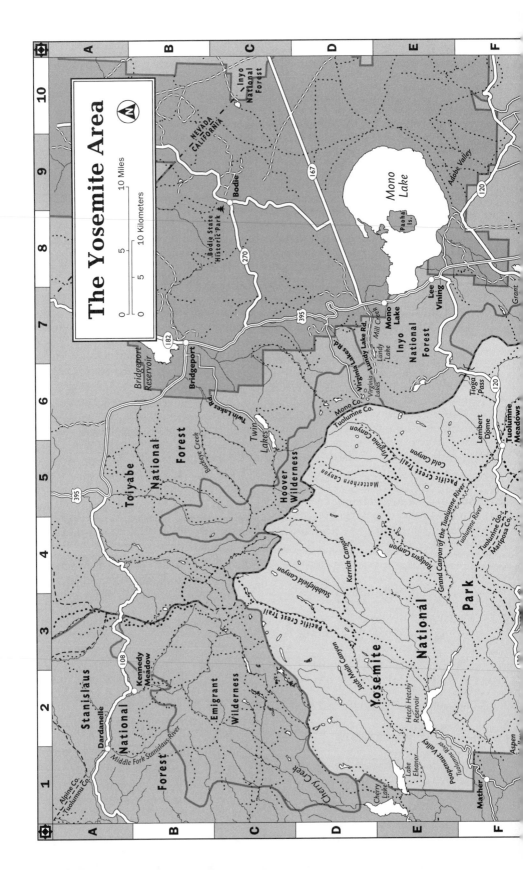

The Yosemite Area

N

0   5   10 Miles

0   5   10 Kilometers

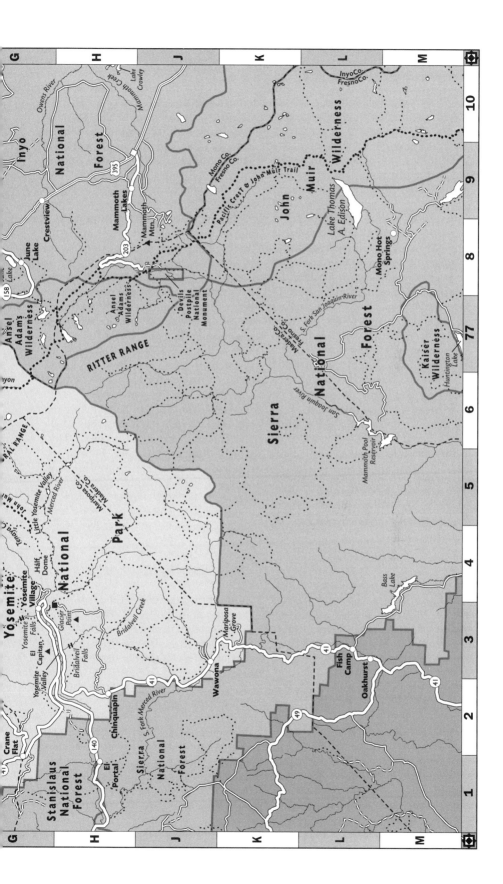

Sonora Pass (State Route 108)

Built in 1901, the Sonora Pass was one of the first highways to cross the Sierra Divide. It has long since been superseded by the highways to its north and south, however, as the easiest route over the mountains. One trip over will tell you why: From Kennedy Meadows over the pass to the Walker River, State Route 108 is the most winding, steep, and gorgeous road you've ever seen. (The pass area looks so much like the Alps it was used as a location for the filming of *For Whom the Bell Tolls*.) It isn't something you'd want to drive a truck or motorhome across. Most visitors stay on the west side of the almost 9,700-foot pass. For almost guaranteed solitude drive the extra few hours to the east slope where you'll find uncrowded hiking, fishing, and backpacking. This route is also a favorite path of cyclists over the Sierra, for exactly the same reasons cars don't like it.

SOUTHERN SIERRA: YOSEMITE TO SEQUOIA/KINGS CANYON

State Route 168

This is the only route into the wilderness of the Sierra National Forest between Yosemite and Sequoia/Kings Canyon, and it's closed in the winter. Huntington and Shaver lakes are both located off of here.

EASTERN SIERRA

Markleeville

On the eastern foot of State Route 4, tiny Markleeville is the county seat of Alpine County. The population of the entire county is less than 1,200, so don't expect any big-city services. Markleeville does, however, have plenty of interesting frontier logging and mining history at the **Alpine County Historical Museum** (tel. 530/694-2317). The museum is open from early summer until fall, Wednesday through Monday, from noon to 5pm. While there is no fee, donations are accepted. Camping, fishing, hiking, biking, and hot springing are the big deal around here—some of the most remote and uncrowded country in the state. While Markleeville doesn't have a bank, it does have the Cutthroat Bar, a redneck delight where the standing offer is that any woman willing to give up her bra can trade it for a genuine Cutthroat T-shirt as long as she's willing to bare-breast it in front of a crowd of slathering regulars. Gee, I wonder why there aren't more takers?

Every year the chamber of commerce sponsors the Death Ride: Tour of the California Alps: 2,500 cyclists from around the country come here to test themselves on the surrounding high passes. For Death Ride registration information or more detailed information about the area, contact the **Alpine Chamber of Commerce**, P.O. Box 265, Markleeville, CA 96120 (tel. 530/694-2475).

Monitor Pass (State Route 89)

Monitor Pass connects Tahoe and summertime State Route 4 traffic with U.S. 395 down the eastern Sierra. During the fall in particular it is a great place to catch the changing colors whether on a bicycle or in your car.

Bridgeport

Bridgeport is the supply center for everything north of Mammoth Lakes. It's no great shakes, but you can get everything from gasoline to food to fishing lures here, as well as food and lodging. More interesting are Bridgeport's weird weekend happenings: Every October brings the Big Mountain Man Rendezvous. No cars are allowed in town and participants dress in period costumes from the pioneer days while competing in shooting contests, musical performances, and craft markets. During the last weekend of June a primitive event of a different type takes over when the annual gathering of the western states Harley Davidson motorcycle clubs roars into town. Outside town are Big Hot Warm Springs, Bridgeport Reservoir, and the Hoover Wilderness. Contact the **Bridgeport Chamber of Commerce,** P.O Box 541, Bridgeport, CA 93517 (tel. 760/932-7500), for info on lodging, camping, and activities. The **Bridgeport Ranger Station,** HCRI Box 1000, Bridgeport, CA 93517 (tel. 760/932-7070), offers wilderness permits, maps, and camping info.

Twin Lakes Road

A major accessway into the Hoover Wilderness and the popular Twin Lakes. Great fishing for brown and rainbow trout.

Virginia Lakes Road

Midway between Bridgeport and Lee Vining, Virginia Lakes Road cuts about 6 miles into the high mountains west of U.S. 395. It passes 10 small lakes, a campground, and the **Virginia Lakes Resort** (tel. 760/647-6484), P.O. Box 1065, Bridgeport, CA 93517, which has a small store, restaurant, and cabins for rent during the summer.

Lundy Lake Road

Lundy Lake, a reservoir, is a major trailhead into the Twenty Lakes Basin and notable on its own for good fishing and camping below the dam on the banks of Mill Creek. **Lundy Lake**

Resort, P.O. Box 265, Lee Vining, CA 93541 (no phone), has cabins, camping, laundry, store, and showers.

Lee Vining

Named for a gold miner, Leroy Vining, who was one of the first to prospect the eastern Sierra, Lee Vining is another small and peaceful supply stop at the intersection of Tioga Pass (State Route 120) and U.S. 395 near the shore of Mono Lake. Camping supplies, gas, food, lodging, and information are available—there's even an art gallery. Visit the **Mono Lake Ranger Station,** P.O. Box 10, Lee Vining, CA 93541 (tel. 760/647-6331), west of the highway intersection on Tioga Road, for maps and information.

June Lake Loop (State Route 158)

Five miles south of Lee Vining, State Route 158 begins its westward loop through the spectacular country around the semideveloped town of June Lake and **June Mountain Ski Resort** (tel. 760/648-7733). Besides skiing and snowboarding at the ski area, June Lake is great for hiking, camping, and fishing. Four lakes—Grant, Silver, Gull, and June—lie inside the loop and are popular for fishing, swimming, and boating. Camping and lodging are available at several different locations. Just to the west of the loop is the huge Ansel Adams Wilderness. Contact the **June Lake Chamber of Commerce,** P.O. Box 2, June Lake (tel. 760/648-7584), for info.

Mammoth Lakes

Though it only officially became a town in 1984, Mammoth Lakes has been the economic center of the eastern Sierra since the ski mountain boomed in popularity during the 1970s. This is where L.A. comes to play in the snow, and

Angelenos drop a lot of cash here to do it, supporting condos, nice restaurants, bars, ski shops, clothing outlets, and all the accoutrements of the glittery Southern California lifestyle. Whether this is a good thing or not is up for interpretation; a lot of old and new Mammoth locals like to complain about the weekend interlopers, but without them most people here would be out of a job. Besides the 2,500-acre ski mountain just outside town, Mammoth also boasts two cross-country skiing centers, dogsledding, a bobsled run, mountain biking, rock climbing, hot springs, numerous lakes, fishing, hiking, Devils Postpile National Monument, and the area's only commercial airport all within a stone's throw.

While the **Mammoth Lakes Visitors Center,** P.O. Box 48, Mammoth Lakes, CA 93546 (tel. 760/934-2571 or 800/367-6572), is ostensibly the place to call for help with lodging, trip planning, etc., the visitors center staff was virtually useless when I called. However, the visitors center itself on the highway into town—look for Perry's Pizza—is a good source of tourist maps and brochures. The people at **Mammoth Mountain Ski Resort,** P.O. Box 24, Mammoth Lakes, CA 93546 (tel. 760/934-2571 or 800/367-6572), offer info on lodging, skiing, and much more, and are *much* more helpful over the phone than the visitors center. Contact the **Mammoth National Forest Visitors Center,** P.O. Box 148, Mammoth Lakes, CA 93546 (tel. 760/934-2505), for hiking maps as well as nature and camping information. **Mammoth Adventure Connection,** P.O. Box 353, Mammoth Lakes, CA 93546 (tel. 800/228-4947), is the place to call if you're interested in climbing lessons, mountain biking tours, dogsledding . . .

Rock Creek Lake and Road

Rock Creek Road is popular for the resort area also known as Tom's Place

where the road turns off U.S. 395. The lake itself is only 63 acres but popular with anglers. Many trailheads leave from the lake into the John Muir Wilderness, popular in winter for cross-country skiing. Camping, fishing, hiking, resorts, boat rentals, and pack station are offered. Contact the **White Mountain Ranger Station** (tel. 760/873-2500), 640 S. Main, P.O. Box 8, Bishop, CA 93545, for more info and questions about fees.

Bishop

Besides being the mule capital of the world (and home of Mule Days, one of the odder annual events you'll ever see), Bishop is a pretty nice little town with lots of places to sleep and eat. It's also nearby a lot of places to play at the back side of Kings Canyon National Park and the southern end of the John Muir Wilderness just west of here on State Route 168. Contact the **Bishop Chamber of Commerce,** 690 N. Main St., Bishop, CA 93514 (tel. 760/873-8405), or the **White Mountains Ranger Station,** 798 N. Main St., Bishop, CA 93514 (tel. 760/873-2500), for more info.

Big Pine/Palisade Glaciers

When you pass through the tiny town of Big Pine, look up at the Palisade Glaciers to the west. These are the southernmost "living" glaciers in North America, which means they are replenished at their top end every winter and continue to break off and melt at the bottom. This is also the most popular ice-climbing area in California (I guess to call ice climbing popular at all is a stretch, but if you are an ice climber, this is a popular place to be one).

Lone Pine and Mount Whitney

Lone Pine lies literally in the shadow of Mount Whitney. It's only 13 miles up

Bishop's Average Temperatures and Precipitation											
	Jan	Feb	Mar	Apr	May	June	July	Aug	Sept	Oct	Nov	Dec
High (°F)	52.9	58.2	63.4	70.9	80.2	90.4	97.5	95.2	88.2	77.1	63.5	55.1
Low (°F)	21.4	25.9	29.5	35.8	43.5	50.8	56.3	53.8	46.8	37.4	27.7	22.1
Precipitation (in.)	1.3	1.0	0.4	0.3	0.3	0.1	0.2	0.1	0.2	0.2	0.5	1.0

Whitney Portal Road to the trailhead where most leave for the trying but technically simple hike to the highest point in the Lower 48. Between town and the sheer wall of the range lie the Alabama Hills, popular with Hollywood directors for the desert landscape and rugged granite boulders—perfect for shooting westerns. Call the **Lone Pine Chamber of Commerce,** 126 S. Main St., Lone Pine, CA 93545, for lodging and other tourist information. Stop by the **Eastern Sierra Interagency Visitors Center** (tel. 760/876-6222) at the junction of U.S. 395 and State Route 136 just south of town for wilderness information, books, or the bathrooms. The **Mount Whitney Ranger Station,** 640 S. Main St., Lone Pine, CA 93545 (tel. 760/876-6200), offers wilderness permits, Mount Whitney climbing permits, maps, and camping information.

Parks & Other Hot Spots

NORTHERN SIERRA: LAKE TAHOE TO YOSEMITE

Lake Tahoe

One of the world's finest alpine lakes, the statistics on Lake Tahoe are resoundingly impressive: It's 12 miles wide, 22 miles long, and about 72 miles around, but that doesn't begin to tell the whole story. More impressive: The lake averages 989 feet deep. That's the average; the deepest point is 1,645 feet deep. You don't lose your watch in this lake and go looking for it. Even though the lake sits high above snowline, as a result of its incredible depth it never freezes (except for a few small, shallow inlets). As winter cools surface water, the colder water sinks and is replaced by warmer water from below. At all times of the year the lake is amazingly clear. Despite an increase in pollution as the population around the lake has exploded in the last 50 years, you can still see a quarter sitting on the bottom in 70 feet of water (assuming you can find a place that's only 70 feet deep to drop it in).

Of course, most of us don't come to Tahoe to drop coins in a lake. We come here to ski, camp, mountain bike, hike, fish, and boat. A lot of visitors also come here to pour money into the Nevada-side casinos, hotels, and brothels just down the road, but that's in Nevada and this is a book about California. Sorry. On the California side you'll just have to content yourself with good clean fun.

For skiers, an interesting option is the interchangeable ticket program among north-shore resorts. For a fixed price you can buy a multi-day ticket that allows you to ski at any of seven downhill or seven cross-country ski areas. For information about all the area resorts and lodging options, or to make reserva-tions, contact the **Tahoe North**

Visitors and Convention Bureau (tel. 800/TAHOE-4-U).

Donner Memorial State Park

2 miles off Interstate 80 on Donner Pass Road. Tel. 530/582-7894. Closed for winter season (Oct-Nov–End of May). Day-use and camping fees.

If you want to learn more about the Donner party, go to Donner Memorial State Park. The Emigrant Trail Museum is a fascinating place to find out more about the Donners, the construction of the first railway over the Sierra, Tahoe history, and the natural history of the Sierra Nevada. Also of note is the Donner Lake campground, and fishing, canoeing, and swimming in the lake itself. Unfortunately you can hear the noise of Interstate 80 from virtually anywhere in the park—ironic when you consider the Donners' forced isolation.

Sugar Pine Point State Park

Just south of Homewood on State Route 89. Tel. 530/525-7982. Open year-round. Day-use and camping fee.

Once the summer estate of turn-of-the-century San Francisco bank tycoon Isaias W. Hellman and his family, Sugar Pine Point is now a fine park with 2 miles of waterfront for swimming, boating, and sunbathing; good hiking and biking; and year-round camping. Also worth noting is Tahoe's only lighthouse and, of course, the Hellmans' outrageous Ehrmann Mansion, which is open for tours in the summer.

D. L. Bliss and Emerald Bay State Parks

Southwest shore between Sugar Pine Point and Camp Richardson on State Route 89. Tel. 530/525-7982. 268 campsites. Flush toilets, showers, picnicking, beach, fishing, boating, hiking. Closed for winter season. Day-use and camping fees.

Two names, one park. Originally two separate parks, the two are now managed together. This shoreline is the most spectacular publicly owned property on the lake. There's really too much here to appreciate in one visit: fantastic hikes, great shore access, and spectacular Emerald Bay marked by tiny Fannette Island, the only island in the lake. The main State Park Headquarters for the Tahoe region is also here. It is a good source of information about other places to visit.

Pope–Baldwin Recreation Area and Tallac Historic Site

Just north of Camp Richardson on State Route 89. Tel. 530/542-4166 (year-round); 530/541-4975 (summer only). Historical buildings, hiking, multi-agency visitors center (summer only), picnic grounds, and cultural center.

The Tallac Historic Site is a publicly owned but privately managed tribute to the days when Tahoe was the place to see and be seen for California's rich and famous. Several incredible old estates have been preserved by the nonprofit **Tahoe Tallac Association** (tel. 530/541-4975) and are open for a variety of events. The Recreation Area offers lake access and several nice trails. One of the most unique trails in the entire state is here: Rainbow Trail, which at one point descends below stream level alongside Taylor Creek. The Forest Service has constructed a Plexiglas wall allowing you to see creek life in a kind of natural aquarium.

Desolation Wilderness

Southwest of Lake Tahoe from D. L. Bliss State Park to U.S. 50. Tel. 530/573-2600. For information contact Forest Service Lake Tahoe Basin Management Unit, P.O. Box 8465, South Lake Tahoe, CA 96158.

Far from desolated, this 64,000-acre wilderness on the southwest shore of Tahoe is so popular that reservations for many backcountry destinations under the quota system often fill up 90 days in advance. Fifty percent of the trail permits are held until the day of departure, though. If you are adamant about going to an exact place, try to reserve in advance. If you are more flexible, you can get away with showing up really early in the morning the day you want to leave. Hikers (or in winter, skiers) looking for tips on where to go in the wilderness or on other Forest Service lands around the lake should visit the Forest Service Center at 870 Emerald Bay Rd.

Kirkwood and Caples Lakes

On the west side of the Carson Pass, 63 miles east of Jackson, large Caples Lake and its tiny neighbor Kirkwood Lake are the main center of summertime camping and boating in the area. No motorboats are allowed on Kirkwood Lake, leaving it to the canoers and kayakers to enjoy. Caples Lake is much larger and motorized fishing boats are allowed. Rental boats are available. Fishing here is best just after the ice

breaks up in spring, but good all season. Several national forest campgrounds surround Caples and trailheads from here make a good launching point for hikes into the Mokelumne Wilderness. For information and maps, contact the **El Dorado National Forest Amador Ranger District** office in Pioneer (tel. 209/295-4251).

Silver Lake

Four hundred feet of elevation lower than Caples, Silver Lake gets warm enough in summer to make an inviting swim and is big enough for waterskiing. Several resorts rent cabins around this blue water and granite boulder jewel. National forest campgrounds (tel. 209/295-4251) around the lake hold plenty of campers but do fill up quickly on summer weekends.

Mokelumne Wilderness

South of State Route 88. Tel. 209/295-4251 (Amador Ranger District in Pioneer).

The Mokelumne Wilderness protects more than 100,000 acres of Sierra High Country. Countless lakes and meadows dot this enormous wilderness, and the huge Mokelumne River Canyon drains it. Miles of good hiking trails make it easy to explore this still uncrowded retreat.

Calaveras Big Trees State Park

Off State Route 4 between Dorrington and Arnold. Tel. 209/795-2334. 129 camping sites. Picnic areas, visitors center, flush toilets, showers, running water. Day-use and camping fees.

Calaveras Big Trees was once thought to be the only place on earth where the giant sequoia grew—more than a thousand grace the park in two groves. Though this is one of the best-preserved forests of giant sequoias, it was here in 1852 that a group of promoters chopped down the Discovery Tree, a 24-foot-diameter giant, building a dance floor on its stump, a bowling alley out of its trunk, and a traveling freak show exhibit out of the shell of its bark—all to show their appreciation for these fantastic trees. John Muir used this horrible example to rally protection for the sequoias.

Numerous trails loop through the park, and the Stanislaus River bisects the 6,300-acre forest. Swimming holes and fishing pools make it a favorite summer getaway. World-class kayaking and rafting happens a few miles downstream below Murphy. In winter the park is open for camping and is often snow-free. If there is snow, the park is open for cross-country skiing.

Lake Alpine

Hidden under a cloak of snow all winter, Lake Alpine bursts out in an explosion of beauty every spring and summer. The several-mile-long reservoir is surrounded by four national forest campgrounds with all the usual amenities. Other nearby camps accommodate the overflow. Boats ranging from kayaks to small motorized fishing boats (15 mph speed limit on the lake) are available to rent at the marina. Trout fishing is good. Trails surround the lake and explore the headwaters of the Stanislaus River. Ebbetts Pass is a few miles beyond here just past Mosquito Lake. Shallow and inhabited by thousands of its namesake, the lake is an important trailhead into the Carson-Iceberg Wilderness south of here.

Pinecrest Lake

Winter or summer, Pinecrest is where the action is on State Route 108. Several hundred campsites are broken up into smaller camps hidden in the trees near the west side of the lake. A boat ramp and marina allow launching of private boats (20 mph limit) and rentals of canoes, sailboats, and fishing boats. The town of Pinecrest has a gas station, grocery store, sporting goods shop, a few restaurants, condos, cabins, and post office. Best, though, is the trail around the roadless back side of Pinecrest Lake. Private cabins reached only by boat or trail are peppered among long stretches of undeveloped granite shoreline. The lake freezes in winter but don't walk or ski on the ice. Water levels change too quickly for the ice to be safe and solid. For forest information contact the **Summit Ranger Station,** 1 Pinecrest Lake Rd, Pinecrest, CA 95364 (tel. 209/965-3434). For lodging information and reservations contact **Pinecrest Lake Resort,** P.O. Box 1216, Pinecrest, CA 95364 (tel. 209/965-3411).

SOUTHERN SIERRA: YOSEMITE TO SEQUOIA/ KINGS CANYON

Yosemite National Park

Visitors center at west end of Yosemite Village Mall in the valley. Tel. 209/372-0200. Yosemite Wilderness Office, P.O. Box 577, Yosemite, CA 95389. Information: Yosemite National Park, P.O. Box 577, Yosemite, CA 95389. Tel. 209/372-0265.

Yosemite National Park tries to be everything to everybody, and often ends up shooting itself in the foot trying. Don't get me wrong. Nowhere on earth is quite like the Yosemite Valley. It's stunning—a natural cathedral of sheer rock, rushing water, and magical light. Unfortunately it's also been overdeveloped by the very people mandated to protect it. Do over a thousand hotel rooms, fast-food joints, postcard shops, and huge traffic jams really add to the nature experience here?

Finding the wild Yosemite takes careful planning, and I've devoted some care to mapping out a strategy for taking on what's arguably the most famous of the country's national parks. See the "Yosemite National Park" feature a little later in this chapter.

Huntington Lake and Shaver Lake

The most popular weekend getaway for people from Fresno, these two lakes off State Route 168 are large enough for waterskiing, windy enough for boardsailing, and surrounded by plenty of good camping, marinas, picnic areas, lodges, and summer cabins. Huntington in particular is a good starting point for hikes into the surrounding national forest. For information contact the **Shaver Lake Ranger Station,** P.O. Box 300, Shaver Lake, CA 93644 (tel. 209/855-5360), or the **Shaver Lake Chamber of Commerce**, P.O. Box 58, Shaver Lake, CA 93644 (tel. 209/841-3350).

Sequoia and Kings Canyon National Parks

Off State Route 180 from Fresno or State Route 198 from Visalia. Information: Sequoia and Kings Canyon National Parks, Three Rivers, CA 93271. Tel. 209/784-1500. Road and weather information: Tel. 209/565-3341.

Once separate, now a single park under unified management, Sequoia/Kings Canyon is one of the most fantastic wilderness areas in the National Park System. Though it gets heavy visitation, nothing in the park compares to the traffic and crowding problems faced by Yosemite. Only the very western segment of the park, home to the sequoia groves and all the park infrastructure, is accessible by road. The rest is covered by seemingly endless expanses of jagged peaks, gorges, rivers, canyons, and alpine meadows. Since you can't just pull over and see all the sights, visiting the park takes a bit of planning, so I've devoted some time to helping you get the most out of this rugged wilderness. See the "Sequoia and Kings Canyon National Parks" feature a little later in this chapter.

EASTERN SIERRA

Grover Hot Springs State Park

Tel. 530/694-2248. 7 days, 9am to 9pm during summer, more limited in winter. Showers, flush toilets, camping, swimming. $5 day use, $14 camping.

A few miles outside Markleeville on Hot Springs Road is the year-round hot spring soaking paradise of Grover Hot

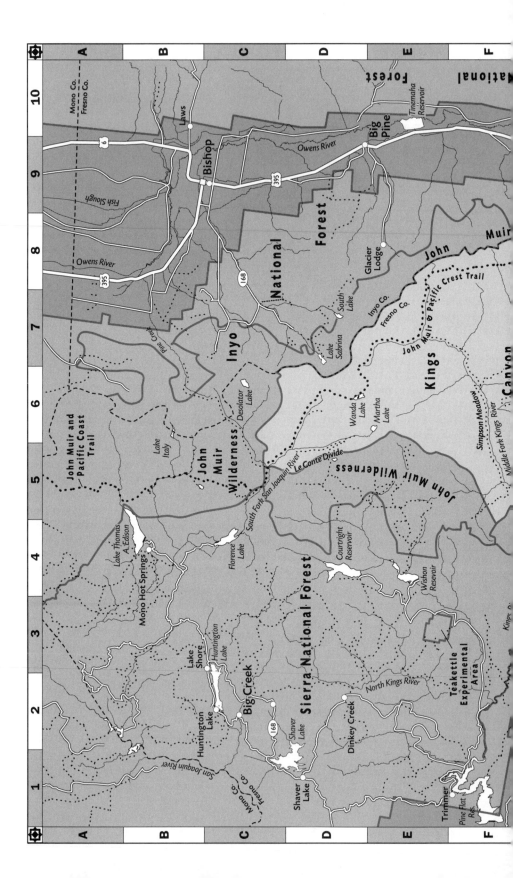

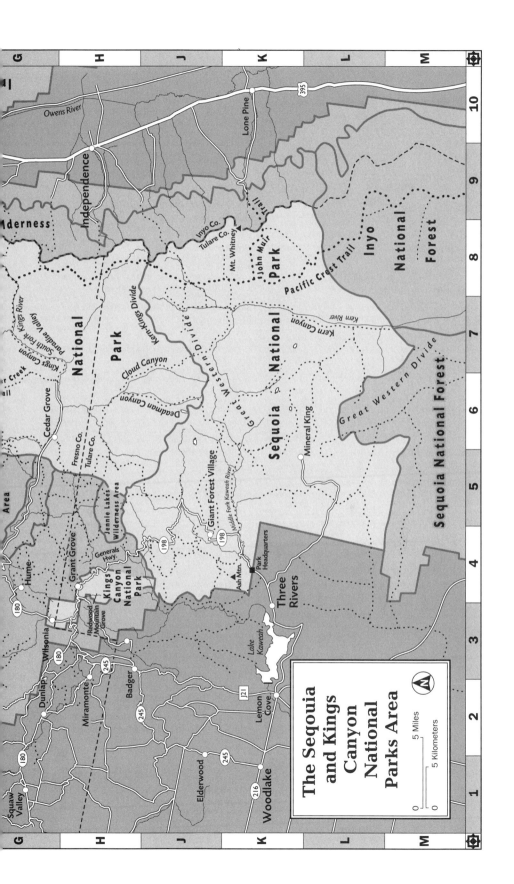

Springs State Park. Though the collection of government-issue concrete pools (bathing suits required) full of both hot and cold water is less than beautiful, a soak at Grover is a great thing after a long day of hiking in the nearby Mokelumne Wilderness. The fee is good all day so you can exit and reenter. Showers and changing rooms are also nice for that complete makeover after several days in the wilderness.

Bodie State Historic Park

Tel. 760/647-6445. 8am to 7pm summer; 9am to 4pm winter. $2. Picnic tables, museum, water in summer only, pit toilets, flush toilets in summer only, ghost town.

Seven miles south of Bridgeport and 14 miles east of U.S. 395 lies Bodie, once the meanest, baddest mining town in the west. Now lying in a state of arrested decay, it's the meanest, baddest ghost town in the west.

Mono Lake

This huge inland sea offers a number of interesting things to do: birding, swimming, canoeing, and hiking are the most popular. Though its surroundings are incredibly stark, sometimes oppressively so, the natural history of Mono Lake is among the most interesting you're likely to find. So is the human history. To get a good view of the 13-mile by 8-mile lake, hike to the top of Black Point Fissures in the **Mono Lake County Park** on Cemetery Road. **Mono Basin National Scenic Area** and **Mono Lake Tufa State Reserve** (tel. 760/647-6331) both protect and allow access to the lakeshore. The Mark Twain Interpretive Trail is a mile-long path explaining many facts

about the lake. Tufa towers—millennia-old pillars of mineral salt formed underwater and left exposed when the lake level receded owing to the Los Angeles Department of Water and Power's freshwater predations—are an interesting sight on the south shore at either the state reserve or the county park, where boardwalks over the muddy shore make them accessible. Though you won't want to get the water in your eyes or open cuts, a soak at **Navy Beach** on the south shore is a popular local cure for aching bones and other ailments. You'll be amazed by the buoyancy of Mono's saline water.

Owens River Headwaters

Between June Lake and Mammoth, Owens River Road cuts east paralleling the headwaters of the river. Several private guest ranches in the area specialize in fly-fishing vacations. Other stretches are accessible to the public. Many great mountain bike rides lace the area.

Devils Postpile National Monument

Tel. 760/934-2289. Closed in winter. No entry fee. $6 shuttle fee required to get into the park from Mammoth Lakes. Camping $6–$8 per night. Pets on leash okay.

Just a few miles outside the town of Mammoth Lakes, Devils Postpile National Monument is home to one of nature's most curious geological freak shows. Formed when molten lava cracked as it cooled, the 60-foot-high blue-gray basalt columns that form the postpile look more like some sort of satanic pipe organ or a jumble of giant pencil leads than anything you'd expect to see made from stone. The three- to seven-sided columns formed underground and were exposed when glaciers scoured this valley in the last ice age some 10,000 years ago. Similar examples of columnar basalt are found in Ireland and Scotland.

Rainbow Falls on the San Joaquin River and Fish Creek Hot Springs are other popular draws, and the Pacific Crest Trail and John Muir Trail both pass through the park on their way north and south. Because of its high elevation (7,900 feet) and heavy snowfall, the monument is open only from summer until early fall. Weather in the summer is usually clear and warm, but afternoon thundershowers can soak the unprepared. Nights are still cold, so bring good tents and sleeping bags if you'll be camping. The Mammoth Lakes region is famous for its beautiful lakes—but unfortunately all that water also means lots of mosquitoes. Plan for them.

From late June until early September cars are prohibited in the monument between 7:30am and 5:30pm to maintain the wild atmosphere of the area. Visitors must take a shuttle bus from the Mammoth Mountain Inn to and from locations in the monument. While it takes some planning, the resulting peace and quiet is well worth the trouble and makes you wonder why the Park Service hasn't implemented similar programs at the Yosemite Valley and other traffic hot spots.

Crowley Lake

One of the state's most productive fishing lakes, Crowley swarms with anglers on the April 1 opening of trout season. The former state record German brown trout was caught here—25 pounds, 11 ounces. The lake is located 11 miles south of Mammoth on U.S. 395. A boat launch fee is required, and fishing regulations change every year, so check them. Waterskiing season runs from July 4 to Labor Day. There is no camping here, but you will find a grocery and bait store. For more information contact the **BLM Bishop Resource Area Office** (tel. 760/872-4881).

Owens River Gorge

The Owens River Gorge is a gorge without a river most of the time as the Los Angeles Department of Water and Power diverts the river south, but the 700-foot walls carved when water did run here remain. Recently the gorge has become a sport climbing destination on par with Joshua Tree and other desert locales. Routes are bolted and generally uncrowded. An unmarked dirt road 20.5 miles south of Mammoth on U.S. 395 connects with Gorge Parallel Road. Turn south and in roughly 2 miles you're there.

Northern Sierra: Lake Tahoe to Yosemite ◆ What to Do & Where to Do It

This is the Sierra that most people know. Often incorrectly called the High Sierra, which properly refers to the southern Sierra from Yosemite to Mount Whitney, the Tahoe to Yosemite region is the most accessible and developed part of the whole range. It's a relatively short drive here from the Bay Area, and a robust tourist infrastructure ensures that any creature comforts won't be overlooked.

Which doesn't mean the area has been spoiled by success: It's just too darn big for that to be true. 20 minutes from the glitter and casinos of South Lake Tahoe you can find yourself all alone by an alpine lake. On State Route 4 and State Route 108, passes that have no connection with either Tahoe or Yosemite, you can find some of the most pristine areas in the entire range. I think the single most beautiful stretch of road I've ever driven might be State Route 108 from Kennedy Meadow to Leavitt Meadow just after the snow has melted. The combination of shimmering aspens, soaring granite peaks rushing with countless cascades, and miles of flower-filled alpine meadows made me feel like a location scout for *The Sound of Music*.

High enough and wild enough to contain incredible hiking, cross-country skiing, and mountain biking, the northern Sierra is a wilderness, but one with plenty of options for people of all different levels of stamina and ability. It doesn't require the same physical stamina and commitment as the remote, untamed parts of the southern Sierra: You need not be Sir Edmond Hillary to have a good time here. Numerous ski resorts, both alpine and nordic, are dispersed throughout the area, and self-guided winter explorers will find no shortage of snow-covered roads, meadows, and backcountry trails to test. Another outstanding feature of this part of the range is the large number of easily accessible lakes and rivers. From the huge expanse of Lake Tahoe to the thousands of diminutive alpine ponds that dot the Sierra, you can do almost anything: fish for giant mackinaw trout, boardsail, swim, or kayak the Truckee River, stopping to flycast for native rainbows.

BIRD WATCHING

Birding in the Sierra Nevada is so wonderful because it isn't something you have to seek out like you would in so many other locations—the generally wild character of the mountains lends itself to surprise sightings. You might be canoeing on Donner Lake and see a family of common mergansers. Hiking along the top of Burst Rock near Dodge Ridge I once heard a sound like an incoming artillery shell only to look up and see a peregrine falcon whoosh past me at 100 mph, wings tucked in full descent mode. It circled back up and did the same thing two more times while I watched from the edge of a 500-foot precipice. Other commonly seen Sierra Nevada species are the osprey, California quail, golden eagle, bald eagle, barn owl, calliope hummingbird, and red-breasted sapsucker. In the High Country the most common birds by far are the audacious stellar jay and the friendly yet dignified Clark's nutcracker. Most Sierra Nevada state and national parks maintain bird lists and often have interpretive programs. *Discovering Sierra Birds* by Edward C. Beedy and Stephen Granholm (Yosemite Natural History Association, 1985) is a great guide to Sierra bird species and habitat.

BOARDSAILING

For Sierra boardsailing, nothing beats **Lake Tahoe.** The lake is big enough that it develops some real wind virtually every afternoon. It's also big enough that you can get in real trouble if you aren't competent. Because of the lake's incredible depth it never really warms up. Even in the warmest part of summer it doesn't rise above the 60s with the exception of certain shallow bays. The best rigging area and access on the California side is at **Sugar Pine Point State Park,** just south of Homewood on State Route 89 (tel. 530/525-7982). Wear a full suit to be comfortable. Several marinas rent gear, and private boardsailing schools operate at various locations around the lake during the summer. Contact the local visitor bureaus for up-to-date suggestions about specific instructors and schools.

The Cow & the Cowbird

Public lands grazing is one of the hot wildlands issues as the so-called wise-use movement butts heads with the Clinton administration over grazing allotments and fees for millions of acres owned by the federal government but leased to private ranchers. One side of the debate calls them welfare ranchers; the other calls them heroes of the West, upholders of a grand old tradition. The truth is probably somewhere in between. While only 3% of the nation's beef is raised on public land, more than 361 million acres are allocated to the cow, mostly marginal grazing land that is only profitable because the government leases it out for a pittance when compared to the cost of private land. The government netted nearly $25 million from grazing fees nationwide in 1981, the same year it spent $58.5 million on the program, a nearly $30 million subsidy for 3% of the country's beef. Since then things haven't gotten any better.

One thing is undeniable: there's a lot of cattle in them there hills and they ain't doing them hills a lot of good. It's a well-known fact that any large, hoofed animal is going to do a lot of damage to the ground it walks on, trampling meadows and muddying streams. It also stands to reason that if you introduce a lot of hungry grazers into an area with limited forage, something is going to lose out, most likely the deer, elk, and bighorn sheep that traditionally ate here. What is less immediately apparent is the damage done when an exotic species, in this case the cow, brings its own parade of parasites, diseases, and companion species with it. Witness the cowbird.

Prior to the 1930s brown-headed cowbirds were not seen in the Sierra. They lived in the ranchland below where they dined happily on their favorite snack, fresh cow dung, but at that time there were very few cattle in the Sierra. When public lands grazing took off after World War I, cows were introduced into the Sierra Nevada, and, not being the type to let all that delicious dookie go to waste, the cowbird came along.

So they eat shit, you ask? What's so bad about that? There's no accounting for taste. Well, truthfully it isn't their table manners that make the cowbird bad neighbors. It's their kids. Following the herd to find its next meal makes the birds too busy to tend their own nests. Instead, the brown-headed cowbird lays its egg in the nest of a smaller native bird where it is incubated by an unsuspecting parent. When the eggs hatch, the larger cowbird chick kills its nest mates, either directly or by outcompeting them for food. At least 22 different native bird species are threatened by the cowbird. One University of California study showed that 22.4% of warbling vireo nests contain a cowbird chick, creating an 80% loss of reproductive potential for the species overall. The vireo is nearly extinct because of the cowbird. The cowbird is here because of the cow. And the cows are here because some rancher is making a nice federal subsidy to have them here.

Lake Alpine on State Route 4 is another popular boardsailing spot without nearly the daunting wind or surface area of Tahoe. **Bear Valley Cross Country** (tel. 209/753-2834) rents gear and can arrange small-group or individual lessons.

Pinecrest Lake on State Route 108 is a great place for learners too, since the lake's low motorboat speed limit keeps interference to a minimum. A long sandy beach perfect for rigging and dry land practice lines the entire east shore. Water temperature is cold.

CANOEING

So many wonderful small lakes dot the Sierra that it is almost easier to say where not to take your canoe than where to take it. It seems like every corner you turn reveals some inviting expanse of blue water. If you have your own boat, just pack a fishing rod, a picnic, and your bathing suit and go crazy. Depending on renting a canoe limits you somewhat, but not too much. Most of the bigger alpine lakes have rental fleets of canoes and small rowboats. **Tahoe Paddle and Oar** (tel. 530/581-3029) in Tahoe City teaches canoeing and has rental boats. **Bear Valley Cross Country** on State Route 4 runs a summertime rental fleet on Lake Alpine, one of my favorite canoeing lakes.

CROSS-COUNTRY SKIING & SNOWSHOEING

If you like the sensation of busting fresh tracks through the woods after a new snowfall, the plentiful snow-covered logging roads and trails of the national forests are marked for winter cross-country skiing. Try the **Castle Peak Trail** off Interstate 80 near Boreal (Sno-Park permit required), or the **Taylor Creek/Fallen Leaf Lake Trail** in the **Pope-Baldwin Recreation Area,** just north of Camp Richardson on State Route 89 (tel. 530/544-5050). **Donner Memorial State Park,** 2 miles off Interstate 80 on old State Route 40 (tel. 530/ 582-7894), often offers ranger-led ski or snowshoe tours, and **Sugar Pine Point State Park,** just south of Homewood on State Route 89 (tel. 530/525-7982), has great skinny-skiing. Or stop by the **Lake Tahoe Visitors Authority** (tel. 800/AT-TAHOE) in South Lake

and pick up complimentary maps of the surrounding area. The Forest Service visitor centers for each individual ranger district (see "Parks & Other Hot Spots") also keep continually updated, excellent maps of trails on their land.

Like its alpine cousin, skinny-skiing on groomed trails is big business here. The granddaddy of California nordic resorts is **Royal Gorge** (tel. 530/426-3871) in Soda Springs with 175 miles of groomed track, numerous warming huts, and a wilderness lodge. Purists might scoff at Royal Gorge's recently installed lifts, which allow access to the upper slopes, but telemarkers love them. At Tahoe, **Squaw Valley** (tel. 530/583-5585), with 30 kilometers of groomed trails, and **Northstar** (tel. 530/562-2475), with 65 kilometers of groomed trails, both maintain Nordic areas in addition to their considerable alpine facilities. **Kirkwood** (tel. 209/258-7248), with 80 kilometers of groomed trails, also doesn't limit itself to just pleasing downhillers. In South Lake, **Lake Tahoe Winter Sports Center** (tel. 530/577-2940) just south of the airport has numerous groomed trails. On State Route 4 the **Bear Valley Cross-Country Center** (tel. 209/753-2834) offers an excellent network of groomed trails, warming huts, and lessons with plentiful nearby lodging.

Castle Peak Trail

6 miles round-trip. Intermediate to advanced. Some difficult downhills and steep climbs. Access: Trailhead is at the Castle Peak/Boreal Interchange on Interstate 80 near Donner Summit. Sno Park permit required to park. Map: USGS Norden and Soda Springs topos.

Castle Peak is extremely popular with cross-country skiers looking to get away from groomed trails and flat tracks. This route will take you up from the trailhead at 7,200 feet to more than 9,000 at Castle

Pass, so be prepared to climb and descend. More experienced skiers use this route as an entry to some really wild backcountry. A great option is to make overnight reservations at the **Sierra Club's Perter Grubb Hut** just a short ski from Castle Pass. Call the **Sierra Club's Clair Tappaan Lodge** (tel. 916/426-3632) for information and reservations.

Taylor Creek

Several loops up to 4.5 miles. Beginner to intermediate. Flat trails through open meadows and aspen groves. Access: 3.5 miles north of South Lake Tahoe on State Route 89. Sno-Park permit required to park. Map: None needed.

The Forest Service maintains this great series of loop trails near Fallen Leaf Lake for the enjoyment of beginning and intermediate skiers. The main two loops—Fallen Leaf Dam Trail and the Sawmill Trail—both offer great views and varied terrain yet are easy enough for all but the most rank beginners. Since they're at only 6,200 feet, snow conditions can be a problem here early or late in the season.

Winnemucca Lake Loop

6 miles. Moderate. Trail begins at summit of Carson Pass just west of Hope Valley and junctions of State Routes 88 and 89. Clearly marked with blue diamonds and pink flagging. Map: Eldorado National Forest map.

One of the best intermediate and advanced trails in the northern Sierra, this loop takes you through some beautiful backcountry, including several perfect telemarking bowls. En route you'll pass frozen Woods Lake and then connect with the snow-covered roadbed of old Highway 88, which you'll follow back to Carson Pass. Several steep pitches

over the length of the trail make it unsuitable for skiers not confident of their turning and descending abilities.

DOWNHILL SKIING & SNOWBOARDING

The Tahoe Basin is the densest concentration of ski resorts this side of Switzerland, 17 of them at last count. An entire book could be dedicated to describing them all. Throw in Iron Mountain and Kirkwood on State Route 88 and you're pushing 20. The options range from ultramodern, ultraglitzy, and ultra-expensive Squaw Valley, known for its difficult advanced runs and home to the 1960 Winter Olympics, to the cruiser's paradise of Northstar at Tahoe, regularly ranked one of the country's best intermediate mountains, all the way down in size to tiny Soda Springs, the entirety of which can be rented by private groups for special events. Virtually all of them have good ski schools, rental packages, and lodging. All Tahoe resorts except for Alpine Meadows now allow snowboarding. You can get a complete listing of Tahoe ski areas with extensive mountain descriptions and current ticket prices by contacting The **Tahoe North Visitors and Convention Bureau** (tel. 800/TAHOE-4-U) or the **Lake Tahoe Visitors Authority** (tel. 800/AT-TAHOE).

Squaw Valley

End of Squaw Valley Road, Olympic Valley. Tel. 530/583-6985 or 800/545-4350; 530/583-6955 for snow conditions. 4,200 lift-served acres (25% beginner, 45% intermediate, 30% expert); 30 lifts including 1 cable car, 1 gondola, 4 high-speed quads, 9 triples, 10 doubles, and 3 surface; 2,850-foot vertical drop. Full-day adult ticket $49.

Were there any justice in the world Evel Knievel would have gotten his start here—it's the Sierra Nevada's semi-official daredevil mountain. Squaw Valley's bread-and-butter are the extremists of the ski world who flock here for the world famous KT-22, the mega-air to be had on Poulsen's Gully, and the seemingly vertical Chute 75, perhaps the steepest trail in Tahoe. Though primarily known as an expert area, great cruisers like Mountain Run attract intermediates, and beginners will love Bailey's Beach, a fantastic bowl. There's also a half-pipe for boarders.

Northstar-at-Tahoe

State Route 267 and Northstar Drive, Truckee. Tel. 530/562-1010; 530/562-1330 for snow conditions. 57 trails (25% beginner, 50% intermediate, 25% expert); 11 lifts including 1 gondola, 3 high-speed quads, 2 triples, 3 doubles, and 2 surface; 2,280-foot vertical drop. Full-day adult ticket $48.

While Northstar originally built its reputation on family skiing (the front side is filled with beginner and intermediate runs), the addition of a high-speed quad lift serving a dozen tree-filled expert trails on the back side is changing that image. The meticulous grooming may turn off many of the bump-lovers who frequent Tahoe, but powder days on the back side shouldn't be missed. Though Village Run gets packed in the afternoons, in the mornings it's almost perfect—a long beginner cruiser. Intermediates will have no shortage of options on the front.

Soda Springs Winter Resort

Off Interstate 80, Soda Springs exit. Tel. 530/426-1010 for info and snow conditions. 16 trails (30% beginner, 50% intermediate, 20% expert); 2 lifts including 1 triple and 1 double, 2 surface tows for snow tubing; 652-foot vertical drop. Full-day adult ticket $16.

They don't have a snow-conditions line, but whoever is working the phones will be glad to look out the window and tell you what the weather's like. That should tell you what to expect at this small, friendly ski area. With the cheapest lift tickets in Tahoe, it's great for beginners. Experts might get a little bored, but if you have a very large family or just a lot of friends, the entire area is available to rent for functions.

Kirkwood Ski Resort

Kirkwood Meadows Drive, Kirkwood. Tel. 209/258-6000; 209/258-3000 for snow conditions. 65 trails (15% beginner, 50% intermediate, 35% expert); 12 lifts including 2 doubles, 7 triples, 1 quad, 2 surface; 2,000-foot vertical drop. Full-day adult ticket $45.

Kirkwood on State Route 88 is a short drive from South Lake, but worlds away in attitude. This is where many local skiers go on weekends. And they come for one thing: the snow, which is arguably the best in the area. With hair-raising descents like The Wall and chutes like Sisters, the terrain is some of the Sierra's best for advanced skiers; and the Bunny Lift services a group of isolated beginner runs, so first-timers won't feel intimidated.

Bear Valley Ski Area

Highway 4, at Mount Reba Road, Bear Valley. Tel. 209/753-2301; option 2 for snow conditions. 67 trails (30% beginner, 40% intermediate, 30% expert); 11 lifts including 2 triples, 7 doubles, and 2 surface; 1,900-foot vertical drop. Full-day adult ticket $35.

Bear Valley near the summit of Ebbetts Pass (State Route 4) is one of the best-kept skiing secrets around. Even skiers

Are Those Mountains the Sierra or the Sierras?

When talking about the large range of mountains east of the Central Valley and west of Nevada, it is common to hear people say they just spent a nice weekend in the "Sierra Nevadas," "Sierras," or "Sierra Nevada Mountains." Though common usage, the first two are technically wrong since there is only one Sierra Nevada in California, and the third makes you sound really dumb. Sierra *means* mountain range, so when you say "I went climbing in the Sierra Mountains" you're saying you climbed the mountain mountains. Duh.

When the Spaniards settling California crossed the coastal range they encountered a huge range of snow-covered peaks to the east and offhandedly named them *La Sierra Nevada:* the Snowy Range. Without exploring the Sierra, they quickly got back to the business at hand: subjugating the Indians, propagating the Catholic faith, and asking around about gold, which doesn't occur in the coastal range but does occur in quantity in the Sierra. Being busy people, the Spaniards didn't have the time or desire to grope around those huge peaks eating pine nuts and trout while looking under rocks, where they would have found gold.

Later, gringos with too much time on their hands did look under rocks and find gold. Others moved here in force in the form of the Gold Rush of 1849. The name confused the hell out of the English-speaking prospectors. American mountains always had names like sports teams: the Rockies, the Appalachians, the Grand Tetons. Our mountains, like us, are a nation of individuals. No one thought to refer to mountain peaks in the collective but singular form. Where a Spanish speaker sees a range made from a bunch of separate mountains, we see a whole bunch of mountains standing together making a range—a subtle difference, sure, but enough to fuel the irresistible urge among Anglophones to call them the Sierras, just like the Rockies.

Just remember Sierra Nevada equals Snowy Range. As in: "I spent the weekend skiing in the Sierra Nevada/Snowy Range," singular.

There, that's easy.

who've been there several times seem not to realize that the steepest advanced runs in California are hidden away in Grizzly and Kodiak bowls *below* the lodge. I came back here in the summer once and was amazed to see waterfalls in the same spot I'd been perfecting my steeps skiing just a few months earlier. Another huge slice of blue diamond cruising runs lies on the back side of Mount Reba. Besides traditional ski and snowboard lessons, Bear Valley Ski Area has a nationally recognized disabled skiers' program.

Dodge Ridge Ski Area

Dodge Ridge Road, Pinecrest. Tel. 209/ 965-3474; 209/965-4444 for snow conditions. 60 trails (20% beginner, 40% intermediate, 40% expert); 12 lifts, including 1 quad, 2 triples, 5 doubles, and 4 surface; 1,600-foot vertical drop. Full-day adult ticket $39.

Dodge Ridge on State Route 108 is a medium-sized mountain trying hard to live down a reputation as a beginners' area. It's still no Kirkwood or Squaw, but new runs make it a perfectly enjoyable place to spend a day for any level skier. Beginners and intermediates love Dodge Ridge: The slopes seem specially designed to instill confidence, and it is rarely crowded. A low base altitude makes Dodge a bad bet late or early in the season unless you're wearing your rock skis.

FISHING

There are a couple of different fishing options in Tahoe and the northern Sierra. Rivers like the Truckee, Walker, Mokelumne, and Stanislaus all offer great fly-fishing, and the alpine lakes are often filled with hungry trout in the early summer after ice-off. Unfortunately the smaller lakes are subject to extreme boom and bust cycles; last year's great fishing lake might now be dead depending on how harsh the winter was. Lake Tahoe offers a Sierra Nevada version of something you usually associate with the ocean— the party boat—only here they're trolling for lake trout instead of mooching for salmon. **Blue Ribbon Fishing Charters** (tel. 530/541-8801) in South Lake Tahoe and **Mac A Tac Charters** (tel. 530/546-2500) in Tahoe City are two of the many charter boats that will take you out trolling for giant Mackinaw trout. Since trolling down where the lake trout dwell takes special gear, and finding them takes a good degree of local knowledge, going with a guided charter is a smart bet.

If you're anxious to do your best *A River Runs Through It* imitation but don't know a backcast from a backhand, **California Fly Fishing** (tel. 800/588-7688) in Truckee can help you learn the basics and guide you to the best fishing water in the Tahoe region. **Ebbetts Pass Sporting Goods** (tel. 209/795-1686) in Arnold near Calaveras Big Trees State Park and the Stanislaus River can recommend

good water and possibly hook you up with a local guide.

HIKES, BUSHWHACKS & BACKPACK TRIPS

DAY HIKES

Granite Lake, Desolation Wilderness

2.5 miles round-trip. Moderate. Short but steep. Access: Park at Bayview Campground off State Route 89 above Emerald Bay. Map: Desolation Wilderness map or USGS Emerald Bay topo.

This brief day sampler of the Desolation Wilderness will show you a little of everything the high country can offer. The trail climbs unrelentingly on the mountain flank above Emerald Bay. While that stinks for walking, it's great for the view. The higher you go, the thinner the lodgepole pine forest becomes, until finally you break through the trees after a little less than a mile. The granite-bouldered viewpoint here gives you a bird's-eye look at Lake Tahoe and Emerald Lake, plus a good chunk of the surrounding area. In another quarter-mile you reach Granite Lake. Lots of shoreline nooks and rocks make for fun exploring and on a hot day a swim will cut the trail dust before you start the downhill trek to your car.

Mount Tallac, Desolation Wilderness

10 miles. Strenuous. Steep, rocky, and slippery. Allow all day. Access: Mount Tallac Trailhead north of Lake Tahoe Visitors Information Center on State Route 89. Map: Desolation Wilderness map or USGS Emerald Bay topo.

In the 5 miles to the summit of Mount Tallac this hike gains almost 3,400 feet at a rather punishing pace. Along the way, though, you'll pass beautiful Floating

Island Lake and Cathedral Lake, cross several creeks, and plunge through a beautiful forest before beginning the grueling climb up the ridgeline to the summit. The last 2 miles are the killer. The footpath is rocky and slippery. No shade helps cool you down. The trail ahead seems to be growing longer, not shorter. Don't despair. A mile away from your goal you'll see the summit and it will look like you'll never reach it. You will, and when you do, you'll be rewarded with an outrageous view. You're standing on a narrow ridgeline summit with a 360° view of the entire Tahoe Basin. Fallen Leaf Lake and Emerald Bay lie to your east. The Desolation Wilderness spreads out behind you. The wind on this almost 10,000-foot summit will probably push you on your way home before too long.

Rubicon Trail, Sugar Pine Point State Park

4.2 miles one way. Easy. Access: Sugar Pine Point State Park Calawee Beach or Emerald Bay. Map: Sugar Pine State Park map.

This is the longest waterfront trail on the California shore of Tahoe. Along the way you pass numerous tempting swimming beaches and granite cliffs where you can see the seemingly bottomless depth of the lake. You'll also meander through a scenic boat-in-only camp. The Rubicon connects Sugar Pine Point State Park with Emerald Bay State Park. Leave a car at the Emerald Bay parking lot or Calawee Beach for a shuttle or do the hike round-trip. This is a great hike to combine with a tour of the Vikingsholm Mansion on the shore of Emerald Bay.

South Grove Trail, Calaveras Big Trees

5.25 miles. Moderate. Access: End of Memorial Parkway in Calaveras Big Trees State Park. Map: Purchase at visitors center or trailhead.

Most visitors to Calaveras Big Trees only visit the easily accessible North Grove, but the most rewarding nature experience with the best trees is actually on the other side of the river in the South Grove. Here, this 5.5-mile loop winds through second-growth sequoia for about a mile before getting into the really good stuff, the old-growth giants. The biggest tree in the park is here: 250-foot Agassiz Tree, named after a Swiss naturalist who was instrumental in protecting the trees. Beaver Creek provides a nice backdrop for the understory of dogwoods, poison oak, and azalea.

Burst Rock to Powell Lake

3.8 miles round-trip. Moderate to strenuous. Access: Off State Route 108 near Pinecrest. Drive to end of unpaved Crabtree Road and Gianelli's Cabin Trailhead. Map: USGS Pinecrest topo.

This is a good half- or whole-day wilderness sampler. Though you're less than 2 miles from your car at Powell Lake, it has the high alpine feel of much harder-to-reach lakes. Of course you won't be alone. This is a very popular hike as well as the main access into a huge section of the Emigrant Wilderness. The highest point of the hike is appropriately the metaphorical high point as well. From the top of 9,150-foot Burst Rock you can see for miles into the surrounding wilderness—a vista of dramatic canyons, blue jewel lakes, and the volcanic spires of the Dardenalles.

Heiser Lake

4.5 miles round-trip. Moderate. Consecutive ups and downs. Access: Mosquito Lake near Ebbetts Pass on State Route 4. Map: USGS Spicer Meadows and USGS Pacific Valley maps.

Short but sweet is the best way to describe this hike. Little Heiser Lake is a tucked-away, tree-lined lake deep enough to support a nice population of trout. Several granite islands make a good goal for a summer-day swim. The trail rollercoasters up and down a few false rises before the final summit and drop into Heiser. None of them are too huge, but the combined effect of all those climbs can be pretty tiring.

OVERNIGHTS

Rubicon Lake, Desolation Wilderness

16 miles round-trip. Moderate. Mostly level. Allow 2 or 3 days. Access: Park at trailhead on State Route 89, 0.1 miles south of Meeks Bay Resort. Map: USFS Desolation Wilderness map. Wilderness permit required.

For an 8-miler in the Sierra Nevada, the hike to Rubicon Lake is remarkably level and easy. The only really steep pitch comes in the last quarter-mile before the lake. Along the way in you pass five other lakes, including several with good campsites if you want to spend the night on the trail. Rubicon Lake is tiny, but good for swimming in the shadow of Jakes Peak. Good campsites are found in the lodgepole pine forest surrounding the lake.

Emigrant Lake, Mokelumne Wilderness

9 miles round-trip. Easy (perfect overnight). Access: Park at Caples Dam Parking Area just off State Route 88. Map: USFS Mokelumne Wilderness map.

Almost half of the 4.5 miles into Emigrant Lake follow the shoreline of beautiful Caples Lake. I suppose it would be possible to cheat and hitch a ride across the lake by boat, but the walk is nice in its own right. Eventually the trail turns and follows Emigrant Creek along a gentle meadow-lined valley lushly vegetated with aspen and wildflowers. A short steep climb tells you that you're almost there. A sometimes dicey rock hop over the lake's outlet creek and you're confronted with the first glimpse of steep-sided Emigrant Lake. Carved by glaciers, steep granite talus cliffs drop straight into the water. Several coves allow fishing and swimming access, but the water is extremely cold until the end of summer when it warms up to just plain cold.

Bull Run Lake

7.4 miles round-trip. Moderate. Allow 2 or 3 days. Access: Take Stanislaus Meadow Trailhead turnoff from State Route 4. Drive as far as conditions allow down the half-mile road (leave low-clearance cars on highway). Map: Carson–Iceberg Wilderness map.

Bull Run Lake was one of my first backpacking experiences as a kid. We built a raft and floated to the rock island in the center of the lake. It fell apart, so we swam back and nearly froze. That night we thought a bear was in camp, but it turned out to be my father snoring. The next day I climbed the mountain behind the lake alone to watch the sun go down and ran back to camp before darkness fell. Great times for a 10-year-old. I've been back since and it's still a magic place for me. The hike in is steep, but you can tolerate 3-plus miles of just about anything to reach a place this beautiful.

KAYAKING

The advent of the sit-on-top kayak has fostered a boom in casual lake kayakers

Mountain Words

When writing about mountains one runs into a little problem: England, where our language developed, isn't known for its great mountain ranges. As a result, English is not a tongue rich in mountain words. Since the United States, on the other hand, has amazing mountains, we've been forced to look elsewhere for our descriptive language or make up our own. Many of the best mountain words have come from French, German, Italian, and Spanish, the Alps and Pyrenees being what they are. These are beautiful, sonorous words, subtle words, words that will teach you to see things in mountains you didn't know were there:

Arête: Sharp-crested mountain ridge
Bergschrund: Series of crevasses
Butte: A solitary, steep hill or small mountain
Caldera: Volcanic crater left by an eruption
Cirque: A steep bowl-like mountain basin
Col: Pass or saddle between mountains
Cordillera: A system of mountain chains

Couloir (Cool-Wahr): A steep, mountainside gorge or gully
Crevasse: A glacial fissure or deep crack
Defile: Narrow pass between hills or cliffs; gorge
Escarpment: Cliff formation
Esker: A gravelly or sandy mountain ridge
Glacier: Slow-moving mass of perennial ice
Hogback: Sharp-crested mountain ridge
Hoodoo: Oddly eroded rock column
Massif: A mountain range section or mass
Moraine: Glacial deposit of rocks and boulders
Moulin: A vertical shaft worn by water pouring though a crack in a glacier
Palisade: Line of cliffs
Piedmont: Area at the foot of a range
Randkluft: Chasm left by a receding glacier
Scree: Rocky debris on a mountain slope
Serac: Jagged glacial ridge or ice fall
Sierra: Chain of mountains with saw-tooth peaks
Talus: Rocky debris below a cliff
Tarn: Small mountain lake with steep sides
Traverse: A place suitable for crossing a mountain face

on Tahoe. You don't need any particular ability to paddle one, and they open doors to places you'd never see otherwise. They're more or less uncapsizable and unswampable, and their low freeboard leaves them less at the mercy of Tahoe's occasionally fierce winds. **Kayak Tahoe** (tel. 530/544-2011) and **Tahoe Paddle and Oar** (tel. 530/581-3029) are both based on the west shore of the lake near some of the best paddling and they provide rental equipment, tours, and instruction.

Whitewater kayakers have several great Class II and III runs available to them on the **Truckee River** before it flows down into Nevada. The **River Ranch Run** is the best, roughly 11 miles of continuous Class II and III. From River Ranch to Truckee, a solid Class III paddler only has to worry about one thing: low-clearance bridges if the water is high. Call either of the shops listed above for detailed route information and recommendations. Other than the Truckee, most good whitewater on

Sierra Nevada rivers occurs farther downriver in the Gold Country canyons. Not that these high mountain stretches don't get run occasionally—they do, and you can find excellent descriptions in Chuck Stanley and Lars Holbek's classic *A Guide to the Best Whitewater in the State of California* (Friends of the River Books, 1984), but these upper runs are volatile and dangerous Class V and VI runs. If you can handle that, you don't need me telling you where to go.

MOUNTAIN BIKING

The northern Sierra has more good mountain bike rides than you could do in a lifetime. Over a century of logging and mining did have one positive outcome: an incredible network of skid trails, mine roads, and grades into some of the most out-there outback of the Sierra. While all wilderness areas and most state parks ban mountain biking, the vast majority of national forest land is open. The most famous ride in the area, Tahoe's mind-bogglingly scenic and challenging Flume Ride, is actually in Nevada beginning in Spooner Lake State Park, but numerous less-well-known rides wind above the California shore as well. A recently booming sport is summertime mountain biking at downhill ski areas. Call me a masochist, but I actually like riding up huge mountains on my own. If you prefer the easy way up, though, **Squaw Valley** (tel. 530/583-6985) will load you and your bike into the tram for a quick blast to the summit. From there it truly is all downhill. **Northstar-at-Tahoe** (tel. 530/562-2248) maintains their cross-country ski trails as a mountain biking park in summer and rents equipment on site. In Tahoe, **City Porter's Ski and Sport** (tel. 530/583-0293) and **CyclePaths** (tel. 530/581-1171) are both great stops to get local trail maps and advice. They also offer guided half-day and full-day mountain bike tours in the surrounding area. In Truckee, **Paco's Truckee Bike and Ski** (tel. 530/587-5561) offers many similar services.

For more detailed descriptions of Tahoe area rides, including the Western States 100, Flume Trail, Paige Meadows Truckee River Loop, and many more, consult Carol Bonser's fantastically in-depth *Mountain Biking the High Sierra: Lake Tahoe–North* (Fine Edge Productions, 1993) and *Mountain Biking the High Sierra: Lake Tahoe–South* (Fine Edge Productions, 1993).

Blackwood Canyon

8–20 miles. Easy to moderate. Access: Park at Blackwood Canyon Trailhead 4 miles south of Tahoe City on State Route 89. Map: USGS Tahoe and Granite Chief topos.

The lower 4 miles of Blackwood Canyon Trail makes a great introductory ride for novice trail bikers. It's a single track all right, but a level and smooth one. For a loop return, head back along the gravel road when you reach Blackwood Creek. More ambitious riders will want to turn left and bike up the Blackwood Canyon gravel road to the top of Barker Pass, 7 miles and 1,500 feet of elevation gain from here.

Sugar Pine Point State Park

Distance varies. Easy. Access: Sugar Pine State Park off State Route 89. Map: Park map.

Though bikes aren't allowed on the foot trails in Sugar Pine State Park, numerous maintenance roads and bike paths make this a good place for kids or beginners to try out their fat wheeler. Several nice loops explore the less-developed portions of the lakeshore.

Flume Trail

24 miles round-trip. Moderate. 2,600-foot elevation gain. Allow at least 6 hours. Access: Drive east on U.S. 50 out of South Lake Tahoe and turn north on Nevada State Route 28. Spooner Lake State Park is 0.5 miles up on your right. Map: USGS Carson City topo.

Okay, we're not in California anymore, but it's impossible to discuss mountain biking in the Tahoe area without mentioning the Flume Ride. If you can, try to ride this on a weekday; it gets jammed on the weekends. But either way, don't miss it. Parts of this trail are grueling—steep inclines on rock-filled sand (keep your weight on your back tire)—but the flume itself is unbelievable. Four and a half miles of perfect single track looking out over Lake Tahoe far below is a worthy reward for any climb. Once you get to the top, ride the little trail down to Marlette Lake for lunch or a swim. Head back up to the trail and then it's all downhill. And yes, logs were once floated along here from man-made Marlette Lake to Lake Tahoe to be milled.

ROAD BIKING

Tour of Lake Tahoe

Distance: 72 miles. Strenuous. Access: Anywhere around Lake Tahoe with a motel room or campsite for you to collapse in at the end of your ride. Map: AAA or any other good Tahoe area road map.

For a 72-mile ride in the mountains, this one is relatively flat (total climb about 3,000 feet). But don't jump into your biking shorts thinking it's going to be easy. First of all, you're over a mile high, so the distance alone is going to feel more like a century. The other challenge, unfortunately, is staying sane through miles of heavily trafficked roads. Sadly, this isn't the kind of road ride where you can get all delirious and wiggly without getting squished by an RV. Several stretches follow nice bike paths, but they crisscross the highway. The worst stretch is State Route 89 above Emerald Bay. The road is narrow with drop-offs, and I swear some people drive it without looking at the road once. For that reason I suggest camping at Sugar Pine Point State Park and riding the Emerald Bay to South Lake Tahoe stretch early in the morning when traffic is light and when you're fresh. From Sugar Pine you take State Route 89 to South Lake, the bike route through town, turn northwest on U.S. 50 (scary), then turn north on Nevada State Route 28 (ahh, relief), cruise the Nevada Shore until Lake Shore Drive takes you through Kings Beach. Get back on State Route 28 until it connects back with State Route 89, and then you're nearly home. I've described the loop counterclockwise because I like it better that way, but feel free to reverse it so you can have the good views—and scary drop-offs—on your side of the road.

ROCK CLIMBING

The bad news is it isn't Yosemite. The good news is it isn't Yosemite. The atmosphere is friendlier and it's far less crowded—it's not quite the "scene" that Yosemite is. The granite this far north has a tendency to be a bit more weathered and crumbly than Yosemite, but that's a bit like complaining that the champagne is a slightly off year of Dom Perignon. **Donner Summit** and **Lovers Leap** are the two major Tahoe areas, and both have numerous routes. **Mountain Adventure Seminars** (tel. 209/753-6556 or 800/362-5462) on State Route 4 offers instruction around Ebbetts Pass.

Donner Memorial Nature Trail

0.5 miles. Access: Donner Memorial State Park. Trail begins at Emigrant Trail Museum.

Though today you can hear the roar of cars and trucks on nearby Interstate 80, this park memorializes one of the most haunting and heart-wrenching tales of California history, the terrible winter spent here by the Donner party after a surprise October snowstorm caught them. Heroic rescue attempts failed, and by spring only 47 of the original 89 members of the party were alive. The survivors were forced to cannibalize their dead to survive. This short trail combines an explanation of the glacial geology that shaped this alpine lake valley with a stop at a carved granite boulder bearing the names of everyone who spent that terrible winter here. Donner Creek runs through the area, a gentle stream perfect for kids to explore on their own.

Calaveras Big Trees North Grove Trail

1 mile. Access: Visitors center and picnic area at park entrance.

This flat, smooth loop through the Big Trees is a good way to see the grandeur of the giant sequoia for those who can't or don't want to hike into the park's more remote South Grove. The self-guided interpretive trail explains the interesting botany of the sequoia, and trailside signs will teach you to recognize common forest plants like the dogwood, hazel, and azalea. The strangest sight of all is the 24-foot-diameter stump of the Discovery Tree, which was used as a dance floor after the tree was felled. Unlike some other sequoia groves, this one has a rather mixed population of Douglas fir, sugar pines, and ponderosa pines, all of which seem diminutive next to the giant sequoia.

Most of the raftable whitewater in the northern Sierra begins lower down in the foothills of the Gold Country. Up high, the rivers are too extreme for most commercial rafting or for rafting period. The Truckee River, however, is a grand exception. Exciting but forgiving Class III rapids run almost nonstop for 10 miles. Contact the **Tahoe North Visitors and Convention Bureau** (tel. 800/ TAHOE-4-U) for a current list of outfitters running the Truckee.

For a bigger adrenaline surge, rafters with some experience in self-bailing paddleboats can bomb the relentless **North Fork of the Stanislaus River** right through Calaveras Big Trees. This highly technical Class IV run has a short season, usually from April until the end of June. The scenery along this run is outstanding: sequoias, waterfalls, deer, blooming azaleas and dogwoods. But you'll probably be too busy trying not to hit that huge hole after you career off that huge rock to really notice. Contact **Whitewater Adventures** (tel. 707/ 255-0761) or **Beyond Limits** (tel. 800/ 234-RAFT) for schedules of commercial trips down this part of the Stanislaus.

Southern Sierra: Yosemite to Sequoia/Kings Canyon ◆ What to Do & Where to Do It

The southern Sierra from Yosemite to Sequoia/Kings Canyon is otherworldly. This, the high roadless area known as the High Sierra, is where John Muir fell madly in love with these mountains. This is his "Range of Light" that inspired so many later writings and galvanized his philosophy of protecting wilderness for wilderness' sake while others were still stuck on the idea that places should only be saved if they are scenic or contain some sort of freak of nature like a funny rock, or a bunch of geysers of interest to tourists (come to think of it, many people are still stuck on that way of thinking).

As a result of the extreme isolation of much of the southern Sierra, it is a hard-core backpacker's and peak bagger's paradise. Very few places in the Lower 48 allow you to get as far "out there" as you can in the John Muir Wilderness and the backcountry of Sequoia/Kings Canyon National Park. But there are also plenty of places that can be explored by day hike, or even from your car. The Yosemite Valley, of course, is popular with day users to the point of damage. Other great places to pack a picnic and make a mellow day of it are Tuolumne Meadows in Yosemite, or Mineral King Valley in Sequoia/Kings Canyon. Climbers will be in heaven with the huge walls of perfect Sierra Nevada granite looming all over the place, whether they're flashing a bouldering problem in the Yosemite Valley or nearing the top of a multi-day climb in the high peaks near Mount Whitney. Probably the only people that will be sorely disappointed by the southern Sierra are mountain bikers, who as a result of the National Parks Service and National Forest Service prohibitions on offroad riding into the wilderness will find their options severely restricted.

BIRD WATCHING

Yosemite Park's elevation ranges from 2,000 feet to over 13,000, enclosing numerous entire plant and animal communities. Of particular interest to birders are the high meadows that provide hunting grounds for raptors such as the great gray owl, golden eagle, and osprey. These meadows are also home to many species of grosbeaks, warblers, and hummingbirds. Occasionally you'll catch a blue grouse wandering the edge of the conifer forest boundary. In the lodgepole and white pine forests around Lake Tenaya you can find numerous pine-nut-and-needle-eating species like the white-headed and black-backed woodpeckers, Clark's nutcracker, and Steller's jay.

Sequoia and Kings Canyon National Parks share similar habitats with Yosemite, including the majestic giant sequoia forests where you might catch a glimpse of a gold-crowned kinglet or a pileated woodpecker.

BOARDSAILING

As the Sierra Nevada becomes taller toward the southern end of the range, large alpine lakes become more scarce. **Lake Tenaya** on Tioga Pass is one popular boardsailing spot—the wind here makes a gorgeous sound as it moans around the lake's granite domes and through the lodgepole pine forest. Tenaya is shallow and rocky, so beware, but the scenery is incomparable. Several good pull-outs and beaches on State Route 120 make for good rigging and launching. **Huntington** and **Shaver lakes** are also popular with boardsailors. Huntington hosts sailing regattas every summer weekend. Call the **Sierra National Forest Ranger District** (tel. 209/855-5360) or **Huntington Lake Resort** (tel. 209/893-3226) for more information about rental equipment and instruction.

CANOEING

As road access and large lakes become more scarce in the southern reaches of the Sierra, so do your opportunities to canoe. **Tenaya Lake** is a great place to paddle, but you'll have to bring your own boat. The same goes for the **Merced River** in the Yosemite Valley, and beware of going too far downriver. Below the El Capitan Bridge the tranquil Merced becomes solid Class III and IV water, no place for a canoe. **Huntington Lake Resort** (tel. 209/893-3226) rents canoes and other small craft on that beautiful alpine lake during the summer.

CROSS-COUNTRY SKIING & SNOWSHOEING

The national parks of the southern Sierra are some of the greatest backcountry skiing regions in the world. Several trans-Sierra routes begin or end here, including the famed **Sierra Haute Route** through Kings Canyon (see "Cross-Country Skiing" under "Eastern Sierra: What to Do & Where to Do It") and **State Route 120/Tioga Pass** in Yosemite. The **Yosemite Cross-Country Ski School** (tel. 209/372-8444) leads guided 6-day trips over Tioga Pass with a cabin-based overnight at Tuolumne Meadows for approximately $435 (not counting return airfare to Lee Vining). Their **Glacier Point overnight ski trip** is a more subdued overnight. You'll ski about 10 miles of groomed track up to Glacier Point, one of the best vistas in the entire park, where your guide cooks dinner and breakfast. No need to pack a tent; lodging is in the new log & stone Glacier Point Lodge. Reservations are required. Skiers not part of the overnight program are welcome to use the groomed track to Glacier Point at no charge. The 20-mile round-trip is a good all-day ski for a strong skier. The ski school is located at the **Badger Pass Ski Area** (tel. 209/372-8430) and also offers rental gear and a full slate of on-site lessons for all abilities, ranging from basic technique to trans-Sierra crossings. If you're on your own, **Crane Flat,** located off the park road about 5 miles southeast of the Big Oak Flat entrance to Yosemite, is another good place to go. Just outside the south entrance to the park, **Goat Camp** (tel. 209/683-4665) has 18 miles of marked national forest ski trails, some of which cross into Yosemite's amazing Mariposa Grove of giant sequoias. A snow-covered trek through these giants is something you'll never forget.

Sierra Summit (tel. 209/233-2500), near Huntington Lake, is a popular downhill resort for the Fresno area crowd, but not many people know about the excellent cross-country skiing in this same neighborhood. Contact the **Hume Lake Ranger Station** (tel. 209/338-2252) to have them send you a trail map of the region.

Two Nordic ski areas operate in Sequoia and Kings Canyon National Parks. Just north of Giant Forest Village, the park's "downtown," **Sequoia Ski Touring** (tel. 559/565-3435) at Wolverton near Giant Forest Village, offers rentals and trail maps for 35 miles of well-marked backcountry trails through the sequoias. In Kings Canyon, **Sequoia Ski Touring** (tel. 559/335-2314) in Grant Grove near the northern entrance to the park provides the same services and an even wider selection of trails. People with their own equipment are welcome on all trails in the park at no cost. Trail maps are available at the visitor centers.

On winter weekends, park rangers at Sequoia/Kings Canyon lead introductory snowshoe hikes (snowshoes provided) at **Sequoia Ski Touring** in Grant Grove (tel. 559/335-2314).

DOWNHILL SKIING & SNOWBOARDING

Well, one thing you can say about skiing in the southern Sierra is that it's easy to decide where you want to go since you only have two choices. There's **Badger Pass** in Yosemite, the oldest ski area in California, or **Sierra Summit** above Huntington Lake. Both mountains allow snowboarding.

Badger Pass Ski Area

Badger Pass, Yosemite National Park. Tel. 209/372-8430; 209/372-1000 for snow conditions. 9 trails (35% beginner, 50% intermediate, 15% expert); 5 lifts including 1 triple, 3 doubles, and 1 surface; 800-foot vertical drop. Full-day adult ticket $22 weekdays, $28 weekends.

Badger is a mountain from the days when advanced skiing meant you knew how to do a stem christie and could stop without falling over or grabbing anything. Skiing's come a long way since then, but Badger just doesn't have the terrain to keep up. It is, on the other hand, a great beginner and easy intermediate mountain and it's cheap. Bring on the kids and families.

Sierra Summit Ski Area

59265 State Route 168, Lakeshore. Tel. 209/233-2500; 209/233-3330 for snow conditions. 20 trails (10% beginner, 65% intermediate, 25% expert); 9 lifts including 2 triples, 3 doubles, and 4 surface; 1,600-foot vertical drop. Full-day adult ticket $25 weekdays, $35 weekends.

In contrast to Badger Pass, Sierra Summit is blessed with a good amount of expert and advanced terrain, but also has enough beginner and intermediate runs to keep everyone happy.

FISHING

Numerous reservoirs in the area offer great lake fishing, particularly **Shaver Lake** on State Route 168. Depending on the season, you'll catch anything from smallmouth bass and catfish to trophy-sized brown and rainbow trout.

In Yosemite, the **Merced River** in the valley is catch and release only. Barbless hooks are required. You can fish for your dinner at various High Country lakes and streams, which are literally leaping with trout. A California license is required and available in the park at the Yosemite Village Sportshop.

Backpackers into the John Muir Wilderness and the backcountry of Sequoia/Kings Canyon will find hundreds of lakes waiting to be fished. Some are dead; others hold relentless schools of trout that will practically maul each other to get at your fly or lure. Trout fishing in the lower altitudes is fairly limited, mostly along the banks of the **Kings** and **Kaweah rivers**. High Country lakes are refuges for rare pure-strain, wild trout and are not stocked with hatchery fish. Before venturing into the High Country, inquire at a ranger station about the area you'll be visiting to find out about closures or specific regulations. A California fishing license is required for everyone over 16 years old. Tackle and licenses are available at several campgrounds and park stores.

HIKES, BUSHWHACKS & BACKPACK TRIPS

The hiking options in Yosemite and Sequoia/Kings Canyon are seemingly endless. If you've completed the hikes below and are still crying for more, consult some of the specialized guidebooks to the area. For Yosemite, *Tuolumne Meadows* by Jeffrey B. Shaffer and Thomas Winnett (Wilderness Press, 1977) and *Yosemite National Park* by Thomas Winnett and Jason Winnett (Wilderness Press, 1983) are two of the best. For Sequoia/Kings Canyon, the

Yosemite National Park

This area first became widely known to white men when a troop of U.S. soldiers in the Mariposa Battalion, sent to chase down a band of Native Americans, stumbled upon this natural wonder and were awestruck by its beauty. They regaled their friends with tales of its impossible geography when they got home, and Yosemite's popularity has been steadily increasing ever since.

It's a place of record-setting statistics: the highest waterfall in North America and three of the world's 10 tallest waterfalls (Upper Yosemite Falls, Ribbon Falls, and Sentinel Falls); the tallest and largest single granite monolith in the world (El Capitan); the most recognizable mountain (Half Dome); one of the world's largest trees (the Grizzly Giant in Mariposa Grove); and literally thousands of rare plant and animal species.

Unfortunately, popularity isn't always the greatest thing for wild places. Over the last 20 years, tourist-magnet **Yosemite Valley** has set records for the worst crowding, noise, crime, and traffic of any California national park.

The park covers more than 1,000 square miles but the majority of visitors flock to the floor of "the valley," a 1-mile-wide, 7-mile-long freak of glacial scouring that tore a deep and steep valley from the solid granite of the Sierra Nevada. It's still one of the most beautiful places on earth, but in summer the place seems like Jellystone Park—a Yogi Bear freak show. To make it worse, the Park Service, which once called for eliminating auto traffic in the valley and reducing infrastructure inside the park, has done the exact opposite, continuing to allow kitchy concession signs, rinky-dink curio shops, an auto repair garage, several hotels, a post office, a small hospital, and last but certainly not least, a jail, to turn Yosemite Valley into an urban mess, albeit a pretty one.

Car traffic in the valley creates bumper-to-bumper gridlock on almost any busy weekend. There have been several plans to cut down on the number of cars permitted to enter the valley, but so far federal authorities have failed to muster the courage to implement them. If you want to enjoy the things that bring all those people to the valley without having to deal with the hordes themselves, come here before Memorial Day or after Labor Day.

If you must go in summer, try to do your part to help out. It's not so much the numbers of people that are ruining the valley but their insistence on driving from attraction to attraction within the valley. Once you're here, park your car and bike, hike, or ride the double-decker shuttle buses that go everywhere in the valley. Bring your own bike or rent one in the park. A wonderful and underused network of bike paths will take you anywhere you want to go with no parking hassles. And you'll get an open-air view while everyone else is honking their horns and craning their necks to see out a car window. (Two of the park's concessions, Curry Village and Yosemite Lodge, rent bikes during summer; for more information on these places, see "Campgrounds & Other Accommodations" later in this chapter.) It may take longer to get from point A to point B, but you're in one of the most gorgeous places on earth, so why hurry?

What most sets Yosemite Valley apart is its incredible geology. The Sierra Nevada was formed between 10 and 80 million years ago when a tremendous geological uplift pushed layers of granite lying under the ocean up into an incredible mountain range. Cracks and rifts in the rock gave erosion a start at carving canyons and valleys. Then, during the last ice age, at least three glaciers flowed through the valley, shearing away at the land, hauling away the rubble, and leaving vertical faces of stone. The last glacier retreated 10,000 to 15,000 years ago, but left its legacy in the incredible number of huge, high waterfalls pouring into the valley from hanging side canyons.

The 7-square-mile valley is really a huge bathtub drain for the combined runoff of hundreds of square miles of snow-covered peaks. From the 4,000-foot-high valley floor, the 8,000-foot tops of El Capitan, Half Dome, and Glacier Point look like the top of the world, but they're small in comparison to the high peaks in the park, some of which rise to nearly 14,000 feet. High country creeks flushed with snowmelt catapult over the abyss left by the glaciers and form an outrageous variety of falls, from tiny ribbons that never reach ground to the torrents of Nevada Falls and Vernal Falls. In concert with the shadows and lighting of the deep valley, the effect of all this falling water is mesmerizing. On a clear spring morning you'll see more rainbows than you can count and hear a bass note of roaring water echoing through the entire valley.

All that vertical stone gets put to use by hundreds who flock to the park for some of the finest climbing anywhere. Sharp-eyed visitors will spot a lot of climbers hanging off the sheer faces of Yosemite's famous walls; among these are the aforementioned El Capitan and Half Dome. Sometimes spending as long as 10 days slung from the rock, the world's best climbers are here to see and be seen proving their mettle. At the base of the big walls you'll find climbers of all abilities practicing moves and belaying techniques on smaller pitches.

The valley is also home to beautiful meadows and the meandering Merced River. When the last glacier retreated, it dammed Merced River with a pile of glacial debris and formed a lake where the valley is now. Eventually sediment from the river filled the lake and created the rich and level valley floor we see today; tiny Mirror Lake, in the upper end of the valley, is all that remains of this once-huge body of water. Float trips—by raft, inner tube, or other conveyance—are a summer staple on the slow-moving Merced.

Deer and coyote frequent the valley, often causing vehicular mayhem as one heavy-footed looky-lou slams on the brakes to whip out the Handi-cam while another rubbernecker, equally mesmerized by Bambi, drives right into him. Metal crunches, tempers flare, and the deer daintily hop away, looking amused at the stupidity.

Bears, too, are at home in the valley. The name *Yosemite* derives from the native *uzumati*, "grizzly bear." Grizzlies are gone from the park now, but black bears are plentiful and make their presence known through late-night depredations of ice chests and food in the campgrounds rather than by posing pretty for the cameras in broad daylight.

The name of nature writer John Muir, one of the founders of the conservation movement, is virtually synonymous with Yosemite. Muir came here from the Midwest in the late 19th century and ended up spending the rest of his life battling for the protection of Yosemite and the greater Sierra Nevada.

Muir won the largest battle of his life when he formed the Sierra Club and convinced President Benjamin Harrison to declare Yosemite a national park in 1890. Later, though, he suffered a critical defeat when the City of San Francisco built a water diversion dam within the park, flooding Muir's beloved

continued

Hetch Hetchy Valley, the glacial splendor of which rivaled Yosemite Valley. Always the opportunist, Muir, lobbying the federal government to declare the entire Sierra Nevada a national park, once spent 3 days swapping tall tales, drinking, and sleeping under beds of pine boughs with the old rough rider himself, President Teddy Roosevelt.

While it's easy to let the tremendous gravity of the valley draw all of your attention there, remember that 95% of Yosemite is wilderness. Very few of the 4 million visitors who come to the park each year ever get more than a mile from their car. That leaves most of Yosemite's 750,000 acres open for anyone adventurous enough to hike a few miles. Even if the valley is the hands-down winner for dramatic freak-of-nature displays, the **Yosemite High Country** offers a more subtle kind of beauty: glacial lakes, roaring rivers, and miles of granite spires and domes. The area around Tuolumne Meadows is my favorite region of the park. This spectacular High Country meadow covers several square miles along the headwaters of the Tuolumne River. Awesome day and overnight hikes lead off into the wilderness in all directions. Miles of uncrowded granite-climbing routes surround you. This is still a pristine place, unaffected by the tour-bus mentality you find in the valley, and the people who come here seem to appreciate that. Tenaya Lake is another popular High Country destination, also a starting point for many great trails to the backcountry. Whether you're here for a week or just a day, both are ideal places for fishing, climbing, or hiking. Since this area of the park is under snow from November through June, the short season we call summer is really more like spring. From snowmelt to the first snowfall, the High Country explodes with wildflowers and long-dormant wildlife trying to make the most of the short season.

The **southwest corner** of the park, with its giant sequoia groves, is also nice. While it's not the wilderness that Tuolumne Meadows is by any means, it is possible to slip into the park's south gate and enjoy a hike among the majestic giants of Mariposa Grove or along Glacier Point Road without having to deal with an overly stressful crowd scene. And just outside the park's southern boundary is Goat Camp, where you can wind through the sequoias on cross-country skis. Also in this part of the park are several meadows and the rushing south fork of the Merced River.

JUST THE FACTS

Getting There. There are four main entrances to the park. Most valley visitors enter through the Arch Rock Entrance Station on State Route 140. The best entrance for Mariposa Grove and Wawona is the south entrance on State Route 41 from Mariposa. If you're going to the country, you'll save a lot of time by coming in through the Big Oak Flat entrance, which puts you straight onto Tioga Road without dealing with the congested valley. The Tioga Pass entrance is only open in summer and is only really relevant if you're coming from the east side of the Sierra, in which case it's your only choice. A fifth, little-used entrance is the Hetch Hetchy entrance in the euphonious Poopenaut Valley, on a dead-end road.

Fees. It's $20 per car per week to enter the park or $10 per person per week for bike, motorcycle, or walk-in. Annual Yosemite passes are $40. Wilderness permits are free, but reserving them requires a $3 fee.

Visitor Centers & Information. There is a central 24-hour recorded information line for the park at 209/372-0200. All visitor-related service lines including visitors centers, campgrounds, ranger stations, hotels, and information can be accessed by touch-tone phone at 209/372-1000. By far the biggest visitors center is the Valley visitors center (tel. 209/372-0299). For interesting biological and geological displays about the High Sierra, as well as trail advice, the Tuolumne Meadows Visitors Center (tel. 209/372-0263) is great. All three can provide you with more information in the form of maps, newspapers, books, and photocopied leaflets than you'll ever read.

Regulations. Rangers in the Yosemite Valley spend more time being cops than being rangers and they have their own jail: Don't do anything here you wouldn't do in your hometown; this isn't the Wild West. Despite the pressure, park regulations are pretty simple. Wilderness permits are required for all overnight backpacking trips. Fishing licenses are required. Utilize proper food storage methods in bear country. Don't collect firewood around campgrounds. No off-road bicycle riding. Dogs are allowed in the park but must be leashed and are forbidden on the trails. Don't feed the animals.

Seasons. Winter is one of the nicest times to visit the valley. It isn't crowded like it is during summer and a dusting of snow accentuates the stark contrasts of all that granite. To see the waterfalls at their best come in spring when snowmelt is at its peak. Fall can be cool but beautiful and much less crowded.

The high country is under about 20 feet of snow from November through May, so unless you are snow camping, summer is pretty much the only season. Even in summer thundershowers are an almost daily occurrence and snow is not uncommon. Mosquitoes can be a plague during the peak of summer but get better after the first freeze.

Avoiding the Crowds. Crowds and summer in the valley go together like salt and french fries, and both will cause your blood pressure to soar. Help alleviate crowding and help yourself by doing whatever you can to visit the valley any time but between Memorial Day and Labor Day—and avoid those holidays like the plague. Otherwise, the best way to avoid the crowd is to head for the backcountry.

Even though they are overworked just trying to keep the peace, Yosemite's wonderful rangers also take time to lead a number of educational and interpretive programs ranging from backcountry hikes to fireside talks to snowcountry survival clinics. Call the main park information number with specific requests for the season and park area you'll be visiting. Also a great service are the free painting, drawing, and photography classes offered spring through fall and holiday weekends in winter at the Art Activity Center next to the Museum Gallery.

GETTING YOUR BEARINGS

The Valley. It's hard to encapsulate the valley into a list of things to see simply because the Yosemite Valley is much more than any sum of its parts. First-time visitors are often completely dumbstruck as they enter the valley from the west. The first two things you'll see are delicate and beautiful Bridal Veil Falls and the immense face of El Capitan, a beautiful and anything-but-delicate 3,593-foot-tall solid-granite

continued

rock. A short trail leads to the base of Bridal Veil, which at 620 feet tall is only a medium-sized fall by park standards, but one of the prettiest.

This is a perfect chance to get those knee-jerk tourist impulses under control early: Resist the temptation to rush around bagging sights like they're feathers for your cap. Instead, take your time and look around. One of the best things about the valley is that many of its most famous features are visible from all over. Instead of rushing to the base of every waterfall or famous rock face and getting a crick in your neck from staring straight up, go to the visitors center (see below) and spend a half-hour learning something about the features of the valley. Buy the excellent *Map and Guide to Yosemite Valley* ($2.50); it describes many excellent hikes and short nature walks. Then go take a look. Walking and biking are the best ways to get around—browse through the walks and hikes listed in this chapter for something that sounds right. To cover distances the park shuttles run frequently and everywhere.

Right in the middle of the valley's thickest urban cluster is the Valley Visitors Center (tel. 209/372-0299), with exhibits that will teach you about glacial geology, history, and the park's flora and fauna. Check out the Indian Cultural Museum next door for a lot of insight into what life in the park was once like. Excellent exhibits highlight the Miwok and Paiute cultures who occupied the park, and the museum has an awesome collection of baskets and other artifacts. Behind the center is a re-creation of Ahwahneechee Village, an Indian village like the ones that once existed here. The Museum Gallery houses a fine number of Ansel Adams works as well as other artists' work. You'll also find much interesting history and memorabilia from the career of John Muir.

If you absolutely must see it all and want to have someone tell you what you're seeing, the Valley Floor Tour (tel. 209/372-1240) is a 2-hour narrated tour by bus or open-air tram (depending on season) of the valley, with narrative on natural history, geology, and human culture. Tickets are $17.50; purchase them at valley hotels or call for advance reservations.

A few hundred yards from the visitors center is the Awahnee Hotel. Unlike the rest of the hotel accommodations in the park, the Ahwahnee actually lives up to its surroundings. (See "Campgrounds & Other Accommodations" later in this chapter for details.)

The best single view in the valley is from Sentinel Bridge over the Merced River. At sunset Half Dome's face functions as a projection screen for all the sinking sun's hues—from yellow to pink to dark purple—and the river reflects it all. Ansel Adams took one of his most famous photographs from this very spot.

The Southwest Corner. This corner of the park is densely forested and gently sculpted in comparison to the stark granite that makes up so much of the park. Coming from the valley, State Route 41 passes through a long tunnel. Just prior to the tunnel entrance is Tunnel View, sight of another famous Ansel Adams photograph, and the best scenic outlook of the valley accessible by automobile. Virtually the whole valley is laid out below: Half Dome and Yosemite Falls straight ahead in the distance, Bridal Veil to the right, and El Capitan to the left.

A few miles past the tunnel, Glacier Point Road turns off to the east. Closed in winter, this winding road leads to a picnic area and visitors center at Glacier Point, site of another fabulous view of the valley, this time 3,000 feet below.

Schedule at least an hour to drive here from the valley and an hour or two to absorb the view. This is a good place to study the glacial scouring of the valley below; the Glacier Point perspective makes it easy to picture the valley below filled with vast sheets of ice.

Thirty miles south of the valley on State Route 41 is the Wawona Hotel and the Pioneer Yosemite History Center. In 1879 the Wawona was the first lodge built in the state reserve that would later become the national park. Its Victorian architecture evokes a time when travelers spent several days in horse-drawn wagons to get to the park. What a welcome stop it must have been. (See "Campgrounds & Other Accommodations" later in this chapter for more information.) The Pioneer Center is a collection of early homesteading log buildings across the river from the Wawona.

One of the primary reasons Yosemite was first set aside as a park was the Mariposa Grove of sequoias. These humongous trees have personalities that match their gargantuan size. Single limbs on the biggest tree in the grove, the Grizzly Giant, are 10 feet thick. The tree itself is 209 feet tall, 32 feet in diameter, and more than 2,700 years old. Totally out of proportion with the size of the trees are the tiny cones of the sequoia. Smaller than a baseball and tightly closed, the cones will not release their cargo of seeds until opened by fire. Many good trails lead through the grove.

The High Country. Of the entire Sierra Nevada, the High Country of Yosemite has the most grandiose landscape. Dome after dome of beautifully crystalline granite reflects the sunlight above deep-green meadows and icy-cold rivers. Tioga Pass (on State Route 120) is the gateway to the High Country. At times it clings to the side of steep rock faces; other times it weaves through canyon bottoms. Several good campgrounds make it a pleasing overnight alternative to summertime crowds in the valley, though use is increasing here too. Unlike the valley, a car is vital to getting around here, as the only public transportation is the once-a-day bus to Tuolumne Meadows. Leaving the valley at 8am, the bus will let you off anywhere along the way. The driver waits 2 hours at Tuolumne Meadows, which isn't much time to see anything, then heads back down to the valley, returning around 4pm. One-way fare is $12, or slightly less to intermediate destinations.

Tenaya Lake is a popular windsurfing, fishing, canoeing, sailing, and swimming spot. The water is very chilly. Many good hikes lead into the high country from here and the granite domes surrounding the lake are popular with climbers. Fishing here varies greatly from year to year.

Near the top of Tioga Pass is stunning Tuolumne Meadows. This enormous meadow, covering several square miles, is bordered by the Tuolumne River on one side and spectacular granite peaks on the other. The meadow is cut by many stream channels full of trout, and herds of mule deer are almost always present. The Tuolumne Meadows Lodge and store is a welcome counterpoint to the overdeveloped valley. In winter the canvas roofs are removed and the buildings fill with snow. You can buy last-minute backpacking supplies here, and there is a basic burgers-and-fries cafe.

The myriad adventures you can have in Yosemite—from easy walks to scaling granite walls, from fishing and float trips to cross-country ski tours—are listed throughout the "Southern Sierra ◆ What to Do & Where to Do It" section. Let your fingers do the walking and have fun.

official park map and guide gives good basic maps for the park, but for serious hiking you'll want to check out *Sierra South: 100 Back-Country Trips in California's Sierra* by Thomas Winnett and Jason Winnett (Wilderness Press, 1993). Another good guide is *Kings Canyon Country*, a hiking handbook by Ginny and Lew Clark (Western Trails Publications, 1985). The Grant Grove and Giant Forest visitor centers both sell a complete selection of maps and guidebooks to the park.

DAY HIKES

Yosemite Falls Trail

7 miles round-trip. Moderate to difficult. Steep, narrow switchbacks. Access: Yosemite Falls Trailhead at Sunnyside Campground. Map: Park map.

The Yosemite Falls Trail zigzags 3.5 miles from Sunnyside Campground to the top of Upper Yosemite Falls. This trail gives you an inkling of the weird vertically oriented world climbers enter when they head up Yosemite's sheer walls. As you climb this narrow switchbacked trail, the valley floor drops away until people below are like ants, but the top doesn't appear any closer. It's a little unnerving at first. Plan on spending all day on this 7-mile round-trip because of the incredibly steep climb.

Nevada and Vernal Falls, Yosemite Valley

7 miles round-trip. Moderate to difficult. Granite steps on the descent can be slippery. Access: Yosemite Valley. Trailhead at Happy Isles near Curry Village. Map: Park map.

This trail is the northernmost reach of the 200-mile John Muir Trail. From the valley floor you hike up the John Muir Trail to the top of Nevada Falls. For one of the most intense perspectives you'll ever get, look right over the brink of the falls. The feeling of vertigo and motion is not for the faint-hearted, but it's certainly a rush. From 2,000 feet above Happy Isles where you began, it's a dizzying view straight down the face of the fall. After taking in the view of the valley below and the strange side-angle perspective of Half Dome, return via the Mist Trail. Much of the Mist Trail consists of steps carved out of granite. Sometimes it's slippery. The trail/staircase descends alongside Nevada Falls and passes through a small flat containing Emerald Pool and the Silver Apron, a tempting-looking water slide above the pool. Just below Emerald Pool the trail descends again right along the rushing cataract of Vernal Falls. On a hot day this trail is a cool wonderland. When the water is really high, though, it can be positively scary.

Tuolumne Meadows to Glen Aulin High Sierra Camp, Yosemite

13 miles round-trip. Moderate. Access: From Tuolumne Meadows Visitors Center, follow dirt road sign "Stables." Park where road veers right. Trailhead on left. Map: USGS Tuolumne Meadows map.

The first part of this hike is striking enough, a flat journey through one of the best alpine meadows in Yosemite. Mule deer often graze in large herds, and you're likely to see waterfowl and large trout in the river. Stop off at Soda Springs and taste the highly effervescent water bubbling out of the ground in the small log-framed spring house. Continuing downstream, you'll leave the meadow and follow the north bank of the river for a couple miles through a mixed conifer forest with lots of small meadows and wildflowers. Soon, the river begins to run faster. You're entering the Grand Canyon of the Tuolumne. The next 2.5 miles down to Glen Aulin are spectacular; the river cascades through roaring cataracts and the trail crosses over the river several times on small bridges. Finally you wind down to Glen Aulin High Sierra Camp, built at the base of roaring Glen Aulin Falls. A small store here sells snacks and drinks, but things are pricey; they came in on mule after all. Take a plunge in the river below the falls and rest before returning back upriver.

If you haven't had enough by Glen Aulin, an option is to continue on to Hetch Hetchy at the bottom of the canyon. There is a convenient trail the whole way down complete with numerous waterfalls and other natural wonders. If you plan on trekking the whole way down, though, plan on spending at least a night or two—it's about 30 miles from Tuolomne Meadows to Hetch Hetchy.

This is only one of many fantastic hikes that depart from Tuolomne Meadows; so many hikes lead from here into the backcountry it is impossible to do them justice. A good day hike is the 5-mile climb to Cathedral Lake. This steep but shady trail passes an icy cold spring and traverses several meadows.

Redwood Mountain Loop, Sequoia/Kings Canyon

6.3 miles. Moderate. Access: Redwood Saddle Trailhead, Kings Canyon National Park Road off State Route 180. Map USGS Giant Forest topo or Sequoia/Kings Canyon Park map.

In stark contrast to the tourist-thronged Giant Forest in this same park, the Redwood Mountain Grove of sequoias lies in a much wilder setting. You're likely to not see many other hikers on this remote trail along the ridgeline of Redwood Mountain. After passing through a stunning sequoia forest the trail descends into the redwood creek drainage. The trees here are thick, some of the biggest in the world. Soon you'll come to a trail junction with a sign pointing you back up to the trailhead through the lush creek valley.

Mineral King, Sequoia/Kings Canyon

Various hikes. Access: Mineral King. Map: Sequoia/Kings Canyon Park map or USGS Mineral King topo.

Many of the Sequoia/Kings Canyon's most impressive hikes are in the Mineral King section in the southern end of Sequoia. Beginning at 7,800 feet, trails lead onward and upward to destinations like Sawtooth Pass and Crystal Lake. The old White Chief Trail departs from here to the now-defunct White Chief Mine. Once a silver mining boomtown in the 1870s, Mineral King was the center of a pitched battle in the late 1970s and early 1980s when developers sought to build a huge ski resort here. They were defeated, and the wilderness remains unspoiled.

Paradise Valley Trail, Sequoia/Kings Canyon

7.5 miles. Moderate. Allow 3 hours. Access: The trailhead is at the end of the dead-end road to Cedar Grove, 6 miles east of Cedar Grove Village. Map: Park map or USGS The Sphinx topo.

The Paradise Valley Trail is a fairly easy day trip by park standards leading to beautiful Mist Falls. The falls are best in the early spring and summer because snowmelt jacks up the quantity of water pouring over the edge.

Copper Creek to Lower Tent Meadows, Sequoia/Kings Canyon

7 miles. Strenuous. Steep. Allow 3.5 hours. Access: 6 miles east of Cedar Grove Village. The trailhead is off of the second parking lot on the other side of the road's end loop. Map: Park map or USGS The Sphinx topo.

Copper Creek Trail immediately rises into the high wilderness around Granite Pass at 10,673 feet. The views of snow-capped peaks and canyons are incredible, but it is one of the most strenuous day hikes in the park. The trail continues beyond Lower Tent Meadows, but unless you're prepared to spend a night or two in the wilderness, it's best to turn around there.

Giant Forest, Sequoia/Kings Canyon

Various hikes. Access: Giant Forest off General's Highway. Map: Park map or USGS Giant Forest topo.

If the altitude and steepness are too much for you at the Copper Creek Trailhead, try some of the longer hikes in the Giant Forest. The entire forest is woven with interlocking loops that allow you to hike as short or as long as you want. The 6-mile Trail of the Sequoias will take you to the grove's far eastern end where some of the finest trees are. A fascinating side trip is the 100-foot walk through the hollow trunk of the Fallen Monarch. The fallen tree has been used for shelter for more than a hundred years and is tall enough inside that you can walk through without bending over.

OVERNIGHTS

The hundreds of square miles of Yosemite wilderness make it a prime location to really get "out there." If you plan on staying in the woods for an extended amount of time, Yosemite Park wranglers can be hired to make resupply drops at any of the backcountry High Sierra camps.

Perhaps the most famous trail in Sequoia/Kings Canyon is the Whitney Portal. Since the trailhead is only accessible from Lone Pine on the east side of the Sierra, however, I have included it with the overnights in that section.

Half Dome Cable Route, Yosemite

17 miles round-trip. Strenuous. Access: Happy Isles Trailhead, Yosemite Valley. Map: USGS Half Dome or Yosemite Park map.

Half Dome may look insurmountable by anyone but an expert rock climber, but thousands every year take the popular cable route up the back side; so many hikers have done this walk that the granite underfoot is grooved and polished from their footsteps. It's almost 17 miles round-trip from Happy Isle on the John Muir Trail and a 4,900-foot elevation gain. Many do it in one day, starting at first light and rushing home to beat nightfall. A more relaxed strategy is to camp in one of the backpacking campgrounds in Little Yosemite Valley just past Nevada Falls. The overnight campsites here fill up early, so try to make wilderness permit reservations well in advance.

Depending on your schedule you either want to camp first and charge up Half Dome in the morning or, in the way I prefer to do things, hike to Little Yosemite, set up camp, blitz the cable route to the summit, and return at dusk to a waiting camp. From Little Yosemite to the top of Half Dome it is a little more than 3 miles, a good portion of it climbing a 46° granite slope. The Park Service has installed steel cables to help you out, and during summer, boards are installed as cross-beams, but they're still far apart. Wear shoes with lots of traction and bring your own leather gloves for the cables. Your hands will thank you. The view from the top is an unbeatable vista of the High Country, Tenaya Canyon, Glacier Point, and the awe-inspiring abyss of the valley below. When you shuffle up to the overhanging lip for a look down the face, be extremely careful not to kick rocks or anything else onto the climbers below who are earning this view the hard way.

Dinkey Lakes

14 miles round-trip. Moderate. Wilderness permits available at Pineridge ranger station. Access: From State Route 168 near Shaver Lake, turn right on road marked Dinkey Creek and Wishon Dam. Drive 13.6 miles to a fork in the road where you bear left toward Courtright Village and Cliff Lake Trailhead. Park at Cliff Lake Trailhead. Map: USGS Blackcap Mountain and Huntington Lake topos, Sierra National Forest map.

The Dinkey Lakes Wilderness in a unique island of alpine High Sierra terrain is separated from the rest of the High Sierra by a lower forested plateau. Several lakes are clustered at the 9,500-foot level below some nearly 11,000-foot peaks. The Cliff Lake Trail climbs steadily but gently for 5 miles, the last stretch a number of switchbacks. Soon you're at Cliff Lake, named for the 400-foot cliffs that provide its backdrop. There are several good campsites here. To get beyond any possible crowd, though, I recommend going over the next pass, about 400 feet of climbing, but worth it. You'll then drop into the Dinkey Lakes Basin where stunning Rock Lake or diminutive Little Lake

make good campsites. Allow an extra day to enjoy the numerous day hikes and good fishing in this area.

HORSEBACK RIDING

Four stables offer scenic day rides and multi-day pack excursions in **Yosemite**: **Yosemite Valley Stables** (tel. 209/372-1000) is open spring through fall. The other three—**Wawona** (tel. 209/375-1000), **Tuolumne Meadows** (tel. 209/372-1000), and **White Wolf** (tel. 209/372-1000)—only operate during summer. Or call High Sierra Reservations: 209/253-5674. Day rides vary from $30 to $60 depending on length. Multiday backcountry trips cost roughly $100 per day and must be booked almost a year in advance.

ICE-SKATING

In winter the **Curry Village Ice Rink** in Yosemite is a lot of fun. It's outdoors and melts quickly when the weather warms up. $5 adults, $4.50 children. Skate rentals available.

KAYAKING

Numerous Class V and VI runs exist on the Kings, Kaweah, and San Joaquin rivers, most of which have been run maybe two or three times total. Only recently, professional outfitters have begun taking experienced kayakers down the Class IV and V **Kaweah** and **Upper Kings rivers.** Contact park headquarters (tel. 559/565-3341) for a current listing of companies running trips. This is one of the wildest, steepest rivers in North America and only for the very adventurous.

To bag a first descent in 1981, my friend Reg Lake with Doug Thompkins and Royal Robins hiked over Whitney Portal, a 21-mile trudge across a 13,777-foot pass,

Sequoia & Kings Canyon National Parks

It's only about 200 road miles be tween Yosemite and Sequoia/Kings Canyon, but the two Sierra Nevada parks are worlds apart. Where the Park Service has taken every opportunity to modernize, accessorize, and urbanize Yosemite, leading to a frenetic tourist scene much like the cities so many of us strive to escape, at Sequoia/Kings Canyon they've treated the wilderness beauty of the park with respect and care. Only one road loops through the park, **Generals Highway,** a narrow, steep, and winding road through the forest that connects the park's two year-round entrances; and no road traverses the Sierra here. The Park Service doesn't recommend taking a large vehicle onto these twisty, precipitous roads. As a result the park is much less accessible by car than most, but spectacular for those willing to head out on foot. Once technically two separate parks, Sequoia and Kings Canyon are contiguous and managed jointly from the park headquarters near Ash Mountain on State Route 198 east of Visalia.

The Sierra Nevada tilts upward as it runs south. Mount Whitney, the highest peak in the Lower 48 at 14,495 feet, soars above the southeast corner of the park, but it is just one of the many high peaks in Sequoia/Kings Canyon. The **Pacific Crest Trail** reaches its highest point here too. Crossing north to south through both parks, it remains at 10,000 feet most of the time and crosses through 12,000-foot-tall passes. For many miles it coincides with the **John Muir Trail,** which runs just inside the park's eastern boundary along the top of the striking east slope of the Sierra, ending just below Mount Whitney. The Kern, Kings, and Kaweah rivers drain this huge High Country expanse, becoming incredible whitewater rafting and kayaking rivers as they descend into the Gold Country. Small High Country lakes are home to some of the only remaining pure-strain golden trout. Bighorn sheep and spotted owl hide away in the craggy peaks and alpine meadows. Bear, deer, and numerous smaller animals and birds depend on the park's miles of wild habitat for summer breeding and feeding grounds.

Besides the snow-covered peaks, rushing whitewater, and plentiful wildlife, Sequoia/Kings Canyon is also home to the largest groves of giant sequoia redwoods in the Sierra Nevada. There are over 75 groves of giant sequoias in the park, but the easiest places to see the park's big trees are **Grant Grove** in Kings Canyon near the park entrance on State Route 180 from Fresno, or **Giant Forest,** a huge grove of trees containing 40 miles of footpaths, near the entrance to Sequoia National Park on State Route 198. Saving the sequoias was the reason Sequoia National Park was created in 1890 at the request of San Joaquin Valley residents, making it America's second oldest national park.

Unlike the coast redwoods, which reproduce by sprouting or by seeds, giant sequoias only reproduce by seed. The tiny cones require fire to open, so it can be decades between generations. Adult sequoias don't die of old age and are protected from fire by thick bark. Most die when they topple in high winds or heavy snows; the huge trees have surprisingly shallow roots. These groves, like the ones in Yosemite, were first thoroughly explored by conservationist and nature writer John Muir.

Sequoia/Kings Canyon is home to the best wilderness in the Sierra Nevada. Few roads go here because there is nowhere to build them; jagged peaks, hollowed-out canyons, and icy rivers are impediments to the smooth laying of asphalt. Hiking and backpacking are what this park is all about: 800 miles of backcountry trails connect gorges, lakes, high alpine meadows, and snowfields; 800 miles of streams and 500 lakes teem with fish. From Lodgepole, you can day hike to Twin Lakes at 9,500 feet. At road's end on the Kings Canyon Highway (open from May to November) you can stand by the banks of the Kings River and stare up at 5,000-foot-tall granite walls rising above the river, the deepest canyon in the United States.

JUST THE FACTS

Getting There. Sequoia/Kings Canyon only has two year-round entrances. State Route 180 from Fresno is the park's north entrance. State Route 198 from Visalia enters the park from the southwest. During summer additional dead-end roads lead into Mineral King, South Fork, and Cedar Grove.

Fees. A $10 fee per car is good for one week's worth of entry at any park entrance. An annual pass is only $20.

Avoiding the Crowds. Most visitors make a loop through the park by entering at Grant Grove and leaving through Ash Mountain or vice versa. To escape the crowds and see less-used areas of the park, enter on one of the dead-end roads to Mineral King, South Fork, or Cedar Grove. The lack of through traffic makes these parts of the park incredibly peaceful even at full capacity, and they are the gateway to the park's best hiking.

Visitor Centers & Information. The main information number for the park is 559/565-3341. There are two year-round visitor centers. Lodgepole Visitors Center (tel. 559/565-3782), open during the summer only, is the largest with a full selection of park information and displays about the history, biology, and geology of this incredible place. Some time spent here will pay off by letting you decide which parts of the widely dispersed park you most want to concentrate on. Grant Grove Visitors Center (tel. 559/335-2856) is in Grant Grove Village, 3 miles from the Big Stump entrance on Highway 180. Ash Mountain Park Headquarters also has a visitors center (tel. 559/565-3719) on State Route 198 east of Visalia. In the summer three additional visitor centers are open: Mineral King (tel. 209/565-3768), Lodgepole, at the southern end of the park west of Three Rivers, and Cedar Grove (tel. 209/565-3793), on State Route 180 west of Hume. Park rangers lead hikes, campfire talks, and slide shows at campgrounds and visitor centers year-round (limited to weekends in winter).

Regulations. Wilderness permits are required for all backpacking trips. For destinations other than Mount Whitney, you shouldn't have any trouble getting wilderness permits the day before you leave on the trail. You can reserve permits in advance in summer only—winter is first come, first served—by writing the park headquarters, or by faxing 559/565-4239. Mountain bikes are forbidden on all park trails. Dogs are allowed but must be leashed. They are not permitted on trails. The Park Service allows firewood gathering at campgrounds, but removing wood from living or standing trees is forbidden.

The Seasons. In the middle to high altitudes where most Sequoia/Kings Canyon visitors are headed, summer is short and the winters are cold. Spring can come as early as April and as late as June. Snow is not unheard of in July and August. Afternoon showers are common. Only the main road through the park is open during winter months when the climate can range from bitter cold to pleasant and changes minute by minute. Be ready for anything when you head into the backcountry on skis. Mosquitoes, poison oak, and rattlesnakes are common in lower elevations during summer.

carrying boats and several days' worth of camping gear. Then they hiked back down to Junction Meadow at 8,000 feet where the Kern begins, and put in. From there it was a mere 37 miles of gnarly Class V whitewater, and they'd bagged the first descent. Amazingly enough others have done the trip since they did it.

For the rest of us mere mortals the Kern below Sequoia National Park is the best bet. **The Forks of the Kern Run** is good Class IV and "easy" V and requires only about a 3-mile hike to the put-in. Below that, you can even drive your car to the launching points. The **Limestone Run** between Johnsondale Bridge and Fairview Dam is a good Class III and IV, and way below here, just outside Kernville, is the best beginner run in the southern Sierra, appropriately named the **Kernville Run.** The exact put-ins and take-outs for each run vary dramatically depending on your ability. Consult the blow-by-blow descriptions in Jim Cassady's *California Whitewater: A Guide to the Rivers* (North Fork Press, 1995) or Chuck Stanley and Lars Holbek's classic *A Guide to the Best Whitewater in the State of California* (Friends of the River Books, 1984) before committing to any of these runs.

Sierra South, 11300 Kernville Rd., Kernville, CA 93238 (tel. 760/ 376-3745), is a kayaking school and shop with an excellent reputation for safe and quality instruction. They teach a full spectrum of whitewater skills from basic paddling to advanced technique.

MOUNTAIN BIKING

If you take a look at a map of the High Sierra from the northern boundary of Yosemite to the southern edge of Sequoia/Kings Canyon, you'll recognize one thing immediately: It's one of the largest continuous wilderness areas in the continental United States, and has wisely been designated almost entirely official wilderness areas or national park. Yay, yippie, yahoo. That protection is a good thing, a great thing, no doubt about it, but it means your mountain bike isn't going to be seeing too much trail action here. You'll have to stick to the lower-elevation areas outside the parks if you really want to ride. Kernville is surrounded by endless miles of Forest Service roads and single track, and the Kern River has countless nice swimming holes to help cut the road dust. With great kayaking, camping, mountain biking, climbing, and rafting, Kernville threatens to become another Moab. Hopefully it will be spared. **Mountain and River Adventures,** 113 Kernville Rd. (tel. 760/376-6553), rents bikes, leads mountain bike tours, and is a great source of local trail knowledge.

ROAD BIKING

Yosemite Valley

8 miles of bike paths plus the valley roads. Map: Park map.

A bicycle makes for the perfect way to see the valley. Eight miles of bike paths in addition to the valley roads make this an even better option. You can rent one-speeds at the Yosemite Lodge or Curry Village for $5 per hour or $16.25 per day. If you want a fancier bike you'll have to bring it from home. All trails in the park are closed to mountain bikes.

ROCK CLIMBING

For many years rock climbing and Yosemite were practically synonymous. The new sport climbing focus has drawn some of the limelight away from Yosemite's amazing granite walls, but it is still an important way station on the cutting-edge climbers' circuit. With its huge expanses of hard and perfectly textured granite, the valley is the most famous climbing spot in the world— a canvas waiting for climbers to paint their routes. Here the big walls like **El Capitan** and **Half Dome** don't simply loom over and surround you. They sink into your subconscious.

The **Salathe Wall,** a staggeringly long multi-day climb up the face of El Capitan, still stands as one of the most important proving grounds for any big-wall climber. So much so that it is widely referred to as "the finest rock climb in the world." Hundreds of other multi-pitch climbs surround the valley. Sitting in a meadow near the Merced River with binoculars, you can scan the high walls; sometimes so many people are climbing that it looks like a family of spiders has invaded.

The valley is amazing, but for the more casual sport climber looking for single-pitch or simple multi-pitch climbs with easy walk-down descents, some of the best routes are in the High Country around Lake Tenaya and Tuolumne Meadows. The routes here were pioneered much later than the valley, many of them in the 1960s. Perhaps that's why you find routes named things like "The Needle and the Spoon" or the even less subtle "Drug Dome." **Lembert Dome** at the east end of Tuolumne Meadows is a favorite spot for introducing climbers to long multi-pitch routes. It's clean and forgiving; an obvious escape route allows you to bug out before the final and scariest pitch if you get freaked.

The **Yosemite Mountaineering School** (tel. 209/372-1244) was one of the first in North America, and continues to set many standards for all levels of climbing instruction. A basic lesson at Yosemite Mountaineering is $100 per person per day and will teach you basic body moves and rappelling and take you on a single-pitch climb. Classes run from early spring through early October in the valley, less in Tuolumne Meadows. Call them to get precise information about their different clinics, lessons, and guide services. Some of the best guidebooks available are Don Reid's *Yosemite Climbs: Free* (Chockstone Press, 1994) and *Yosemite Climbs: Big Wall* (Chockstone Press, 1993).

There is no climbing school in Sequoia/Kings Canyon, but **Mountain and River Adventures** (tel. 760/232-4234) teaches rock climbing and can point experienced climbers to the local hot spot, a series of needle-like granite extrusions known appropriately enough as the Needles.

WALKS & RAMBLES

Yosemite Falls

0.25 miles. Access: Yosemite Valley Visitors Center.

Yosemite Falls is within a short stroll of the visitors center. You can actually see it better elsewhere in the valley, but it's really impressive to stand at the base of all that falling water. The wind, noise, and blowing spray generated when millions of gallons catapult 2,425 feet through space onto the rocks below are sometimes so strong you can barely stand on the bridge below.

Mirror Lake, Yosemite Valley

2 miles. Access: Take shuttle bus to trailhead from Curry Village.

Mirror Lake is a stunning natural reflecting pond near the base of Half Dome and the Vernal Falls, Nevada Falls Trail. The already tiny lake is shrinking every year as it fills with silt, becoming meadow, but the reflections of the valley walls and sky on its surface remain one of the valley's most tranquil sights. Twilight here is amazing. As the valley turns pink and purple, the changing sky is reflected by the lake. Often, it seems like you can hardly tell which one is the real sky. The walk to the lake is flat and easy. To add a little distance to it and get away from the paved trail, circle the lake on the dirt path.

Hazelwood Nature Trail, Sequoia National Park

1 mile. Access: Giant Forest Village.

This short and easy loop explains some of the interesting facts of the sequoia forest: how their cones must be heated by fire to release the seeds, how old they are, what this area was like when the often 2,000-year-old sequoias that tower here were mere sprouts. Then, if you're feeling ambitious, many miles of trail lead off into the wilder reaches of Giant Forest.

Congress Trail Loop, Sequoia National Park

2-mile loop. Access: Lodgepole Visitors Center.

The 2-mile Congress Trail Loop in the Giant Forest will take you to the base of the General Sherman Tree, the largest living thing in the world. Single branches on the General Sherman are more than 7 feet thick. Each year the General Sherman grows enough wood to make a 60-foot-tall tree of normal dimensions. Other trees in the grove are nearly as large and many of the peaceful-looking trees have also been saddled with strangely militaristic and political

monikers like General Lee and Lincoln. Longer trails lead to remote reaches of the grove and nearby meadows.

Moro Rock

0.5 miles round-trip. Access: Giant Forest Village.

Near Giant Forest Village, Moro Rock is a 6,724-foot-tall granite dome formed by exfoliation of layers of the rock. A quarter-mile trail scales the dome for a spectacular view of the adjacent Kaweah Canyon. The trail gains 300 feet in 400 yards, so be ready for a climb.

WHITEWATER RAFTING

The **Kern** and **Kaweah** are both run by commercial raft outfitters. More than 60 miles of whitewater are runable on the Kern, most of it Class III and IV. The most demanding Kern run is the **Forks of Kern,** requiring a hike in (the rafts go on mules) and then a powerful run of IV to V-plus rapids, many of which must be scouted and often portaged. For a first-timer or family trip, the **Powerhouse Run** through Kernville is a perfect introduction.

The Kaweah is a beautiful and volatile river. The river is pure snowmelt draining Sequoia National Park, so wetsuits are required. It's cold and steep; a swim here could be deadly. Since the river isn't dam controlled, the season is short. Reserve trips early. Most out-fitters require that you have previous Class V paddle raft experience.

The following outfitters lead runs down the Kern and Kaweah: **Sierra South** (tel. 760/376-3745; Powerhouse run only), **Whitewater Voyages** (tel. 800/488-RAFT), **Kern River Tours** (tel. 760/379-4616), and **River Travel Center** (tel. 800/882-RAFT; free booking service for all California rivers).

Eastern Sierra ◆ What to Do & Where to Do It

The eastern Sierra puts on display the startling contrasts between the Great Basin high desert and the abrupt, soaring peaks of the Sierra. From Lone Pine it is only 13 miles to the base of Mount Whitney—the highest peak in the Lower 48—but 10,000 feet practically straight up to the 14,495-foot summit. Whitney is not alone; five other peaks over 14,000 feet surround it. Another five 14,000-foot peaks are located just outside Big Pine, 50 miles north, and another, White Mountain, is just to the east. In all, 13 of the state's 14 peaks taller than 14,000 feet are here within a geological stone's throw of the Owens Valley (Mount Shasta in the Cascades being the 14th).

It's a bit of geographic irony that the lowest point in North America is only 60 miles from here—Badwater in Death Valley. Besides being the tallest, the peaks of this end of the Sierra are some of the most dramatic in the country—soaring spires, high granite cirques, the southernmost living glacier in the United States, hanging valleys, waterfalls, dramatic ridgelines—kin in form and spirit to Wyoming's Grand Tetons.

Because of the dramatic vertical contrast, one can cover a lot of different types of geography in a single trip. It is actually possible to start a backpacking trip in scrub desert, climb the summit of Mount Whitney, descend into lush sequoia redwoods on the west slope, and soak your weary bones in a riverside hot spring all in a few days. In winter, when State Route 120 closes, the ski crossing from Crane Flat in Yosemite to Lee Vining following the roadbed is the favorite haute route across the range.

BALLOONING

Weather permitting, **Mammoth Balloon Adventures,** P.O. Box 8561, Mammoth Lakes, CA 93546 (tel. 760/934-7188), flies year-round from the meadows outside town. Their sunrise flight is the most popular and also least likely to be scrubbed by the high winds that pick up in the late morning and afternoon. Reservations are requested.

BIRD WATCHING

Two hundred ninety-five separate bird species have been spotted at Mono Lake. More than 50,000 California gulls come each spring to breed on the lake's two major islands. Other seabirds use Mono as a staging area for winter migrations. As many as 800,000 eared grebes have been known to gather here in the fall before heading south. Other migratory species include waterfowl like green wing and cinnamon teal, Canada geese, loons, common mergansers, and bufflehead. Besides the county park and state park, many quiet side roads lead to remote wetlands. Go past Mono Lake County Park on Cemetery Road to the DeChambeau Ponds, where you can see many local species in the ponds and scope the breeding island from a clear vantage point.

To the north of Mono Lake, the ghost town of Bodie is a great raptor viewing spot. Vultures no longer circle over town waiting for the scraps of the next gunfight, but plenty of golden eagles, horned and burrowing owls, and red-tailed hawks hunt the surrounding scrub desert while sage grouse strut the empty streets.

BOARDSAILING

This side of the Sierra has plenty of wind but not nearly enough large bodies of water to make boardsailing a popular option. If, by some fluke of transport, you happen to be here and have your gear with you, I'd recommend **Crowley Lake**. It's open enough to get some real wind and big enough that you won't be tacking every 15 feet. You will, however, have to contend with trout fishermen, lots of them, and waterskiers. **June Lake** is also a good sailing lake without so much boat traffic. Any number of other smaller lakes *could* be sailed, but none really stand out.

BOBSLEDDING

Bobsledding. Are you out of your mind? Well, no.

Bobsledz International (tel. 760/934-7533), a commercial bobsledding operation, has mellowed out the course, tuned down the sleds, and brought bobsledding to the masses. For a fee, you and your friends can take the T-bar up and slide down their specially designed bobsled run to your heart's content. I wish I could say I did it and it's great, but when I was in Mammoth, Bobsledz International was buried 15 feet deep under the biggest storm in decades and their sleds were going nowhere. To find it, head out of Mammoth Lakes toward Mammoth Mountain on State Route 203. It's 1.5 miles south of town on the right.

CANOEING

With hundreds of lakes small and large accessible by car, the Mammoth area is a canoeing heaven. If you don't have your own boat, rent one at Lake Mary's **Pokonobe Lodge** (tel. 760/934-2437), or at Silver Lake's **Silver Lake Rentals** (tel. 760/389-0057).

For a totally different canoeing experience, sign up for one of the **Mono Lake Committee** (tel. 760/647-6595) canoe tours. Led by local environmentalists and ecologists, these tours are given each weekend morning in the summer. Only 12 spots are open each morning and the trips leave early to beat the blasting winds that pick up in the afternoon. You'll see seabird nesting islands, tufa towers, brine shrimp, and a whole lot of other things you've probably never even imagined. Call ahead to reserve a spot and get directions to the put-in place. If you have your own boat and decide to do it yourself, put in at Navy Beach off State Route 120 on the south shore. Keep a large (1-mile) buffer zone between yourself and the nesting birds to prevent them from panicking and crushing eggs.

CROSS-COUNTRY SKIING

The eastern Sierra boasts some amazing cross-country skiing. The snow here is dryer and lighter than on the west slope, so you'll stand less chance of becoming mired in the mythical Sierra cement. Terrain ranges from groomed flat tracks to the ultimate Sierra haute route through Kings Canyon National Park with lots in between.

BACKCOUNTRY

The mining and logging history of the eastern Sierra has laced the range with countless dirt roads that go unplowed in the winter, perfect for self-guided backcountry skiing. Possibilities range from an easy ski to a beautiful hot spring to hair-raising plunges down the couloirs of the Sherwins.

Belated Gold Rush: Settling the Eastern Sierra

The Owens Valley/eastern Sierra area was one of the last regions settled in California. Spanish settlers never crossed the Sierra from the west, leaving the native Paiutes in peace to hunt the herds of pronghorn antelope and deer. After Mexico seceded from Spain in 1821, however, the Mexican government began to lose its grip on California, leaving a power vacuum that the United States would seize as an opportunity to expand its territory. Between 1825 and 1845, explorers like Peter Ogden, Jedediah Smith, Joseph Walker, and Captain John Fremont led expeditions that mapped the Great Basin and crossed the Sierra Nevada but established no settlements on the eastern side. Even the Gold Rush left the southeastern Sierra unsettled. Then, as now, the best mountain pass for wagon trains and heavy traffic was Donner Pass, north of Lake Tahoe, and settlers streamed that way leaving the land to the south unexplored until later. Until the boomtown growth of Los Angeles in the second half of this century made Mammoth the closest major mountain resort to millions of people, this side of the Sierra was a peaceful backwater.

Leroy Vining, from whom the present-day town of Lee Vining gets its name, was the first to cross back over the range and begin serious gold exploration on this side. He found gold, though not in the quantities being extracted from the placer fields and hard rock mines of the west slope, but enough to make other miners take notice and begin their own explorations.

By the 1880s the initial Gold Rush was petering out on the west slope and thousands crossed back over the Sierra in search of new gold deposits. Mammoth City, a town of 2,000 on the site of modern-day Mammoth Lakes, boomed and busted between 1878 and 1881 at an incredible cost in human suffering when a fire destroyed most of the town during a harsh winter and miners were left to fend for themselves without substantial shelter.

Near Mono Lake, the gold and silver mining community of Bodie fared better. At one point more that 30 mines employed 10,000 miners and created a booming economy of vice based on hookers, whisky, and guns. Sixty-five bars and brothels competed with only two churches for the townspeople's attention. Murders were so common they scarcely rated mention in the paper. The town's own people bragged that it was the most lawless place on earth, and for a few years it probably was. More than $30 million worth of gold and silver was scraped out of the hills above town, but by 1890 most of the mines were closed. The turn of the century left Bodie a ghost town, much of which remains preserved in Bodie State Historic Park.

Avalanche danger is high in this part of the Sierra; heavy snows, steep pitches, and changing weather make for perfect avalanche conditions. Before heading into the backcountry, make yourself aware of local conditions by calling the nearest ranger station. I once was snowed in at Tamarack Lodge for 4 days when an avalanche buried the snowplow (a huge Caterpillar tractor) up to its roof and closed Lake Mary Road. The driver was okay, but then again, he was inside the cab of a huge tractor. A lone skier wouldn't have fared so well.

Certain trailhead parking areas now fall under the category of California Sno-Park and you need to purchase a permit to park there or you'll get a hefty fine. Daily or annual Sno-Park permits can be bought in most sporting goods and ski shops.

Strong intermediate and advanced skiers may want to tackle something a little more intense than the standard single-day backcountry trips and try a multi-day trek. But unless you are an expert on winter camping, emergency first aid, avalanche dangers, and alpine weather conditions, setting out alone and unprepared can be extremely dangerous. Contact **John Fisher, Mountain Guide** (tel. 760/873-5037), P.O. Box 694, Bishop, CA 93515, who will provide guidance. **Alpine Skills International** (tel. 530/426-9108), P.O. Box 8, Norden, CA 95724, teaches multi-day advanced ski mountaineering courses each spring in the Palisade Glacier area to prepare strong skiers for the challenges of High Country crossings. *Backcountry Skiing in the High Sierra* by John Moynier (Chockstone Press, 1992) is also a great guidebook to the more advanced backcountry skiing in the southern Sierra, including the High Route and other trans-Sierra crossings.

The following listings are organized roughly from north to south.

Bodie State Park

Distance depends on how far from the park the road is closed by snow. Strong beginner/intermediate. Varied trails. Access: 7 miles south of Bridgeport, turn east on State Route 270. Park is in 13 miles; road will probably be closed a short distance before.

It's a simple thing to ski into Bodie down the summertime road and you're likely to have it all to yourself. Nothing could be more ghostly than this ghost town blanketed with snow during a winter storm. The weather here sucks in winter and you'll understand why the people left.

Obsidian Dome Trails, June Lake Area

Approximately 10km of trails but varies widely with snow conditions. Strong beginner/intermediate. Varied trails. Access: 11 miles north of Mammoth Lakes on U.S. 395. Forest Road 2S10. Park just off highway.

All trails begin with a 0.3km ski west from the trailhead until you reach a large meadow. Here trails branch off into three loops, two beginners and an intermediate. The beginner trails circle through trees and small meadows. The intermediate loop climbs gently to a great view of Obsidian Dome, a large volcanic dome. The loop circles counterclockwise and returns to the parking area.

Shady Rest Loop, Mammoth Lakes

7.4km of trails. Beginner. Flat. Access: Trail begins at the USFS Visitors Center on State Route 203 as you enter Mammoth Lakes. Park in the Forest Service lot.

One of the most popular beginning ski areas in Mammoth Lakes, the Shady Rest Loop begins practically at the **USFS Visitors Center** (tel. 760/934-2505) door. Stop by the center first and pick up the brochure describing the several loops that wind through a grove of Jeffrey pines. Crowded on weekends, this is a great place for a midweek ski.

California's Great Salt Lake

Mono Lake, just east of Yosemite National Park, is a remarkable inland sea and one of the most troubled ecosystems in the state. The first pioneers to see this great saline lake in the 1800s described it as lifeless and hideous, the Dead Sea of California; but the Kutsadika Paiute tribe of Native Americans who lived here knew different. Brine fly grubs, a fantastic source of protein, were their chief staple, and they traded them with neighboring tribes for acorns.

Though the lake's water is so saline only brine shrimp can live in it, and the surrounding salt plains so brutal as to only support brine flies, this seeming lack of diversity creates an interesting and delicate ecosystem. Those swarming brine flies that you'll find so annoying on your visit are food for the 85% of California's seagull population that comes here to nest each spring, as well as another 300 bird species that nest here in lesser numbers. Because the brine shrimp's traditional predators—fish—can't survive here to cull their numbers, they multiply with such fecundity that by the middle of summer the lake is teeming with an estimated 4 trillion of the tiny shrimp. At the same time the fledgling gulls reach maturity and turn to this rich and plentiful food source while they begin to fly and forage for themselves, generally the most dangerous time for young birds. Soon they are strong enough to fend for themselves and migrate back to their more traditional habitat, the ocean and bays of the West Coast.

Hot Creek, Mammoth Lakes

16km round-trip. Beginner/intermediate. Gentle ups and downs. Access: 3 miles south of town on State Route 203, turn left on Fish Hatchery Road. Continue to sign for Hot Creek. Park where road ends, depending on snow levels, and continue on the snow-covered road on skis.

Four miles out of town near the Mammoth Airport, Hot Creek is one of the most popular winter attractions for skiers, snowshoers, and, unfortunately, snowmobilers. From the end of the road you'll have no trouble following other tracks on the slightly pitched trail. Clouds of steam should be visible to your left in all but the worst conditions. Eventually you'll pass a gate (if the snow isn't too deep) and slope downhill. About 1km later you'll see Hot Creek with the bubbling thermal springs feeding it. The USFS discourages people from bathing in the creek as certain areas reach 210°, but hundreds of people ignore the warning every year and have a great time. If you choose to take a dip, be extremely careful; people have died here. To return to your car, follow the same route in reverse.

Inyo Craters, Mammoth Lakes

8km round-trip. Intermediate. Some ups and downs. Access: From State Route 203 turn right on Mammoth Lakes Scenic Loop. Parking area in 3.5 miles on north side of road.

Begin by skiing a short distance down the snow-covered road. You'll see a blue diamond marker on the right saying Inyo Craters. Follow blue diamonds through a few zigzags and then the trail becomes more obvious. In about 3km is the final ascent to the summit of the craters. While the trail is easy, some very steep cornices and drop-offs are nearby. Be careful. The view is worth the climb. Return the way you came.

Red Cones Trail, Mammoth Lakes

17.5km round-trip. Advanced intermediate/ advanced. Large elevation changes. Access: Tamarack Lodge at the end of Lake Mary Road.

Though you'll ski right through the Tamarack area on your route, resist the temptation of those groomed tracks and follow the free public access corridor up the snow-covered roadbed of Lake Mary Road until you reach Horseshoe Lake 5km later. It's a gentle but steady climb with beautiful views back toward town and of the surrounding peaks. Once you reach Horseshoe Lake, begin looking for the blue diamond trail that leaves from the north end of a large flat expanse (no, not the frozen lake) that is a summer parking lot. Follow the blue diamonds another 4km up through a rolling forest. Red Cones summits are hidden until you are nearly upon them. You'll break out of the trees and climb a few hundred yards to the summit where on a clear day you can see incredible distances in every direction.

Rock Creek (Tom's Place to Rock Creek Road)

6 to 8km round-trip. Beginner/intermediate. 400-foot elevation gain. Access: 17 miles south of Mammoth Lakes on 395, turn off at Tom's Place on Rock Creek Road. In a little more than 5 miles you'll see the Sno-

Park Area (fee required) and East Fork Campground.

From the parking area ski the 3km uphill to Rock Creek Lodge. You're in a steep canyon, so be aware of avalanche danger. When you reach the lodge you can either turn around and head home, or ski another kilometer (intermediate) or so to the Twelve Peaks View, a striking spot with a view of some of the biggest peaks in the Sierra Nevada and all the valleys below. Return to your car the way you came.

OVERNIGHTS

Sierra Haute Route (Independence to Kings Canyon)

51 miles total over 7–9 days. Advanced. Guides strongly recommended. Access: Trailhead begins at Symmes Creek and ends at Wolverton Cross-Country Ski Area inside Sequoia/Kings Canyon National Parks.

There are more-famous multi-day routes in North America, but the High Route, with 40 miles of backcountry skiing over 10,000 feet, is widely held to be the best high-altitude crossing in the Lower 48. Above treeline for all but a few miles of its course, the High Route has a little of everything the advanced skier could ask for: high traverses, several 12,000-foot-plus passes, open bowls, unbelievable scenery, and great snow. It can be heaven or it can be hell, depending on the weather you encounter, but there's no place in the state like this: views for literally hundreds of miles, untracked powder, 4,000-foot downhills, and probably not another person within miles. Following the boundary between Sequoia and Kings Canyon National Parks along the divide between the Kings and Kaweah rivers, the route climbs from the Symmes Creek Trailhead at 6,300 feet outside Independence to the route's high point at 13,000-foot Milestone Pass. After days above treeline the trail ends as you ski down into the giant sequoia groves of the national park's Giant Forest. For a good primer on routes and resources, read *Backcountry Skiing in the High Sierra* by John Moynier (Chockstone Press, 1992).

NORDIC SKIING CENTERS

Two well-managed Nordic skiing operations are within close distance of Mammoth Lakes. **Tamarack Lodge and Cross-Country Ski Area** (tel. 760/934-2442) has 30 miles of groomed trails in the stunning Mammoth Lakes Basin at the very end of Lake Mary Road. With rentals, nice lodgings, lessons, and a four-star restaurant on the edge of a stunning winter wilderness, Tamarack is a great all-in-one resort. The groomed runs are arranged in a series of interlocking loops with dual tracks spaced wide enough apart that you can skate in the middle. Most of the larger loops are relatively flat and marked "beginning." To spice things up you can take the steep connector trails, marked blue or black, between loops. Beyond that, miles of backcountry skiing in the Lakes Basin begins where the groomed trails end. Adult ski passes are $15 per day, and afternoon passes are $10.

DOGSLEDDING

Dogsled Adventures (tel. 760/934-6270) runs daily half-hour and hour-long sled tours (weather and snow conditions permitting) from the Mammoth Mountain Inn next door to the Main Lodge of Mammoth Mountain. For between $40 and $70, depending on the length of the trip, you'll be trundled in a sled driven by a professional musher and pulled by 10 specially bred dogs on a tour of the Minaret Vista Loop. An interesting side trip is to visit the Dogsled Adventures Kennel, the only professional breeding kennel for sled dogs in California. Most of the puppies are spoken for well ahead of time, so you'll be safe from impulse buying.

DOWNHILL SKIING & SNOWBOARDING

For better or worse, downhill skiing is the economic engine that drives the part of the eastern Sierra around Mammoth Mountain. If it weren't for skiing, the town of Mammoth Lakes would have no reason to exist. Almost 2,000 people are directly employed by the ski area and tourist traffic supports many more. Though it's 350 miles away, this is where Los Angeles comes to play in the mountains. It's interesting to spend an entire week here: Monday through Friday it's a nice mountain town filled with nice mountain people. Friday night the glitter and clamor of Los Angeles comes roaring up U.S. 395 in a thousand ski-racked luxury wagons, the condos light up, the mountain is a sea of speeding neon, and the Ralph Lauren Polo outlet does brisk business. Come Monday the hordes go home and it's a mellow mountain town again.

A different kind of boomtown was born in the 1930s when Dave McCoy, a hydrologist for the Los Angeles Department of Water and Power, was sent into these mountains to measure winter snowfall. He discovered that Mammoth Mountain gets more snow than any other like-sized peak in the Sierra, more than 25 feet per year, and some of the best.

Starting with a Model A engine-powered rope tow, McCoy eventually turned Mammoth Mountain and its smaller sister June Mountain into one of the biggest skiing operations in the country with the longest season. In

1995, a record snow year, the mountain opened in November and was still open into August. The ski area regularly stays open until late May or June. And since both June and Mammoth are owned by the McCoy family, they are run on a completely interchangeable lift ticket system—two mountains for the price of one. Make sure to ask about package deals when you call.

Mammoth Mountain

1 Minaret Rd., Mammoth Lakes, CA 93546. Tel. 760/934-2571 for tickets; 760/934-6166 for snow conditions. 150 named trails (30% beginner, 40% intermediate, 30% expert); 30 lifts including 7 high-speed quads, 3 quads, 7 triples, 10 doubles, 2 gondolas, and 1 poma; 3,100-foot vertical drop. Full-day adult ticket $49.

Though named after a fossilized woolly mammoth skeleton found years ago near what is now the base lodge, Mammoth is mammoth in the other meaning of the word too: 11,053-foot summit elevation, 3,500 skiable acres, 30 modern lifts, 150 trails, and some of the woolliest terrain of any California ski area. Any talk of the mountain being a certain percentage beginner, a certain percentage intermediate, and a certain percentage advanced is pretty much beside the point; there's too much of all of it for any one person to ski in a weekend.

Maybe it is the Southern California surfer influence, maybe just economic prudence, but Mammoth was a snowboard-friendly mountain back when everyone else was telling boarders to beat it. It has several full-time snowboarders on the ski patrol staff as well as a nationally recommended snowboard school and a full supply of quality gear for sale and rent in the base lodges. On the drawing board for 1996 is a half-pipe and trick area just for snowboarders.

June Mountain

85 Boulder Rd., June Lake, CA 93529. Tel. 760/648-7733 for tickets; 760/934-2224 for snow conditions. 35 trails (35% beginner, 45% intermediate, 20% advanced); 8 lifts including 2 high-speed quads, 5 doubles, and 1 rope tow; 2,590-foot vertical drop. Full-day adult ticket $40.

Forty-five minutes to the north of Mammoth, June Mountain is the place to get away from the glitz and glam, not to mention the crowd, of Mammoth. At 10,135 feet, June Mountain is no small potato, yet somehow feels much more intimate than the mammoth Mammoth. It also has better weather. When the wind closes most of Mammoth, come here and you'll likely find more manageable conditions.

The first thing you'll see driving into the base area is a daunting wall of advanced runs. Don't worry—the top half of the mountain is where all the intermediate and beginning runs are located. A tram will take you up and down.

For snowboarders, June has one of the best half-pipes in the country and all sorts of trick riding props. This was the first California mountain to open all its terrain to snowboarders and remains a leader on the snowboard scene.

FISHING

Despite the wholesale looting of most of the water on this side of the Sierra by the Los Angeles Department of Water and Power, the eastern Sierra and Owens Valley remains an incredible trout fishery. Fly fishermen flock to Bishop to cast the few remaining stretches of the Owens River, and each spring hundreds of boats troll for trophy trout on Lake Crowley. It is a changed landscape from what it once was, but still a beautiful and rich one.

Virtually every species of trout can be caught here including the rare golden trout and cutthroat trout. Trophy German brown and rainbow trout have come out of too many lakes to even bother mentioning here. Just go look at the photos in Tamarack Lodge or the marina at Crowley Lake and you'll get the picture. For detailed recommendations of where to satisfy your particular fishing itch, call one of the following shops: **Mammoth Sporting Goods** (tel. 760/934-8474), **The Trout Fly** (tel. 760/934-2517), or **Village Sports Center** (tel. 760/934-8220).

Two resorts cater to fly fishermen on private stretches of catch-and-release creeks. **Hot Creek Ranch** (tel. 760/935-4214) has 2.5 miles of private frontage on Spring Creek as well as easy access to the public areas of Hot Creek. With cabins, a fly shop, and beautiful views, you could drive in once and never want or need to leave.

Alpers Ranch (tel. 760/648-7334) is farther north of Mammoth Lakes near the headwaters of the Owens River. Several miles of the Owens are available for ranch guests to catch and release. Ranch owner Tim Alpers allows catch-and-keep fishing on a pond where he raises trout to plant in local lakes and rivers. Accommodations are in simple cabins and a small store is on site.

HIKES, BUSHWHACKS & BACKPACK TRIPS

Two of the most famous West Coast trails, the John Muir Trail and the Pacific Crest Trail, run through this area and lure hikers from all over, but you can find just as much solitude and beauty on hundreds of other hikes and overnights. The ranger stations for each particular section of the eastern Sierra are a good place to ask for hikes geared toward a special interest or

ability level as there aren't really any great general-interest hiking guidebooks to this area other than R. J. Secor's *The High Sierra* (The Mountaineers, 1992), and it concentrates largely on peak bagging.

DAY HIKES

San Joaquin Ridge, Devils Postpile

4 miles round-trip. Moderate. Steady uphill and then back down. Allow 3 hours. Access: Minaret Vista parking lot on State Route 203 past Mammoth Mountain. Map: Devils Postpile map.

To get that High Country feeling without too much actual climbing, San Joaquin Ridge is a great hike. Shortly after beginning the hike in a lodgepole pine forest you'll break through treeline and remain here most of the hike. Above treeline doesn't mean barren, though, and during the summer you'll find an incredible garden of tiny wildflowers and rock-clinging lichen. After about 2 miles of steady uphill along this rocky ridge, you'll reach an unnamed 10,255-foot summit. Soak up the view and return the way you came.

Convict Lake Round-Trip

3 miles. Easy. Good for kids though there are a few spots with steep drop-offs. Allow several hours and you'll have time to play. Access: Take Convict Lake Road to lake. Park near boat ramp. Trail circles lake.

For a leisurely afternoon that combines a hike with a picnic, some fishing, or a nice swim, this is a great choice. Hike either direction around the lake. A boardwalk will help you cross the boggy meadow where the creek enters the lake. For swimming, fishing, etc., shoreline access is better along the northwest side of the lake.

Little Lakes Valley

4 to 8 miles depending on turnaround. Moderate. Allow lots of time for exploring. Access: From U.S. 395 drive to dead end of Rock Creek Road at Mosquito Flat. Map: Inyo National Forest map.

Little Lakes Valley is one of those magical remnants of the glacial age: Surrounded by peaks and ridges that tower several thousand feet above the valley floor, this glacial valley is sprinkled with 40 lakes, streams, and beautiful meadows. From the trailhead it is about 2 miles to Long Lake. From here it is about another 2 miles to the crystalline Gem Lakes. There's plenty in between. Pack a picnic and just explore the area. You won't be let down.

Lundy Lake to Crystal Lake and May Lundy Mine

6 miles round-trip. Moderate. Allow 4 hours. Access: North of Lee Vining on U.S. 395, turn west on Lundy Lake Road. Drive 3 miles until the road forks. Take the left fork and park near the gate below the dam. Map: Inyo National Forest map.

This hike grants a glimpse of the hard-scrabble life of a hard-rock miner. As you climb the 2,000-foot elevation gain to the May Lundy Mine, you'll feel for the poor suckers who spent years scouring gold from these hills. When the climb passes the cascading falls look for evidence of the old waterwheel and pipes in the creek. At Crystal Lake you'll find the remains of a small town: boarding houses, cabins, old stores, and the old stamp mill that crushed ore brought down from the May Lundy. The lower tunnel of the May Lundy is located at 11,000 feet on the slope of Lake Canyon and other shafts are much higher. Oneida Lake is behind the old settlement. Return the way you came.

Rainbow Falls, Devils Postpile

4 miles round-trip. Moderate. Allow 2.5 hours. Access: Via Devils Postpile shuttle bus. Map: Devils Postpile National Monument map.

From the separate Rainbow Falls Trailhead (stay on the shuttle past Agnew Meadows) this short hike will take you to the edge of spectacular Rainbow Falls, where the entire middle fork of the San Joaquin River catapults 101 feet off a lava cliff. The falls is more notable for the sheer volume of water pouring over it than anything else, though it is one of the highest falls outside the Yosemite Valley. A small trail leads to swimming and fishing holes below the base of the falls.

Thousand Island Lake Loop, Devils Postpile

18 miles. Strenuous. Allow all day and pack a flashlight just in case. Access: Agnew Meadows Trailhead (take Devils Postpile Shuttle from Mammoth Mountain Inn). Map: Devils Postpile and John Muir Wilderness maps.

Eighteen miles is one hell of a long day, especially at high altitude, but this is one of the finest loop hikes in the world. Taking its name from a strange lake at the headwaters of the San Joaquin River speckled with hundreds of small granite islands, the loop begins following the San Joaquin River Gorge for 7 steady uphill miles, puts you at Thousand Island Lake in time for lunch and a swim, and then sends you home via the High Trail (trail junction 1 mile below the lake on the river trail). The High Trail takes you far above the river gorge on a ridge overlooking the surrounding peaks. Since the last bus leaves the

The Owens Valley Water Wars

little history is crucial to any understanding of contemporary water politics on the eastern slope of the Sierra Nevada. At the turn of the century, Los Angeles was a sleepy little city with lots of orange trees, nice beaches, and virtually no water. Not such a bad place really, but a group of "visionary" city businessmen and politicians had a different idea about the future of L.A. Led by city water-czar William Mulholland and with the complicity of the *Los Angeles Times,* the city began to pursue a two-pronged strategy of scaring people in Los Angeles into believing there was a drought and they'd soon be drinking sand if something weren't done, and using underhanded techniques like lawsuits and physical threats to condemn land and purchase water rights from ranchers in the Owens Valley. By November 1913, the first water flowed into the Owens Valley Aqueduct destined for the so-called City of Angels. Though local opponents went as far as bombing the aqueduct 17 times in protest, the plug had been pulled on the Owens Valley and there was no going back. The ranching economy withered, and the formerly lush valley was transformed into a desolate, dusty place dominated by an alkali flat where Owens Lake once was.

Owens Lake was only the first place to fall to quench L.A.'s thirst. By 1930, Mulholland's aqueduct had created blossoming growth in L.A. and the city numbered over 1 million citizens. Still convinced that they needed more water for more growth, city residents voted in 1930 to expand the Owens Valley Aqueduct all the way to Mono Lake. By 1941, every major tributary to the inland sea had been diverted south.

As a result, the level of the lake began dropping and the ecology of the lake suffered. One of the two largest bird-breeding islands became a peninsula as the water level dropped, and coyotes ravaged the nesting bird population. Increasing salinity also affected lake species. By the 1970s, a band of loosely knit environmentalists, local residents, and ranchers began to take on the Los Angeles Department of Water and Power, first with guerrilla theater actions and protests, later with lawsuits. One of these lawsuits, which reached the state Supreme Court in 1983, would impact all California environmental battles.

The justices ruled that all the natural resources in the state—lakes, rivers, beaches, open space, the air—are owned by the people and must be managed by the state for the good of the people. Called the Public Trust Doctrine, this legal precedent established the right of citizens' groups to sue for compensation or injunction whenever and wherever the public trust is infringed. It soon became one of the most powerful tools for environmental protection.

The Owens Valley is still an artificial desert, while Los Angeles is an artificial oasis. Because of court rulings the level of Mono Lake has stopped dropping and the ecological damage has been stabilized, but no real agreement has been reached between the warring factions about what the final level will be and how much water can be diverted.

Agnew Meadows lot around 5:30pm, either hoof it out in time or plan to drive in to Agnew before the 7:30am cut-off time for private traffic into Devils Postpile.

Lake Sabrina to Hungry Packer Lake

12.6 miles round-trip. Moderate. 3 or 4 days. Access: From Bishop follow State Route 168 west where a sign says North Lake and South Lake. At 9 miles you'll pass a ranger station where wilderness permits are available. Follow the signs until you reach the Sabrina Basin hikers' parking lot. Map: Inyo National Forest map and Mount Goddard topo.

Lake Sabrina Basin is the more popular name for the Middle Fork Bishop Creek Drainage, the largest drainage in this part of the Sierra. This incredible glacier-carved bowl has more than 40 lakes between the altitude of 9,000 and 12,400 feet. The north and south forks of Bishop Creek have almost 60 more. During peak season, from July 1 to September 15, the Forest Service limits the quota of hikers allowed into Sabrina Basin to enhance the wilderness experience and protect habitat. With some planning, though, you should have no trouble getting a permit for this hike.

Because no trails lead from Sabrina Basin to Kings Canyon National Park, the middle fork doesn't see quite the heavy use that the other Bishop Creek drainages do. From the parking area walk south 0.5 miles to the signed trailhead. As the trail skirts the east shore of Lake Sabrina you'll have a good view of what's to come through stunted pines and junipers. In a mile or so you'll be joined by the George Lake Trail. Steer right and head up a switchbacked trail

to Blue Lake. Beautiful and close to the trailhead, Blue Lake is a popular lay-over and destination in its own right, but keep going. You'll cross Blue Lake's outlet creek and continue along the west shore. The trail gets faint and heads in several directions. You want to bear west toward Emerald Lakes and then Dingleberry Lake—13,435-foot Mount Haeckel is a good landmark because it is just behind your destination. Just above Dingleberry you'll have to cross the middle fork (be careful in early season). The trail heads over a ridge where you can see most of the middle fork below. Soon you'll cross the outlet creek of Hungry Packer and climb to the lake's basin. Campsites are plentiful and the fishing is good. Many good day hikes round out a long weekend here.

Mount Whitney

22 miles round-trip. Difficult. 10,000-foot elevation gain/loss. The longest overnight of your life. Access: Take Whitney Portal Road from Lone Pine until it dead-ends. Map: USGS Mount Whitney topo.

You wouldn't think that the highest point in the Lower 48 could be reached by walking up a clearly marked trail with no technical climbing required, but that's exactly what Mount Whitney is, a walk up. From Whitney Portal Road you'll follow the Whitney Trail, a virtual super-highway, through an astounding number of switchbacks until it intersects with the John Muir Trail. You'll probably want to camp as high up the Whitney Trail as you can at Trail Camp, beyond which the only water is snow. In the morning it is 2 miles of switchbacks to the John Muir Trail and another 2 miles to Whitney Summit. At 14,494 feet, this is the highest you can get in the continental United States. A hut and outhouse mark the summit. Even though the walk up is relatively easy, be aware of any symptoms of acute mountain sickness such as nausea, confusion, loss of coordination, and headache. If any in your party are experiencing these symptoms, turn around and head down. They'll improve quickly as you lose altitude.

The hardest thing about the Whitney Trail is securing a permit to do it. The Forest Service only accepts applications for summit permits by mail and strictly enforces the system. Conceivably you could do the whole hike in one day and circumvent the permit process, but you better be in really good shape before attempting it. Almost half the people who attempt Whitney, including those who camp partway up, don't reach the summit. Weather, altitude, and fatigue can all conspire to stop even the most prepared party. Send your application to the rangers' office in Lone Pine in the spring to guarantee a permit for the summer. The address is Mount Whitney Rangers Station, 640 S. Main St., Lone Pine, CA 93545 (tel. 760/876-6200). Make sure to include the date you want and the number in your party. You can also receive a permit by writing to the rangers' office at Sequoia National Park, Ash Mountain, P.O. Box 10, Three Rivers, CA 93271 (tel. 209/565-3341). When parking is a problem at the trailhead, the chamber of commerce in Lone Pine runs a shuttle.

HORSEBACK RIDING

Horses are big business on this side of the Sierra and there are lots of businesses just itching to take you on a pack stock trip of the High Sierra or a short day ride. These are the biggest, but many other smaller operators are available seasonally or part-time:

◆ **Agnew Meadows Pack Station,** Minaret Vista Road (tel. 760/934-6633), offers 2-hour, half-day, and extended overnights into the wilderness around Devils Postpile.

◆ **Mammoth Lakes Pack Outfit,** Lake Mary Road past Tamarack Lodge (tel. 760/934-2434), leads 3- to 6-day backcountry trips all over the eastern Sierra. Trips tailored to individual groups. They also run horseback riding and wilderness photography workshops.

◆ **McGee Creek Pack Station,** McGee Creek Road, Crowley Lake (tel. 760/935-4324), specializes in long backcountry trips into the John Muir Wilderness through McGee Canyon.

◆ **Mike Morgan's Bishop Pack Outfitters** (tel. 760/873-4785) in Bishop leads 2-hour, half-day, and all-day rides into the Sabrina and Humphrey basins. They also offer a dinner ride by special request for large groups.

◆ **Red's Meadow Resort and Pack Station** (tel. 760/934-2345) offers overnights, multi-day trips, and dinner wagon rides near Rainbow Falls, Red's Meadow, and Red's Meadow Hot Springs.

◆ **Sierra Meadows Ranch** (tel. 760/934-6161), practically in the town of Mammoth Lakes, is a complete equestrian center oriented toward daily events rather than overnight pack trips. Sleigh rides are given in winter.

◆ **Wolf Creek Pack Station** (tel. 702/345-6104) in Markleeville specializes in backcountry fishing, hunting, and camping trips in the Mokelumne Wilderness.

HOT SPRINGS

The violent volcanism that is still forming the Sierra Nevada has one very soothing and gentle side effect: hot springs. The eastern slope is positively dripping with them. Besides well-known ones like Hot Creek near the Mammoth Airport, and Grover Hot Springs State Park outside Marklee-ville, hundreds of others dot the landscape. *Great Hot Springs of the West* (Capra Press, 1993) is a good guide to developed springs in the whole west, but for the really out-there and hidden springs you'll need to seek out local advice. For obvious reasons locals are sometimes loath to reveal their secret skinny-dipping spot to the first yahoo to stagger up to them on a street corner bellowing, "Where are all the cool hot springs?" Take a more subtle approach and you might be rewarded with some great surprises.

MOUNTAIN BIKING

Nowhere in the state is as well suited to the serious mountain biker, and nowhere is as unforgiving. Rides out here usually begin somewhere around 9,000 feet and head up. For someone coming from any of California's sea-level population centers the effect is like having one of your lungs removed, and I don't care how bad-ass you think you are. Also, except for right around Mammoth, rides in the eastern Sierra tend to take you a long way from nowhere and then a little far-ther. Know how to fix anything that can break on a ride or you'll find yourself 25 miles from help and walking. Of course, the bright side is that you can do a 50-mile bike ride and never see another cyclist. And where else can you bike to the top of a 14,000-foot peak or out into a desert filled with hidden hot springs?

Far and away the best local guide-book for any sport on the eastern Sierra is Don and Reanne Douglass's *Moun-tain Biking the High Sierra: Mammoth Lakes and Mono County* (Fine Edge Productions, 1992). Bike shops all over California carry guidebooks and they provide a great balance of mile-by-mile road and trail directions and interesting narrative. If you are really serious about biking the eastern Sierra, buy this book.

Mammoth Mountain Bike Park

Various trails for all levels of ability. Access: Mammoth Mountain Ski Area (1 Minaret Rd., Mammoth). Map: Mammoth Mountain map.

When the snow finally melts off Mam-moth Mountain, generally in July, the ski company turns Mammoth into a mountain biking park. For a price, you and your bike can ride the lifts to the top of Mammoth Mountain and spend the 3,000 and something feet of vertical you just cheated headed down any num-ber of trails. Each year at the beginning of July the mountain is host to the Grundig World Cup/Reebok Eliminator National Moutain Biking Champion-ships, where you can watch clinically insane pros hurtle down the kamikaze hill pushing 70 and 80 mph. The moun-tain also rents bikes and will sell you any parts for your own bike you break trying to mimic those pros.

Inyo Craters Loop

8 miles. Moderate. Heavily wooded and geographically confusing. Access: From Mammoth Scenic Loop park at Forest Road 3S22 or 3S30.

A whole mess of fire and jeep roads cut through this area and it's likely you'll get lost. So what. Just remember that the Scenic Loop is to the southeast and have a good time. Ideally you'll be able to follow the signs marking the trail to the top of Inyo Craters. You'll have to walk your bike to the edge of the craters themselves. These mini-volcanoes are the youngest major geologic feature in the Sierra Nevada, probably only about 1,500 years old. Several hundred feet deep, the craters blew more than 5 million tons of debris in a violent explosion of volcanic gas. Think about that on your ride back to town.

Deadman Creek to June Lake

About 20 miles. Difficult. Good route finding required. Grueling rocky climb and single-track descent. Access: Upper Deadman Campground. Map: Inyo National Forest map.

This all-day ride is the high road for advanced cyclists between Mammoth and June lakes. There are many ways to hook up with the trail in the before-mentioned mess of jeep trails near Inyo Craters. Either way, what you're looking for is Upper Deadman Campground. (Use your Forest Service map.) From there the narrow dirt road continues up for about 5.5 miles until reaching a ridge and veering into the headwaters of Deadman Creek. In another mile the road shoots uphill again and gets really rocky. At 7 miles (after a hellacious climb) you crest out in the very headwaters of the Owens River, where the water pouring out of all those taps in Los Angeles gets its start. The road peters out in the debris of an old avalanche. A hiking trail leads from the nearby knoll down into June Lake for several miles of tough and bushy single track.

Upper Owens River Gorge Loops

Distances vary. Easy. Mostly flat roads and trails. Access: North and east of Tom's Place, take Road 4S02 off U.S. 395. Park immediately.

A number of relatively flat and easy loops take advantage of the numerous roads and trails out to the Owens River Gorge, a dramatic rift carved by the river into soft volcanic stone. This is also a famous climbing area. It may appear barren at first glance, but the sagebrush plain is home to hawks, deer, burros, and the occasional pronghorn. From U.S. 395 the gorge is north and slightly west toward Crowley Lake. Head off across the sagebrush plains and hills until the earth opens in front of you. Head up-or downstream on the rim or take the hand-carved trail to the canyon bottom and follow the creek upstream to Crowley. A paved road will take you to the canyon rim. Return to U.S. 395 when you've had enough. I know these directions are really nondirections, but the beauty of this spot is that you are able to explore so many options on a whim and the road will always be to your south. Go ahead, get lost. Then figure out which way south is and take a fire road that way. Wow, look, a highway and your car.

Shady Rest to Lookout Mountain

16 miles round-trip. Moderate. Paved and well-graded dirt road. Access: Shady Rest Campground off State Route 203 in Mammoth Lakes. Map: Inyo National Forest or Mammoth Lakes tourist map.

This is a good first ride to get acclimated to the elevation before heading for the bigger stuff. In 16 miles you only gain about 1,000 feet, yet the view of the surrounding area is fantastic. The route is entirely paved or well-graded dirt. As you climb Lookout Mountain, the last 2 miles to the summit are steep but not unreasonable and the road-bed is good. When you reach the top the Sierra Nevada is to your west and the White Mountains to the east. You should be able to see for miles on a clear day.

ROAD BIKING

There really aren't many paved roads on this side of the Sierra, so the ones that are, tend to be popular with cars too. Unless you're training for some gnarly road race and want to ride skinny wheels at altitude (many great road racers do train here for the hills, altitude, and good weather), I recommend using a mountain bike or at least a good cross bike, even for road rides, simply because there are so many tempting dirt roads and side paths you won't want to miss.

Long Valley Crowley Lake Road Ride

16 miles round-trip. Easy. Moderately hilly. Access: Crowley Lake Drive junction with U.S. 395. Crowley Lake Road parallels U.S. 395 south to Tom's Place and Rock Creek Road.

Moderate hills and light traffic make this a perfect ride to get acclimated to the thin air here. You're between the freeway and the mountains with amazing views in every direction and a perfect spot to call the sag wagon (from Tom's Place) if the altitude is slaying you. Return to your car the way you came.

Rock Creek Road

16 to 24 miles round-trip. Very difficult. Serious high-altitude climbs. Access: Park at Tom's Place 17 miles south of Mammoth Lakes on U.S. 395.

Okay, so yesterday you rode Crowley Lake Road and it didn't even make you sweat. Drive or ride back out to Tom's Place and ride up Rock Creek Road and back. The 3,000-foot elevation gain

within 12 miles will put the fear into you, especially considering you started at about 9,000 feet. When you're not dying from exertion, take a look around; this is one of the prettiest glacial valleys in the Sierra, filled with meadows of flowers and lakes jumping with trout. Rock Creek Lake has a store where you can buy some food or a drink before flying back down to Tom's Place or continuing another 4 miles to the end of the road at Mosquito Flat. Then head for home. Hope you have good brakes.

Death Ride Tour of the California Alps

48 to 130 miles. Difficulty: Read the name. Access: Town of Markleeville.

Every summer 2,500 registered riders pay good money to come to Markleeville and ride till they practically drop. This beautiful and little-used part of the Sierra has endless opportunities for self-torture. Luckily, it's a tour, not a race, and you have several different options. Contact the Alpine County Chamber of Commerce, P.O. Box 265, Markleeville 96120, for information and registration (tel. 530/694-2475).

BIKE RENTALS

Several shops in the area rent mountain bikes. In Mammoth Lakes call **Kittredge Sports** (tel. 760/934-7566), or **Village Sports Center** (tel. 760/934-8220). In Bishop call **Bikes of Bishop** (tel. 760/ 872-3829).

ROCK CLIMBING & MOUNTAINEERING

Long a destination for hard-core adventurers who came to ice climb and mountaineer on the huge peaks of the Palisades and the Whitney Massif, the eastern Sierra has also suddenly boomed as a sport-climbing area. Though relatively new to the scene, the Owens River Gorge is beginning to eclipse Joshua Tree as Southern California's favorite sport-climbing outpost. Plentiful granite domes and spires around Mammoth Lakes provide more rock-climbing options.

There are several local guidebooks with route maps to areas like Rock Creek, Buttermilk, and the Owens Gorge. Check out *Rock Climbs of the Sierra East Side* by Erret Allen and Alan Bartlett (Chockstone Press, 1988), *Owens Gorge Climbs* and *Mammoth Area Rock Climbs* by Marty Lewis, or *Climber's Guide to the High Sierra* by Steve Roper (Sierra Club Books, 1976). For more advanced backcountry mountaineering and a wonderful index of peaks and their history, read *The High Sierra* by R. J. Secor (The Mountaineers, 1992).

SNOWSHOEING

Snowshoeing is back in fashion with the invention of smaller, lighter shoes that enable you to more or less run with snowshoes on. I, frankly, don't see why in the hell you'd want to run with snowshoes on, but then I never really got into jogging with ankle weights either. **The Great Outdoors** (tel. 760/924-2070) in Mammoth Lakes rents snowshoes, and the Tamarack Resort hosts the Great Snowshoe Race, a 10-kilometer race around the lakes basin, every January.

WALKS & RAMBLES

Hot Creek

1 mile. Well-traveled paths. Access: From U.S. 395 turn on Hot Creek Hatchery Road and drive to the Hot Creek Overlook (about 3 miles).

People flock here year-round to soak in the hot spring creek but Hot Creek it-

Swim at Your Own Risk

Sign at Hot Creek, the most popular hot spring in the Mammoth lakes area:

Twelve people have lost their lives in Hot Creek since 1968 and many more have been seriously injured. Some of the hazards are scalding water, broken glass, arsenic in the water, sporadic high pollution, sudden temperature changes, unpredictable eruptions, unstable ground. It is recommended that you remain on paved and wood paths and that you do not enter the water. Some of the more dangerous areas are fenced. However, new hazards are a constant threat. Please use extreme caution.

self is a lot more than just a bubbling bathtub. This officially designated Wild Trout Stream is home to a great population of native trout, and fishing is catch and release only. Bald eagles are commonly sighted in the winter. During spring and summer the dramatic cliffs are home to nesting swallows and other small birds. Cougars are rarely seen, but leave their sign in the form of paw prints and scat. Park at the Hot Creek Overlook and follow the trail down the hill. Dirt and wooden paths lead through the beautiful and striking thermal site with geysers and bubbling pools. You can hike either direction up and down the creek to get away from the crowd that is probably here for the spring.

Mono Lake Mark Twain Interpretive Trail

1 mile. Boardwalk trail. Access: From State Route 120 turn off at road to South Tufa

Area–Navy Beach. Trail starts in parking area.

Interpretive signs quoting Mark Twain on this 1-mile boardwalk trail explain Mono Lake while the trail winds through some of the best tufa towers and past a hot spring. The trail ends at Navy Beach, a popular area for taking a Mono Lake swim. Don't get the water in your eyes.

Devils Postpile

Various trails. Access: Devils Postpile National Monument Visitors Center.

There's more to Devils Postpile than a bunch of rocks, no matter how impressive they might be. Located on the banks of the San Joaquin River in the heart of a landscape of granite peaks and crystalline mountain lakes, the 800-acre park is a gateway to a hiker's paradise. Short paths lead from here to the top of the Postpile, and to Soda Springs, a spring gushing cold carbonated water.

Campgrounds & Other Accommodations

CAMPING

Ninety-nine percent of the places covered in this chapter are public land, controlled by either the National Forest Service, the National Parks Service, or the State Parks Department. While phone numbers and addresses vary for individual parks and jurisdictions, bookings for campground reservations are centralized through the PARKNET reservation service. For all state parks call 800/444-PARK (many Forest Service campgrounds are non-reservable). To reserve campsites in Yosemite, Sequoia/Kings Canyon, and Devil's Postpile national parks call 800/365-CAMP.

NORTHERN SIERRA: LAKE TAHOE TO YOSEMITE

Donner Memorial State Park

2 miles west of Truckee on Donner Pass Road. Tel. 530/582-7892. 150 sites. Flush toilets, showers, running water, picnic tables. Dogs okay on leash. $16 per night. Reserve through PARKNET (800/444-PARK).

Set along Donner Lake in exactly the same location that the ill-fated Donner party met their tragic fate, you'd find it hard to believe that this beautiful spot was the site of such a horrible tragedy. With good fishing, canoeing, and cross-country skiing, the only drawback is the drone of Interstate 80 that runs nearby.

Sugar Pine Point State Park

18 miles north of South Lake on State Route 89. Tel. 530/525-7982. 175 campsites. Flush toilets, showers (summer only), store and laundry (in town), fire pits, picnic tables. Dogs on leash permitted. Open year-round. $12–$16 per night. Reservations recommended in summer only (800/444-PARK).

This huge state park positively crawls with tourists in the summer. Reserve well in advance. Nice beaches and great lakefront hiking. If you're bringing a boat, ask about the boat-in campground, far removed from the hustle and bustle of the main camping area.

East Silver Lake

State Route 88 near Carson Pass. Tel. 209/ 295-4251 (Eldorado National Forest). 62 sites. Pit toilets, running water, boat ramp, store, marina. Pets on leashes okay. $10 per night. Reserve through PARKNET, (tel. 800/280-CAMP).

Silver Lake gives the feeling of being in the backcountry even though it is easily reached by road. Great fishing, swimming, and hiking into the Mokelumne Wilderness. The campground is wooded and some sites front the lake.

Lake Alpine

29 miles east of Arnold on State Route 4. Tel. 209/795-1381 (Stanislaus National Forest). 4 campgrounds with a total of nearly 100 sites. Flush toilets, showers, picnic tables, fire pits, boat launch, grocery store, rental boats, laundry. Pets on leashes okay. Summer only. $14 per night. No reservations.

Lake Alpine on the Stanislaus River is one of the prettiest man-made lakes I've ever seen. Numerous fingers of granite reach into the lake, making perfect casting points. Several great hikes go into the Emigrant Wilderness from here or around the lake.

Pinecrest Lake

Pinecrest Lake Road off State Route 108 at 5,600 feet. Tel. 209/965-3434 (Stanislaus

National Forest Summit Station). 200 sites. Running water, flush toilets, grocery store, boat ramp and marina. Pets on leashes okay. $15 per night. Reservations recommended (tel. 800/280-CAMP).

Pinecrest is another beautiful Sierra lake that could fool you into believing it's not a reservoir except when the water level drops. A great trail circles the lake. Fishing is good for rainbow trout. Popular with small-boat sailors because of the 20 mph speed limit. Downstream from the dam, the Stanislaus River offers great fly-fishing.

YOSEMITE NATIONAL PARK

All car campsites in Yosemite can be reserved up to 8 weeks before date of arrival through the **PARKNET** ticket service (800/365-CAMP). During the busy season all valley campsites sell out within hours of becoming available on the service.

Yosemite Valley Car Campgrounds

In the village. Tel. 209/372-0299. 404 sites. Drinking water, flush toilets, pay phones, fire pits, and a heavy ranger presence. Showers are available for a cost at Curry Village. Only Upper Pines allows pets on leashes. $15 per night.

If you are expecting a real nature experience, skip camping in the valley unless you like experiencing nature with 4,000 of your closest friends.

The five car campgrounds in the valley are always full except in the dead of winter. All are located along the Merced River. North Pines, Upper Pines, Lower Pines, and Lower River allow small RVs (less than 35 feet). Upper River is for tents only.

Sunnyside Campground, Yosemite Valley

In the village on the west side. Tel. 209/372-0299. 35 sites. Drinking water, flush toilets, pay phones, fire pits. Showers are available for a cost at Curry Village. No pets. $3 per night.

Sunnyside is the only walk-in campground in the valley and fills up with climbers since it is only $3 per night. Hard-core climbers used to live here for months straight, but the Park Service has cracked down on that. It's still a much more bohemian atmosphere than any of the other campgrounds.

Wawona and Bridal Veil Creek

Near the south entrance to the park. Tel. 209/372-0302. 210 sites. Drinking water, flush toilets, pay phones, fire pits. $10 per night. Reservations accepted in summer.

Outside the valley things start looking up for campers. Two campgrounds near the south entrance of the park, Wawona and Bridal Veil Creek, offer a total of 210 sites with all the amenities. Wawona is open year-round. Because it sits well above snowline at more than 7,000 feet, Bridal Veil is open summer only.

Crane Flat

20 miles southeast of Big Oak Flat entrance on Big Oak Flat Road. Tel. 209/372-0302.

141 sites. Water, flush toilets, fire pits. $15 per night. Open May–Oct. Reservations.

Crane Flat, Hodgdon Meadow, and Tamarack Flat are all in the western corner of the park near the Big Oak Flat entrance. Crane Flat, set at 6,200 feet, is the nearest to the valley, about a half-hour drive.

Hodgdon

Adjacent to the Big Oak Flat entrance. Tel. 209/372-0302. 105 sites. Water, flush toilets, fire pits. Pets okay on leash. $15 per night. Reservations.

Hodgdon Meadow is directly adjacent to the Big Oak Flat entrance at 4,800 feet. It's one of the least crowded low-elevation car campgrounds, but there's not a lot to do here.

Tamarack Flat

Off Tioga Pass Road near the Big Oak Flat entrance. Tel. 209/372-0302. 52 sites. No water, pit toilets, fire pits. No pets. $6 per night. No reservations. Open June–October.

This is one of the least-known car campgrounds in the park. Open June through October, Tamarack Flat is a bargain at $6 per night.

Tuolumne Meadows

Tuolomne Meadows. Tel. 209/372-0302. 314 tent and RV sites, 25 walk-in sites. Water, flush toilets, pay phones, fire pits. Showers available nearby. Pets okay. $15 per night; $2 per night for walk-in sites. Summer only.

Tuolumne Meadows is the largest campground in the park at more than 300 spaces, but it absorbs the crowd well and has all the amenities, including campfire programs and slide shows in the outdoor amphitheater. Half the sites are reserved in advance. The rest are set aside for first-come first-served.

White Wolf

West of Tuolumne Meadows. Tel. 209/ 372-0302. 87 sites. Water, flush toilets, hot showers, pay phone, fire pits. Pets okay on leash. $10 per night. Summer only.

White Wolf is the other full-service campground in the High Country. It has a drier climate than the meadow and doesn't fill up as quickly.

Porcupine Flat and Yosemite Creek

Near Toulomne Meadows. Tel. 209/ 372-0302. No water, pit toilets, fire pits. No pets. $6 per night. No reservations. Summer only.

The High Country's two primitive car camps, Porcupine Flat and Yosemite Creek, are the last to fill up in the park.

SHAVER LAKE AREA

Rancheria Camp, Huntington Lake

20 miles north of Shaver Lake on State Route 168. Tel. 209/855-5360 (Sierra National Forest). 150 sites. Flush toilets, running water, store, picnic tables, fire pits. Pets on leashes okay. $14 per night. Reserve by calling 800/280-CAMP.

One of a half-dozen camps surrounding beautiful Huntington Lake, this one is the best of the bunch. Nearby

is Rancheria Falls, a good day hike. Fishing and boating on the lake are great.

Camp Edison

On Shaver Lake, State Route 168. Tel. 209/ 841-3444. 252 sites. Flush toilets, show-ers, motorhome hookups, boat ramp, rent-als, bait shop. Pets okay. $15–$22 per night. Call for reservations.

It's a zoo, but so is Shaver Lake. Other campgrounds are available around the lake but they're all pretty comparable. Still, it's a great place to come for fishing and boating. Open year-round but the best season is May through November.

SEQUOIA AND KINGS CANYON NATIONAL PARKS

There are 13 campgrounds in the park, by far the most convenient and economical accommodations here. Only Lodgepole on the Kaweah River in Sequoia accepts reservations. Others are first-come, first-served and often fill up on weekends. Three campgrounds, Azalea, Lodgepole, and Potwisha, are year-round. The rest are open from snowmelt through September. Even in summer, campers should prepare for rain and possible snow. Bring a good tent and warm sleeping bags.

Lodgepole

5 miles northeast of Giant Forest on the Marble Fork of Kaweah River. Tel. 209/ 565-3341. 260 sites. Running water, flush toilets, showers, public phones, fire pits.

Pets okay on leash. $16 per night. Reservations are through PARKNET (tel. 800/365-CAMP).

This is one of the main campgrounds in the park, and with more than 200 sites, tends to be one of the noisiest. It is within a short stroll of restaurants, gas stations, and the main visitors center. If you're seeking solitude, lace up your hiking boots.

Dorst

14 miles northwest of Giant Forest on Dorst Creek. Tel. 209/565-3341. 219 sites. Running water, flush toilets, public phones, fire pits. Pets okay on leash. $16 per night.

This is the park's other main campground, though it only stays open from June to September. It's set on Dorst Creek at 6,700 feet near a backcountry trailhead.

Foothills / Mineral King Area Campgrounds

Near Giant Forest Village. Tel. 209/565-3341. 143 sites total. Facilities vary. Pets okay on leash.

Smaller and more peaceful are South Fork, Potwisha, Buckeye Flat, Atwell Mill, and Cold Springs. South Fork, Atwell Mill, and Cold Springs, with no water and pit toilets, are $8 per night. The others, with flush toilets, running water, and public phones, charge $14.

Cedar Grove Area Campgrounds

Near Cedar Grove Village. Tel. 209/565-3341. 351 sites total, plus 4 group sites. Running water, flush toilets, fire pits. Pets okay on leash. $12 per night.

Campers in the remote Cedar Grove area near the Kings Canyon River Gorge can choose from Moraine, Sentinel, Sheep Creek, Canyon View, and Canyon View Group Camp. All five sit at 4,600 feet and are convenient to some of the park's best hiking. The small Cedar Grove Village offers a restaurant, store, showers, and gas.

Grant Grove Area Campgrounds

Near Grant Grove. Tel. 209/565-3341. 360 sites total. Running water, flush toilets, fire pits. Pets okay on leash. $12 per night.

Three campgrounds in the Grant Grove area will put you near the Sequoias without the noise and crowds of Giant Forest Village. Sunset, Azalea, and Crystal Springs are all set at 6,600 feet. Showers are available at Grant Grove.

EASTERN SIERRA

Car camping in the eastern Sierra still remains a fairly pristine experience (other than the car) with few of the hassles associated with other parts of the state. There are so many national forest campgrounds here (24 in Mammoth/June Lakes alone) that you can always find a site—some of the lesser-known areas have the best camping. The national forest ranger stations for the area you want to visit are the best sources of information about specific camps and activities. The Inyo National Forest map that covers this entire area shows all campgrounds and is worth the $2 investment.

Lundy Creek

The closest decent campground to Mono Lake, Lundy Creek is just east of U.S. 395, 5 miles north of Lee Vining. 51 sites. Pit toilets, no water. Pets okay. $5 per night. No reservations.

It's a moonscape, but you wouldn't be visiting Mono Lake if you didn't like moonscapes. The campground, set on the shore of Lundy Lake, is nothing special, and you wouldn't come here except for the fact that you want to check out Mono Lake, but it does the trick. Purchase any supplies you may need in Lee Vining.

June Lake Oh! Ridge Camp

Right on the shore of June Lake, this national forest campground has it all. 148 sites. Flush toilets, running water, laundromat. Dogs okay on leash. $10 per night plus $7.50 reservation fee (tel. 800/280-CAMP).

It's huge but it's nice. This is the summertime equivalent of downtown in Camping USA. If you don't mind company, the fishing is great, the swimming is great, and the boating is great. Even if you do mind the company, there are plenty of good hikes into the surrounding hills where you will lose the crowd.

Twin Lakes

4 miles outside the town of Mammoth Lakes on the shore of beautiful Twin Lakes. 95 sites. Flush toilets, running water. Dogs okay. $11 per night. No reservations.

There are actually several campgrounds around Twin Lakes with a grocery store,

laundry, great fishing, and hiking. Trophy fish come out of these two lakes every year and they are popular with canoers and boaters. No swimming in Lower Twin Lake. It is the town water supply.

Rock Creek Lake

7 miles from Tom's Place on Rock Creek Road. 28 sites. Flush toilets, running water. Dogs okay. $8 per night. No reservations.

It gets cold up here at 9,600 feet, but the scenery is worth it. Countless great hikes head into the hills and the fishing is good.

Big Trees

In the Bishop Creek Drainage 11 miles from U.S. 395 on State Route 168. 9 sites. Flush toilets, running water. Dogs okay. $8 per night. No reservations.

One of the most popular backpacking and hiking destinations in the whole area surrounds you here. Lake Sabrina and hundreds of other lakes are up the road. Mountain bikers can explore several dirt roads.

INNS & LODGES

NORTHERN SIERRA: LAKE TAHOE TO YOSEMITE

Sierra Club Clair Tappaan Lodge

2.4 miles east of Interstate 80 on Donner Pass Road. Take Soda Springs/Norden exit. P.O. Box 36, Norden, CA 95274. Tel. 530/426-3632. Inexpensive.

This rambling wood-shake lodge hearkens back to the days when the Sierra

Club was the world's greatest hiking club. The dorm-style bunkrooms, private rooms, and family suites are all rustic and beautiful. The lodge has its own hot tub, library, kitchen, and dining room. Three family-style meals per day are included in the rates, which begin at $35 per night for dorm accommodations. Winter cross-country ski rental available.

Rainbow Lodge
(Royal Gorge Nordic Center)

6 miles west of Soda Springs on State Route 40. P.O. Box 1100, Soda Springs, CA 95728. Tel. 530/426-3661. Inexpensive. Some rooms share baths.

Built in 1925 with lots of cheap labor, the dramatic timber and granite construction of this lodge makes you feel like it could have been built by giants. A fine restaurant and bar are here, so you'll have plenty to do after a hard day's ski.

YOSEMITE NATIONAL PARK

Ahwahnee Hotel

Yosemite Valley. Tel. 209/252-4848. Reservations recommended. Extremely expensive.

The grand Ahwahnee Hotel is one of the most romantic and beautiful hotels in California if not the world. The native-granite and timber lodge was built in 1927 and reflects an era when grand hotels were, well, grand. Fireplaces bigger than most Manhattan studio apartments warm the immense common rooms. Parlors and halls are filled with Native American rugs and antiques. With its ballroom, pool, tennis, gourmet dining, outstanding views, and high-digit price tag, it's a special-occasion sort of affair. Rooms are booked a year in advance. Try to reserve one of the cottages, which cost the same as the rooms in the main hotel but are more spacious. And don't worry about what you're wearing unless you're going to dinner—this is Yosemite after all.

Wawona Hotel

By the south entrance, 45 minutes from the valley. Tel. 209/252-4848. Reservations recommended. Moderate.

The next best thing (and much more affordable) is the Wawona Hotel near the south entrance. Now a National Historical Landmark, the Wawona is a romantic throwback to another century. That has its ups and downs. Private bathrooms were not a big hit yet in the 19th century and rooms were small to hold in heat. Still, the Wawona is a great place to play make-believe. It offers a restaurant, pool, stables, and a lounge.

Yosemite Lodge

Yosemite Valley. Tel. 209/252-4848. Reservations recommended. Moderate.

Yosemite Lodge is the next step down in Yosemite Valley accommodations. It's actually a huge complex, not a lodge, with an array of accommodations ranging from luxurious suites with outdoor balconies and striking views of Yosemite Falls to one-room cabins with shared baths in a separate building. There is a pool. Two restaurants and a cafeteria serve mediocre meals.

Curry Village

Yosemite Valley. Tel. 209/252-4848. Reservations recommended. Moderate to inexpensive.

Curry Village is the valley's low-rent district. This compound of almost 200 cabins and almost 400 tent cabins varies widely in quality. Some have private baths. Others share campground-style bathrooms. Ironically the oldest cabins are the nicest. Shoddy construction gives the others a slapped-together appearance, not to mention making them cold and drafty in winter. The tent cabins have wood floors and canvas walls. Without real walls to stop noise, the tent cabin areas lack any sort of privacy, but they're fun in that summer camp way. You'll have to sustain yourself with fast food from the Curry Village shopping center; no cooking is allowed in the rooms.

High Sierra Camps

Reservations through High Sierra Reservations, Yosemite Park and Curry Co., 5410 E. Home Ave., Fresno, CA 93727 (tel. 209/454-2002).

Yosemite's five backcountry High Sierra Camps are an intriguing option bridging the gap between backpacking and staying in a hotel. These wilderness lodges are simple tent cabins and cafeteria tents located in some of the most beautiful, remote parts of the park. The five camps—Glen Aulin, May Lake, Sunrise, Merced Lake, and Vogelsang—make for good individual destinations. Or you can link several together, since they're arranged in a loose loop about a 10-mile hike from each other—a nice wilderness circuit. Overnight rates include a tent cabin, breakfast, dinner, bathrooms, and showers. High Sierra Camp reservations are accepted beginning in December for the following summer and usually book solid by January.

SHAVER LAKE AREA

Mono Hot Springs Resort

End of State Route 168 at the edge of the John Muir Wilderness. P.O. Box 215, Lake Shore, CA 93634. Tel. 559/325-1710. Cabins $65 per night and up. Groceries and restaurant nearby.

This private hot spring resort on the edge of the Ansel Adams Wilderness might just be the ultimate tonic for city-induced stress syndrome. With hot mineral baths, massage, rustic cabins (reasonably priced), and good food, you'll decompress in no time. And nobody can beat Mono Hot Springs for location. Hiking into the John Muir Wilderness from here is extraordinary. Call well in advance for reservations. The season is short and weekends are filled early.

SEQUOIA AND KINGS CANYON NATIONAL PARKS

Lodging in the park ranges from rustic one-room cabins with no bath or heat to a luxury motel. None of the complexes are very big. All lodging in the park is operated by the park concessionaire, **Sequoia Guest Services,** P.O. Box 789,

Three Rivers, CA 93271 (tel. 209/561-3135). Call or write for information and reservations.

The heaviest concentration of accommodations is in Giant Forest, where you'll find something in every price and taste range. Grant Grove offers a variety of cabins with private or shared baths. Cedar Grove is the site of an 18-room motel. Each room has its own bath and two queen-sized beds.

EASTERN SIERRA

Tamarack Lodge and Cabins

Twin Lakes Road. Tel. 800/237-6879 in California, 760/934-2442 elsewhere. 25 cabins, 11 rooms. $75–$360 per night. AE, MC, V. No pets.

Located on the shore of Twin Lakes, this beautiful old lodge is a cross-country ski resort in winter and a lakeside hotel in summer. The restaurant has been written up by *Bon Appetit* and the prices reflect its four-star quality. Rooms in the timbered lodge are quaint but the walls are a little thin. The upstairs suite in the lodge is a veritable palace and perfect for a family or two. The restaurant and a large common room centered around a beautiful fireplace occupy the entire bottom floor. About a dozen cabins with kitchens and baths are scattered around the grounds. In winter they are secluded and can be a little hard to get in and out of during big storms, but they're very romantic.

Red's Meadow Resort

Tel. 760/934-2345 or 760/873-3928. Inexpensive. Open summer only.

Lodging is in cabins at this resort right in the gateway to the Ansel Adams Wilderness and Devils Postpile. Trout fishing on the San Joaquin is a popular pastime as are hikes into the backcountry. There is a store on the premises and a cafe if you don't feel like cooking.

Alper's Owens River Ranch

Tel. 760/648-7334, summer; 760/647-6652, winter. Inexpensive.

Favored by fly fishermen for its private frontage on the Owen's River, Alper's is a fairly simple but beautiful collection of cabins on a cattle ranch. Prices are really reasonable and change with season.

7

The Gold Country

EW PERIODS IN TIME HAVE CAPTURED THE AMERICAN IMAGINATION like the Gold Rush of 1849. The promise of gold to be had just for a little sweat and digging was exactly the kind of Horatio Alger dream needed to fuel the usurpation of California from the Mexicans and Native Americans to whom it previously belonged. As long as it was a desolate wilderness, they could have the durn place, but once it became known that thar's gold in them there hills, thousands of Yankees descended on the place and California was well on its way to becoming the Golden State. These days a few hardy miners still chase their dreams of hitting the mother lode, but most people here are riding a different kind of boom, the real-estate boom of the early '90s that turned former mining camps like Sonora and Angels Camp into fashionable enclaves of Bay Area and Los Angeles equity refugees. Along with espresso, art galleries, and BMWs, the new wave of Gold Country pioneers have a lot of free time on their hands and an appetite for recreation. As a result, camping, fishing, river rafting, hiking, and mountain biking enjoy a popularity like never before in this area. It's not that any of those things are new here, just that suddenly there are a lot more people living here and doing them regularly.

The Lay of the Land

Gold was first discovered in California at Sutter's Mill on the American River in the foothills above Sacramento. In keeping with history the Gold Country is commonly defined as the region from 1,000 to 3,000 feet in altitude along the west slope of the Sierra Nevada even though gold was found in many other regions of the state in later years. From Quincy in the north to Oakhurst in the south, this is a region of dry rangeland and oak hillsides interspersed with large canyons cut by such major California rivers as the Feather, American, Tuolumne, and Merced. Black bear and mule deer use this snow-free strip as a wintering area to escape the cold winters of the High Sierra. Rattlesnakes abound, and the plant community is pretty rough and tumble: a thorny, prickly mix dominated by a hardy chaparral cover on the hillsides, blackberry- and poison-oak-covered riverbanks, and the occasional cluster of pines and firs. Spring, however, brings out the Gold Country's flashier side; the grassy hillsides explode in a display of golden California poppies beginning in early May. By the time the June heat arrives they are gone.

Orientation

Highway 49

Though every major road over the Sierra passes through the Gold Country, it is Highway 49 that embodies the spirit of the 49ers (no, not the football team, the miners) who settled this tough country. Winding almost 300 miles from Portola to Oakhurst, Highway 49 is a road-tripper's delight, going through great old mining towns like Jackson and Angels Camp and over long stretches of isolated cattle country. Often the road switchbacks down steep river canyons before crossing on some high bridge and winding back up the other side. This is not a road for people prone to car sickness, but it is a great way to unwind from the urban superhighway mentality.

Auburn

Auburn is pretty much the northern end of what is traditionally considered the Gold Country. The American River runs practically through Auburn with great whitewater, and Folsom Dam is just a few miles downstream. My favorite feature of the Auburn area, though, is the half-mile-long, 800-foot-high Foresthill Bridge, built to connect the tiny community of Foresthill with Auburn when Auburn Dam was to be constructed. The dam was put permanently on hold when a huge earthquake fault was discovered nearby, but the bridge stands as a monument to man's impudent desire to control nature in ways it often refuses to be controlled. In June, downtown is the finish line of the Western States 100, a sadistic foot race from Squaw Valley to here through the Granite Chief Wilderness. For Auburn information contact the **Auburn Chamber of Commerce,** 601 Lincoln Way, Auburn, CA 95603 (tel. 916/885-5616). The **Foresthill Ranger District Office** can be reached at 22830 Foresthill Rd., Foresthill, CA 95631 (tel. 916/367-2224).

Coloma

Coloma is a summertime whitewater mecca, and becomes almost unbearably crowded—still, it's a great Gold Rush–era town. It was near Coloma that John Marshall triggered the Gold Rush of 1849 by announcing to his workers, "Boys. By god, I believe I have found a gold mine." Earlier that morning he had spotted some shining flecks in the tail-race of a sawmill he was building for John Sutter on the South Fork of the American River. The **Marshall Gold Discovery State Historic Park** (tel. 530/622-3470) nearby still offers gold panning. The **Coloma Outdoor Discovery School** (tel. 530/621-2298) is a special environmental learning center for children that offers 3-day programs October through May.

Placerville

Once a rough-and-tumble mining town known alternately as Hangtown, Placerville today is more or less a glorified western theme park truck stop, an off-ramp from the U.S. 50 Corridor to the slow lane of Highway 49. For Placerville information contact the **El Dorado County Chamber of Commerce,** 524 Main St., Placerville, CA 95667 (tel. 530/621-5885).

Jackson

Far from a ghost town, Jackson was and still is one of the most stable mother lode cities. The Mokelumne River runs nearby, and the Camanche and Pardee reservoirs offer nearby fishing and camping. Also worth a visit is the interesting **Indian Grinding Rocks State Historic Park** (tel. 209/296-7488). For Jackson information contact the **Amador County Chamber of Commerce** on Highway 49, P.O. Box 596, Jackson, CA 95642. (tel. 209/223-0350).

Angels Camp

Immortalized by Mark Twain's story "The Celebrated Jumping Frogs of Calaveras County," Angels Camp is another weird example of life following art. Twain *made up* the story of the jumping frog jubilee, a fantastic tall tale about bored miners and the stupid things they'll do for fun. Angels Camp, of course, couldn't leave well enough alone and actually started holding the frog-jumping contest in 1928. Now it's a famous tourist draw every May. For information contact the **Calaveras County Lodging and Visitors Association,** 1301 S. Main St., P.O. Box 637, Angels Camp, CA 95222 (tel. 800/CAL-FROG).

Columbia and Sonora

Columbia is a fantastic state park encompassing an entire 19th-century mining village. The town is still "alive": tours, exhibits, and shops relive the Gold Rush. Sonora is a booming foothill town on State Route 108 and Highway 49. It's gone a little hog wild since Bay Area refugees discovered it in the late '80s. Now you can't throw a rock without hitting a bed and breakfast or a fancy cafe, but the change has actually been nice. For information contact the **Tuolumne County Visitors Bureau,** 55 W. Stockton St., P.O. Box 4020, Sonora, CA 95370 (tel. 209/533-4420). The **Stanislaus National Forest Headquarters** can be reached at 19777 Greenley Rd., Sonora, CA 95370 (tel. 209/532-3671).

Mariposa

Mariposa is the gateway to the Yosemite Valley to most people who whiz through here at top speed, but it merits its own visit. Great cycling surrounds the town, and the town's mining history exhibit at the county fairgrounds is really interesting too. For information visit the **Mariposa County Chamber of Commerce** at the corner of Highway 49 and State Route 140, P.O. Box 425, Mariposa, CA 95338 (tel. 209/966-2456). The **Mariposa Ranger District,** P.O. Box 747, Mariposa, CA 95388 (tel. 209/966-3638), is at the same corner.

Oakhurst

What little there is to say about Oakhurst is probably best said by the talking grizzly statue downtown at the corner of State Route 41 and Route 426. This is the end of the mother lode and the Gold Country. Like Mariposa, Oakhurst is largely a way station on the journey into the south entrance of Yosemite. For information visit the **Eastern Madera County Chamber of Commerce,** 49015 Rd. 426, Oakhurst, CA 93644, (tel. 209/683-7766).

Parks & Other Hot Spots

While Yosemite National Park to the southwest (see Chapter 6, "The Sierra Nevada") garners most outdoor attention in this neck of the woods, the Gold Country still has a fair amount of outdoor offerings, particularly if **whitewater** is your thing. The **American River** runs practically through the town of Auburn. In summer the small city of Coloma is transformed into the Grand Central Station of **river rafting.** Traffic Jams back up the streets and the South Fork of the American River. The **Marshall Gold Discovery State Historic Park** (tel. 530/622-3470), also in town, has great **swimming** in the American River, and nice **hiking** trails past the old historic buildings.

The **Mokelumne River** runs near Jackson, and **Camanche and Pardee reservoirs** are two popular **fishing** and **camping** lakes surrounded by more than 15,000 acres of public land. A really interesting state park here is the **Indian Grinding Rocks** (tel. 209/296-7488), a meadow containing a limestone mesa

that is marked by more than 1,100 ancient mortar-and-pestle grinding holes. The grinding rock (*Chaw'se* in the Miwok language) is the largest in the United States. A museum and Native American roundhouse are also here.

Beyond the jumping frog contest, other good reasons to visit Angels Camp are the fantastic whitewater of the **Stanislaus River,** nearby **Moaning Cave and Mercer Caverns** (The county gets its name—*Calaveras,* which means "skulls" in Spanish—from these caves, once a sacred Miwok burial site), and miles of great **bicycling.** South of Sonora on Highway 49 is some of the state's best whitewater, the famous **Tuolumne River,** as well as two huge reservoirs: **Lake Don Pedro** and **Lake McClure.**

While Mariposa is primarily a stopping point on the way to Yosemite, there is some great **cycling** in the surrounding area. Northeast of Oakhurst before you come to Yosemite National Park, a large swath of Sierra National Forest cut by dirt roads and seldom-used trails offers a good alternative to the crowds of Yosemite. **Bass Lake,** a beautiful, tree-circled reservoir owned by Pacific Gas and Electric, is a popular **fishing, swimming, and waterskiing** lake just outside Oakhurst. Contact the Bass Lake Ranger District (tel. 209/683-4665) for information about the lake and national forest.

What to Do & Where to Do It

BIRD WATCHING

The oak woodlands and chaparral communities of the Gold Country foothills are an important habitat for numerous species including **woodpeckers, raptors,**

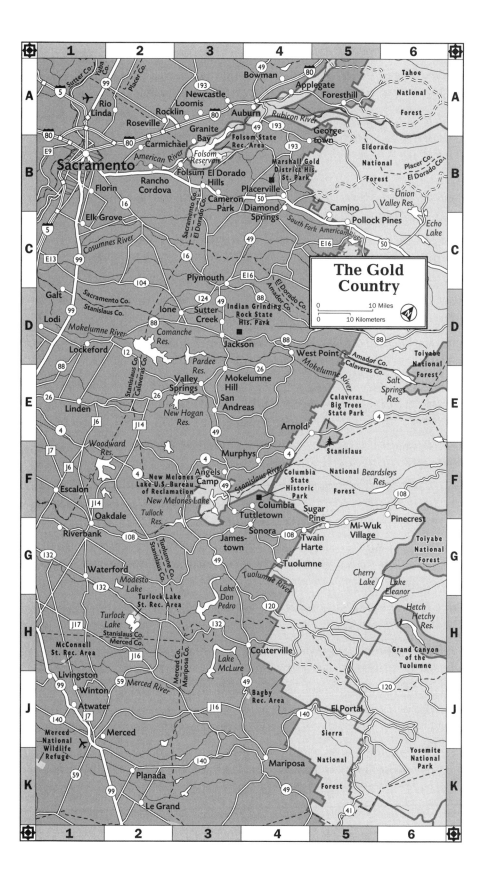

The Gold Country

0   10 Miles

0   10 Kilometers

and **owls**. Not surprisingly, the acorn woodpecker is one of the most common species you'll see here, almost as common as the California quail that seem to scamper out from under every bush. You might also spot the hairy woodpecker, Nuthall's woodpecker, and downy woodpecker in the oak forests, and spot large raptors like the red-tailed hawk, northern goshawk, and golden eagle. A special treat is the occasional twilight sighting of great horned, western screech, and northern pygmy owls. Wild turkey have become common in the foothills in the last few decades, and sometimes you'll spot them right in the middle of Highway 49. Public land is less common here in the rolling ranch country than high up in the Sierra, but several places offer good access: **Hangtown Gold Bug Park** (tel. 530/642-5232) in Placerville (62 acres of woodland), **Indian Grinding Rock State Historic Park** (tel. 209/296-7488) near Jackson, and the numerous public parks around **Bass Lake.**

FISHING

Whether you're a fly fisherman looking for a perfect patch of river or a bass buster searching for bucket-mouthed hogs, the Gold Country probably has what you're looking for. As they tumble through the foothills, the **American, Mokelumne, Stanislaus, Merced, and Tuolumne rivers** all offer great trout fishing. Local seasons and closures change from river to river and from mile to mile on certain rivers like the Tuolumne, where sections are closed or are catch and release only.

Lake fishermen have a hard time deciding where to go in this neck of the woods. Depending on the season (and the water level) the large foothill reservoirs like **Folsom Reservoir, Lake Don Pedro, Lake McClure,** and **Bass Lake** are hot spots for trout, Kokanee salmon, largemouth and smallmouth bass, crappie, and catfish.

GOLD PROSPECTING

It's hard to visit the Gold Country and not get a little itch of the greed that drove the rush. Panning is harder than you might think; standing around waist deep in gold water can sap your enthusiam right off if you don't know what you're looking for. Luckily, a number of outfitters are just itching to take you out and show you how to do it right. (For a price. This is a gold rush after all.) Try **Columbia State Park Hidden Treasure Gold Mine** (tel. 209/532-9693), **Gold Country Prospecting** in Placerville (tel. 530/622-2484), **Gold Prospecting Expeditions** in Jamestown (tel. 209/984-4653), or **Jensen's Pick and Shovel Ranch** in Angels Camp (tel. 209/736-0287).

HIKING

Hiking is hard in this area for the simple reason that much of the land is private, and that which isn't private is so darn steep and desolate that you'd be really hard-pressed to walk up or down it without falling off. The river canyons are the only real choice, and they are often impassable. There are good hikes that reach back into some of the remote river canyons, however.

Western States Pioneer Express Trail, Auburn State Recreation Area

3 miles round-trip, but 20-some miles possible. Moderate. Access: End of Driver's Flat Road at Ruck-A-Chucky Campground. Map: Auburn State Recreaton Area map.

Beginning at the Ruck-A-Chucky Campground, this trail heads upstream about 200 feet above the Middle Fork of the

How to Pan for Gold

Find a gold pan—ideally a 12- to 15-inch steel pan. Place the pan over a burner, or better yet, in a campfire. This will darken the pan, making it easier to see any flakes of placer gold. On a stream, find some gravel, sand, or dirt that looks promising or feels lucky. Fill the pan nearly full and then place it under water and keep it there while you break up the clumps of mud and clay and toss out any stones. Then grasp the pan with both hands. Holding it level, rotate it in swirling motions. This will cause the heavier gold to loosen and settle to the bottom of the pan. Drain off the dirty water and loose stuff. Keep doing this until gold and heavier minerals called black sand are left in the pan. Carefully inspect the black sand for nuggets or speck traces of gold. When you find gold, immediately rush to San Francisco and scream "Gold! Gold! Gold!" at the top of your lungs. This will inevitably start the next Gold Rush.

You can dredge from June 1 to October 15. A dredging permit is required. Apply at Regional 2 Headquarters, California Department of Fish and Game, 1710 Nimbus Rd., Rancho Cordova, CA 95670 (tel. 916/358-2900). Or you can sign up for one of the many tours offered in Gold Country towns. See "Gold Prospecting" above.

American River. Down below you can see dark deep pools broken up by the occasional riffle. Look for heron and other water birds waiting to catch trout in the shallows. In about three-quarters of a mile you'll see roaring Ruck-A-Chucky Falls, one of the most feared rapids on the Middle Fork. A small side trail leads down to the falls for a close-up look at the action. Careful, though, the water-worn rocks around the falls get really slippery. Continuing up the main trail you'll pass over Ruck-A-Chucky and descend again. This time you come out near a nice sandy beach and an inviting swimming hole. Give in to the temptation, but don't forget what's downstream. Sometimes blackberry vines along the river offer up a perfect feast. Return the way you came.

KAYAKING

For a really strong kayaker this is heaven; the **Class IV and V** South Fork of the Tuolumne, Cherry Creek, North Fork of the American, and North Fork of the Stanislaus are some of the finest whitewater in the west. More moderate **Class II and III** runs are the **Chili Bar Run** on the South Fork of the American, the **Electra Run** on the Mokelumne near Jackson, and sections of the Merced between Yosemite and Lake McClure. Don't hop into your boat on any of these rivers because you *think* it is safe to go downstream; numerous easy Class III sections lead into harrowing Class V sections, and knowing where to take out is imperative. *California Whitewater: A Guide to the Rivers* by Jim Cassady (North Fork Press, 1995) is the definitive mile-by-mile guidebook to all these rivers and is well worth the purchase.

California Canoe and Kayak, 8631 Folsom Blvd., Sacramento, CA 95826 (tel. 800/366-9804), runs 2-day introductory kayak classes on the lower American, a beginning class on the South Fork, as well as intermediate and advanced classes. The school operates out of several locations in the Bay Area and Sacramento.

The River Store, 1032 Lotus Rd., Lotus, CA 95651 (tel. 530/626-3435), is the center of the whitewater kayaking scene on the South Fork of the American. No lessons, but great information and plenty of gear for sale.

For a copy of the *Boating Trail Guide to the North and Middle Forks of the American River,* a publication showing put-in and take-out sites, rapids and their difficulty rating, and emergency information, phone the **Whitewater Management Office** (tel. 530/885-5648). For river conditions contact the **California River Flow Hotline** (tel. 800/952-5530).

MOUNTAIN BIKING

Mountain biking in the Gold Country is still relatively untapped. Unfortunately much of the area is private property or too steep to ride, but there are some great exceptions, including the Merced River ride, one of my favorite rides in the world. Shorter rides like the Western State Pioneer Express Trail through Auburn State Recreation Area along the American River, or the single-track Darrington Trail circling Folsom Lake, are great for getting the feel of the area.

For other mountain biking adventures, contact the local ranger district in the area you'll be visiting. They know the ins and outs of public access, and can point you to great mining roads and trails into little-known spots. Particularly attractive is the Stanislaus National Forest above Sonora and near Groveland.

Merced River Ride

28 miles round-trip. Moderate. Gravel road. Access: Where State Route 140 joins the Merced River 20 miles west of Yosemite, take the one-lane bridge across the river. Follow the dirt road downstream until you find a suitable parking place. Map: Mariposa County road map.

For the first 14 miles the dirt road sticks with the river: perfect views of one of the best Class III and IV whitewater runs on the river, great swimming holes, stunning side canyons, even a few national forest campgrounds if you should decide to do it overnight. I like to ride it down and back, but it is possible to hook up with Highway 49 by Bear Valley and arrange a car shuttle. (Why you'd do this I don't know, as the drive is much worse than the ride.) The only drawback to this ride is that the road is open to cars, so you must be alert and try not to run them over—trust me, you'll be going faster than they are.

Western State Pioneer Express Trail

14 miles. Moderate. Access: Trail begins at Highway 49 bridge over American River. Map: Auburn State Recreation Area map.

The Western State Trail is a long-distance trail connecting Sacramento with Carson City, Nevada, a remnant of the days when trails, not highways, were how most people crossed the Sierra Nevada. These days the trail is open to hikers and horses, with only certain sections open to cycling. This section along the banks of the American River is one of the finer ones. Deep swimming holes will entice you off your bike and the foothill scenery is really nice. For entertainment keep your eye peeled for rafts careening down Murderer's Gorge Rapid.

Darrington Trail

7.8 miles. Moderate to difficult. Steep and rocky single track; intermittent creek crossings. Access: Trail begins at Skunk Hollow Trailhead on Pilot Hill–Salmon Falls Road. Map: Folsom Lake State Recreation Area map.

The Darrington Trail flanks the shore of Folsom Lake. It's steep here, so sections of the trail are not for the faint-hearted. Much of the ride is on open grasslands, and in the summer the heat can be intense. Bring plenty of water for this one.

ROAD BIKING

With Highway 49 weaving its way up and down throughout the area, the Gold Country is a great place to hit the blacktop.

Highway 49

Anywhere from 20 to 200 miles. Moderate to difficult. Steep sections, busy traffic throughout. Access: Anywhere along Highway 49. Map: AAA road map or equivalent.

Sinuous Highway 49 makes a great bike tour from end to end, and the towns along the route are spaced just the right distance apart so that you can make an unsupported ride sleeping in a hotel or B&B every night. If you decide to do it, plan to ride between March and the middle of June. After June you can pretty much forget about riding here until the end of September when the 100° days finally abate.

American River Bikeway

32 miles one way. Moderate. Access: Begin at Beal's Point Campground in Folsom Lake State Recreation Area (tel. 916/988-0205). Map: Sacramento County road map.

One of the most well-used and beautiful bike routes in California is the American River Bikeway that travels from Beal's Point Campground in Folsom Lake State Recreation Area all the way to Sacramento, 32 miles west. Following the north bank of the American, you get beautiful views of the river and down into the Central Valley. Parts of the Sacramento end of the trail are unsafe at night, so plan to have plenty of time and a shuttle or ride waiting.

WALKS & RAMBLES

Marshall Gold Discover State Historic Park Walking Tour

Distance depends on you. Access: Coloma historic quarter.

This is a ramble in the best sense of the word: The historic quarter of Coloma doesn't lend itself to directed, goal-oriented trekking. Instead, take an hour or two and wander around. You'll find a mining museum, with exhibits of ore carts and stamp mills—as common in their day as computer monitors and fax machines are in ours—plus plaques explaining the various methods used to extract gold. Standing close by is the old Wah Hop Store, a left-over from the days when Chinese laborers built the stone walls and embankments you see all over the mother lode. Across Highway 49 on the banks of the South Fork of the American you can explore a replica of John Sutter's Sawmill where James Marshall discovered gold on January 24, 1848, and set off the rush that would leave California a vastly different place. Near the south end of town take little Cold Springs Road to the cemetery, where the oldest grave marker dates back to 1850; many others followed soon after, grim testimony to the hard lives of the prospectors.

Indian Grinding Rock State Historic Park Tour

0.75 miles. Access: Visitors center on Volcano Road, 1.5 miles south of State Route 88 near Jackson.

By combining the nature walk self-guided trail (get brochures at visitors center) with a stop at the huge grinding rock and the reconstructed Miwok village, a visitor can quickly get a picture of the way the Native Americans lived in harmony with their ecosystem here. The numerous oaks that still shade the trail were the main staple of the Miwok, and nearby forests provided game and construction materials for their cedar bark houses.

WHITEWATER RAFTING

Not too long ago river rafting in the Gold Country was pretty limited because the rivers here were simply too tough to take commercial passengers down. Well, that's changed. Improvements in raft design and a more gonzo attitude among outfitters has opened all but the most insane Gold Country whitewater to commercial rafts. Almost every commercial rafting company in the state runs at least one of the Gold Country canyons, and for many this area is their bread and butter. There are literally more river rafting companies in California than there are runable rivers—at last count about 40 full-time outfitters. Overall the quality of service is really good; with that kind of competition the bad ones are weeded out fast. For a list of outfitters operating on a particular river, or just for general information, contact the **River Travel Center**, Box 6, Point Arena, CA 95468 (tel. 800/882-7238). They are a booking service for all outfitters on all rivers in California (at no charge to you) and are extremely knowledgeable about the sport.

Several outfitters are known for a certain specialty: **Beyond Limits Adventures**, P.O. Box 215, Riverbank, CA 95367 (tel. 800/234-RAFT), is best known for its Team Extreme trips for thrill-seeking rafters who want to tackle

Class V whitewater, but it also offers beginning and intermediate-level trips. **ARTA** (the American River Touring Association), Star Route 73, Groveland, CA 95321 (tel. 800/323-ARTA), is one of California's oldest outfitters. They've been around since 1963 and offer runs on virtually every California river and many out of state as well.

EASY RUNS

◆ **South Fork American River (Chili Bar and Gorge sections)**   This moderate Class II and III run through the Gold Country around Coloma is the best introductory whitewater in the state and is extremely popular to the point of overcrowding. More than 50 rapids—great gravel bar, wave train whompers—keep things exciting but never become technical or unforgiving. Most runs done with guide-directed paddle rafts.

◆ **Mokelumne River (Electra Run)** This 5-mile run near Jackson is a great one for kids. The water is all Class II-plus, meaning you can send junior out for a spin in one of the inflatable kayaks that outfitters bring along on these trips and not worry about him missing a take-out and going over Death Trap Falls. Short enough to run twice in a day.

DIFFICULT RUNS

◆ **Middle and North Forks of the American (Oxbow to Mammoth Bar, Chamberlain Falls, and Giant Gap)** Mostly heavy Class IV pool and drop rapids with the exception of the sketchy Giant Gap Run (Class V). These three runs are all popular for rafters looking for a step up in the excitement level. Giant Gap is several steps up: You hike 2 miles down a trail and then bomb almost 14 miles of constantly technical whitewater. Outfitters require previous experience on at least Class IV water before they'll take you on this one.

◆ **North Fork Stanislaus River (Sourgrass to Calavaras Big Trees)** Some of the world's most beautiful Class III boating now lies buried under New Melones Reservoir, but these 5 miles of Class III and IV-plus rapids are far upstream of the dam's reach. The season is short for the Stanislaus because of sporadic upstream releases, but the ride is worth it—5 miles of constant whitewater through beautiful rock canyons and sequoia forests, and past striking waterfalls.

◆ **Middle Fork Stanislaus River (Dorrington to Camp 9)** Like the Giant Gap run on the American, this run also requires a 2-mile hike 3,000 vertical feet down to the river to access 10 miles of almost constant Class IV to V-plus action. This is a relatively new commercial run, only offered in the last 3 or 4 years. You should have some experience with heavy water before signing on for one of these trips.

◆ **Tuolumne River (Lumsden Launch to Ward's Ferry Bridge)** The longtime classic of heavy-water California rafting. From put-in to take-out the Tuolumne dishes out nearly constant Class IV whitewater, including Clavey Falls, one of the biggest drops in western whitewater, but what's most stunning is the scenery. This stretch of the Tuolumne has been declared a Wild and Scenic River, and certainly deserves it. Don't be surprised to see bear, mule deer, or even a golden eagle. You can do this run in a day, but many outfitters offer it as a 2- or 3-day overnight run to get in some exploring up Cherry Creek, do a little fishing, and enjoy the beauty of this gorge.

◆ **Merced River (El Portal to Bagby)** Just outside of the Yosemite National Park Arch Rock entrance on State Route 140, the Merced River enters about 30 miles of really amazing Class III to IV-plus whitewater. For the first half the road runs alongside the Merced, perfect for motorists to watch the action, but a little distracting as a wilderness experience for the boaters. Downstream of Briceberg the road and river go separate ways and the canyon is one of the most beautiful you've ever seen. Also part of the National Wild and Scenic River System.

Campgrounds & Other Accommodations

CAMPING

Camping is a great way to go here year-round. Winter nights can get cold, even snow, but other days are clear and beautiful. It's always a gamble, but the lack of crowds could be your jackpot. Spring is beautiful almost without fail—wildflowers, clear skies, the whole package. Summer and early fall are a little too hot for my taste, unless I happen to be camped right near a river or lake. Luckily most campgrounds in the area *are* located right on rivers or lakes. Mosquitoes and ticks can be a problem, but they're nothing compared to the poison oak. It grows everywhere in the river bottoms, usually mixed in with blackberry vines just to tempt you. Rattlesnakes are common, but not really a problem as long as you give them the space they deserve. If you see them, please don't smash, chop, shoot, or otherwise maim them just because they scare you. You scare them too. Let them slither away and you can both live happily ever after.

Auburn State Recreation Area

1 mile south of Auburn on Highway 49. Tel. 530/885-4527. 53 tent sites; 22 boat-in sites, dispersed throughout park. Pit toilets, no piped water. Dogs okay. Reservations only for boat-in sites, call PARKNET (tel. 800/444-PARK; reservation fee charged); other sites are first come, first served; $7–$9 per night.

Just outside the reach of Sacramento's urban sprawl, Auburn State Recreation Area is a great place to get a little taste of wilderness. The park offers 42,000 riverfront acres along the American River, which runs through the park, with some of the river's most difficult rapids easily visible to hikers. Good fishing, biking, and swimming too.

Indian Grinding Rock State Historic Park

11 miles northeast of Jackson on State Route 88, then 1.5 miles south on Pine Grove–Volcano Road to the park. Tel. 209/296-7488. 23 sites. Flush toilets, running water. Pets okay. $10–$12 per night.

This park reminds you that before the Gold Rush there was another civilization living here in a way very different from ours. The Miwok museum and the enormous grinding stone area is fascinating. You can stay in some 20 campsites, but for a change stay in one of the park's five bark houses, built in the traditional Miwok way out of cedar poles and bark. They sleep about six. Call ahead for an application. Other park offerings include petroglyphs, a nature trail, reconstructed Miwok houses, and a sweat lodge.

Glory Hole

Midway between Angels Camp and Sonora on Highway 49 on the shore of New Melones Reservoir. Tel. 209/536-9094. 140 sites. Flush toilets, piped water, showers, boat ramp. Pets okay. No reservations; $14 per night.

New Melones kind of gives me the creeps. I just can't help thinking about all the great whitewater that used to run through here before the Stanislaus River was dammed to create this rather tepid reservoir; and in the fall the lake drops, exposing a huge bathtub ring of mud. It is the best place to camp in the Angels Camp to Sonora corridor, though. If you're a boater, you'll love it here. Nearby is a cabin where Mark Twain supposedly lived for a winter.

River Ranch Campground

5 miles northeast of the tiny town of Tuolumne on Buchanan Road. Tel. 209/928-3708. 55 sites. Flush toilets, piped water, showers, store, laundry. Pets okay. Call ahead for reservations; $14 per night.

In contrast to most of the other campgrounds in the area, this privately operated camp seems a bit overdeveloped, but it's pretty nice. The best feature is the Tuolumne River, which runs past here with good fishing and swimming.

INNS & LODGES

Virtually every small town on Highway 49 has at least one and probably two or three funky old B&Bs, some of them dating all the way back to the Gold

Rush. For complete references call the chamber of commerce in the area you're going to visit. The following are some of the ones I think are really neat.

Coloma Country Inn

345 High St., Coloma, CA 95613. Tel. 530/622-6919. 5 rooms (3 with private bath), 2 suites. $90–$130 double; $130–$185 suite. No credit cards.

Located in the middle of a state park (albeit a state historical park), this restored 1852 country farmhouse on 5 acres is a great place to spend a night away from your tent. And it's quite romantic. The two suites are in a separate cottage; one has a full kitchen. There's a pond complete with ducks, bicycles available for guest use, and innkeeper Alan Ehrgott is a balloon pilot. You can sign up for an hour-long flight with this 12-year veteran.

The Murphys Hotel and Lodge

457 Main St., Murphys, CA 95247. Tel. 209/728-3444. 29 rooms. $70–$80 and up. All major cards.

During the Gold Rush years, this was the grandest hotel in California outside of San Francisco. As a result, numerous famous and infamous characters of that period stayed here and played here: Mark Twain, Horatio Alger, Ulysses S. Grant, Daniel Webster, J. P. Morgan, and even stage coach bandit Black Bart were guests. In keeping with the Wild West history of the place, the bar downstairs has been known to party well into the night. Murphys is about 10 miles east of Angels Camp on State Route 4.

8

The Northern Mountains

I'S OFTEN OVERLOOKED THAT NOT ALL OF CALIFORNIA'S BEST MOUNTAIN wilderness is in the Sierra Nevada. I guess that's easy to understand when you take into consideration the grandeur of the Sierra, the distribution of much of the state's population near the Sierra, and the relative impenetrability of the Klamaths and Cascades to the automobile.

Still, it is a mystery how so many people can drive along Interstate 5 on a clear day, see the Trinity Alps to their west and the obvious, in fact, startling, Mount Shasta just a few miles east of the highway, and never bother to explore the possibilities here.

Of course, the people who *do* come to the state's northern mountains aren't going to cry any tears over the lack of crowds, nor are the people who live here. They know about the awesome kayaking, trout fishing, backpacking, backcountry skiing, climbing, camping, and a million other things to do here, and they probably aren't anxious for many more people to hear about it.

Maybe it's because most of the land is simply national forest and national wilderness, not glamorous, big-name national parks. Maybe it's because people were scared off by Bigfoot rumors in the 1970s and tales of renegade pot growers in the 1980s. Who knows? But anyone who drives 5 hours from the Bay Area to trudge along behind an ant trail of other hikers on an overcrowded Yosemite pathway when they could have driven 5¹/₂ hours to the Trinity Alps and been all alone is missing out.

Since the white man came to these parts, area history has been a sad litany of abuse and exploitation. First explored by Peter Ogden in 1828 and 2 years later by Jedediah Smith, the area wasn't really heavily explored until the 1850s Gold Rush. The Gold Rush brought destructive hydraulic mining that ripped up riverbeds and banks with enormous spouts of water to free trapped gold. Hard-rock mines yanked millions of dollars from the hills. Towns like Happy Camp, Scott Bar, Orleans, and Somes Bar were the final outposts of miners seeking their fortune from these remote canyons and hillsides.

Later, logging became the next big boom. It's hard to believe, but virtually every tree in the Klamaths was cut down between the early part of this century and the 1980s, when the last old growth was chopped. The trees you see growing now are second and third growth. Though today almost 2 million acres are included in the Klamath, Siskiyou, and Six Rivers national forests, and management practices are improving slowly, rampant clear-cutting and destructive mining practices continue. The people who live here walk a thin line between their ties to and love of the land and the necessity of balancing economic needs against ecological concerns.

The Lay of the Land

The Klamath Mountains reach from southern Oregon about 130 miles into northwestern California. The range includes the Siskiyous, Salmons, Marbles, Scott Bars, and Trinity Alps. The glaciated Trinity Alps are the highest and most dramatic part of the Klamaths, reaching heights of 8,000 feet. The Klamaths were formed together with the Sierra Nevada about 225 million years ago as the floor of the Pacific Ocean began to slide under the North American continent. The wreckage of the ocean bottom crumpled up like bent sheet metal and formed the beginnings of the range. It took millions of years for these pipsqueak mountains to achieve a respectable size, and then around 140 million years ago the Sierra split into two.

The northern third drifted 60 miles northwest to become the Klamaths. The other two-thirds, of course, became the Sierra Nevada. At the time the entire Central Valley would have been under water, and the Klamaths were probably an island chain for a few million years. While the Sierra shot skyward again in a dramatic surge of uplift that began about 3 million years ago, which has yet to subside, and was then scoured by glaciers to form the great mountain valleys, the Klamaths remained relatively stable; hence their more eroded and confused topography. Still, the Klamaths bear many similarities to their southern brethren: Geologists like to describe the rock layers in the two ranges as matching up like the type in a newspaper page torn in two. During the Gold Rush some of the richest deposits in California were actually found here, not in the Sierra Nevada, and individual rock specimens from both ranges are virtually identical.

Plants and animals in the northern mountains include many of the same species to be found in the evergreen forests of the Sierra, only here they have much more room to move around. Because the Klamaths are relatively low and their terrain more varied, there exists an abundance of richly productive evergreen forest, thickly wooded river valleys, and fertile meadow grasslands. Black bear, deer, cougar, eagles, hawks, and other large animals are common sights. Salmon and steelhead, though endangered due to dam building and siltation caused by clearcutting the hillsides, still return to the Klamath, Smith, Trinity, and Salmon rivers each year to spawn.

Orientation

Using Interstate 5 as a dividing line, you can bisect the northern mountains into two manageable pieces. On the west you have the Klamaths, a series of ranges with very blurry boundaries and distinctions between them. The Trinity Alps, covering hundreds of square miles of forest, meadows, and above-treeline rocky peaks, are the largest and most important of the Klamath ranges. Trinity County, in which the Trinities lie, has the distinction of being the only county in California without a single traffic light or parking meter, though it does have more than 400 miles of hiking trails and several of the best whitewater rivers in the state.

On the east side of Interstate 5 between Redding and the Oregon border lies a high plateau dotted with the southernmost peaks of the Cascade Range, most importantly Mount Shasta and Mount Lassen, both dormant (but not dead) volcanoes. Shasta rises nearly 10,000 feet from the surrounding countryside to a summit height of more than 14,000 feet, dwarfing everything for miles around. Though they seem like small fry next to Shasta, the other surrounding mountains are great: deep forests, open range, fantastic fly-fishing, hiking, and whitewater. Farther north and east the Modoc Plateau becomes flatter until you hit Tule Lake and the Walker Mountains.

Weaverville

The county seat of Trinity County, Weaverville, population 3,500, is the big city in these parts—a beautiful town of Gold Rush–era Victorians, brick storefronts, and the oldest continually used Chinese temple in California. If you're going into the Trinity Wilderness, rafting the Trinity River, or visiting Trinity Lake (creative naming, huh?), you'll probably pass through Weaverville coming or going. For information contact the **Trinity County Chamber of Commerce,** 317 Main St., Weaverville, CA 96093 (tel. 916/623-6101 or 800/421-7259).

Yreka

The only town with a population over 5,000 people in the entire central northern area, Yreka was founded by proud ranching and mining pioneer stock and remains much the same. The county seat of Siskiyou County, it is home to the **Siskiyou County Museum,** 910 S. Main (tel. 530/842-3836), the **Klamath National Forest Interpretive Museum and Headquarters,** 1312 Fairlane Rd. (tel. 530/842-6131), and a stunning display of gold nuggets at the **Siskiyou County Courthouse,** 311 4th Street (call the museum for info). For Yreka information, contact the **Yreka Chamber of Commerce,** 117 W. Miner St. (tel. 530/842-1649 or 800/ON-YREKA).

Mount Shasta City

This tiny town of about 1,000 citizens is one of those wonderful mountain towns seemingly crafted for the traveling wilderness bohemian. There's a health food store here with good hippy staples like soy milk and granola; several good restaurants; climbing, bicycling, and ski shops (try **The 5th Season,** 300 N. Mount Shasta Blvd., Mount Shasta, CA 96067; tel. 530/926-3606,

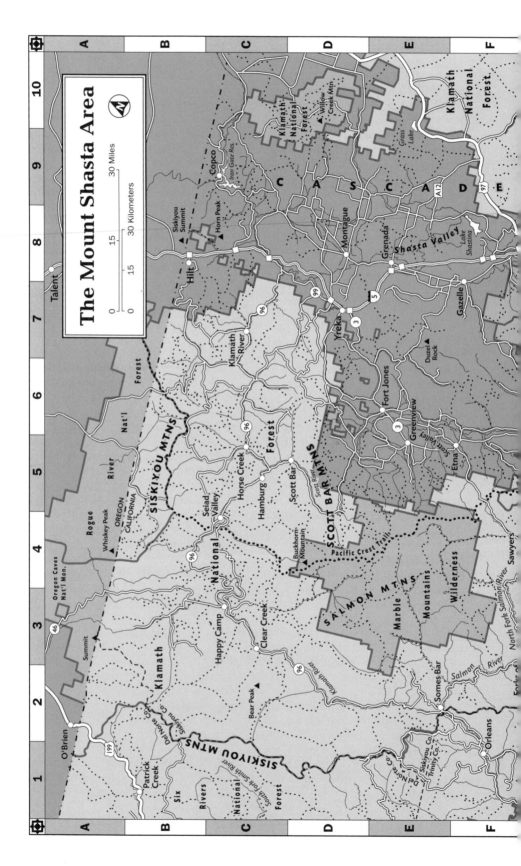

The Mount Shasta Area

N

0   15   30 Miles

0   15   30 Kilometers

Mount Shasta City's Average Temperatures and Precipitation												
	Jan	Feb	Mar	Apr	May	June	July	Aug	Sept	Oct	Nov	Dec
High (°F)	42.1	47.3	50.9	57.9	67.0	75.4	85.1	83.3	77.5	65.4	50.9	43.9
Low (°F)	25.5	28.6	29.6	33.2	39.6	46.2	50.7	49.0	44.3	37.4	30.8	26.7
Precipitation (in.)	7.2	5.7	4.2	2.8	1.6	0.8	0.3	0.5	0.9	2.0	5.2	6.0

for all of the above); art galleries; and a used-book store. For information contact the **Mount Shasta Visitors Bureau,** 300 Pine St. (tel. 916/926-4865 or 800/926-4865).

McCloud

This tiny lumber town about 6 miles off Interstate 5 on State Route 89 is going through a rejuvenation. The mills and lumber jobs that were lost in the 1980s are slowly but surely being replaced by an economy driven by people looking to escape the big city. Excellent fishing, and whitewater boating on the McCloud River, draw plenty of visitors, some of whom seem to be staying and refurbishing the beautiful old homes sold for next to nothing when the economy faded. The lesser-known summer estate of William Randolph Hearst is near here on the McCloud River. The Nature Conservancy also manages a nature preserve along 7 miles of McCloud River frontage.

Parks & Other Hot Spots

Trinity Alps Wilderness

West of I-5. Access: From State Route 299, State Route 3, and any number of smaller roads between them. Tel. 530/623-6106 (Big Bar Ranger Station). The wilderness has no facilities; the surrounding towns and national forest campgrounds have everything under the sun.

Designated by Congress in 1984, the Trinity Alps Wilderness is the second largest in California—more than 500,000 acres. The wildest and least-charted country in the state is here. Though 400 miles of trail explore the wilderness, huge blocks can only be reached by blazing your own trail.

Trinity Lake

With 150 or so miles of wooded shoreline, Trinity Lake is a popular fishing, camping, and waterskiing lake. The lake is actually named Clair Engle Lake after the U.S. Senator Clair Engle who ramrodded the water project through as budget-fattening pork. The dam drowned several small towns, and the antipathy left behind is such that nobody, and I mean nobody, who lives near here calls the lake Clair Engle. For information contact the **Weaverville Ranger District Office,** State Route 299 in Weaverville (tel. 530/623-2121).

Salmon and Klamath River Drainage

The Klamath is the largest and longest river in Northern California, reaching from the Oregon border near I-5 all the way to Klamath in Redwood National Park. Roads follow the Klamath most of the way and most of the surrounding land is national forest. There are countless places to fish, camp, hike, and run whitewater. The Salmon, a tributary to the Klamath, is a designated wild and scenic river and holds some of the most striking whitewater in the state. For information contact the **Six Rivers National Forest** (tel. 707/442-1721) or the **Klamath National Forest Headquarters,** 1312 Fairlane Rd., Yreka, CA 96097 (tel. 530/842-6131).

Marble Mountain Wilderness

West of I-5 via State Route 96 or State Route 3. Tel. 530/842-6131 (Klamath National Forest Headquarters).

Another of the Klamath Ranges, the Marbles aren't nearly as high as the Trinities, but are extremely well forested and lush. The wilderness, with 250,000 acres and little visitor use, spans between the Marble and Salmon mountains, but you won't know the difference. Marble Valley, Sky High Valley, and Spirit Lake are some of the more popular backcountry camps, but with this much land and this few visitors, crowding is never a problem.

Mount Shasta

The Native Americans believed Shasta was the home of the Great Spirit. Today, things haven't changed at all. A number of New Age religions center around the mountain, and it is considered one of the energy spots of the universe. Some of us just come here to climb, ski, and hike, but even that is somewhat of a holy experience. A ski area once existed on the flanks of the mountain but repeated avalanches took

care of that. Now the Mount Shasta Ski Park is located on a much tamer adjoining mountain. The 14,162-foot summit of the real thing can be reached in a single day hike with no really technical climbing involved. You do, however, need an ice axe, crampons, and a hell of a lot of willpower. There is talk of building a trail around the base of the mountain, but it is currently incomplete.

Castle Crags State Park

Castle Crags Exit from I-5. Tel. 530/235-2684. Camping, picnicking, showers, restrooms, store. Fees required.

There's 6,000 acres of hiking, camping, and fabulous rock climbing here just south of Shasta City. The Pacific Crest Trail passes through the park and the Sacramento River runs nearby.

Ahjumawi Lava Springs State Park

3.5 miles north of McArthur; accessible only by boat. Put in at PG&E Rat Farm launching area 4 miles north of McArthur on Main Street. Tel. 530/335-2777. Environmental camping.

This unique park contains the outlet of an underground river that drains Tule Lake, 50 miles away. Accessible by boat only, the 6,000 acres are open for exploration by canoeists and boaters.

Burney Falls, Hat Creek, Fall River Mills

State Route 299 northeast of Shasta City. State Park: $5 day use; $14 camping.

Just north of Lassen on State Route 299, these three rivers arguably offer the best trout fishing in the entire state. The town of Burney is well equipped with fly-fishing shops and several fishing guides. Hat Creek is one of the best fly-fishing streams in the nation. For information contact the **Burney Chamber of Commerce**, P.O. Box 36, Burney, CA 96013 (tel. 530/335-2111).

McArthur–Burney Falls Memorial State Park

6 miles north of State Route 299 on State Route 89. Tel. 530/335-2777. Hiking, camping.

15 miles northeast of Burney is McArthur–Burney Falls Memorial State Park where a huge spring-fed waterfall pours over a richly mossy 129-foot cliff into a deep pool below. More impressive than the height of the falls is the fact that 100 million gallons of water pour over them each day.

Shasta Lake

When it is full, which in recent decades has been a rare thing, Shasta Lake on the Sacramento River is huge: 30,000 acres and 370 miles of shoreline. Hundreds of houseboats cruise the lake, and it is extremely popular with skiers and fishermen. There are several marinas in different arms of the lake. The **Shasta–Cascade Wonderland Association** (tel. 530/365-7500 or 800/326-6944) is an excellent source of boat rental, lodging, camping, and activity information about the lake.

Lassen Volcanic National Park

State Route 89. P.O. Box 100, Mineral, CA 96063. Tel. 530/595-4444. Camping, restrooms, showers, cross-country ski rental, natural history museum, backcountry camps, wilderness lodge.

Though it is a lot like Yellowstone with its geothermal wonders, Lassen is one of the least-visited national parks. Those who do visit tend to stick to the loop road and rarely venture into the backcountry. Big mistake. The park contains boiling lakes, great hiking (150 miles of trail), a backcountry lodge, fishing, and in the winter, great cross-country skiing. See Lassen feature later in this chapter.

Lava Beds National Monument

Loop road through park begins and ends on State Route 139 south of Tulelake. P.O. Box 867, Tulelake, CA 96134. Tel. 530/667-2283. Camping, interpretive center, ranger-led hikes, restrooms. Day-use and camping fees.

From above, this park looks like a windblasted, rugged lava bed with a few scrubby hills and trees. Well, it is. It's what you don't see on first glance that makes this park remarkable—hundreds of lava tube caves, many open for your exploration. Lava tube caves are fairly simple to navigate, unlike limestone caverns, and so even the novice spelunker can have a great time here. The history of the park is really interesting too. It was here that the last band of Modoc Indians led by Captain Jack stood off the U.S. Army for 6 months in 1873 before being starved out, tricked, and executed. See Lava Beds feature later in this chapter.

What to Do & Where to Do It

There's good birding all over the northern mountains: everything from the endangered and controversial spotted owl to the brown sparrow calls this area home. But the big news in these parts is the incredible numbers and diversity of **waterfowl** you can see at **Tule Lake and the Lower Klamath Lake Wildlife refuges,** almost 100,000 acres of wetlands and agricultural fields. They are an incredible breeding ground for the geese and ducks that congregate in stunning numbers during the spring and fall migrations. By official estimate, 45,000 ducks and 2,600 geese are hatched and reared here every year. The number of adult waterfowl stopping through reaches the millions. During the winter, when birding for waterfowl is slow, Tule Lake and Lower Klamath are the site of a winter congregation of between 500 and 800 bald eagles, and a lesser number of golden eagles. For a complete list of birds and information about self-guided tours of the refuges by canoe or on foot, contact Refuge Manager, Klamath Basin National Wildlife Refuges, Route 1, Box 74, Tulelake, CA 96134 (tel. 530/667-2231).

CANOEING

One of California's most unique state parks, **Ahjumawi Lava Springs State Park** (tel. 530/335-2777), is inaccessible by foot or car and perfectly suited to exploration by canoe. The Pit River Indians, who were the original residents of this huge spring-fed freshwater lake, creek, and wetland system, named it *Ahjumawi:* "where the waters come together." The waters originate from huge lava springs in enormous upwelling of cold, clear water that seems to turn every shade of blue and green while reflecting striking views of Mount Shasta, Mount Lassen, and the surrounding area. Boaters can camp overnight at any of nine backcountry sites. Put in at the PG&E Rat Farm launching area 4 miles north of the town of McArthur on Main Street.

CROSS-COUNTRY SKIING & SNOWSHOEING

Expert backcountry skiers have their work cut out for them on the flanks of **Mount Shasta,** where you can climb as high as your skills and legs will take you. For beginners, the area between Bunny Flat and the Sierra Club hut is a safe and relatively easy place to practice your first backcountry skills. If the hills are too daunting, continue up the unplowed Everitt Memorial Highway beyond Bunny Flat. Since an avalanche peeled the old ski lifts off the mountain at the former downhill ski area, Caltrans no longer plows the last 3 miles of road. The **House of Ski,** 1208 Everitt Memorial Highway (tel. 530/926-2359), is on your way up to the mountain and rents a full line of cross-country gear.

Lassen Volcanic National Park (tel. 530/595-4444) is an amazing place to check out on skis or snowshoes. Snow closes the park road in November and most years it doesn't open until June, so cross-country skiers have their run of the park. Snowmobiles were once allowed but are now forbidden. Marked trails of all skill levels leave from Manzanita Lake at the north end of the park and Lassen Chalet at the south. Most visitors come to the southwest entrance where the ski chalet offers lessons, rental gear, and a warm place to stay. Popular trips are the beginners' trails to Lake Helen or Summit Lake. More advanced skiers can make the trek into Bumpass Hell, a steaming valley of sulfuric mud pots and fumeroles. A popular overnight is

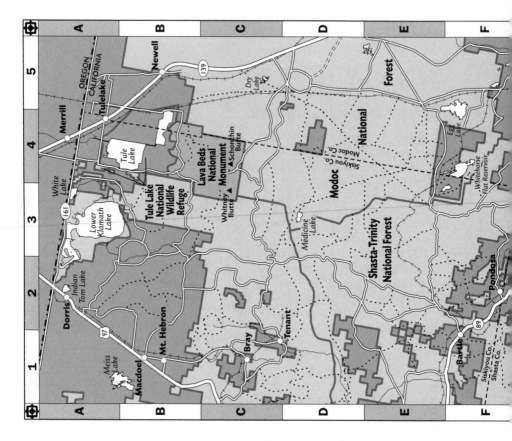

to ski the 30-mile course of the park road from the north entrance through the park to the chalet, but doing this involves a long car shuttle. Because of the remoteness and dangerous geological features of the park, rangers require that all skiers register at the trailheads whether they are heading out for an overnight or just the day. For more information call Lassen Ski Touring. Park staff also lead snowshoe hikes into the park emphasizing ecology and winter survival.

The following resorts offer groomed trails, rental equipment, and lessons: **Mount Shasta Nordic Center,** 5 miles east of Shasta City on State Route 89 (tel. 530/926-8610); and **Lassen Ski Touring,** State Route 36 at southwest entrance to Lassen Volcanic National Park.

DOWNHILL SKIING & SNOWBOARDING

Mount Shasta Ski Park

104 Siskiyou Ave., Mount Shasta City. Tel. 530/926-8610; 530/926-8686 for snow conditions. 21 trails (20% beginner, 60% intermediate, 20% expert); 3 lifts including 2 triples and 1 surface. Full-day adult ticket $31 weekends and holidays, $26 weekdays, $18 on Tuesday.

The Native Americans believed Mount Shasta was the home of the Great Spirit and left it to higher powers, never climbing above timberline. When the white man built a ski area on the flanks of Shasta in 1958, the Indians remained

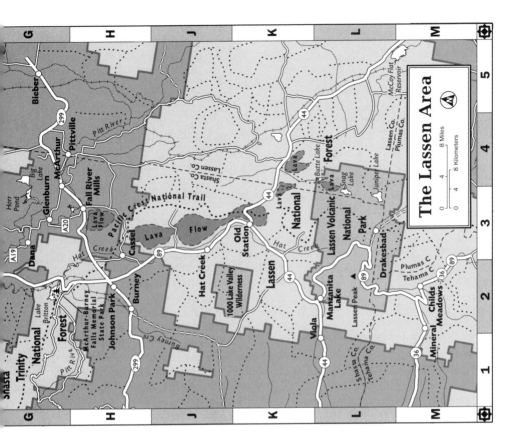

The Lassen Area

8 Miles
8 Kilometers

confident that it wouldn't last. It didn't, but the Great Spirit took a while to take his revenge. Avalanches and bad weather kept the mountain closed much of the time and the resort always trod a thin line between profit and insolvency, but it always held on. Then, in 1978, a huge avalanche swept most of the chairlifts from the mountain. That did the trick, and the ski bowl closed for good.

In 1985 a new resort opened on Mount Shasta, this time below timberline and hopefully out of the range of the Great Spirit's wrath. Snowmaking and night skiing are recent additions, and the resort is looking to expand even more. There's a little bit of everything here, and yes, snowboarding is allowed.

FISHING

The fly-fishing in this part of the state is simply among the best anywhere in the world. The most famous trout fishing rivers here are **Hat Creek, Fall River, McCloud River, Pit River,** and **Burney Creek.** The Trinity, Salmon, and Klamath once supported huge runs of steelhead and salmon, but dams and siltation caused by clearcutting of the forest have drastically reduced their number. For guides and specific information about any of the above rivers, call the nearest chamber of commerce.

Lake fishermen will go crazy with pleasure on **Lake Shasta** just trying to figure out what to chase. The enormous reservoir on the Sacramento River has a surface area of 30,000 acres and more than 370 miles of shoreline. Spring and summer are the best fishing seasons when the lake warms and fish go into feeding mode. Deep-water trollers pull out trophy-sized rainbow trout, while fishermen working the shallows often score big with largemouth and smallmouth bass. To keep the kids happy, Lake Shasta has a huge population of crappie that will practically jump into your boat during the spring. Call the **Shasta–Cascade Wonderland Association** (tel. 530/365-7500 or 800/326-6944) for information about boat rentals or tackle shops.

HIKES, BUSHWHACKS & BACKPACK TRIPS

DAY HIKES

Mount Eddy Summit and Deadfall Lakes

9.5 miles round-trip. Moderate to strenuous. Access: Trailhead at dead end of Forest Road #17, 14 miles west of Edgewood/Gazelle exit off I-5 north near Weed. Map: USGS Mount Eddy topo.

The best place to appreciate the splendor of Mount Shasta isn't on Shasta itself, but rather from the summit of 9,025-foot Mount Eddy. Rising above a mixed forest of red and white fir, Jeffrey and ponderosa pine, and numerous smaller deciduous species, Mount Eddy was the site of a now-abandoned national forest lookout because of its astounding views of the Trinity Mountains to the west and Shasta to the east. This trail is a segment of the Pacific Crest Trail. After the first 2 miles of hiking through forest, you'll hit a basin containing three small lakes: Upper, Middle, and Lower Deadfall lakes. Middle has great sunbathing rocks and deep spots perfect for a cool-off swim.

After the lakes the Mount Eddy Trail begins steadily climbing; the total elevation gain on this hike is almost 3,000 feet. Several steep switchback sections might require some work, but the view will keep you going. After enjoying the summit, return the way you came.

McCloud River Preserve

5-plus miles round-trip. Moderate. Access: In McCloud turn south on Squaw Valley Road. Follow for 12 miles and past McCloud Reservoir until you come to a dirt road signed AH-DI-NA. Follow signs to AH-DI-NA Campground and go past campground to end of road. Map: Shasta–Trinity National Forest map; Nature Conservancy brochure.

Access to the McCloud River is really difficult in most places; private land lines much of the area. Thanks to the Nature Conservancy's reserve in the McCloud River Canyon, however, hikers and fishermen can enjoy this spring-fed stream. Wandering downriver from the reserve entrance, you'll pass through a nice forest of oak and maple mixed with the occasional large Douglas fir. Keep your eyes peeled for wildlife: the Nature Conservancy has documented the presence of wolverines, mountain lions, and black bears here. More likely you'll see a bald eagle or a small herd of deer grazing by the river. Continue downstream until you reach the signed boundary of the Conservancy's wildlife study area, which is off-limits to visitors. Return the way you came.

Whitney Butte Trail, Lava Beds National Monument

6.8 miles round-trip. Moderate. Access: 2 miles north of the visitors center, take the turnoff for Merrill Cave. The trailhead is at the end of the road. Map: Free brochure available at visitors center.

Lava Beds National Monument

Lava Beds is one of those places that takes a while to grow on you. It's a desolate, windy place: high plateaus, spikey buttes, and rolling hills covered with lava cinders, coyote bush, and tortured-looking junipers. Miles of land just like it cover most of this corner of California. So why, asks the first-time visitor, is this a national monument? The answer lies underground.

The ground here is like Swiss cheese, so porous in places that it actually makes a hollow sound. When lava pours from a volcano it doesn't cool all at once; the outer edges cool first and the core keeps flowing, forming underground tunnels like a giant pipeline system. More than 200 lava tube caves lace the earth at Lava Beds: caves that are open to the public to explore on their own or with park rangers (see "Spelunking" under "What to Do & Where to Do It"). Whereas most caves lend themselves to a fear of getting lost with their huge chambers, multiple entrances, and bizarre topography, these are simple, relatively easy-to-follow tunnels with little room to go wrong. The feeling once inside is that this would be a great place for a game of hide-and-seek.

In the winter of 1872 a band of 53 Modoc Indians held off a siege by more than 1,000 well-armed U.S. cavalrymen for nearly 6 months using the lava tube tunnels as hideouts in a deadly game of cat and mouse. The Modocs, who had left a reservation where they were forced to live with a rival tribe, returned here to their traditional homeland and demanded their own reservation. General E. R. S. Canby was charged with returning them. By May 1873, weakened by starvation and exhausted, almost all the Modocs had been captured or killed. On June 1, 1873, their leader, "Captain Jack," surrendered with the last of his tribe. On October 3, 1873, he and three other Modoc leaders were hanged. The surviving members of his band were banished to an Oklahoma reservation. There's very little of historical note remaining to see aboveground here besides a white cross marking the spot where General Canby was killed during surrender meetings with the Modocs, an act that led to the final blood bath.

A hike to Schonchin Butte (0.75 miles, one way) will give you a good perspective on the wildly stark beauty of the monument and nearby Tulelake Valley. Wildlife lovers should keep their eyes peeled for terrestrial animals like mule deer, coyote, marmots, and squirrels. Birders can attempt to spy bald eagles, 24 species of hawks, and enormous flocks of ducks and geese headed to the Klamath Basin, one of the largest waterfowl wintering grounds in the Lower 48. Sometimes the sky goes dark with ducks and geese during the peak migrations.

Park elevations range from 4,000 to 5,700 feet, and this part of California can get cold, even snow, any time of year. Summer is the best time to visit with average temperatures in the 70s; winter temperatures plunge down to about 40° during the day and as low as 20° by night. Summer is also the best time to participate in ranger-led hikes, cave trips, and campfire programs. Check the visitors center bulletin board for schedules.

Whitney Butte Trail leads from Merrill Cave along the shoulder of 5,000-foot Whitney Butte to the edge of the Callahan Lava Flow along the park boundary. Though stark, the views from this trail are some of the most spectacular in the park: over a foreground of jagged lava and hardscrabble juniper bushes, you can look out onto the huge expanse of Tule Lake Wildlife Refuge and the Warner Mountains to the east.

Lyons Trail, Lava Beds National Monument

8.2 miles. Strenuous. Access: Trailhead begins at visitors center. Map: Park map.

The 8.2-mile (one way) Lyons Trail spans the wildest part of the monument where you are likely to see plenty of wildlife. Besides numerous birds of prey like red-tailed hawks, kites, and the occasional bald eagle, you might see the large herds of mule deer grazing on the greenery that grows among the brutal-looking lava flows and pumice fields.

Lassen Peak Trail, Lassen Volcanic National Park

4.8 miles round-trip. Moderate. Access: Trailhead is on Park Road, 7.5 miles past the south park entrance. Map: Lassen Trails booklet available at visitors center.

Probably the most popular hike in Lassen is the 2.5-mile climb from the Park Road to the top of Lassen Peak. The trail may sound short, but it's steep and generally covered with snow until late summer. At 10,457 feet in elevation, though, the view of the surrounding wilderness you'll get from the summit is worth every step of the way. On clear days it's possible to see south all the way to Mount Diablo near Oakland and north into the Cascades.

Cinder Cone Trail, Lassen Volcanic National Park

4 miles round-trip. Moderate. Access: Trail begins at the Butte Lake campground at the far northeast corner of the park. Map: Lassen Trails booklet available at Visitors Center.

Cinder Cone in the northeast corner of the park is best reached from the Butte Lake campground at the far northeast corner of the park. If 4 miles seems too short, you can extend the hike (and shorten the drive) by walking in about 8 miles from Summit Lake on the Park Road. Now dorment, Cinder Cone is generally accepted as the source of mysterious flashing lights that were seen by early settlers to the area in the 1850s. Black and charred-looking, Cinder Cone is bare of any sort of life and surrounded by dunes of multi-hued volcanic ash.

Pacific Crest Trail Day Hike, Lassen Volcanic National Park

10 miles round-trip. Moderate. Access: Trail begins at Drakesbad on the Warner Valley Road in the southeast corner of the park. Map: Lassen Trails booklet available at visitors center.

A 17-mile segment of the Pacific Crest Trail cuts through the park and can be accessed via the Warner Valley Road or by a long hike from Hat Lake. The most interesting section of the trail for non–through hikers is the 5-mile segment south of Drakesbad that leads toward the park's southern boudary via Boiling Springs Lake and Terminal Geyser. This little-visited part of the park is actually one of the most spectacular geothermal displays this side of Yellowstone, and you're likely to have it to yourself.

OVERNIGHTS

Trinity Alps Overnight, Alpine Lake

18 miles round-trip. Allow 3 or 4 days. Strenuous. Steep and rocky. Access: Trail begins at Bridge Camp, 2 miles up Stuart Fork Road from Trinity Alps Resort. Map: USGS Rush Creek Lakes and Siligo Peak topos.

This is a nice backpack for a long weekend. The forest service campground at Bridge Camp is a nice layover before beginning your hike early in the morning. You quickly leave the beautiful Stuart Fork of the Trinity and begin a relentless climb. The first 5.5 miles aren't so steep, but after you pass the trail junction at Oak Flat and follow the Alpine Lake Trail, you'll gain almost 3,000 feet in just a little over 3 miles. The payoff? Well, you get to camp beside a beautiful alpine lake in a glacial valley. Great day hikes surround the area. If you feel like breaking up the hike in or out, there's a really nice campsite on the Stuart Fork just about a quarter-mile west of the Stuart Fork/Alpine Lake Trail junction that makes for a pleasant halfway break.

HORSEBACK RIDING

Coffee Creek Ranch, HC 2, P.O. Box 4940, Trinity Center, CA 96091 (tel. 530/266-3343), is located right on Coffee Creek with every possible dude ranch activity you could think of (and a few you probably couldn't think of). It has a heated pool, fishing pond, square dancing, and, of course, a huge stable of beautiful horses waiting to be ridden into the surrounding mountains.

For a more rugged adventure, the **Hank Pritchard Cattle Drive,** in Manton (tel. 530/474-3355), does the *City Slickers* thing, bringing soft city folk along on a genuine multi-day cattle drive and making them do real work for a change. They do two trips each year; one begins June 1, the other October 15.

KAYAKING

If what you dream of is miles and miles of Class III and IV water, with relatively easy portages around the hard stuff, this is your neck of the woods. For an intermediate kayaker, the runs are almost limitless: **the Lower Klamath, the Trinity, the McCloud River, the Upper Sacramento between Lake Shasta and Lake Siskiyou, the Salmon.** Mixed in with all the *easy* water are some gnarly stretches of Class IV-plus and Class V: **the Gorge Run of the Salmon, Burnt Ranch Gorge on the Trinity, the Upper Klamath,** any of which will keep all but the most jaded boater happy.

The best resource for mile-by-mile descriptions of any of these rivers is either *California Whitewater* by Jim Cassady and Fryar Calhoun (Cassady and Calhoun, 1985) or *A Guide to the Best Whitewater in the State of California* by Lars Holbec and Chuck Stanley (Friends of the River, 1988). Kayakers seeking instruction would do well to contact **Otter Bar Lodge** which is widely considered to be one of the best and certainly the most luxurious kayaking school in the world (see sidebar). **Cutting Edge Adventures** in Mount Shasta, P.O. Box 1334, Mount Shasta, CA 96067 (tel. 530/926-4647), runs two 5-day kayak clinics each summer on the Klamath. Evenings are spent camping on the river, and all gear is carried by rafts.

Otter Bar Lodge

One of the most pleasant weeks of my entire life was spent at Otter Bar Lodge on the Salmon River (often called the Cal Salmon to differentiate from the Salmon River in Idaho). Peter and Kristy Sturgis started Otter Bar as just a wilderness lodge. Peter was—and still is—a hotshot whitewater kayaker, so his boating buddies kept coming here for the fantastic whitewater on the Salmon and the nearby Klamath. One thing led to another, and now 15 years later, Otter Bar Lodge is widely considered to be among the top three kayaking schools in the nation and unequivocally the most luxurious. The lodge is a beautiful, hand-built work of art, the fruit of years of Sturgis's labor. It has four double rooms, two cabins, multiple decks, a wood-burning hot tub, and my favorite, an outdoor shower where I once watched a golden eagle circle while I washed my hair. The food is delicious, so good in fact that *Bon Appetit* has written about Otter Bar. You will not suffer a lack of creature comforts here.

Teaching at Otter Bar is done in small groups of three or less, and the emphasis is placed on practical hands-on river learning rather than repetitive drills in the pond. Sturgis employs a rotating corps of some of the best kayakers in the world as his instructors. Groups rotate days with instructors to benefit from a variety of different teaching styles. During my session we rotated between three instructors.

Creek Hanauer is a mid-40s local resident who lives up the river from Otter Bar. He has a gift for the gab and an easy way of laughing at his own and everyone else's follies. Creek was great at letting you make a mistake, but then would explain perfectly what you'd done wrong and how to avoid it in the future. His wealth of local natural and human history made him a great river companion.

Reg Lake, at 51, is somewhat of a legend in kayaking circles. He's done numerous first descents around the globe and spends half the year sea kayaking around South America. The Zen master of the instructors, Reg on a river is a living example of excellence through economy of motion. Rivers have taught him a lot over the years, and he was very into letting the river do the teaching, sometimes to the point that I wanted to strangle him. "What am I doing wrong, Reg?" I'd ask after a sound thrashing. "Why don't you try it again and let the river show you?" Well, Reg, because I figured I'd let you save me the trouble. Inevitably he'd relent and share some brilliant nugget of kayak technique, but not before you threatened to shove a paddle up his nose.

Brennan Guth was the youngest instructor at 25, but somehow has found enough time to fit in stints as a mountaineering instructor and professional river guide. He's worked with Native American tribes in Idaho and finished a degree in philosophy at the University of Montana. All this in between running some of the hardest whitewater in the world. By far the most gonzo boater I've ever seen, Brennan is a genius of technical, cutting-edge kayaking and his teaching style reflects it: precise, insightful, and calm in the face of what seemed to the rest of us to be overwhelming hardship. He's also got a killer wit and is a great conversationalist about almost any subject.

Each day they'd take us down increasingly harder stretches of river. By virtue of being the third best boater in our nine-person session, when the groups were divided up I wound up being the worst kayaker in the hardest group. Michael and Kristin, my fellow students, were a young married couple who'd recently escaped the Bay Area to live in Mount Shasta. Michael was pretty much unstoppable. Throw a rapid in front of him, any rapid, and he'd run it. Flip him over, he'd pop back up smiling. Kristin and I, on the other hand, took turns reassuring each other that we probably wouldn't die and really were doing this for fun. When one of us would take a beating, screw up our Eskimo roll, and swim, we'd laugh together and exchange knowing looks. Meanwhile, Michael was looking for bigger, faster thrills and seemed a little dissatisfied with the pace of things.

The high point for all of us came on the last day when Brennan led the three of us down a section of the Klamath that a week earlier would have spelled certain destruction. At the top of a scary-looking rapid named Aikens Creek, the run called for us to ferry out to a mid-river boulder, catch the eddy behind the boulder, then peel out downriver around some rocks and slam through a long and pretty scary-looking wave train that emptied into a big pool. Brennan probably ran it backward just for kicks, but for the rest of us it was pretty intense. Even Michael looked a little put off by it.

I caught the eddy easily enough, looked over my shoulder at Brennan and Kristin who'd already made it through, and then, mysteriously, flipped over. Hanging there, about to run the biggest rapid of my life backward and upside down, I had a moment of incredible calm and clarity. I took inventory of my situation. . . .

"Andrew," I told myself underwater, "if you screw up now it's curtains for you."

That out of the way, I did what they'd been coaching us to do all week: I set up my roll, went through my mental checklist to make sure I was doing it right, then snapped my paddle and body around in an amazing display of grace and coordination I didn't know I had in me. Next thing I knew I was upright, paddling like a son of a bitch to keep from slipping backward over the lip of the rapid. After hiding out in the safety of an eddy for a minute, I caught my breath and ran it, this time flawlessly.

That rapid was a huge mental victory for me. The worst possible thing that could happen to me did, and I handled it fine. The fear that had been holding me back all week left me, and that day my kayaking improved fivefold. On the last rapid of the day I got slammed over a 4-foot drop, punched through a huge wave still upright, and actually caught air. When I landed, I wiped out and rolled up laughing so hard I nearly choked. That, to me, is what it's all about.

Otter Bar Lodge, Forks of Salmon, CA 96031, tel. 530/462-4772; www.outterbar.com. One-week sessions, $1,590 per person including all meals, equipment, and instruction.

MOUNTAIN BIKING

The mountain bike is king here—not surprising in an area where you can count the number of stoplights on both hands and where there's at least as many dirt roads as paved ones. In the **Klamath National Forest** you could literally ride a new logging road every day for a year and never cover the same ground twice. That's not even taking into account all the single track. The option is there for extended multi-day touring through all the northern mountain areas. National forest campgrounds are plentiful, and small towns are fairly evenly spaced to restock on food every day or two.

For a really cushy stay at a beautiful wilderness lodge with awesome guided mountain bike rides every day, look into **Otter Bar Lodge** (tel. 530/462-4772) on the Salmon River. This famous kayaking school has branched out in recent years to include a mountain biking program. You'll bike to secluded swimming holes, up to fire lookouts, and descend as many miles of single track as you could ever stand. It's expensive, close to $1,590 per person per week double occupancy, but Otter Bar provides all meals and equipment, and the staff is great. (See "Otter Bar Lodge" feature and look under "Camping & Other Accommodations" for more information.)

Siskiyou Lake Loop

11 miles. Easy. Flat. Access: Begins where North Shore Road turns to dirt 3 miles west of Mount Shasta City. Map: Shasta–Trinity National Forest recreation map.

Though this ride is almost entirely on gravel and dirt roads, and never gains more than 80 feet of elevation, there is one tricky spot: the ford through the headwaters of the Sacramento River. From the parking area follow North Shore Road around the lake. At the intersection of North Shore Road and Dead End Road, you'll want to go straight on North Shore. After crossing a bridge over Deer Creek and then riding through another small stream, you should see a dirt road to the left that has been blocked off to car traffic. It will take you to the Sacramento River. Carry your bike across. (In high water you may not be able to ford the river. Be careful!) Continue back along paved Barr Road, which will follow the south shore back around and over the dam to your starting point. At the dam take a look down into Box Canyon, the dramatic gorge below.

The Ride Around Mount Shasta

63-plus miles. Extremely difficult. Elevation gain moderate, but the ride is long and rough on dirt and gravel roads, plus 2 hellish miles along a railroad grade. Access: Park your car in downtown Mount Shasta City and ride south on Mount Shasta Boulevard. Map: Shasta–Trinity National Forest recreation map.

Even though this route is relatively flat with only one serious climb, don't go into it ill prepared. It's long and very trying. The climate around Mount Shasta is so weird and varied that you could leave Mount Shasta City in warm sunshine and get snowed on when you reach the other side of the mountains. Since you'll be riding on dirt forest service roads that may or may not be currently open to logging trucks and woodcutters, stay alert for traffic. Take a lot of water, full tool kit, extra tubes, and plenty of food—the only town on the route is Mount Shasta City.

Along the route you'll pass from evergreen forest to volcanic moonscape, and then through a long stretch of high desert in the rain shadow of hulking Mount Shasta. Along the eastern side of the mountain many small streams drain the mountain. With a water pump filter, these could save you a lot of weight in carrying extra bottles of water. For the most current information on the conditions of fire roads on this route, contact the staff at **The 5th Season, 300 N. Mount Shasta Blvd.** (tel 530/926-3606), or the **Mount Shasta Ranger District,** 300 Pine St. (tel. 530/926-4511).

ROAD BIKING

Lassen Volcanic National Park Metric Century

62 miles round-trip (100km). Strenuous. Access: Lassen Chalet just inside southwest entrance of park. Map: Lassen Volcanic National Park map.

This road is only open 6 months of the year, but during those 6 months it is simply one of the greatest metric century rides in the world. Starting at the chalet, you'll tour through beautiful wooded countryside with occasional views of Mount Shasta and Lassen Peak. In the first 10 miles you'll climb almost 2,000 feet to crest the 8,512-foot Park Road summit. (If you're feeling really ambitious it is a short hike from here to the top of Mount Lassen.) Early in the season watch for ice on the road near here. Now you'll descend through more striking alpine scenery and pass the occasional bubbling mud pot or sulfur vent, eventually reaching Manzanita Lake at Lassen Park's northwest corner. Manzanita Lake is a stunning spot to rest; Lassen Peak makes a spectacular backdrop to this large, tree-encircled gem. Don't linger too long because from here you have to climb almost 3,000 feet back up to the Park Road summit before you can coast back to the chalet and your car.

ROCK CLIMBING & MOUNTAINEERING

The jagged granite spires of the **Castle Crags** are the easternmost vestiges of the Klamath Range, which was once joined with the Sierra Nevada before dramatic geological forces drove the two ranges apart. The climbing here is very similar to the Sierra too: good clean routes on granite domes and spires with single faces as tall as 1,500 feet. Numerous shorter routes are popular with sport climbers. There is so much variety here it would be hard to get tired of the place. Perhaps the greatest treat of climbing the crags is the exquisite view of Mount Shasta and the surroundings you get from the top. For specific routes and climbing advice, contact **The 5th Season** (tel 916/926-3606) in Shasta City.

SPELUNKING

The caves at **Lava Beds National Monument** (tel. 530/667-2282) are open to the public with little restriction or hassle. All you need to see most of them is a good flashlight or headlamp, sturdy walking shoes, and a sense of adventure. Many of the tunnels are entered by ladders or stairs, others by holes in the side of a hill. Once inside, walk far enough to round a corner, then shut off your light. Imagine the Modocs, knowing they're surrounded, sitting here waiting for the cavalry. Then imagine the cavalry knowing that anywhere they go the ground could open to a bunch of armed and desperate men. A chilling impasse, to say the least.

One-way **Cave Loop Road** just to the southwest of the visitors center is home to many of the best cave hikes. About 15 lava tubes have been marked and made accessible. Two of the caves are ice caves, where the air temperature remains below freezing all year and ice crystals form on the walls. If exploring on your own gives you the creeps, check out **Mushpot Cave.** Almost adjacent to the visitors center, this cave has been outfitted with lights and a smooth walkway; you'll have plenty of company. Hardened spelunkers will find enough remote and relatively unexplored caves in the monument, many requiring specialized climbing gear, to keep themselves busy.

Climbing Mount Shasta

Mount Whitney and its surrounding peaks may be higher, but as far as the experience of climbing a *mountain* goes, nothing in the state rivals 14,162-foot-tall Shasta. Unlike the other mountains over 14,000 feet in the state, Shasta stands all by itself, a perfect cone rising 10,000 feet above the surrounding countryside. Ask any kid to draw you a mountain and they'll draw you something that looks remarkably like Mount Shasta, a perfect triangle standing over a seemingly flat plain.

Though just about anyone in good physical condition can climb Shasta by the popular Avalanche Gulch Route, it's not something to be taken lightly. You won't need a rope, but most of the climb is on ice and snow, meaning that crampons and ice axe are indispensable.

In a normal snow year, the prime climbing season on the mountain is from early June through late July or early August. Too early, and you'll be slogging through waist-deep soft snow on your way to the summit. Too late in the season, and after a few miles of slipping and sliding on scary pumice and scree slopes,

you'll be making pacts with the devil just to get off the mountain. What you want is to find the whole route covered in nicely hardend sun-and-wind-packed snow, making for a smooth walk all the way to the top. Not to mention that if the mountain is covered with snow, you get to slide down, something I don't recommend trying on rock.

The winter of '94–'95 was an incredible snow year on Shasta, and the mountain was still covered in late August when my friend Kristin Williams and I set out for the summit at 3am under a full moon. Hiking through the pines above the Bunny Flat parking area, the moonglow gently lit Avalanche Gulch and Casaval Ridge, and we were able to sleepwalk our way up the mountain without flashlights.

Two miles later the Sierra Club cabin at Horse Valley popped out of the darkness. This stone hut was built over a century ago, and its weathered walls have sheltered many great campfire storytelling sessions. Since it was now about 4 am, Kristin and I refrained from waking everybody up and asking them to tell us great campfire stories. Instead,

WALKS & RAMBLES

Bumpass Hell, Lassen Volcanic National Park

1.5 miles. Access: Trailhead clearly marked on Lassen Park Road. Map: Lassen National Park map.

The beginning of this walk leads you through a quiet and peaceful meadow of wildflowers and chirping birds before depositing you right in the middle of Bumpass Hell, a churning, roaring, stinking display of volcanic power. The bubbling mud pots and hot springs here cover acres. Stay on the path: Bumpass Hell is named for a hunter who fell in a mud pot and lost his leg.

Clear Creek, Mud Creek Trail

1.5 miles. Access: Near McCloud; in flux at press time. Contact Shasta Ranger Station for latest road status. Map: Shasta–Trinity National Forest map.

we filled our water bottles at the spring-fed tap (about 2 gallons each, there's no water above here unless you melt it) and stumbled on up the Olberman's Causeway, an amazing elevated path built of huge flat rocks by one of the original caretakers of the Sierra Club hut.

From the hut to the summit it is only 4.1 miles, but more than 6,000 vertical feet. The stone pathway soon gave way to well-packed snow. By sunrise we were at 10,400 feet on the frozen "shores" of Helen Lake, a semi-glacial tarn that is only a lake in years of extremely light snow. Though we'd been walking on snow and ice for almost 2 miles now, Lake Helen is where the climb really begins.

After a breakfast of Power Bars and oranges, we strapped on our crampons and pulled out the ice axes. Ahead we could see several other parties strung out along the 2,500-foot snowfield leading to the top of Avalanche Gulch and the red pumice cliffs of Red Banks. In the 15 minutes it took us to eat and gear up, it looked like they moved about half an inch.

"Doesn't it look like they're not going anywhere?" I asked Kristin, feeling a little giddy and cocky as I looked down at the base of the mountain way below. "We'll pass those guys no problem."

About an hour later I was where those people had been, on a 40° slope of sun-cupped icy snow, and it was me who was barely moving. They, on the other hand, were nowhere to be seen. No doubt they were on top snapping summit pictures and jeering the slowpokes behind them. To the casual observer it must have looked like Kristin and I had fallen asleep standing upright, but if they looked closely, they might have been able to discern the rhythm of our forward progress: Pick up ice axe . . . drive ice axe into snow . . . shuffle left foot up 4 inches to new ice axe placement . . . follow with right foot . . . lean on ice axe . . . gasp like a carp . . . pick up ice axe . . . every 20 steps stop to drink water or eat. God, I've never seen anything go on as long as that snowfield. Luckily, the views below us were beautiful and kept us entertained while we wheezed and popped our way upward.

Avalanche Gulch is narrow and steep at the top. Soon we were working our way over a slight headwall and into a

continued

The remote Clear Creek and Mud Creek drainages on the south side of Shasta are good places to get a look at the different ecosystems of the mountain in one compact area. From here you'll explore the pine forests of the mountain flanks, pass mountain hemlock and running meadows, and see where a mudflow in 1960 nearly slid into the little logging town of McCloud. Several waterfalls grace the area. On the mountain above you can see the Konwakiton and Wintun glaciers, permanant ice fields cut with numerous crevasses and ice falls.

WHITEWATER RAFTING

This area gives the rivers of the Sierra Nevada a good run for their money. The **Klamath and Trinity rivers** in particular are popular with commercial outfitters. The Klamath is the best late summer whitewater in the state; its steady flow is controlled by a dam in Oregon. The Trinity, too, is kept at a steady narrow chimney through the Red Banks. Kristin, who'd been feeling bad for the last hour or two, suddenly got her second wind and bolted ahead out of sight. Me? I lost my wind and got scared. One slip here might not have meant death, but wouldn't have been a cakewalk either.

Looking from the bottom you think that once you crest the Red Banks it's just a hop, a skip, and a jump to the summit. Ha! After the Red Banks you still have more than 1,000 feet of altitude to climb, most of it in a single rock-covered nightmare called Misery Hill. We'd been hiking in beautiful sunshine the whole way when, as if on cue, we hit Misery Hill and suddenly, boom, we were socked in by a thick cloud bank. Great, I thought, you mean I climbed all this way to look at the inside of a cloud? That's right brother, said the mountain, as it started throwing 60 mph gusts at us just to stir up the mix.

After conferring for a second and deciding we were in fact up for it, we decided to bolt for the summit. After hauling my ass up Avalanche Gulch, I thought Misery Hill looked like something you'd see at a putt-putt golf course. At least I couldn't fall off it, or if I could, the clouds prevented me from peering morbidly into the abyss. Inexplicably, I was feeling strong and fast.

Kristin, on the other hand, started to feel really sick. As we stumbled across the last ridge to the summit it was so windy that we had to hunker down and brace with our ice axes when the 60 to 70 mph gusts hit and stagger onward whenever they let up; but I noticed Kristin was bracing in the calm periods and trying to walk during the wind blasts. Occasionally she'd wander in a small circle and look confused. By the time we reached the base of the summit col, a 50-foot-tall pile of rocks that is the actual highest point on Shasta, it was obvious that my climbing buddy was in a bad way. She had all the classic symptoms of altitude sickness. Slurring her words, Kristin told me she was about to vomit and collapse and that I should go on. Then she staggered up to some guy coming up behind us, took off his sunglasses, and stared into his eyes with a crazed look. There was no time for a picnic or a nice session of yodeling. We snapped a hasty almost-summit shot and before you could say "Acute Mountain Sickness" we'd shed our crampons and were lurching arm in arm back down the rocks of Misery Hill.

From the base of Misery Hill you can glissade—the nice-sounding French word for sliding on your butt—all the

pace by releases from Lewiston Dam. Depending on your ability and desire for thrills, you might choose a single-day Class III trip down the **Lower Klamath** or **Upper Sacramento.** Looking for something a little more hairy? Try the **Salmon** in early spring (it is a wild river with a very short season), the **Burnt Ranch Gorge of the Trinity** (Class V, scary water), or the **Upper Klamath** (Class IV-plus).

Numerous rafting companies run all these rivers. Contact the local chamber of commerce or the **River Travel Center,** Box 226, Point Arena, CA 95468

tel. 800/882-7238, for complete listings, prices, and recommendations.

Campgrounds & Other Accommodations

Bridge Camp, Shasta—Trinity National Forest.

2.5 miles up the Stewarts Fork Trinity River from Trinity Reservoir on Trinity Alps Road way to wherever you run out of snow. Kristin mysteriously pulled a Hefty garbage sack out of her pack, stuck her legs through it, sat down, and was gone. I followed right behind, but I was too gripped with fear to keep up. I used my ice axe as a brake the whole way down and even then I thought I was a goner once or twice. I don't know what she did to maintain control but I swear that from above Kristin looked like an Olympic luger, just a cloud of snow quickly pulling away from me, the occasional arm or leg sticking out. By the time we hit Lake Mary, the thicker air and the adrenaline blast had made her as good as new. What took us 13 hours to hike up took exactly an hour and a half to slide down. We were lucky that there was snow almost to the Sierra Club hut. A month later and we'd have been walking down.

When we got to the car at sunset, a mid-40s, crystal-clutching, New Age couple in a Honda Accord was blaring what sounded like the soundtrack to *Close Encounters of the Third Kind* on their car stereo while they intermittently made out and stopped, appearing to be seized by the cosmic vibes of the mountain.

"How far did you hike?" they leaned out and asked between smooching sessions.

"Oh, up there, a little ways" said Kristin, gesturing vaguely at the mountain and throwing her ice axe onto the sopping pile of our gear.

Behind us the summit glowed purple in the sunset and we giggled like kids driving back to town.

PRACTICALITIES

Rent crampons, ice axes, mountaineering boots, and any other climbing gear you'll need at **The 5th Season,** 300 N. Mount Shasta Blvd. (tel. 530/926-3606). The staff there is a good source of general mountain wisdom and lore.

The Mt. Shasta Book by Andy Selters and Michael Zanger (Wilderness Press, 1990) gives accurate and easy-to-understand descriptions of all the major climbing routes up Shasta and ski mountaineering areas on the volcano. It comes with a redrawn Mount Shasta topographical map covering the whole mountain, rather than splitting it into two separate quadrants like the USGS maps.

Note: We did the hike in one day, leaving our car at 3 am and returning at about 7pm. It can be done, but it hurts. Next time I'm going to bivouac at least as high as the Sierra Club hut and possibly as high as Lake Helen to make the summit hike less of a grueling ordeal.

off State Route 3. Tel. 530/623-2121. 10 sites. Pit toilets, running water. Pets okay, horse corrals available. $4 per night, no reservations.

This small campground is a world apart from the hustle and bustle that characterizes most camping near Trinity Lake. The Stewarts Fork tumbles by the camp, providing numerous swimming holes. This is also the trailhead for the Stewarts Fork Trail into the Trinity Alps Wilderness.

Castle Crags State Park

6 miles south of I-5, Dunsmuir exit. Tel. 530/235-2684 or 530/225-2065. 64 sites. Flush toilets, showers. Pets okay. $12–$14 per night. Call MISTIX (800/444-PARK) for reservation, fee charged.

With the granite spires of the Castle Crags looming over you, Mount Shasta in the distance, and the Sacramento River running nearby, this is a hard spot to beat.

Lassen Volcanic National Park

Stashed away in the far northeastern corner of California, Lassen Volcanic National Park is a remarkable reminder that North America is still forming, and that the ground below is alive with forces of creation and, sometimes, destruction. Mount Lassen is the southernmost peak in a chain of volcanoes, including Mount Saint Helens, that stretches all the way from British Columbia; though dormant, the chain is still very much alive.

Mount Lassen last awoke in May 1914, the beginning of a cycle of eruptions that spit lava, steam, and ash until 1921. The eruption climaxed in 1915 when Lassen blew its top, sending a mushroom cloud of ash 7 miles high that was seen for hundreds of miles. The peak itself has been dormant for 65 years now, but the area still boils with a ferocious intensity; hot springs, fumaroles, mud pots, and geysers are all indicators that Lassen hasn't had its last word. Monitoring of geothermal features in the park shows that they are getting hotter, not cooler, and some scientists take this as a sign that the next big eruption in the Cascades is likely to happen here.

Until then, the park gives visitors an interesting chance to watch a landscape recover from the massive destruction brought on by the last eruption. To the north of Lassen Peak is the aptly named Devastated Area, a huge swath of volcanic destruction steadily repopulating with conifer forests. Forest botanists have revised their earlier theories that forests must be preceded by herbacious growth after watching the Devastated Area immediately revegetate with a diverse mix of eight different conifer species, four more than were present before the blast.

The Lassen area was inhabited by four groups of Indians before the arrival of whites. The Atsugewi, Maidu, Yana, and Yahi all used portions of the park as their summer hunting grounds. The white man's diseases and encroachment into their territory quickly decimated

The only drawback is that I-5 runs nearby and can sometimes be heard. Plenty of nearby places to explore.

Lake Siskiyou Camp

On Barr Road across I-5 from Mount Shasta City. Tel. 530/926-2610. 300 sites. Flush toilets, running water, showers, store, boat rentals, laundry. Pets okay. $16.50–$22.50 per night. Reservations accepted.

Lake Siskiyou is a great place to camp with kids. The sandy beach and warm water make it an inviting swim. Fishing on the lake is good, and motorized boats are prohibited. Since the lake was built for the sole purpose of recreation, it stays full all summer long. Great hikes and mountain biking into the nearby hills.

Indian Well, Lava Beds National Monument

0.75 miles from the park headquarters. Tel. 530/667-2282. 40 sites. Picnic table, fire ring, cooking grill, pit toilets, no water. During summer, water and flush toilets are available. $10 per night in summer; $6 per night in winter. No reservations.

their population. By the turn of the century, they were thought to be gone from the wilds of the Lassen area. In 1911, however, a nearly naked Native American man was discovered by butchers at a slaughterhouse in Oroville. When they couldn't communicate with him, the sheriff locked the man in a cell. News of the "Wild Man" found a receptive audience among anthropologists at the University of California in Berkeley who quickly rescued the man. Ishi, as he came to be known, turned out to be the last of the Yahi tribe and lived at the UC Museum of Anthropology for 5 years before succumbing to tuberculosis. Ishi, through sharing his knowledge with anthropologist Alfred Kroeber and others, is responsible for much of what is known about California Indian culture.

The 106,000-acre park is a place of great beauty. The flora and fauna here are an interesting mix of species from the Cascade Range, which stretches north from Lassen, and species from the Sierra Nevada, which stretches south. The resulting blend accounts for an enormous diversity of plants: 715 distinct species have been identified in the park. Though it is snowbound in winter, Lassen is an important summer feeding ground for transient herds of mule deer and numerous black bears.

In addition to the volcano and all its geothermal antics, Lassen Park includes miles of hiking trails, huge alpine lakes, large meadows, cinder cones, lush forests, a cross-country ski area, and great camping. Only one major road, State Route 89, the Park Road, crosses the park in a 39-mile half circle with entrances and visitors centers at either end. Three-quarters of the park is designated wilderness.

The highlight of Lassen is of course the volcano and all of its offshoots: hot springs, fumaroles, mud pots, etc. It is possible to see many of the most interesting sites in a day, making Lassen an excellent short detour from Interstate 5 or U.S. 395 on the way to or from Oregon. The *Road Guide to*

continued

If you really want to stay inside Lava Beds, there isn't much in the way of selection. Fortunately, Indian Well, the park's only campground, is great. In the winter particularly, it lacks in facilities, but with 20 lava tube caves nearby just waiting to be explored, who's complaining about having to use a pit toilet.

Lassen Volcanic National Park Campgrounds

P.O. Box 100, Mineral, CA 96063. Tel. 530/595-4444. 7 car campgrounds with 375 sites total. Various facilities. Fees vary from $8–$14. Reservations only for Lost Creek Group Campground (fees charged).

Car campers have their choice of seven park campgrounds, more than enough to handle the trickle of visitors who come to Lassen every summer. So few people camp in Lassen that there is no reservation system except for the Lost Creek Group Campground, and stays have a generous 14-day limit. Sites do

Lassen Park (available at park visitors centers) is a great traveling companion that will explain a lot of the features you'll see as you traverse the park.

Bumpass Hell, a 1.5-mile walk off the Park Road in the southern part of the park, is the largest single geothermal site in the park: acres of bubbling mud pots cloaked in a stench of rotten-egg-smelling sulfur. The name comes from an early Lassen traveler, Bumpass, who lost a leg after he shortcut through the area while hunting and plunged into a boiling pool. Don't make the same error in judgment.

Sulphur Works is another stinky, steamy example of Lassen's residual heat. Two miles from the southwest park exit, the ground roars with seething gases escaping from the ground.

Boiling Springs Lake and **Devils Kitchen** are two of the more remote geothermal sites located in the **Warner Valley** section of the park that can be reached by hiking from the main road or entering the park through Warner Valley Road from the small town of Chester.

Most Lassen visitors drive through in a day or two, see the geothermal hot spots, and move on. That leaves 150 miles of trails and expanses of back-country to the few who take the time to get offroad. The *Lassen Trails* booklet, available at the visitors centers, gives good descriptions of some of the most popular hikes and backpacking destinations. Anyone spending the night in the backcountry must have a wilderness permit issued at the ranger stations. For more information, see "Hikes, Bushwhacks & Backpack Trips" under "What to Do & Where to Do It."

Canoes, rowboats, and kayaks can paddle any of the park lakes except Reflection, Emerald, Helen, and Boiling Springs. Motors, including electric motors, are strictly prohibited on all park waters. Park lakes are full of trout and fishing is popular. You must have a current California fishing license.

In winter, the park becomes a cross-country skier's fantasy. Snow closes the park roads, leaving skiers and snowshoers with their run of the place. See "Cross-Country Skiing & Snowshoeing" under "What to Do & Where to Do It" for more information.

JUST THE FACTS

Visitors Centers & Information. Most visitors enter the park at the southwest

fill up on weekends, so your best bet is to get to the park early Friday to secure a place to stay. If the park is packed, there are 43 campgrounds in surrounding Lassen National Forest, so you'll find a site somewhere.

By far the most "civilized" campground in the park is at Manzanita Lake, where you can find hot showers, electrical hookups, and the like. When Manzanita fills up, rangers open the Crags Campground overflow camp about 5 miles away. It is much more basic. On the southern end of the park you'll find Southwest Campground, a walk-in camp directly adjacent to the parking lot to Lassen Chalet.

The two remote entrances to Lassen, Warner Valley and Butte Lake, have their own campgrounds. Butte Lake has flush toilets, no showers, and charges a fee. The two remaining campgrounds, Juniper Lake and Warner Valley, are primitive, with pit toilets and no water, but the price is right—free. Backcountry camping traffic is light and is allowed almost anywhere. Ask about closed areas when you get your wilderness permit.

entrance station, drive through the park, and leave through the northwest entrance, or vice versa. Two other entrances lead to remote portions of the park. Warner Valley is reached from the south on the road from Chester. Butte Lake entrance is reached by a cut-off road from State Route 44 between State Route 89 and Susanville. There are no entrance fees to the park. Ranger stations are clustered near each entrance and provide the full spectrum of interpretive displays, ranger-led walks, informational leaflets, and emergency help. The largest visitors center is located just outside the northwest entrance station before Manzanita Lake. The park information number for all requests is 530/595-4444, or write Lassen Volcanic National Park, P.O. Box 100, Mineral, CA 96063-0100.

Regulations. Because of the dangers posed by the park's thermal features, rangers ask that you remain on trails at all times. Fires are allowed in campgrounds and the backcountry, but please make sure they are dead before leaving them. Mountain bikes are prohibited on all trails.

Seasons. Modoc County (Lassen National Park does not lie in Lassen County) is one of the coldest places in California. Winter lasts from late October and doesn't release its grip until June. Even in the summer, plan for possible rain and snow. Temperatures at night can drop below freezing at any time. Winter, however, shows a different and beautiful side of Lassen that more people are starting to take advantage of. Since most of the park is over a mile high, and the highest point is 10,457 feet high, snow accu-mulates in incredible quantities. Don't be surprised to find snowbanks lining the Park Road into July.

Avoiding the Crowds. Lassen is one of the least-visited parks in the Lower 48, so crowd control isn't as big a consideration here as at other places. Other than Fourth of July and Labor Day weekend, you won't encounter anything that could rightly be called a crowd. Even then you can escape the hordes simply by skipping the popular sites like Bumpass Hell or Sulphur Works and heading a few miles down any of the backcountry trails.

Trinity Alps Resort

Location: Just off State Route 3, 1750 Trinity Alps Road, Trinity Center, CA 96091. Tel. 530/286-2205. 43 cabins. Cabin rentals average $495–$955 per week in summer. Credit cards accepted.

The Trinity Alps Resort reminds me of something out of the 1920s: a family resort where people get together for group hikes and campfire sing-alongs, big kids flirt on the beach, younger kids are fascinated by trying to catch the savvy trout that live downstream. It was in fact built in the 1920s but recently underwent a major renovation. The cabins here are rustic but beautiful. There's a store, horseback rides, rec room, and video games.

Otter Bar Lodge

14026 Salmon River Rd., Forks of Salmon, CA 96031. Tel. 530/462-4772. Exclusive wilderness lodge/kayaking school. Maximum occupancy 14 guests. One-week stays, roughly $1,590 per person depending on activities. Reserve well in advance by calling the lodge. Credit cards accepted.

Otter Bar is well known in the kayaking world for its excellent instruction, awesome location, and, last but certainly not least, cushy accommodations and excellent food. When you're there, you know you're in the middle of nowhere. Right on the Salmon River, Otter Bar has great swimming and mountain biking in addition to the whitewater kayaking program. See "Otter Bar Lodge" feature and "Mountain Biking" under "What to Do & Where to Do It" for more information.

Drakesbad Guest Ranch, Lassen Volcanic National Park

Inside Lassen Volcanic National Park at the end of a dead-end road. Send queries to California Guest Services, 2150 N. Main St. #5, Red Bluff, CA 96080.

Tel. 530/529-1512. 19 rooms. Restaurant, hot spring pools. Doubles begin at $185, meals included. Credit cards accepted. Open mid-June to mid-October. Reserve well in advance.

This incredible wilderness lodge was built around the turn of the century in one of the most remote parts of the Lassen backcountry. Today little has changed. Drakesbad is deluxe in the way that only a place with no electricity or phones can be. At night, guests read by kerosene lamps and huddle under hand-stitched quilts in the rough-hewn pine rooms. Full meal service is available and very good. Daily horseback rides are scheduled to a variety of scenic park locations every day, but it's hard to beat where you are; Drakesbad is surrounded by meadows, lakes, streams, and mature forests. If you're in the mood to hike, hundreds of miles of trail leave from your doorstep. When that is over, you can slip into the 116° hot spring pool to soak away any sore muscles. Unbeatable.

9

The North Coast

NORTH OF THE BAY AREA'S SPHERE OF INFLUENCE LIES A WEIRD and wild coast. Between Jenner, at the mouth of the Russian River, and the Oregon Border, the California coast is a land of deep dark forests, slimy banana slugs, tiny timber and fishing towns, Bigfoot, pot-growing hippies, redneck loggers, crashing surf, and salmon as big as rottweilers. That's the stereotype at least. Some of it is even true. The North Coast of California is a bizarre conglomeration of everything good about the state, everything weird under the sun, and a healthy (or is it unhealthy?) dose of human and ecological tragedy.

Maybe it's the weather that sets the North Coast apart. California, after all, is the Golden State: sunshine, Malibu Barbie, the Beach Boys. But from San Francisco to the Oregon border, California is the land of gum boots and Gore-Tex, not bikinis and Coppertone. Your skin is more likely to erode away in the rain than to get burned in the sun. Whatever it is, the North Coast is the outlandish cousin of the California that people who grew up on *Gidget* and *The Brady Bunch* imagine.

Much of the year the thick coastal fog lies over the land like a soggy wool blanket, dripping slowly but constantly onto the land below. From this constant moisture, the world's original drip irrigation system, springs a verdant world of thick forests, huge rivers, and dramatically eroded coastline. Of course, half the time you can't see any of it through the fog, which cloaks the area in an omnipresent fuzziness that softens everything and washes the color out of a landscape filled with bright reds and greens and blues. There is a certain serene beauty about the fog, though, that makes you focus on the things in front of you without distraction. Given that it receives an average of 80 to 135 inches of rain a year, most of it in the form of a slow drizzle, a sunny day on the North Coast is nothing less than spectacular, inducing a dropped-jaw feeling of "You mean that's what's out there in the fog?" as you marvel at a stand of redwoods or the striking violence of waves crashing into a rocky headland.

Once predominant, now endangered, the defining feature of the North Coast is still the redwood forest. When the coast redwood was first noted as a species in 1794, it is estimated that 2 million acres of the trees covered much of the coast between Santa Cruz and the Oregon line. By 1965 that number was down to 300,000 acres, so the state and federal governments set aside almost 110,000 acres in Redwood National Park. Cutting on private land continued, though. Today a heated battle over cutting down the last 5,000 acres of privately owned old-growth redwoods has reached a feverish pitch.

The fate of the last significant private stand of old-growth redwoods is locked in a three-way battle of the wills between environmentalists, who wish to see the spectacular grove known as the Headwaters Forest preserved; a junk bond tycoon named Charles Hurwitz who presently owns Pacific Lumber, which in turn owns the Headwaters Forest and wants to cut it down; and the federal government, which is looking into the possibility of aquiring the Headwaters Forest

in return for forgiving some of the $250 million in debts the federal government claims Hurwitz owes for his role in the collapse of an FDIC-insured savings and loan in which he owned a controlling interest.

Hurwitz claims that even though he was the majority partner in both, asset A, the Headwaters Forest, can't be held liable for his debts from collapsed asset B, United Savings and Loan. He wants to chainsaw the forest and pocket the profits with his left hand, while his right hand claims it is too broke to pay any debts. The government is suing. Environmentalists are staging a two-pronged legal and guerilla action campaign to stop further logging of the Headwaters Forest. And Hurwitz? Well, Hurwitz is a master of the poker face, and no one really knows what he's about to do.

The economy here was once based on a seemingly stable tripod of three natural resources: timber, salmon, and marijuana. All over the North Coast loggers, lumber mill workers, fishermen, and pot growers existed happily side by side (in fact, often they were the same person), and the money they earned was the foundation for most area business: the car dealers, restaurants, gas stations, and supermarkets. Then the system collapsed. Silt and dirt eroded into the rivers from logging clear-cuts year after year, covering up the gravel needed by the king and silver salmon for their spawning beds. With very few new salmon being born, the fishery plummeted and has yet to recover. Then in the mid-1980s, the big timber companies discovered that they could save money by shipping raw logs to Japan to be processed in high-tech automated lumber mills and then shipping the finished lumber back here to sell, rather than paying the local mill workers union wages. With the loss of those mill jobs, the timber economy seized up and has never recovered. Which left the North Coast standing on one leg, and a dubious one at that. Pot growing didn't go over very well with law enforcement during the Reagan-Bush–era "War on Drugs," and after a few seasons of massive raids, helicopters buzzing overhead, and midnight arrests of prominent local citizens, the big growers left, running off to wherever it is that dope growers go when the heat gets too bad. And that's where it stands now. The North Coast exists largely on an economy of tourism and retirement money from people fleeing the urban life of L.A. and San Francisco. Meanwhile, there are a lot of unemployed fishermen and timber industry workers sitting on their hands waiting for things to take a turn for the better, and a lot of pot growers sitting in jail. Not the way the American Dream was supposed to turn out.

The Lay of the Land

All problems aside, the North Coast is still some of the most beautiful country around, and the opportunities for outdoor sports are almost limitless. The most striking thing here is the fact that most of the coast is still wild. From Eureka to Rockport, for example, there are only three roads that reach the beach in a 75-mile stretch of coast, and 4,000-foot-tall mountains rise straight out of the sea. Within that area is the longest undeveloped stretch of wilderness coast in California, the Lost Coast: 24 miles of plunging cliffs, secret waterfalls, cobblestone beaches, redwood trees, an abandoned lighthouse, and huge crashing surf. It is a backpacker's paradise. The numerous fire roads and trails of the King Range Conservation Area are perfect for extended mountain biking forays. All along the North Coast, state and national parks allow great access to the ocean and the

mountains of Sonoma, Medocino, Humboldt, and Del Norte counties.

The general topography of the North Coast is one of extremely steep mountains rising straight out of the sea. Only in a few spots do you find a large coastal plain, usually near the mouths of rivers such as the Smith or the Klamath, or where large dune fields have formed around bays and lakes. The largest coastal plain surrounds Humboldt Bay and Arcata Bay near the mouth of the Eel River. Eureka, the largest town on the North Coast, fills the central portion, and farms line much of the rest. Most places on the coast, though, are pretty much straight up and down. Highway 1 south of Leggett along the Medocino and Sonoma coast is an excercise in patience and steady nerves as you wind up and down huge sections of sinuous road with scarcely a foot or two of asphalt between you and a thousand-foot fall. It's worth the effort, though. Isolation has left much of the North Coast a window into the past: small towns of Victorian houses, seaside ranches, redwood trees looming high on the ridges, and the constant crashing of ocean waves against a rugged, rocky shoreline.

Orientation

Arranged south to north.

Bodega Bay

This small town and snug harbor is a busy fishing port and home to a 128-campsite county park on the beach (tel. 707/875-3540); a beautiful high headland perfectly situated for whale watching; and the **Bodega Marine Laboratory** (tel. 707/875-2211), a University of California marine research station offering public tours from 2pm to 4pm every Friday.

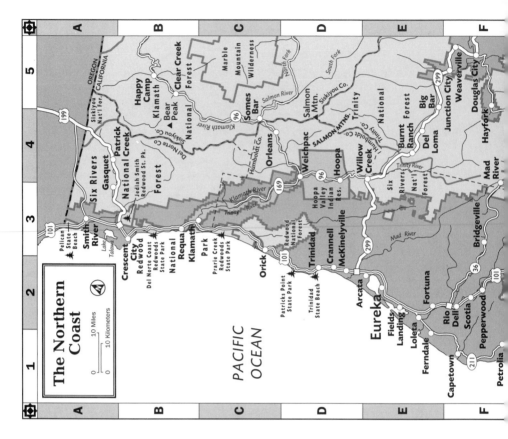

The Northern Coast

10 Miles
0
10 Kilometers
0

PACIFIC OCEAN

Jenner

Situated at the mouth of the Russian River, this tiny town has long been a successful summer resort. The 110-mile-long Russian River drains into the sea here through an impressive estuary and sandbar system.

Point Arena

Port Arena is the site of the only boat launch between Bodega Bay and Fort Bragg. It's also home to the 115-foot-tall **Point Arena Lighthouse** (tel. 707/882-2777), built in 1870. Tours are offered from 11am to 2:30pm daily. **Arena Cove** is a popular and highly localized surf spot.

Mendocino and Fort Bragg

These two towns constitute the "urban" centers of coastal Mendocino County.

Both support numerous B&Bs, fine restaurants, art galleries, and other tourist services. Mendocino is quaint and precious. Fort Bragg is sort of Medocino's redneck cousin, and in my opinion a lot more fun. For information, contact the **Fort Bragg–Medocino Chamber of Commerce,** 332 N. Main, P.O. Box 1141, Fort Bragg, CA 95437 (tel. 707/961-6300 or 800/726-2780).

Eureka and Arcata

The largest town on the North Coast by a long shot, Eureka is a heavily industrialized port city. Until fairly recently a nuclear power plant and several pulp mills were the town's biggest employers. The port of Humboldt Bay is an important harbor—one of the largest between San Francisco and the Columbia River. Since the economy has been in a slump the last 10

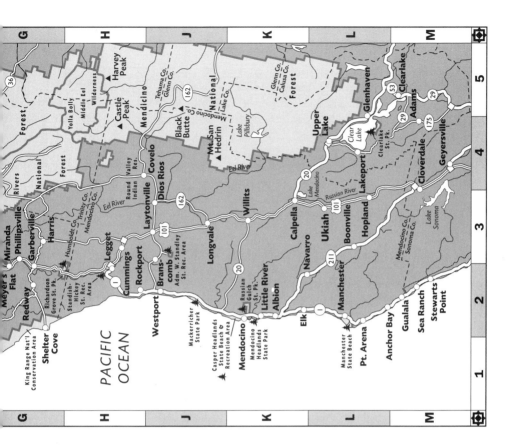

years, property crime has become a problem here. Arcata, a small community on the north end of the bay, is Eureka's alter-ego. Home to Humboldt State University, one of the most counterculture schools in California, Arcata is a bohemian artist and student community.

Crescent City

A hardscrabble logging and port town of 3,500, Crescent City has had a tough history. In 1964 a tsunami caused by an earthquake in Alaska sent 12-foot waves roaring inland a quarter-mile through the business district of Crescent City. Nearly the entire waterfront was leveled and numerous people were killed. In 1972 a freak typhoon destroyed much of the town again. Crescent City is now rebuilt, but has the look of a town that expects to get leveled every decade.

Besides the port, the biggest business in Crescent City is Pelican Bay Maximum Security Prison, where the baddest of the bad in the California prison system are sent.

Parks & Other Hot Spots

Arranged south to north.

Sonoma Coast State Beaches

Between Jenner and Bodega Bay on Highway 1. Russian River Ranger District Station. Tel. 707/875-3483.

A series of more than 20 separate beaches, accessways, coves, and coastal trails. Most units of the park are free with

Eureka's Average Temperatures and Precipitation											
	Jan	Feb	Mar	Apr	May	June	July	Aug	Sept	Oct	Nov	Dec
High (°F)	54	55	55	56	58	60	61	62	62	61	58	55
Low (°F)	41	43	43	45	48	51	52	53	51	49	45	42
Precipitation (in.)	6.2	5.0	5.2	2.8	1.8	0.6	0.2	0.3	0.8	2.9	5.8	6.3

the exception of the Bodega Head Campground and Russian Gulch State Beach.

Salt Point State Park

20 miles north of Jenner on Highway 1. Tel. 707/847-3221. Boat launch, campground, restrooms, beaches. Open year-round. Camping fee.

Salt Point is one of the best-known dive sites on the Sonoma coast—the spear fishing and abalone diving are excellent, but be aware of the underwater reserve boundaries. Less well known is the fact that the 4,300-acre park contains substantial upland areas laced with great hiking and riding trails. Not immediately adjacent to the park but nearby is the Kruse Rhododendron State Reserve, a stunning 300-acre rhododendron forest that blooms from April to June. Call Salt Point for information.

Manchester State Park

0.5 miles north of Manchester on Highway 1. Tel. 707/937-5804. Diving, camping, hiking. Open year-round. Day-use and camping fees.

This 1,400-acre beach park has a large number of sand dunes and a long sandy beach. Good diving and surfing.

Van Damme State Park

3 miles south of Mendocino on Highway 1. Tel. 707/937-5804. Diving, camping, hiking. Open year-round. Day-use and camping fees (no fee for beach use).

A very popular campground located across Highway 1 from a small sandy beach and the mouth of the Little River. Good diving in the offshore underwater preserve and nice hiking in the upland portion of the park.

Russian Gulch State Park

2 miles north of Mendocino on Highway 1. Tel. 707/937-5804. Diving, camping, hiking. Open year-round. Day-use and camping fees (no fee for beach use).

Once a rough-and-tumble port for timber schooners, Russian Gulch is now one of the most beautiful parks on the California coast. The camping here is spectacular, tucked into a forested canyon. Hiking trails lead around the headlands and pass a huge, 200-foot-wide ocean blowhole.

MacKerricher State Park

3 miles north of Fort Bragg on Highway 1. Tel. 707/937-5804. Diving, camping, hiking. 15-acre freshwater lake. Open year-round. Day-use and camping fees (no fee for beach use).

MacKerricher has one of the longest sandy beaches in Mendocino County, though the beach is somewhat severed from the rest of the park by an elevated logging haul road. Lake Cleone is good for freshwater fishing and canoeing. The campground here, like most state parks in the area, is extremely nice.

Sinkyone Wilderness State Park

For maps and information contact Eel River State Parks District Office, P.O. Box 100, Weott, CA 95571. Camping, backpacking, beaches.

This spectacular 7,312-acre park of undeveloped coastline begins where Highway 1 turns inland to Leggett. A one-lane dirt road through the park is passable during good weather, and several good campsites are located on the beach. A 17-mile coastal backpacking trail runs the length of the park.

The "Lost Coast" and King Range National Conservation Area

For information contact Eureka Resource Area, U.S. Bureau of Land Management, 1695 Heindon Rd., Arcata, CA 95521. Tel. 707/825-2300. Camping, backpacking, beaches, mountain biking.

This incredible area is probably the wildest piece of coastline in the Lower 48. Other than the tiny town of Shelter Cove, there is no population in the entire 63,000-acre area, a steep and densely forested range of 4,000- to 5,000-foot peaks rising right out of the sea. It's

possible to hike the entire length of the Lost Coast from the Mattole River to Shelter Cove as a 3- to 5-day backpack trip. Other good backpacking trails are located back in the King Range.

Humboldt Redwood State Park

45 miles south of Eureka on U.S. 101. Tel. 707/946-2409. Camping, hiking, mountain biking, restrooms, showers, visitors center. Open year-round. Fees for some park areas.

The largest redwood park in the state park system, Humbolt Redwood State Park is a stunning 51,000-acre forest containing more than 40% of the remaining old-growth coastal redwoods. Some groves are easy to reach; others require long hikes and offer the rare chance to visit these huge trees in solitude. Thirty miles of the Eel River runs through the park, a popular summertime fishing, canoeing, and swimming spot. The park contains a total of 250 campsites, which fill up quickly.

Humboldt Lagoons State Park and Harry A. Merlo State Recreation Area

31 miles north of Eureka on U.S. 101. Tel. 707/488-2041. Camping, boating, hiking. Open year-round; visitors center only open in summer.

Three lagoons lie inside these two parks. During heavy storms, two of the lagoons overflow into the ocean, carving huge channels in the beach, and dropping the lagoon water levels by up to 6 feet an hour. The surf and tides repair the beach.

Redwood National Park

South of Crescent City on U.S. 101. Information: 1111 Second St., Crescent City, CA 95531. Tel. 707/464-6101. Hiking, camping, beaches, biking, visitors center. Encompasses three state parks: Del Norte Coast Redwoods, Jedediah Smith Redwoods, and Prairie Creek Redwoods. Open year-round. Day use and camping fees for some portions of park.

The establishment of Redwood National Park in 1968 consolidated several state parks, federal reserves, and privately owned forests into this huge tribute to what much of the North Coast looked like before intensive logging cropped the old-growth forests. Most people whiz through here on U.S. 101, stop to take a few pictures, and carry on. Take some time and explore the more remote portions of the park. It's worth it. See the "Redwood National Park" feature a little later in this chapter.

Smith River National Recreation Area

For maps and other information contact the Gasquet Ranger District Office, 10600 Highway 199 North, P.O. Box 228, Gasquet, CA 95543. Tel. 707/457-3131.

Long eyed by dam developers as the last entirely free-running river in the entire state, the Smith River was recently declared a Wild and Scenic River and protected by the 305,000-acre Smith River Recreation Area. Almost a third of the area is old-growth Douglas fir forest. Great fishing, hiking, camping, and whitewater rafting and kayaking.

What to Do & Where to Do It

BIRD WATCHING

The combination of remnant old-growth forests, large coastal wetlands, and the presence of a rich marine environment make the North Coast one of the most diverse birding spots in the state, overshadowed only by Point Reyes. **Lake Earl** just south of Crescent City is a good spot to scope **shorebirds** and **migrating waterfowl.** Look for Aleutian goose, canvasbacks, wood duck, and green-winged teal, plus sandpipers, phalaropes, and other beach dwellers.

Redwood National Park is home to several **endangered species** that dwell in the old-growth forest. The marbled murrelet is a seagoing bird that only comes ashore to nest in the crowns of redwood trees. Also residing in the park is the endangered spotted owl. The listing of the owl as endangered caused an uproar among logging towns in California and Oregon, where "Save a Logger, Eat a Spotted Owl" bumper stickers became the hot accessory for a while.

Trinidad Beach a few miles north of Arcata is the southernmost spot where you can regularly spy the tufted puffin. Large offshore rocks are frequented by nesting puffins and storm petrels.

CANOEING

The **Eel River** in **Humboldt Redwood State Park** is one of the few long stretches of river in coastal California gentle enough to paddle in an open canoe. Water levels can drop dramatically in late summer, so spring and early summer are the best. Few pleasures can match paddling through dense redwood groves on a sunny day. Contact **Adventure's Edge** in Arcata (tel. 707/822-4673) or **Burke's Canoe Trips** in

Forestville (tel. 707/887-1222) for rentals and current advice on the best stretches of river.

FISHING

Once upon a time salmon and steelhead were so plentiful in North Coast rivers that it was almost hard not to catch them. Habitat loss from dams and destruction of their spawning grounds by logging-induced erosion, however, have sent the number of salmon and steelhead plummeting. In some rivers the annual run has fallen from the hundreds of thousands into the hundreds. Many long-time local residents I know have stopped fishing for salmon altogether, figuring that the fish have enough problems already. If you feel you must catch a steelhead or a salmon you certainly won't be alone—hundreds of fishermen line local riverbanks every winter—but you will do better if you hire a guide. The **Smith River,** which is the northernmost river in California, is the best place to catch salmon and steelhead since the Smith hasn't been dammed, and logging damage to its watershed has been light compared to other areas. **Smith River Salmon and Steelhead Trips,** 2095 U.S. 199, Hiouchi, CA 95531 (tel. 707/458-4704 or 800/248-4704), offers excursions with all tackle provided, as well as expert guides, and will arrange multi-day packages with meals and lodging.

HIKES, BUSHWHACKS & BACKPACK TRIPS

For an excellent source of thousands of miles' worth of well-written trail listings and maps of the North Coast, check out the *Hiker's Hip Pocket Guides to Mendocino, Humboldt, and Del Norte Counties,* which you can order from Bored Feet Publications, P.O. Box 1832, Mendocino, CA 95460 (tel. 707/964-6629). Written by Bob Lorentzen, a former timber cruiser for the logging companies turned guidebook author, the Hip Pocket Guides are a stunning example of local knowledge and familiarity with this beautiful area.

DAY HIKES

Pygmy Forest Loop, Salt Point State Park

5-mile loop. Moderate. Most of the hike is on fire roads. Access: Salt Point State Park. Trail begins in Woodside Camp on east side of Highway 1. Map: Salt Point State Park map.

Though most of this hike follows fire roads and utility corridors—not normally my favorite hiking paths—it's worth noting because it passes through one of the most unique botanical displays you'll see. By following the North Trail uphill, within 1.5 miles you'll enter the pygmy forest from which this trail gets its name. Here you'll find a profusion of 15-foot pine trees and 5-foot cypress trees. Well, so what? There's 15-foot-tall trees in every Christmas tree lot. Yes, it's true, but these are hundred-year-old old-growth trees, which due to highly acidic, nutrient-poor soil, never grew taller than your average 5-year-old tree in richer forests. If that doesn't do it for you, don't worry, there are other things to see on the hike. After exiting the pygmy forest, you'll enter a beautiful grass prairie that is spectacular in springtime. Watch for deer here. Leaving the prairie you'll descend through second-growth redwoods until the trail turns and follows Highway 1 back to Woodside Camp.

Russian Gulch Trail, Russian Gulch State Park

6 miles round-trip. Moderate. Little elevation gain. Access: Park near campground on east side of Highway 1, 2 miles north of

Mendocino. Trail departs from the camp-ground. Map: Russian Gulch State Park map.

Russian Gulch is one of the most beautiful coastal canyons on the entire California oceanfront. This trail begins just above Russian Gulch Cove and follows a park access road and the loop trail 3 miles back into a lush redwood forest. At the far end of the trail you'll find a beautiful waterfall, which the loop trail circles. Return the way you came, and take some time to poke around the stunning ocean headlands and cliffs on the beach side of the park.

10-Mile Beach Trail, MacKerricher State Park

You guessed right, 10 miles. Moderate. Access: Laguna Point parking area at MacKerricher State Park. Map: MacKerricher State Park map.

It's hikers' good fortune that a wild 1982 storm washed out several sections of the beachfront haul road at MacKerricher Beach. Once upon a time, logging trucks roared back and forth along the beach road, taking logs to the nearby mill, but now, due to two washed-out sections, the elevated road is closed to motorized traffic and makes a perfect walking route. My advice is to walk the first half of this route on the sand of Mac-Kerricher Beach, taking plenty of time to poke around tide pools and watch the seals that often haul out here. When you reach the mouth of the 10-Mile River, you can return via the road. While you were walking on the beach you probably didn't notice the fantastic sand dunes that lie on the inland side of the haul road. Well, now is your chance. Check out Sand Hill Lake, and Inglenook Fen (a fancy English word for swamp). Both are beautiful marsh and wetland areas where you'll often spot waterfowl. Whenever you tire of walking through the soft dune sand, the haul road offers an easy walking surface back to your car.

Friendship Ridge, Coastal Trail Loop, Redwood National Park

7.5 miles. Moderate. Some steep climbs, seasonal creek crossings. Access: Park at Fern Canyon Trailhead, end of Davison Road off U.S. 101 in Prairie Creek Redwoods State Park. Map: Redwood National Park or Prairie Creek Redwoods map.

This is possibly the most varied and beautiful hike in Redwood National Park. Beginning at the Fern Canyon Trailhead, you'll follow the Coastal Trail north from the trailhead. Soon you'll come to a fork where you'll veer right and follow the Friendship Ridge Trail. For the next 3 miles you'll walk through a magical fern and redwood forest, interspersed with lush meadows and grasslands. Occasional ridgetop sections grant you views in all directions. After about 3 miles of this you'll join the West Ridge Trail, which will soon descend the Butler Creek watershed through old-growth forest and arrive at Butler Creek Camp. From here it is a simple thing to follow the Coast Trail back south. This time, instead of weaving high through the trees, you skirt the fringe of high ocean cliffs and beach. Several short spur trails to the left lead to beautiful waterfalls if you have the time and energy left for a short detour. While walking this stretch, keep your eyes peeled for the elk that live in this area. Give them wide berth if they are blocking the trail—they've been known to stand their ground. The Coast Trail will take you back to the junction where you veered onto Friendship Ridge 7 miles ago. Continue back to the Fern Creek Trailhead where you left the car.

OVERNIGHTS

The Lost Coast

25 miles one way. Strenuous. Scrambling over boulders, miles of sandy beach walking, stream crossings. Allow 3–4 days. Access: From U.S. 101 in Fortuna take Ferndale exit and follow signs to Petrolia. In Petrolia take Lighthouse Road to its dead end at the Mattole River mouth. Map: Trails of the Lost Coast, California Coastal Foundation.

The Lost Coast is one of the most famous and most daunting hikes in California. This is the longest completely wild stretch of coastline in the Lower 48. From the Mattole River to Shelter Cove 25 miles south you'll cross some 15 creeks, climb over huge boulders, scramble up eroded cliffs, camp near crashing surf on black sand beaches, and be amazed by the utter wildness of this place. You can do this hike in either direction, but most choose to do it north to south with the prevailing wind at their back. Since you're walking along the beach much of the way, it is important to be aware of the tides—several places along the route are impassable on a high tide. Also, be constantly aware that large rogue waves are common in the North Pacific, and can easily reach high above the normal waterline. If you look out to sea and see a really big wave looming, walk up the beach a little and give it some space—it certainly beats swimming with your pack on. Other hazards to be alert for are poison oak, which is everywhere, and the numerous timber rattlesnakes that live in driftwood piles on the beach and surrounding meadows. The local timber rattlers are small almost to the point of being cute, but they're very venomous. Three or four days of hiking through paradise will eventually lead you out of the wilderness at Shelter Cove, a tiny fishing and vacation-home village. This is where you want to leave your second car for the shuttle, or have your ride waiting.

Since you're following the beach the entire way, a more useful resource than the map is the *Hiker's Hip Pocket Guide to the Humboldt Coast* by Bob Lorentzen (Bored Feet, 1992), which contains a lengthy mile-by-mile description of the route and hazards that existed at the time of publication. For more information contact the Bureau of Land Management in Arcata (tel. 707/825-2300).

Redwood Creek Overnight, Redwood National Park

16 miles round-trip. Moderate to difficult. Little elevation change, but in spring or fall stream crossings can be a problem. Access: Turn right off U.S. 101 onto Bald Hills Road. In approximately 0.5 miles turn right on turnoff to trailhead parking in another 0.5 miles. Map: Redwood National Park map.

This hike is a beauty. What you're in for is a wilderness trek to the tallest grove of sequoias in the world, the aptly named Tall Trees Grove. En route you'll pass through a primeval forest of giant ferns, dogwood, alders, and willows (and poison oak—watch out). Occasional openings near Redwood Creek, or in the periodic meadows along the route, will really give you the perspective to appreciate these stunning trees from a distance. Though most of this area is old growth, you'll pass through a few sections that were logged before the government created the park—the contrast is striking, even though the second growth is quite beautiful. Just before you reach the Tall Trees Grove, after about 8 miles of hiking, you'll crest a small hill to the high point of the hike, 290 feet above sea level. From here you get an incredible perspective on the grove. The bottoms

Redwood National Park

When he was governor of California, Ronald Reagan once said that if you've seen one redwood, you've seen them all. He couldn't have been more wrong. Redwood National Park is living proof. While he was right that a 367-foot-tall coast redwood (the world's tallest, located in the Tall Trees Grove) does in fact look pretty much like the next one, Reagan was guilty of not seeing the forest for the trees.

It's impossible to explain the feeling you get in the old-growth forests of Redwood National Park without resorting to Alice-in-Wonderland comparisons. Like a tropical rain forest, the redwood forest is a multistoried affair, the tall trees being only the top layer. Everything is so big, misty, and primeval; flowering bushes cover the ground, 10-foot-tall ferns line the creeks, and the smells are rich and musty. It's so Land of the Lost that you can't help but half expect to turn the corner and see a dinosaur.

When Archibald Menzies first noted the botanical existence of the coast redwood in 1794, more than 2 million acres of redwood forest carpeted the North Coast. By 1965, heavy logging had reduced that to 300,000 acres and it was obvious something had to be done if any redwoods were to survive. The state created several parks around individual groves, and in 1968 the federal government created Redwood National Park.

The 110,000-acre park offers a lesson in bioregionalism. When the park was first created to protect the biggest coast redwoods, the federal government allowed loggers to clear much of the surrounding area. Redwoods in the park began to suffer as the quality of the Redwood Creek drainage declined from upstream logging. In 1978 the government purchased the entire watershed, having learned that you can't preserve individual trees without preserving the ecosystem they depend on.

No one has ever lacked for things to do at Redwood National Park. Everything from river kayaking to bird watching is available here. In addition to the redwoods, the park includes miles of coastline, several miles of rivers and streams, a herd of elk, three California state parks, and several small towns.

A number of scenic drives cut through the park. Steep, windy **Bald Hills Road** will take you back into the Redwood Creek watershed and up to the shoulder of 3,097-foot Schoolhouse Peak. Don't even think of driving a motor home up here or pulling a trailer. The partially paved 8-mile **Coastal Drive** wanders among redwood groves and along the banks of the Klamath River. The southern section is okay for RVs, but don't go past Alder Camp Road going north or Flint Ridge heading south. Watch for the old World War II radar tracking station disguised as a barn and farmhouse to fool the Japanese.

One of the most striking aspects of the park is its herd of Roosevelt elk, usually found in the appropriately named Elk Prairie at the southern end of the park. These gigantic deer can weigh 1,000 pounds and the bulls carry huge antlers from spring to fall. Elk are also sometimes found at Gold Bluffs Beach—it's an incredible rush to suddenly come upon them out of the fog or after a turn in the trail. Several hundred black bears call the park home but are seldom seen. Unlike those at Yosemite and Yellowstone, these bears are still afraid of people. Keep them that way by observing food storage etiquette while camping and by disposing of garbage properly.

The park's beaches vary from long white sand strands to cobblestone pocket coves. The water temperature is in the high 40s to low 50s year-round and it's often rough out there, so swimmers and surfers should be prepared for adverse conditions. **Crescent Beach** is a long sandy beach just 2 miles south of Crescent City that's popular with beachcombers, surf fishermen, and surfers. Just south of Crescent Beach is **Endert's Beach,** a protected spot with a hike-in campground and tide pools at the southern end of the beach.

High coastal overlooks (like **Klamath Overlook** and **Crescent Beach Overlook**) make great whale-watching outposts during the December and January migration. The northern sea cliffs also provide valuable nesting sites for marine birds like auklets, puffins, murres, and cormorants. Birders will also thrill at the park's freshwater lagoons. They are some of the most pristine shorebird and waterfowl habitat left and are chock-full of hundreds of different species.

The area streams are some of the best steelhead trout and salmon breeding habitat in California. Park beaches are good for surf casting but be prepared for heavy wave action. A California fishing license is required, and you should check with rangers about any special closures before wetting a line.

JUST THE FACTS

Fees. Admission to the national park is free, but to enter any of the three state parks (which contain the best redwood groves), you'll have to pay a $6 day-use fee. It's good at all three.

Visitor Centers & Information. The headquarters for Redwood National Park is located at 1111 Second St., Crescent City, CA 95531. For 24-hour information about the park, telephone 707/464-6101. The Hirouchi Information Center is a good place to begin your visit to the national park if you are approaching it from the east at its north end; it is closed in winter. Three state parks lie inside Redwood National Park: Del Norte Coast Redwoods (tel. 707/464-6101), Jedediah Smith Redwoods (tel. 707/464-6101), and Prairie Creek Redwoods (tel. 707/464-6101).

Seasons. Frankly, all those huge trees and ferns wouldn't have survived for 1,000 years if it didn't rain one heck of a lot. Just count on rain or at least a heavy drizzle, then go ecstatic when the sun comes out. It can happen anytime. Spring, of course, is the best season for wildflowers. Summer is foggy (it's called "the June gloom" but often includes July). Fall is the warmest, sunniest (relatively!) time of all, and winter isn't bad, though it is cold and some park facilities are closed. A storm can provide the most introspective time to see the park, since you'll probably be alone. And after a storm passes through, sunny days often follow.

Safety. The North Coast used to be one of those places where people left their keys in the ignition in case someone had to move their car. But no more. Lock your car and put valuables in the trunk or take them with you.

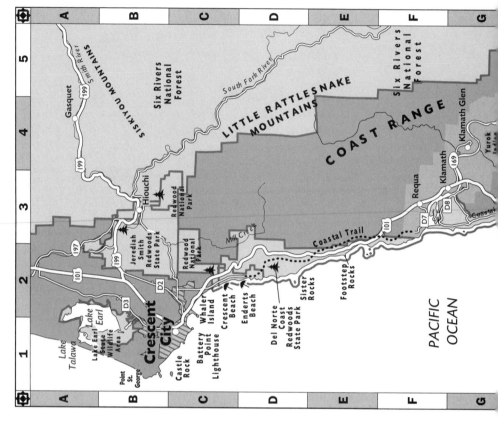

of the trees are way down there, way down, almost 300 feet down, but when you look straight out you notice that the tops of many are higher than you are. This is probably the closest thing you'll ever feel to being in the top of one of the trees. From here a small bridge will carry you into the grove, but from below, these giants look pretty much like every other redwood tree—tall. Camp downstream at least 0.5 miles away from the bridge on one of the many fine sandbars of Redwood Creek. There are bears in the area, so hang your food. The bridges on Redwood Creek are only installed from May 15 to September 15. For about a month before and a month after that you can probably ford the creek when the bridges are gone, but from the end of October to the beginning of April you don't want anything to do with this hike. The rain is horrendous, and the creek crossings are extremely dangerous.

KAYAKING

Whitewater kayakers will enjoy runs like the Class II and III **Russian River** in Sonoma County, which is the closest real whitewater to the Bay Area, the 32-mile **Wilderness Run on the Middle Fork Eel, the Pigeon Point Run of the Trinity,** and all three forks of the **Smith River. Adventure's Edge** (tel. 707/822-4673) in Arcata is a great store specializing in whitewater kayaks and canoes.

In **Redwood National Park** (tel. 707/464-6101) kayakers can join park rangers for a 4-hour float down the Smith River twice a day Thursday through Monday during June and July when water levels are prime. A $6 donation is requested. Reserve a space at the

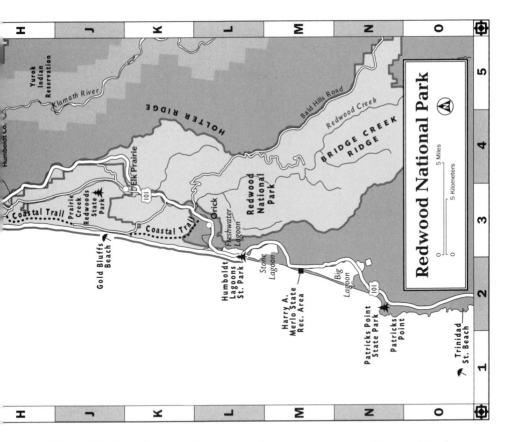

Hiouchi Visitors Center at the north end of the park no more than 2 days in advance. Experienced boaters are free to enjoy the Smith and a number of other creeks on their own.

MOUNTAIN BIKING

Mountain biking the North Coast can be incredibly rewarding or excruciatingly frustrating, often both on the same ride. The same rain that makes this country so beautiful can quickly turn roads and trails into a quagmire. That wonderful single track you follow down through a redwood forest can become a poison oak–choked hell ride when you reach the bottom. Still, this is some of the least explored and most potentially rewarding riding in the whole state. Come prepared for rain and mud and bring lots of spare

parts 'cause you'll probably destroy a few things with all the goo caked to your bike.

Arcata Community Forest

2–10 miles. Moderate. Access: Park at end of California Street near Humboldt State University in Arcata. Follow dirt road until trails begin branching off. Map: Arcata Community Forest map.

The Arcata Community Forest is the favorite playground of Humboldt State students. All trails, single track and fire road, are open to bicycling, but be aware that they are also heavily used by walkers and hikers. Numerous trails make this a perfect place for a day of exploring the watersheds of Janes Creek and Jolly Giant Creek through second-growth redwood forests.

Whiskey Flat Out and Back, Humboldt Redwoods State Park

10 miles. Moderate. Dirt road, gentle climb. Access: Trailhead is near Albee Creek Campground on Mattle Road, Humboldt Redwoods State Park. Map: Humboldt Redwoods State Park map.

The bad news about this ride is there's something blocking the potentially dramatic views on almost the entire ride. The good news is *what* is blocking your view—huge groves of old-growth redwoods. From the trailhead you'll ascend the Grasshopper Road for about a mile, then turn right on Squaw Creek Ridge Road. You'll follow this through a fairly constant and gentle climb until you reach Whiskey Flat Trail Camp. The camp is named after a prohibition-era bootleggers' camp that once graced the spot. Return the way you came.

SCUBA DIVING

We use the term *scuba diving* loosely here, since most diving on the North Coast is done without tanks. Why, you ask, would anyone want to dive up here without tanks? Well, it's really quite simple: a good 90% of diving in Sonoma and Mendocino County is done in pursuit of the red abalone, and California Fish and Game regulations strictly prohibit taking abalone while diving with tanks. So free-diving is the name of the game. That doesn't mean you can't dive with tanks; in fact, the scuba diving is quite good, but most people don't. Either way, the big problem here is getting to the ocean front, and once you're there, getting in through the surf zone. For that reason the following dive sites are the most popular on the coast.

Stillwater Cove. 14 miles north of Jenner. Stillwater Cove is the most popular beginning diving spot on the entire North Coast. The reason, of course, is immediately apparent: the cove is protected from high swells from almost any direction and is generally calm and safe to enter. Underwater the terrain is a little less spectacular than some other sites in the area, but that's the price you pay for easy access. The rocky outcroppings on the north and south sides of the cove have the best fish and invertebrate life.

Salt Point. 20 miles north of Jenner. Salt Point State Park is famous throughout California for its fantastic abalone diving. The two most popular dive sites are Gerstle Cove and South Gerstle Cove. Both are fairly well protected from all but a heavy northwest swell. Gerstle Cove is a game preserve, so you can look but you can't touch. Check out the incredible beds of strawberry anemones here. South Gerstle is open to abalone diving and spearfishing and is good for both.

Russian Gulch. 2 miles north of Mendocino. The farther north you go the harder the diving gets. Russian Gulch is one of the last really desirable dive spots on the Mendocino coast. The beach inside the state park cove makes for easy water entry. The cove is long and well protected, though as you explore the outer areas you'll find it prone to fairly heavy surge. Good abalone diving and spearfishing.

SEA KAYAKING

If you're venturing out on the open sea here you better know what you're doing. The entire North Coast is exposed to whatever storm conditions the Gulf of Alaska is dishing out, and the surf can go from nonexistent to booming in a matter of an hour. Don't go paddling up here if you're not comfortable with that possibility. Still, the payoff of going out is well worth the effort—you'll see a rare perspective on this rocky and wild coast. Bird-watchers will like the numerous offshore nesting rocks, and it is entirely likely that you will see whales, sea otters, and other wildlife.

Force Ten, P.O. Box 167, Elk, CA 95432 (tel. 707/877-3505), located in Elk, a small town on the Medocino coast, offers several different options for beginning through advanced kayakers. Beginners can take advantage of owner Steve Sinclair's expertise by signing up for one of his K-2 tours—a tandem kayak thrill tour of the rocky Medocino sea caves, wave channels, and seabird and seal rookeries. He'll take the back seat and handle the tricky stuff; you stay in front and paddle or just hold on for the ride. Force Ten also offers even wilder and woollier "Storm Surf" tours for intermediate and advanced sea kayakers.

WALKS & RAMBLES

Kruse Rhododendron Loop

2.25 miles. Access: Follow signs off Highway 1 onto Kruse Ranch Road. Trailhead at dead end. Map: Kruse Rhododendron State Reserve map.

The rhododendron is usually just one of many plants growing in the understory of a dark forest dominated by Douglas fir and redwoods, but here logging and several large fires have opened the forest to more sunlight and consequently more rhododendrons. The best time for

this walk is in spring, when the flowers are in full bloom. Other trails lead from here into surrounding Salt Point State Park.

Gold Bluffs–Fern Canyon Loop, Redwood National Park

0.75 miles. Access: Trail begins at end of Davison Road in Prairie Creek Redwoods State Park. Map: Redwood National Park or Prairie Creek Redwoods State Park map.

This spot is one of the most otherworldly locations you're likely to ever see. Walking through Fern Canyon, an unbelievably lush grotto of sword, five-finger, and maidenhair ferns cut by a babbling brook, it's easy to imagine a dinosaur or some other prehistoric beast lumbering across the trail. The trail wanders back and forth through this always-dripping landscape ripe with the thick, earthy aroma of decomposing wood and prospering ferns. Gold Beach, which this walk reaches, was the site of a minor gold rush when miners found some gold in the beach sand. The boom soon became a bust when it turned out there wasn't enough gold here to be worth mining.

WHALE WATCHING

The wild seas cut down drastically on the number of whale-watching charters on the North Coast, but it is done. **King Salmon Charters,** 1875 Buhne Dr. #67, Eureka, CA 95503 (tel. 707/442-3474), often runs trips off the Humboldt coast.

Land-based whale watching is particularly fine in the Sonoma and Mendocino stretch of shoreline. Here, high cliffs make it easy to find an elevated perch from which to sight the passing whales. Each March, Medocino has its

Thar She Blows!

If you're lucky, in an afternoon spent whale watching you'll catch the whales performing a few classic moves. You may see their powerful flukes rising out of the water in preparation for a dive. You will certainly see their spouts, formed by the condensed moisture of their exhalation, which can rise 10 to 15 feet in the air and be seen from 10 miles away. Occasionally you may see their heads popping out above the surface for a look around (spyhopping), or their whole bodies lurching right out of the water in what's called a breach. Why they perform the last two is a mystery. Some speculate that when they spyhop they're actually checking coastal landmarks. As for breaching, who knows? Perhaps it's sheer jubilation.

annual whale festival, a wine-tasting, chowder-chomping good time including plenty of staring out to sea from the Mendocino bluffs looking for those telltale puffs of spray.

Campgrounds & Other Accommodations

CAMPING

Salt Point State Park

20 miles north of Jenner on the Sonoma coast. 140 sites. Flush toilets, running water. Pets okay. $16 per night. Reservations through MISTIX (tel. 800/444-PARK).

Salt Point is the most popular state park with divers since you can camp and dive all at the same spot. Don't overlook the great hiking on the other side of Highway 1, where the park extends way back into the hills.

MacKerricher State Park

On the beach about 5 miles north of Fort Bragg. 153 sites. Flush toilets, running water, showers. Pets okay. $16 per night. Reservations through MISTIX (tel. 800/444-PARK).

MacKerricher is unique to the Mendocino coast as one of the few places where a long beach fronts the ocean without large cliffs. The campsites are located back in a pleasant forest a short walk from the beach and 20-acre Lake Cleone, which offers good freshwater fishing for trout. North of the park lies an enormous field of sand dunes.

Stone Lagoon Boat-In, Humboldt Lagoons State Park

Boat-in only. Launch boats at the parking area 3 miles south of the Redwood Information Center on U.S. 101. The campground is 0.75 miles away, across the lagoon. Tel. 707/488-2041. No water, pit toilets, picnic tables, fire rings. No pets. $7 per night. No reservations.

An interesting camping option is the boat-in campground at Stone Lagoon in Humboldt Lagoons State Park. Reachable only by canoe, kayak, or rowboat, it is on the bank of the lagoon and a short walk to the ocean beach.

Redwood National Park Camping

South of Crescent City on U.S. 101. Information: 1111 Second St., Crescent City, CA 95531. Tel. 707/464-6101. Various facilities. Encompasses three state parks: Del Norte Coast Redwoods, Jedediah Smith Redwoods, and Prairie Creek Redwoods. Open year-round. Day-use and camping fees for some portions of park.

Five small campgrounds are located in the national park proper. Four are walk-in camps and are free, but you must get a permit from the visitors center in advance. The fifth, a car-camping strip along the freeway at Freshwater Lagoon, requests an $8 donation.

Most car campsites are in the **Prairie Creek and Jedediah Smith state parks,** which lie entirely inside the national park. Sites there are $12–$16 per night and can be reserved by calling the state's infuriating MISTIX reservation system (tel. 800/444-7275), which requires an additional $6.75 reservation fee. Be prepared to deal with a truly annoying computer when you call and know exactly what campground and, if possible, which site you would like. (The state park service has promised improvements in this system, but we'll see.)

Farther from the park attractions but also farther from the crowds are four **National Forest Campgrounds** in the mountains above the park. Sites are $8 per night and can be reserved by calling 800/280-2267—where an actual person can help you make decisions.

INNS & LODGES

Rachel's Inn

North Highway 1 (P.O. Box 134), Mendocino, CA 95460. Tel. 707/937-0088. 9 rooms. July–Oct, weekends and holidays year-round $120–$220; Monday–Thurs (Nov–June) $96–$190. Rates include breakfast. Credit cards.

Two miles south of Mendocino, this B&B is set on an acre of land that abuts 82 acres of Van Damme State Park (tel. 707/937-5804). The ocean is very close and a beach is a short walk away. Two things make this inn so special. One is Rachel herself, a solicitous host who loves the Mendocino coast and who was responsible for organizing against the threat of offshore oil drilling in the 1980s. The second is that unlike most inns in town, it's *not* decorated in Laura Ashley style. Instead, it has a refreshing contemporary style, modern art for decoration, and an emphasis on comfort. From the house, guests can walk down to the cove, and there's also a trail from the house across the headlands. Rachel cooks a superb breakfast of huevos rancheros or something similar, plus fruit, baked goods, and cereals. The main house, built in the 1860s, contains four rooms, including the parlor suite, which has its own sitting room with piano and ocean view. The South Room is a state-of-the-art unit for the disabled, with an extra large shower with seat into which you can wheel a wheelchair.

Benbow Inn

445 Lake Benbow Dr., Garberville, CA 95542. Tel. 707/923-2124 or 800/355-3301. Fax 707/923-2897. 55 rooms, 1 cottage. $115–$325. AE, DISC, MC, V.

This national historic landmark was designed by Albert Farr in 1925 overlooking the Eel River, off U.S. 101; pretty Benbow Lake State Park is right out the front door. It's built in a mock Tudor style, and guests enter to a grand hall with cherrywood wainscoting. Rooms in the main building have fireplaces, TVs, private entrances, patios, and some have VCRs, too. A comfortable annex, with elegant woodwork, was added in the 1980s. Bicycles are available.

Trinidad Bed & Breakfast

560 Edmonds St. (P.O. Box 849), Trinidad, CA 95570. Tel. 707/677-0840. 2 rooms, 2 suites. $105–$125 double; $145–$155 suite. Rates include breakfast. MC, V. Closed Dec–Jan.

Set 175 feet above the ocean, the site was selected because of its sweeping views; on a clear day, you can see up to 65 miles of the rugged coastline. Your hosts are Paul and Carol Kirk, innkeepers who have created what many visitors think is the most charming inn around. Rooms contain antique dressers, modern beds, and ocean views. The larger of the two suites has a wood-burning fireplace. Decor throughout is an eclectic mix of New England–style antiques and more recent reproductions.

Redwood AYH Hostel, Redwood National Park

14480 U.S. 101, near Klamath. Tel. 707/482-8265. 30 beds. Very inexpensive.

This is the only lodging actually within Redwood National Park. This turn-of-the-century inn has kitchen facilities, three showers, and 30 beds in shared rooms. The staff leads nature walks and is well versed in local history.

Index

◆ A ◆

Abalone diving, 43, 256, 266
Adventures Aloft, 2, 121
Adventure's Edge, 258, 264
Agnew Meadows Pack Station, 195
Ahjumawi Lava Springs State Park, 229, 231
Ahwahnee Hotel, 206
Alamere Falls, 47
Alper's Owens River Ranch, 191, 208
Alpine County Historical Museum (Markleeville), 140
Alpine Lake, 4, 146, 153, 237
    camping, 201
Alpine Skills International, 186
American Bike Rental, 41
American River, 10, 14, 210, 212, 214–16, 218–19
American River Bikeway, 217
American Wilderness Experience, 16
American Youth Hostels, 16, 64, 270
Andrew Molera State Park, 95, 98, 103, 104–5, 107, 111
    camping, 112
    trails, 99, 109–10
Andrew Molera State Trail, 109
Andrew Molera Walk-In Campground, 112
Angel Island, 23, 33–34
    camping, 59
Angels Camp, 211
Annandel State Park, 118, 124
Año Nuevo State Preserve, 62, 68–69, 76, 82

Anthony Chabot Regional Park, 35–36, 60
Aquarius Dive Shop, 81, 107
Aquatic Adventures of Big Sur, 107, 108
Arana Gulch, 70
Arcata, 254–55
Arcata Community Forest, 265
Arch Rock, 51
Arena Cove, 254
Arroyo Seco, 114
Arroyo Seco Road, 94
Asilomar, 87
Asilomar State Beach, 73–74, 83
Auburn, 210
Auburn State Recreation Area, 214–15, 216
    camping, 220
Audubon Canyon Ranch, 32, 48
Avalanche Gulch Route, 242–45

◆ B ◆

Backroads, 12, 16, 125
Badger Pass Ski Area, 166, 167
Baker Beach, 22, 28, 39, 43
Balconies Cave, 102
Bald eagles, 3, 37, 91, 98, 152, 199, 231, 234, 235, 236
Bald Mountain, 124
Bale Grist Mill, 125
Barlow Flat Camp, 101
Bass Lake, 49–50, 212, 214
Bay Area Bike and Car Rentals, 39
Bean Hollow State Beach, 29

Bean Hollow State Park, 29
Bear Gulch Cave, 101, 111
Bear Gulch Trail, 110–11
Bear Gulch Visitors Center, 98, 102, 106
Bear Valley Cross Country Center, 153, 154
Bear Valley Ski Area, 6, 156–57
Bear Valley Trail, 50–51
Bear Valley Visitors Center, 46, 47, 48
Beltane Ranch, 128
Benbow Inn, 269
Beringer Vineyards, 123
Berkeley Marina, 55
Berkeley Windsurfing and Snowboards, 55
Berry Creek Falls, 76
Beyond Limits, 164, 218
Bicycle Trails Council of Marin, 52
Big Basin State Park, 62, 69
    camping, 85
    trails, 76, 78, 83
Big Pine, 142
Big Sur River, 91, 98, 101, 109, 112–13
Big Sur River Gorge, 108, 110
Big Sur Station, 95–96
Big Trees, 205
Bikes of Bishop, 198
Bird Island, 78
Bishop, 142, 143, 186, 195, 198
Bishop Creek Drainage, 194, 205
Bixby Bridge, 94, 104
Black Diamond Mines Regional Preserve, 36
Blackwood Canyon, 162
Blue Lake, 194
Blue Ribbon Fishing Charters, 158
Bluff Trail, 99
Bobsledz International, 184
Bodega Bay, 253, 254
Bodega Marine Laboratory, 253
Bodie State Historic Park, 150, 183–84, 185
    trails, 186
Bohemian Grove, 50
Boiling Springs Lake, 248
Bolinas, 26, 53

Bolinas Ridge Trail, 52
Bothe-Napa State Park, 125
Bottcher's Gap, 103, 112
Brannan Island State Recreation Area, 121, 126
Bridal Veil Creek Campground, 202
Bridal Veil Falls, 171, 172
Bridge Camp (Shasta-Trinity National Forest), 244–45
Bridge Creek Trail, 77
Bridgeport, 140–41
Bridgeport Ranger Station, 141
Bridgeport Reservoir, 141
Briones Regional Park, 36
Buena Vista Winery, 123
Bugaboo Mountain Sports, 80
Bull Run Lake, 160
Bumpass Hell, 231, 242, 248
Burke's Canoe Trips, 258–59
Burney Creek, 233
Burney Falls, 229–30
Burnt Ranch Gorge, 14, 237, 244
Burst Rock, 152, 159
Butano State Park, 29, 41
    camping, 59
    trails, 40–41
Butano Trail Camp, 40–41
Butte Lake, 236, 248, 249
Butterfly Grove, 83–84
Butts Canyon, 126

◆ **C** ◆

Calaveras Big Trees North Grove Tail, 164
Calaveras Big Trees State Park, 145–46
    trails, 159, 164
Calaveras Ranger District, 137
Calawee Beach, 159
California Alps, Death Ride Tour of the, 198
California Canoe and Kayak, 10, 215
California Department of Fish and Game License Section, 7
California Fly Fishing, 158
California River Flow Hotline, 216
Calistoga mud baths, 127, 128

Calistoga Spa Hot Springs, 128
Camanche Reservoir, 211, 212
Cambria Beach, 98
Camp Edison, 203
Cannery Row (Monterey), 65, 81
Capitola, 64, 75, 85
Capitola Beach, 82
Capitola Pier, 75
Capitola Wharf, 64
Caples Lake, 145, 160
Captain John's Deep Sea Fishing, 40
Carmel Beach, 83
Carmel-by-the-Sea, 68
Carmel River State Beach, 74
Carson-Iceberg Wilderness, 146
Carson Pass, 134, 137, 145, 155
Cascade Range, 225, 247
Castle Crags, 241
Castle Crags State Park, 229
    camping, 245–46
Castle Peak Trail, 154–55
Castle Rock State Park, 30–31, 42, 80
Cathedral Grove, 50
Cathedral Lake, 159, 175
Cave Loop Road, 241
Cayucos Beach, 98
Cedar Grove Campgrounds, 204
Chabot, Lake, 35–36, 60
Chardonnay Sailing Charters, 81, 85
Chase Reef, 81
Chateau St. Jean, 123
Cherry Creek, 14, 215
Chili Bar Run, 215, 218
Chimney Rock, 47
China Beach, 43
Chris' Fishing Trips, 85
Cinder Cone Trail, 236
City Porter's Ski and Sport, 162
Clear Creek, 242–43
Clear Lake State Park, 118, 120, 121
Cleone, Lake, 257, 268
Cliff House, 43–44
Cliff Lake Trail, 177
Club Ed, 75, 83
Coast Camp, 60
Coast Guard Breakwater, 73, 82

Coast Ridge Road, 99–100, 103–14
Coast Trail
    Golden Gate National Recreation
        Area, 39, 43–44
    Point Reyes National Seashore, 47
    Redwood National Park, 260
Coffee Creek Ranch, 237
Coit Reservoir, 56
Coloma, 210–11, 217
Coloma Country Inn, 221
Coloma Outdoor Discovery School, 211
Columbia, 211
Columbia State Park Hidden Treasure
Gold Mine, 214
Condor Gulch Trail, 101
Cone Peak, 91, 105
Congress Trail Loop, 182
Convict Lake, 191
Copper Creek Trail, 176
Cowbirds, 153
Cowell's Beach, 75, 83
Coyote Point Recreation Area and
        Museum, 28, 38–39
Crane Flat, 166
Crane Flat Campground, 202
Crescent Beach, 263
Crescent Beach Overlook, 263
Crescent City, 255
Crissy Field, 3, 22, 28, 37–38, 39, 48
Crowley Lake, 151, 184, 190, 191, 198
Crowley Lake Road, 198
Crystal Lake, 192
Curry Village, 207
Curry Village Ice Rink, 177
Cutting Edge Adventures, 237
CyclePaths, 162
Cypress Grove Loop, 84

 D

Darrington Trail, 216–17
Davenport Bluffs, 14
Davenport Landing Beach, 82
Deadfall Lakes, 234
Deadman Creek, 11, 197
Death Ride Tour of the California Alps,
    198

Deetjen's Big Sur Inn, 115
Del Monte Forest, 68
Delta, the. *See* Sacramento Delta
Delta Meadows River Park, 120–21
Del Valle, Lake, 55
Desolation Wilderness, 145
    trails, 158–59, 160
Devils Kitchen, 248
Devils Postpile National Monument,
    135, 150–51
    camping, 200
    trails, 191, 192, 194, 200
Devil's Slide, 22, 26
Dingleberry Lake, 194
Dinkey Lakes, 177
Dipsea Loop, 49, 50
D. L. Bliss State Park, 144
Dr. Wilkinson's Hot Springs, 127, 128
Dodge Ridge Ski Area, 157–58
Dogsled Adventures, 189
Domaine Chandon, 122
Donner Lake, 144, 154, 200
Donner Memorial Nature Trail, 164
Donner Memorial State Park, 144, 154
    camping, 200
    trails, 164
Donner Pass, 185, 200
Donner Summit, 134, 136, 163
Don Pedro, Lake, 212, 214
Dorst Campground, 204
Drakesbad Guest Ranch, 250
Drakes Beach, 47, 54
Drake's Estero, 51
Dunes State Beach, 29
Duxbury Reef, 53

◆ E ◆

Eagles, bald, 3, 37, 91, 98, 152, 199, 231,
    234, 235, 236
Earl Lake, 258
Earthquake Trail (Point Reyes National
Seashore), 46, 54
East Bay Regional Parks District, 20,
    34–35, 40, 55
    Headquarters, 34
East Bay Wilderness System, 55

Eastern Sierra Interagency Visitors
    Center, 143
East Silver Lake, 201
Ebbetts Pass, 134, 137, 163
Ebbetts Pass Sporting Goods, 158
ECHO: The Wilderness Company, 16
Ecology Loop Trail (The Presidio), 38
Eel River, 253, 258, 264
El Capitan (Yosemite National Park),
    168, 169, 171–72, 181
Electra Run, 215, 218
Elephant seals, 62, 68–69, 76, 82
El Granada Beach, 29
Elkhorn Slough, 3, 72, 74–75, 82
    trails, 74, 75, 84
Elkhorn Slough Interpretive Center, 75
Elkhorn Slough Interpretive Trail, 84
Elkhorn Slough National Estuarine
    Research Reserve, 72
Emerald Bay State Park, 144, 159, 163
Emerald Lake, 158, 160
Emerald Pool, 174
Emeryville Sport Fishing, 40
Emigrant Lake, 160
Emigrant Trail Museum, 144
Emigrant Wilderness, 159, 201
Endert's Beach, 263
Epic Adventures, 106
Esalen Institute, 103, 115–16
Estero Trail, 51
Eureka, 253, 254–55

◆ F ◆

Fallen Leaf Lake, 154, 155, 159
Fallen Leaf Lake Trail, 154, 155
Fall River, 229–30, 233
Fanny Bridge, 137
Farallon Islands Shark Project, 44
Feather River, 210
Fern Canyon Loop, 267
Fern Creek Trail, 49, 50, 260
Fernwood Park, 112–13
    5th Season, 225, 241, 245
Fish Creek Hot Springs, 151
Fisherman's Wharf (Monterey), 65
Five Fingers Loop Trail, 74–75

Floating Island Lake, 158–59
Flora Springs Wine Co., 122–23
Flume Trail, 11, 162, 163
Force Ten, 267
Forest of Nisene Marks State Park, 11, 71, 79–80
    trails, 77, 78–79
Fort Bragg, 254
Fort Point National Historic Site, 28, 39, 43, 45
Francis Beach, 29
Franks Tract State Recreation Area, 121
Freeline Design, 83
Friendship Ridge Trail, 260
Fuller's Cove, 108

◆ **G** ◆

Gablian Mountains, 90, 91, 97
Garrapata Beach, 14, 98, 106
Garrapata State Park, 14, 95, 98, 106, 111
    trails, 109
Gem Lakes, 102
General Sherman Tree, 182
Generals Highway, 178
Geological Survey, U.S., 17, 131–32
Getaway Bicycle Tours, 125
Giant Forest, 8, 176, 178
Glacier Point, 166, 169, 170, 172, 173
Glen Aulin Falls, 175
Glen Aulin High Sierra Camp, 8, 174–75, 207
Glen Camp, 60
Glory Hole Campground, 220
Goat Camp, 166, 170
Gold Beach, 267
Gold Bluffs Beach, 262, 267
Gold Country Prospecting, 214
Golden Gate Audubon Society, 47
Golden Gate Bridge, 20, 22, 38, 39, 42
Golden Gate National Recreation Area, 20, 26, 28, 30–31, 33, 43
    Headquarters, 23, 39
    Marin Headlands, 20, 33
    trails, 43–44
Golden Gate Park, 42

Golden Gate Raptor Observatory, 37
Golden Haven Hot Springs Spa, 128
Gold panning, 214, 215
Good Time Bicycle Co., 125
Gorge Run, 237
Gorge Trail, 108, 110
Granite Creek, 106
Granite Lake, 158
Granite Pass, 176
Grant Grove (Kings Canyon National Park), 178, 179
    camping, 204
Grant Lake, 141
Gray Pine Trail, 124
Gray Whale Cove State Beach, 28
Great Beach (Point Reyes), 46
Great Outdoors, The, 199
Greyhound Rock County Park, 75
Grizzly Giant, 168, 173
Grover Hot Springs State Park, 147, 150, 196
Gull Lake, 141

◆ **H** ◆

Half Dome, 168, 169, 172, 176–77, 181
Half Dome Cable Route, 176–77
Half Moon Bay, 14, 22
Half Moon Bay State Beach, 29
    camping, 58
Hangtown Gold Bug Park, 214
Hank Pritchard Cattle Drive, 237
Harbin Hot Springs, 125
Harding Park, 40
Harry A. Merlo State Recreation Area, 257
Hassle Free Loop, 49
Hat Creek, 229–30, 233
Hazelwood Nature Trail, 182
Headlands Trail, 109–10
Headwaters Forest, 252
Heiser Lake, 159–60
Helen, Lake, 231, 243, 248
Henry Cowell Redwoods State Park, 69
    camping, 85
    trails, 77

Henry W. Coe State Park, 36–37, 56–57, 60
  trails, 56, 58
High Peaks Trail, 7–8, 101
High Sierra Camps, 207
Highway 49, 214, 217, 220–21
Hodgdon Meadow, 202
Hoover Wilderness, 141
Horseshoe Lake, 188
Hot Creek, 131, 187, 191, 199
Hot Creek Ranch, 191
Hot Pursuit Sport Fishing, 40
House of Ski, 231
Hubcap Ranch State Historic Landmark, 126
Huckleberry Botanic Regional Preserve, 35
Humboldt Lagoons State Park, 257
  camping, 268–69
Humboldt Redwood State Park, 257, 258, 266
Hume Lake Ranger Station, 166
Hungry Packer Lake, 194
Huntington Lake, 147, 165
  camping, 203
Huntington Lake Resort, 165, 166

◆ **I** ◆

Ilsanjo, Lake, 120, 124
Indian Grinding Rock State Historic Park, 211, 212, 214
  camping, 220
  trails, 217–18
Indian Well, 246
Inverness, 46
Inyo Craters, 187–88
Inyo Craters Loop, 196–97
Inyo National Forest, 197–98, 204
  trails, 192, 194
Iron Mountain, 155

◆ **J** ◆

Jack London State Park, 120
Jackson, 211, 212
Jackson Flats Trail, 40

Jacks Peak Regional Park, 73
  trails, 78
James V. Fitzgerald Marine Reserve, 28–29
Jedediah Smith State Park, 269
Jenner, 254
Jensen's Pick and Shovel Ranch, 214
Jewel Lake, 56
John Fisher, Mountain Guide, 186
John Muir Trail, 8, 135, 151, 174, 178, 191, 194
John Muir Wilderness, 142, 165, 167, 195
Julia Pfeiffer Burns State Park, 96–97
  camping, 112, 113–14
  trails, 100
June Lake, 141, 184, 186, 197
  camping, 205
  trails, 11, 141, 186, 197
June Lake Loop (State Route 158), 141
June Lake Oh! Ridge Camp, 205
June Mountain, 189–90
June Mountain Ski Resort, 141
Juniper Canyon Trail, 102
Juniper Lake, 248
Junipero Serra Peak, 91, 103

◆ **K** ◆

Kaweah River, 167, 177, 178, 182–83
Kayak Connection, 82
Kayak Tahoe, 161
Kelly Reservoir, 56
Kenneth C. Patrick Visitors Center, 47
Kern River, 177, 178, 180, 182–83
Kern River Tours, 182
Kernville Run, 180
King Range National Conservation Area, 253, 257
King Salmon Charters, 267
Kings Canyon National Park. *See* Sequoia and Kings Canyon National Parks
Kings River, 167, 177, 178
Kirby Park, 72, 82
Kirk Creek, 109, 111
Kirk Creek Campground, 114

Kirk Creek Trail, 100–101
Kirkwood Lake, 145
Kirkwood Ski Resort, 6, 154, 156
Kittredge Sports, 198
Klamath Basin National Wildlife
    Refuges, 231
Klamath National Forest, 238–39
Klamath National Forest Headquarters,
    225, 229
Klamath National Forest Interpretive
Museum, 225
Klamath Overlook, 263
Klamath River, 228–29, 237, 243–44, 262
Kruse Rhododendron State Reserve,
    256, 267
Kule Loklo, 46

❖ **L** ❖

Lagunitas Creek, 32
Lake Merced Boating and Fishing Co.,
    40
Lake Sabrina Basin, 194
Lake Tahoe region, 6, 11, 130, 136,
    143–44, 154–55, 155–58, 162, 163
Lake Tahoe Visitors Authority, 136, 154,
    155
Lake Tahoe Winter Sports Center, 154
Land's End, 43–44
Lassen Peak Trail, 236
Lassen Ski Touring, 232
Lassen Volcanic National Park, 230,
    231–32, 241, 246–49
  camping, 247–48
  trails, 236, 242
Lava Beds National Monument, 230,
    235, 241
  camping, 246
  trails, 8, 234, 236
Ledson Marsh, 120, 124
Lee Vining, 141, 185, 205
Lembert Dome, 181
Lighthouse Point, 64, 70, 84
Limantour Beach, 47
Limantour's Estero, 51
Limekiln Creek State Park, 97

Limestone Run, 180
Lincoln Avenue Spa, 128
Little Heiser Lake, 159–60
Little Lakes Valley, 192
Little Sur River, 91, 98
Little Yosemite, 55–56
Livewater Surf Shop, 53
Lodgepole Campground, 203–4
Lodgepole Visitors Center, 179
Loma Prieta Grade, 77
London (Jack) State Park, 120
Lone Pine, 142–43, 183, 195
Long Valley, 131, 198
Lookout Mountain, 197–98
Lose-the-Crowd Loop, 49
Los Padres National Forest, 91, 96, 97,
    103–4, 105
  camping, 114
  trails, 99–100
"Lost Coast," 253, 257
  trails, 8, 11, 261, 266
Lover's Lane, 39
Lovers Leap, 163
Lover's Point, 73, 82
Lower Klamath Lake Wildlife Rufuge,
    231
Lower Tent Meadows, 176
Lundry Creek Campground, 204–5
Lundy Lake, 141, 192
  camping, 204–5
Lundy Lake Resort, 141
Lyons Trail, 236

❖ **M** ❖

McArthur-Burney Falls Memorial State
    Park, 230
Mac A Tac Charters, 158
McCloud, 228, 243
McCloud River, 228, 233, 234, 237
McClure, Lake, 212, 214, 215
McClures Beach, 47
McGee Creek Pack Station, 195
MacKerricher State Park, 256–57
  camping, 268
  trails, 260

McNee Ranch State Park, 28
McWay Falls, 108, 110, 112
Mammoth Adventure Connection, 142
Mammoth Balloon Adventures, 2, 183
Mammoth Lakes, 2, 11, 141–42, 151, 185,186–88, 189–90, 198, 199
  camping, 204, 205
  trails, 186–88, 197
Mammoth Lakes Pack Outfit, 195
Mammoth Lakes Visitors Center, 142
Mammoth Mountain, 189–90
Mammoth Mountain Bike Park, 196
Mammoth National Forest Visitors Center, 142
Mammoth Sporting Goods, 191
Mammouth Mountain Ski Resort, 142
Manchester State Park, 256
Mangels House, 87
Manresa Beach State Park, 71
  camping, 86
Marble Mountain Wilderness, 229
Marina State Beach, 73
Marin Headlands, 20, 33
Mariposa, 211
Mariposa Grove, 166, 170, 173
Markleeville, 137, 140, 195, 198
Marlette Lake, 163
Marshall Gold Discovery State Historic Park, 211, 212, 217
Mary, Lake, 184
Matt Davis Trail, 49
Mattole River, 257, 261
Maverick's, 22, 43
May Lake High Sierra Camp, 207
May Lundy Mine, 192
Meadowood Resort, 127
Medocino, 267–68
Memorial County Park, 41
Mendocino, 254
Merced, Lake, 39, 40
Merced Lake High Sierra Camp, 207
Merced River, 165–66, 167, 169, 172, 214, 215, 219
Merced River Ride, 216
Mercer Caverns, 212

Mike Morgan's Bishop Pack Outfitters, 195
Mike's Bike Center, 52
Mill Creek, 106
Mineral King, 165, 175, 204
Mirror Lake, 169, 181–82
Missing Link Bicycles, 56
Mission Cliffs, 42
Mississippi Reservoir, 56
Mist Falls, 175
Moaning Cave, 212
Mokelumne River, 158, 214, 218, 219
Mokelumne Wilderness, 145, 201
  trails, 160
Molera Point, 100, 109, 111
Molera Trail Rides, 103
Monarch butterflies, 70, 83–84
Monastery Beach, 64, 74, 80, 81
Monitor Pass, 140
Mono Basin National Scenic Area, 150
Mono Hot Springs Resort, 207
Mono Lake, 3, 133, 135, 141, 150, 183, 184, 185, 187
Mono Lake Committee, 184
Mono Lake Mark Twain Interpretive Trail, 150, 199–200
Mono Lake Ranger Station, 141
Mono Lake Tufa State Reserve, 150
Montara Area Beaches and Parks, 28–29
Montara Lighthouse, 28
Montara State Beach, 28
Monterey Bay Aquarium, 65
Monterey Bay Area Rare Bird Alert, 72, 75
Monterey Bay Kayaks, 81–82, 108
Monterey Pier, 75
Monterey Sport Fishing, 75, 85
Monterey Submarine Canyon, 61, 65, 82
Monument Trail, 58
Morgan Horse Ranch, 46
Moro Rock, 182
Mosquito Lake, 146
Moss Landing, 64–65, 82
Moss Landing State Beach, 72, 75, 82
Mountain and River Adventures, 180, 181

Mount Carmel Trail, 99
Mount Diablo Fire Interpretive Trail, 58
Mount Diablo State Park, 21, 36
    camping, 60
    trails, 55, 57, 58
Mount Diablo Summit Ride, 57
Mount Eddy Summit, 234
Mount Lassen, 130, 225, 246. *See also*
       Lassen Volcanic National Park
Mount Livermore, 23
Mount Saint Helens, 126, 131–32
Mount Shasta, 11, 223, 225, 229, 231,
    240–41
    climbing, 242–45
    skiing, 6, 232–33
Mount Shasta City, 225, 228
Mount Shasta Nordic Center, 232
Mount Shasta Ranger District, 241
Mount Shasta Ski Park, 6, 232–33
Mount Tallac, 158–59
Mount Tamalpais State Park, 33, 40
    camping, 50, 59–60
    trails, 8, 48–49, 51–52
Mount Toro, 63
Mount Whitney, 130, 142–43, 165, 178,
    183
    trails, 194–95
Mount Whitney Ranger Station, 143
Mud baths, in Calistoga, 127, 128
Mud Creek Trail, 242–43
Muir, John, 20, 50, 130, 146, 164–65,
    169–70, 172, 178
Muir Beach Overlook, 54
Muir Woods National Monument, 33, 50,
    52–53
    trails, 49, 50, 52–54
Murphys Hotel and Lodge, 221
Mushpot Cave, 241

◆ **N** ◆

Nacimiento Road, 105
Napa Valley, 122–23, 125–26,
    126–27
    wineries, 122–23, 125
Napa Valley Bike Tours, 125

Native American Celebration, 46
Natural Bridges State Beach, 69–70,
    83–84
Nature Conservancy, 16–17
Nature Trail (Pfeiffer Big Sur State
    Park), 110
Navy Beach, 150, 184, 200
Nevada Falls, 169, 174, 182
New Brighton State Beach, 70–71
    camping, 85–86
New Easy Rider, 40
Nisene Marks. *See* Forest of Nisene
    Marks State Park
North Grove Trail, 164
Northstar-at-Tahoe, 6, 154, 156, 162

◆ **O** ◆

Oakhurst, 210, 212
Obsidian Dome Trails, 186
Ocean Beach, 13, 22, 23, 37, 43
Oceanic Society, 45, 47, 54
Ocean Pinnacles, 81
Ocean View Trail, 49
Ohlone Trail, 34
Old Coast Highway, 104
Old Haul Road, 41
Old Landing Cove Trail, 77
Old Railroad Grade, 52
Olema, 46
Olema Ranch Campground, 59
Olympic Circle Sailing School, 43
Oneida Lake, 192
Oristimba Wilderness, 56
Otter Bar Lodge, 10, 237, 238–39, 240,
    249–50
Outfitters, 14–17. *See also specific*
    outfitters
Outward Bound USA, 16
Owens Lake, 193
Owens River, 190, 191, 197, 208
Owens River Gorge, 151, 197, 199
Owens River Headwaters, 150
Owens Valley, 131, 135, 183, 185, 190,
    193
Owens Valley Aqueduct, 193

◆ **P** ◆

Pacheco Pass, 130
Pacifica, 13, 26, 43
Pacifica Beach, 13, 26
Pacific Crest Trail, 8, 135, 151, 178, 191, 234, 236
Pacific Currents, 53
Pacific Edge Climbing Gym, 106
Pacific Grove Marine Gardens Fish Refuge, 73
Pacific Grove Museum of Natural History, 65, 68
Pacific Muir Beach Overlook, 54
Pacific Valley Area, 97
Pacific Yachting, 81
Paco's Truckee Bike and Ski, 162
Pajaro Valley Wetlands, 72
Palisade Glacier, 142, 186
Palo Colorado Road, 94
Panorama Ridge Trail, 99
Panoramic Highway, 26, 49, 53
Panoramic Highway Trail, 49
Pan Toll Campground, 59–60
Paradise Point Marina, 128
Paradise Valley Trail, 175
Pardee Reservoir, 211, 212
Partington Cove, 97, 100, 106, 108
Partington Ridge, 100
Pelican Lake, 51
Perimeter Trail (Point Lobos), 77–78
Pescadero Creek County Park, 29–30
Pescadero Marsh, 29, 37
    trails, 44–45
Pescadero State Beach, 29, 37, 44–45
Pfeiffer Beach, 96, 98, 107–8, 109, 111
Pfeiffer Big Sur State Park, 90, 95
    camping, 113
    trails, 110
Pfeiffer (Julia) Burns State Park, 96–97, 100, 112, 113–14
Pfeiffer Falls, 110
Pickett's Junction, 137
Pigeon Point Lighthouse, 64, 87
Pigeon Point Run, 264
Pillar Point Harbor, 22, 29

Pinecrest Lake, 146, 153–54
    camping, 201
Pinecrest Lake Resort, 146
Pine Ridge Trail, 101, 103
Pinnacles National Monument, 3, 90–91, 97–98, 102, 105–6
    camping, 114
    trails, 7–8, 101, 102, 110–11
Pit River, 233
Placerville, 211
Plaskett Rock, 106
Pleasure Point, 70, 82
Pleasure Point Inn, 87
Point Año Nuevo Elephant Seal Colony, 68–69, 76
Point Arena Lighthouse, 254
Point Bonita Lighthouse, 44
Point Lobos Perimeter Trail, 77–78
Point Lobos State Reserve, 64, 74, 78, 81, 84
    trails, 77–78, 84
Point Pinole Regional Shoreline, 34, 55
Point Piños Lighthouse, 68, 84
Point Reyes Bird Observatory, 32, 48
Point Reyes Lighthouse, 47, 54
Point Reyes National Seashore, 3, 14, 22, 31–32, 32, 43, 46–47, 48, 54
    camping, 60
    trails, 47, 50–51, 54
Point Reyes Station, 46
Point Sur Lighthouse State Park, 95, 111
Pokonobe Lodge, 184
Pomonio State Beach, 29
Pope-Baldwin Recreation Area, 144–45, 154
Pope Valley, 126
Porcupine Flat Campground, 203
Port Arena, 254
Portola State Park, 30, 41
Powell Lake, 159
Powerhouse Run, 182
Prairie Creek State Park, 269
Presidio, The, 26, 28, 38–39
    trails, 38–39, 45
Presidio Army Museum, 39
Pygmy Forest Loop, 259

❖ **R** ❖

Rachel's Inn, 269
Railroad Slough, 121
Rainbow Falls, 151, 192
Rainbow Lodge, 206
Rainbow Trail, 144–45
Rancheria Camp, 203
Randy's Fishing Trips, 75–76, 85, 98–99
Red Cones Trail, 188
Red's Meadow Resort and Pack Station,
    195, 208
Redwood AYH Hostel, 270
Redwood Creek, 261, 264
Redwood Creek Trail, 53–54
Redwood Mountain, 175
Redwood National Park, 252, 258,
    262–63, 264–65, 270
    camping, 269
    trails, 260, 261, 264, 267
Redwood Nature Trail (Big Basin State
    Park), 83
Redwood Regional Park, 35
Ribbon Falls, 168
Richardson Bay, 33–34, 48, 53
Ridge Trail, 77
Rio Del Mar Beach, 71
Rio Vista, 118, 121
River Inn, 94, 108
River Ranch Campground, 220
River Ranch Run, 161
River Store (Lotus), 216
River Travel Center (Point Arena),
    182–83, 218, 244
Robert Sibley Volcanic Regional
    Preserve, 35
Rockaway Beach, 26, 43
Rock Creek, 188
Rock Creek Lake, 198, 205
Rock Creek Road, 142, 188, 198
Roosevelt Beach, 29
Rose Peak, 34
Royal Gorge Nordic Center, 154, 206
Rubicon Lake, 160
Rubicon Trail, 159
Ruck-A-Chucky Falls, 215
Russian Gulch, 266

Russian Gulch State Park, 256
    trails, 259–60
Russian Gulch Trail, 259–60
Russian River, 254, 264

❖ **S** ❖

Sabrina, Lake, 194, 195, 205
Sacramento Delta, 118, 120–21, 121, 124,
    128
Sacramento River, 230, 237, 244
Saddle Mountain Recreation Park, 86
Sailing Educational Adventures, 42
Salathe Wall, 181
Salinas River, 72–73, 75, 91
Salinas River Wildlife Area, 72–73, 75
Salmon River, 10, 14, 228–29, 237, 244
Salt Point State Park, 256, 266
    camping, 268
    trails, 259
Sam's Fishing Fleet, 85
Samuel P. Taylor State Park, 32, 59
San Andreas Fault, 32, 46, 54
San Bruno Mountain State and County
    Park, 28
San Bruno Ridge Trail, 56
Sand Point Overlook, 78–79
Sandy Beach County Park, 121
San Francisco School of Windsurfing, 39
San Gregorio State Beach, 29
San Joaquin Ridge, 191
San Joaquin River, 118, 151, 177, 192,
    200
San Joaquin River Gorge, 192
San Lorenzo River, 69, 75, 79
San Mateo Memorial County Park,
    29–30
San Pedro Beach, 26
San Simeon Beach, 98
Santa Cruz County Conference and
    Visitors Council, 64
Santa Cruz Pier, 75
Santa Cruz Sport Fishing, 85
Santa Cruz Surfing Museum, 64
Santa Cruz Yacht Harbor, 70, 80–81
Schonchin Butte, 235
Schwan Lake, 70

Scott Creek Beach, 82
Seabright Beach, 82
Seacliff Beach, 71
Sea Lion Cove, 78
Sea Otter Rocks, 106
Sea Trek Ocean Kayaking Center, 53
Sequoia and Kings Canyon National
     Parks, 147, 165, 167, 178–79, 180
  accommodations, 207–8
  camping, 200, 203–4
  cross-country skiing, 166, 188–89
  trails, 8, 167, 173, 175–76, 178–79, 182
Sequoia Ski Touring, 166
     17-Mile Drive, 63–64, 68, 80
Shady Rest, 197–98
Shady Rest Loop, 186
Shamrock Charters, 75, 85
Sharks, white, 13, 43, 44, 75, 82
Shasta-Cascade Wonderland Association,
     230, 234
Shasta Lake, 230, 233–34
Shasta-Trinity National Forest, 244–45
Shaver Lake, 147, 165, 167, 207
  camping, 203
Sierra Club, 16, 20, 47, 103, 130, 169
  Clair Tappaan Lodge, 155, 205–6
  Horse Valley Hut, 242–43
  Perter Grubb Hut, 155
Sierra Haute (High) Route, 166, 188–89,
     192
Sierra Meadows Ranch, 195
Sierra National Forest, 140, 177
Sierra National Forest Ranger District,
     165
Sierra South, 10, 180
Sierra Summit Ski Area, 166, 167
Silverado Trail, 125
Silver Lake, 141, 145, 184
  camping, 201
Silver Lake Rentals, 184
Sinkyone Wilderness State Park, 257
Siskiyou County Museum, 225
Siskiyou Lake, 237, 240
  camping, 246
Six Rivers National Forest, 229
Sky Camp, 60

Skyline Nature Trail, 78
Skyline to the Sea Trail, 76, 78
Slide Ranch Tidepools, 54
Smith River, 258, 259, 264
Smith River National Recreation Area,
     258
Smith River Salmon and Steelhead
     Trips, 259
Soberanes Point, 111
Soberanes Point Trail, 109
Soda Springs Winter Resort, 156
Sonoma Cattle Company, 120
Sonoma Coast State Beaches, 255–56
Sonoma Valley, 123, 125
Sonora, 211
Sonora Pass, 134, 140
Soquel Demonstration Forest, 80
Sorensen's Resort, 137
Southern San Mateo Coast Beaches and
     Parks, 29, 37
South Grove Trail, 159
Spinnaker Sailing, 39, 42–43
Squaw Valley, 6, 154, 155–56, 162
Stagnaro's Fishing Trips, 75
Stanislaus National Forest, 216
Stanislaus River, 137, 146, 158, 164, 212,
     214, 215, 219
Start to Finish, 52, 56
Steamer's Lane, 70, 82
Steep Ravine Trail, 8, 48–49, 60
Stewarts Fork Trail, 245
Stillwater Cove, 266
Stinson Beach, 32–33, 53
  trails, 48–49
Stone Lagoon, 268–69
Sugar Bowl Ski Resort, 6
Sugarloaf Ridge State Park, 120, 124, 126
Sugar Pine Point State Park, 144, 152,
     154, 162
  camping, 200–201
  trails, 159
Sulphur Works, 248
Summit Ranger Station, 146
Sunnyside Campground, 202
Sunset Beach State Park, 71, 86
Sunset Trail Loop, 76

Sweeney Ridge, 40
Sweeney Ridge Preserve, 37
Sykes Hot Spring, 98, 101

◆ **T** ◆

Tahoe, Lake, 130, 136, 143–44, 152, 154,
    158, 161, 163. *See also* Lake
    Tahoe region
Tahoe North Visitors and Convention
    Bureau, 136, 143–44, 155, 164
Tahoe Paddle and Oar, 154, 161
Tallac Historic Site, 144–45
Tall Timbers Chalets, 126–27
Tamarack Flat, 202
Tamarack Lodge, 189, 208
Tan Bark Trail, 100
Taylor Creek, 144–45, 154, 155
    10-Mile Beach Trail, 260
Tenaya Lake, 165, 170, 173, 181
Thousand Island Lake Loop, 192, 194
Tilden Nature Area, 56
Tilden Regional Park, 34–35, 56
Tioga Pass, 134, 135, 166, 173
Tomales Bay State Park, 32
Tomales Point, 43, 51
Trinidad Beach, 258
Trinidad Bed & Breakfast, 270
Trinity Alps, 224, 225, 228, 237, 249
Trinity Alps Overnight, 237
Trinity Alps Resort, 249
Trinity Lake, 228, 245
Trinity River, 14, 237, 243–44, 264
Truckee, 136–37
Truckee River, 137, 158, 161, 164
Tule Lake, 3, 225, 231
Tuolumne Meadows (Yosemite National
    Park), 165, 170, 171, 173, 177, 181
    camping, 202–3
    trails, 8, 174–75
Tuolumne Meadows Visitors Center, 171
Tuolumne River, 173, 212, 214, 215, 219
Twenty Lakes, 141
Twin Lakes, 205, 208
Twin Lakes Beach, 82
Twin Lakes Road, 141
Twin Otters, Inc., 81

◆ **U** ◆

Upper Owens River Gorge Loops, 197

◆ **V** ◆

Valley View Trail, 110
Van Damme State Park, 256
Venice Beach, 29
Ventana Campground, 113
Ventana Double Cone, 103
Ventana Inn, 115
Ventana Wilderness, 91, 94, 96, 98, 103
    trails, 99, 100–101, 103
Venture Quest, 82
Vernal Falls, 174
Vicente Flat Trail, 100–101
Village Sports Center (Mammoth
    Lakes), 191, 198
Vintage Inn, 127
Virginia Lakes, 141
Vogelsang High Sierra Camp, 207

◆ **W** ◆

Wacky Jacky, 40
Waddell Beach, 3, 69, 75, 82
Waddell Creek, 69, 78
Walker Mountains, 225
Warner Valley, 248, 249
Warren Richardson Trail, 124
Wawona Campground, 202
Wawona Hotel, 173, 206
Weaverville, 225, 228
Weaverville Ranger District Office, 228
West Cliff Drive, 84
Western States Pioneer Express Trail,
    214–15, 216
Whaler's Cove, 74
Whiskey Flat Out and Back, 266
White Mountain, 183, 189
White Mountain Ranger Station, 142
Whitewater Adventures, 164
Whitewater Voyages, 182
White Wolf, 203
Whitney Butte Trail, 234, 236
Whitney Portal, 176, 177–78
Whitney Trail, 194–95

Wildcat Beach, 51
Wildcat Camp, 51, 60
Wildcat Canyon Regional Park, 34, 56
Wildcat Gorge Trail, 56
Wilderness Run, 264
Wilder Ranch State Park, 11, 69, 77, 79
Willow Creek, 98, 106, 108, 109
Windsurf Del Valle, 55
Wineries, 122–23, 125
Winnemucca Lake Loop, 155
Wolf Creek Pack Station, 195
Woods Lake, 155
Wreck Beach, 107

◆ ◆

Yosemite Creek, 203
Yosemite Cross-Country Ski School, 166

Yosemite Falls, 168, 174, 181
Yosemite Falls Trail, 174
Yosemite Lodge, 206–7
Yosemite Mountaineering School, 181
Yosemite National Park, 146–47, 165–73,
    177, 180
  accommodations, 206–7
  camping, 201–3
  rock climbing, 180–81
  trails, 8, 167, 174–75, 176–77, 181–82
Yosemite Valley, 165, 168, 171–72, 180,
    206–7
  camping, 201–2
  trails, 174, 181–82
Yosemite Valley Visitors Center, 171, 172
Yreka, 225

FROMMER'S® COMPLETE TRAVEL GUIDES

Alaska
Amsterdam
Arizona
Atlanta
Australia
Austria
Bahamas
Barcelona, Madrid & Seville
Belgium, Holland & Luxembourg
Bermuda
Boston
Budapest & the Best of Hungary
California
Canada
Cancún, Cozumel & the Yucatán
Cape Cod, Nantucket & Martha's Vineyard
Caribbean
Caribbean Cruises & Ports of Call
Caribbean Ports of Call
Carolinas & Georgia
Chicago
China
Colorado
Costa Rica
Denver, Boulder & Colorado Springs
England
Europe
Florida

France
Germany
Greece
Greek Islands
Hawaii
Hong Kong
Honolulu, Waikiki & Oahu
Ireland
Israel
Italy
Jamaica & Barbados
Japan
Las Vegas
London
Los Angeles
Maryland & Delaware
Maui
Mexico
Miami & the Keys
Montana & Wyoming
Montréal & Québec City
Munich & the Bavarian Alps
Nashville & Memphis
Nepal
New England
New Mexico
New Orleans
New York City
Nova Scotia, New Brunswick & Prince Edward Island
Oregon
Paris
Philadelphia & the Amish Country

Portugal
Prague & the Best of the Czech Republic
Provence & the Riviera
Puerto Rico
Rome
San Antonio & Austin
San Diego
San Francisco
Santa Fe, Taos & Albuquerque
Scandinavia
Scotland
Seattle & Portland
Singapore & Malaysia
South Pacific
Spain
Switzerland
Thailand
Tokyo
Toronto
Tuscany & Umbria
USA
Utah
Vancouver & Victoria
Vermont, New Hampshire & Maine
Vienna & the Danube Valley
Virgin Islands
Virginia
Walt Disney World & Orlando
Washington, D.C.
Washington State

FROMMER'S® DOLLAR-A-DAY GUIDES

Australia from $50 a Day
California from $60 a Day
Caribbean from $60 a Day
England from $60 a Day
Europe from $50 a Day
Florida from $60 a Day

Greece from $50 a Day
Hawaii from $60 a Day
Ireland from $50 a Day
Israel from $45 a Day
Italy from $50 a Day
London from $75 a Day

New York from $75 a Day
New Zealand from $50 a Day
Paris from $70 a Day
San Francisco from $60 a Day
Washington, D.C., from $60 a Day

FROMMER'S® PORTABLE GUIDES

Acapulco, Ixtapa & Zihuatanejo
Alaska Cruises & Ports of Call
Bahamas
California Wine Country
Charleston & Savannah
Chicago

Dublin
Las Vegas
London
Maine Coast
New Orleans
New York City
Paris

Puerto Vallarta, Manzanillo & Guadalajara
San Francisco
Sydney
Tampa & St. Petersburg
Venice
Washington, D.C.

FROMMER'S® NATIONAL PARK GUIDES

Family Vacations in the
   National Parks
Grand Canyon

National Parks of the
   American West
Yellowstone & Grand Teton

Yosemite & Sequoia/
   Kings Canyon
Zion & Bryce Canyon

FROMMER'S® GREAT OUTDOOR GUIDES

New England
Northern California

Southern California & Baja
Pacific Northwest

FROMMER'S® MEMORABLE WALKS

Chicago
London

New York
Paris

San Francisco
Washington D.C.

FROMMER'S® IRREVERENT GUIDES

Amsterdam
Boston
Chicago

London
Manhattan

New Orleans
Paris

San Francisco
Walt Disney World
Washington, D.C.

FROMMER'S® DRIVING TOURS

America
Britain
California

Florida
France
Germany

Ireland
Italy
New England

Scotland
Spain
Western Europe

THE COMPLETE IDIOT'S TRAVEL GUIDES

Boston
Cruise Vacations
Planning Your Trip to Europe
Hawaii

Las Vegas
London
Mexico's Beach Resorts
New Orleans

New York City
San Francisco
Walt Disney World
Washington D.C.

THE UNOFFICIAL GUIDES®

Branson, Missouri
California with Kids
Chicago
Cruises
Disney Companion

Florida with Kids
The Great Smoky &
   Blue Ridge
   Mountains

Las Vegas
Miami & the Keys
Mini-Mickey
New Orleans

New York City
San Francisco
Skiing in the West
Walt Disney World
Washington, D.C.

SPECIAL-INTEREST TITLES

Born to Shop: Caribbean Ports of Call
Born to Shop: France
Born to Shop: Hong Kong
Born to Shop: Italy
Born to Shop: New York
Born to Shop: Paris
Frommer's Britain's Best Bike Rides
The Civil War Trust's Official Guide
   to the Civil War Discovery Trail
Frommer's Caribbean Hideaways
Frommer's Europe's Greatest Driving Tours
Frommer's Food Lover's Companion to France
Frommer's Food Lover's Companion to Italy
Frommer's Gay & Lesbian Europe

Israel Past & Present
Monks' Guide to California
Monks' Guide to New York City
New York City with Kids
New York Times Weekends
Outside Magazine's Guide
   to Family Vacations
Places Rated Almanac
Retirement Places Rated
Washington, D.C., with Kids
Wonderful Weekends from Boston
Wonderful Weekends from New York City
Wonderful Weekends from San Francisco
Wonderful Weekends from Los Angeles

NOTES

NOTES